Implementing DevSecOps with Docker and Kubernetes

An Experiential Guide to Operate in the DevOps Environment for Securing and Monitoring Container Applications

José Manuel Ortega Candel

www.bpbonline.com

FIRST EDITION 2022

Copyright © BPB Publications, India

ISBN: 978-93-5551-118-8

LIMITS OF LIABILITY AND DISCLAIMER OF WARRANTY

To View Complete
BPB Publications Catalogue
Scan the QR Code:

Dedicated to

My parents and brothers

About the Author

Jose Manuel Ortega has been working as a software engineer and security researcher, focusing on new technologies, open source, security, and testing. His aim has been to specialize in Python and DevOps security projects with Docker. He is currently working as a security tester engineer, analyzing and testing the security of applications. He has collaborated with universities and the official college of computer engineers, presenting articles and holding conferences. He has also been a speaker at national and international conferences. You can find his conferences and talks related to Python, Security, and Docker on his personal site - `http://jmortega.github.io`

About the Reviewers

Ajay Bhaskar, a DevOps enthusiast, is always eager to learn new technologies related to automating application lifecycle management. He has also reviewed Cloud Analytics using Microsoft Azure Stack. He loves R&D and has a keen interest in inventing or optimizing and implementing solutions.

Prajeesh Prathap is an experienced technologist who specializes in building web scale, cloud native applications with special interest in event-driven, distributed systems. Prajeesh currently works as the platform and operations teams' manager for IT&Care in the Netherlands, specializing in setting up the containerized environments, CI/CD using Azure DevOps, observability platforms etc. He is a regular speaker at numerous technology conferences and has authored courses on Reactive Microservices in .NET Core and Continuous Delivery with VSTS & PowerShell DSC.

Acknowledgments

First and foremost, I would like to thank everyone at BPB Publications for giving me the opportunity to publish this book, which tries to cover some of the technologies that we can find within the DevSecOps ecosystem.

I would also like to thank my teachers and friends at the University for giving me the ability to continuously learn in a world that becomes increasingly complex. Lastly, I would like to thank the editors, reviewers, and publishers for carrying out this project successfully.

Preface

In the last few years, the knowledge of DevSecOps tools in IT companies has increased due to the growth of specific technologies based on containers like Docker and Kubernetes. Docker is an open source containerization tool that makes it easier to streamline product delivery, and Kubernetes is a portable and extensible open source platform for managing workloads and services. The primary goal of this book is to create a theory and practice mix that emphasizes on the core concepts of DevSecOps, Docker containers and Kubernetes clustering from a security, monitoring, and administration perspective.

This book is helpful for learning the basic and advanced concepts of Docker containers from a security point of view. The book is divided into 14 chapters and provides a detailed description of the core concepts of DevSecOps tools: Docker containers and Kubernetes platforms.

Chapter 1 introduces DevSecOps challenges, methodologies, and tools as a new movement that tries to improve the security of applications. The idea of DevSecOps is to take security as a requirement in the application design, development, and delivery process.

Chapter 2 introduces main container platforms, like Docker and Kubernetes, that provide infrastructure for both the development and operations teams. The idea of this chapter is to introduce the main technologies that will be used throughout the book and other alternatives for containers, like Podman.

Chapter 3 covers topics like how Docker manages images and containers, the main commands used for generating our images from Dockerfile, and how we can optimize our docker images by minimizing their size and, in turn, reducing the attack surface.

Chapter 4 explores security best practices and other aspects like Docker capabilities, which containers leverage in order to provide more features, such as the privileged container. We will also review Docker Content Trust and Docker Registry in this chapter; they provide a secure way to upload our images in Docker Hub Platform and private registry. Finally, we will review other registries like Harbor and Quay.

Chapter 5 walks us through Docker daemon, AppArmor, and seccomp profiles, which provide kernel-enhancement features to limit system calls. We will also review tools like Docker Bench Security and Lynis, which follow security best practices in the Docker environment, and take a look at some of the important recommendations that can be followed during auditing and Docker deployment in a production environment.

Chapter 6 discusses best practices for building container images securely. In addition to ensuring that your container is properly configured, you must ensure that all image layers in a container are free from known vulnerabilities. This is done through tools that perform a static scan of images in the Docker repositories. We will also review some open source tools, like Clair and Anchore, in this chapter to discover vulnerabilities in container images.

Chapter 7 explores attack vectors that can affect container deployments with Docker and covers topics like Docker Container threats and system attacks that can impact Docker applications. We will review examples of attacks and exploits that could target running containers. Additionally, we will review specific CVE in Docker images and understand how we can get details about specific vulnerabilities with the Vulners API.

Chapter 8 teaches us about Docker secrets and the essential components of Docker networking, including how we can communicate with and link Docker containers. We will also review other concepts that Docker uses for exposing the TCP ports that provide services from the container to the host so that users accessing the host can access the services of a container, like port mapping.

Chapter 9 covers Docker container monitoring as an important part of the maintenance of applications for getting metrics about application behavior. This chapter introduces some of the open source tools available for Docker container monitoring, such as cadvisor, dive, and sysdig falco.

Chapter 10 introduces some of the open source tools available for Docker container administration, like Portainer, Rancher, and Openshift.

Chapter 11 looks at Kubernetes architecture, components, objects, networking model, and different tools for working with Kubernetes, explaining minikube as the main tool for deploying a cluster.

Chapter 12 discusses Kubernetes security patterns and best practices for securing components and pods, applying the principle of the least privilege in Kubernetes.

Chapter 13 talks about Kubernetes security and Kubernetes Bench for Security project as an application that checks whether Kubernetes is implemented securely by executing the controls documented in CIS Kubernetes Benchmark guide. We will also review main security projects for analyzing security in Kubernetes components and critical vulnerabilities discovered in Kubernetes in the last few years.

Chapter 14 covers capabilities, which are recommended to be implemented when running Kubernetes in production. We will first analyze observability and monitoring in the context of Kubernetes, and then we will review Kubernetes dashboard for getting metrics in your cluster. Finally, we will look at the Kubernetes stack for observability and monitoring with Prometheus and Grafana.

Code Bundle and Coloured Images

Please follow the link to download the
Code Bundle and the *Coloured Images* of the book:

https://rebrand.ly/43164f

The code bundle for the book is also hosted on GitHub at **https://github.com/ bpbpublications/Implementing-DevSecOps-with-Docker-and-Kubernetes**. In case there's an update to the code, it will be updated on the existing GitHub repository.

We have code bundles from our rich catalogue of books and videos available at **https://github.com/bpbpublications**. Check them out!

Errata

We take immense pride in our work at BPB Publications and follow best practices to ensure the accuracy of our content to provide with an indulging reading experience to our subscribers. Our readers are our mirrors, and we use their inputs to reflect and improve upon human errors, if any, that may have occurred during the publishing processes involved. To let us maintain the quality and help us reach out to any readers who might be having difficulties due to any unforeseen errors, please write to us at :

errata@bpbonline.com

Your support, suggestions and feedbacks are highly appreciated by the BPB Publications' Family.

Did you know that BPB offers eBook versions of every book published, with PDF and ePub files available? You can upgrade to the eBook version at www.bpbonline.com and as a print book customer, you are entitled to a discount on the eBook copy. Get in touch with us at :

business@bpbonline.com for more details.

At **www.bpbonline.com**, you can also read a collection of free technical articles, sign up for a range of free newsletters, and receive exclusive discounts and offers on BPB books and eBooks.

Piracy

If you come across any illegal copies of our works in any form on the internet, we would be grateful if you would provide us with the location address or website name. Please contact us at **business@bpbonline.com** with a link to the material.

If you are interested in becoming an author

If there is a topic that you have expertise in, and you are interested in either writing or contributing to a book, please visit **www.bpbonline.com**. We have worked with thousands of developers and tech professionals, just like you, to help them share their insights with the global tech community. You can make a general application, apply for a specific hot topic that we are recruiting an author for, or submit your own idea.

Reviews

Please leave a review. Once you have read and used this book, why not leave a review on the site that you purchased it from? Potential readers can then see and use your unbiased opinion to make purchase decisions. We at BPB can understand what you think about our products, and our authors can see your feedback on their book. Thank you!

For more information about BPB, please visit **www.bpbonline.com**.

Table of Contents

As a result, this multicultural and multidisciplinary automated security environment makes security an issue that affects everyone and not just a single team. This is one of the main engines of DevSecOps.

The following image shows how we are introducing security in DevOps:

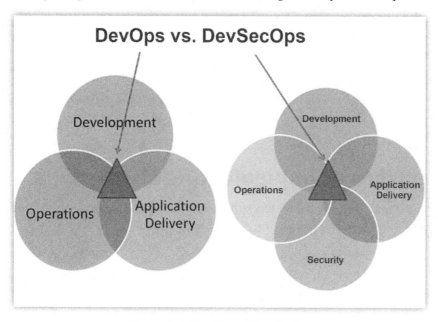

Figure 1.1: *DevOps vs DevSecOps*

Getting started with DevSecOps

The speed at which organizations want to launch software products, especially with DevOps, needs you to have the right tools and processes in the right place. It is in those cases that DevSecOps brings greater value to organizations by incorporating privacy and security into DevOps practices, while allowing you to continue operating with an enhanced level of cybersecurity.

DevSecOps is an initiative that aims to adopt security practices to include them in the DevOps process. Gartner provides a more precise definition: *"DevSecOps is the integration of security in DevOps development in the most fluid and transparent way possible. Ideally, this is done without reducing the agility or speed of developers or without requiring developers to change their tools in the development environment."*

These are the practices of how DevSecOps is implemented:

- Integrate security tools in the development integration process
- Prioritize security requirements as part of the product's backlog

- Collaborate with the security and development teams on the threat model
- Review infrastructure-related security policies prior to deployment

In those circumstances, applying a DevSecOps methodology is the best option for organizations as it incorporates best practices into the core of the software product development cycle. It does this by integrating security practices into all areas of software development, from infrastructure and continuous integration to deployments and continuous delivery of applications.

In addition, applications should follow information security best practices, including issues like data integrity, availability, and confidentiality, helping developers become aware of how to code in a secure way and the need to understand security best practices.

Advantages of implementing DevSecOps

The DevSecOps philosophy makes all team members, regardless of whether a security is their specialty, aware of the need to apply best practices in this matter.

All this will contribute to adding value to the projects carried out. They are not only intended to be functional and easy to use, but security is taken into account as an element of the development process to create secure code. This will allow vulnerabilities to be detected faster and improve responsiveness and patching to any security threat.

Here are some of the benefits of implementing DevSecOps:

- Early identification of potential vulnerabilities in the code is encouraged.
- Greater speed and agility in applying security in all phases of development.
- Throughout the development process, tools and mechanisms are provided to quickly and efficiently respond to changes and new requirements.
- Better collaboration and communication between teams involved in development, as in DevOps.

In this way, tasks related to application security can be subject to automation and monitoring mechanisms if security elements are integrated from the early stages of development.

In addition, the different teams in charge of development and operations become familiar with the security factors and apply them from the beginning, preventing possible security breaches. So, secure and stable versions of software are created in a short time, and these can be made directly available to customers. This means both customers and organizations benefit from the new possibilities.

DevSecOps lifecycle

Just like DevOps proposes the integration of tools to ensure the correctness of the code throughout the development cycle, DevSecOps suggests the integration of security tools as part of the continuous integration and deployment processes.

The integration of these tools make up pipelines known as **application security pipelines**, which can be abbreviated as app sec pipelines. These pipelines may include phases like code review automation, security testing, security scans, monitoring, and automated report generation.

This is the lifecycle and the flow of different phases in the DevSecOps ecosystem where the security process will be part of the entire life cycle:

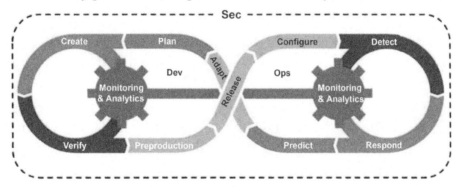

Figure 1.2: DevSecOps life cycle

With the final result of this pipeline, the requirements specification phase, and the implementation, configuration, and deployment of all the tools involved, we can execute the complete DevSecOps cycle, securing each of the phases with specific tools and integrating the entire process with continuous feedback in each phase.

The main benefits of this new culture of operations, development, and security are:

- More automation up front reduces the chances of mismanagement and lowers errors.
- According to Gartner, *"DevSecOps can lead to security functions such as Identity and Access Management (IAM), firewall, and vulnerability scanning being programmatically enabled throughout the DevOps lifecycle, leaving security teams free to establish policies."*
- Security incidents are reduced and security is improved through shared responsibility between all teams.
- Vulnerability remediation costs are reduced.

When we integrate security into the development process instead of a layer that's added later, we allow the power of agile methodologies to be harnessed by DevOps and security professionals with the aim of avoiding blocks to generate secure code.

ShiftLeft security

DevSecOps practice consists of including security in DevOps to adopt the good practices and benefits that the latter offers in development processes. To do this, it proposes to carry out a security shift left, incorporating security practices from the earliest stages of the development cycle.

These practices begin with the training and awareness of developers, as well as the involvement of stakeholders, being essential to the commitment of all parties regarding the security of the software.

Security must be considered from the design phase to avoid delay in project delivery. To reconcile agility and security, the solution lies in implementing security from the beginning of the project and not after it is completed.

Integrating security into an agile development cycle should start as early as possible, that is, in the requirements definition phase. This approach, called **Security Shift Left**, includes an orientation toward the principle of the security approach, allowing the software development process to have a totally secure workflow at each stage of the project development cycle.

For this, it is necessary to include the integration of security in the operational and development processes through the implementation of automatic systems and processes that are not only capable of detecting and alerting of security problems but also of reacting in case they detect a vulnerability.

DevSecOps methodologies

With a DevSecOps methodology, the objective is to integrate application security within the development cycle working with agile development methods linked to continuous delivery and continuous integration tools. Security requirements, which are often high, must be part of the process from the development phase to achieve this.

In this sense, efficient communication is necessary between the teams in charge of security, development, and IT operations. So, the interdisciplinary nature of the process is key to achieving a good implementation.

With the DevSecOps methodology, security mechanisms are already integrated in the early stages of development. This way, the time to launch can be dramatically shortened without having to compromise on security.

In fact, the security level tends to increase by incorporating the corresponding measures from the early stages instead of applying them as a security kit on the already closed product.

Applying the DevSecOps methodology

There are six important components in the DevSecOps methodology:

- **Code analysis**: Deliver the code incrementally, with the aim of being able to detect vulnerabilities quickly.
- **Change management**: Increase speed and efficiency by allowing changes to come from any source, and then determine if these changes are beneficial through a review process.
- **Compliance monitoring**: Be ready for an audit at any time (RGPD).
- **Threat research**: Identify potential emerging threats with every code update and respond quickly.
- **Vulnerability analysis**: Identify new vulnerabilities with code analysis, pentesting, and architecture analysis, and then analyze the response and patching times.

Security training: Train systems and development teams in good security practices.

It is important to note that the aforementioned falls mainly on the security team, but *one of the greatest principles of DevSecOps is to decentralize security* so that it becomes one more requirement in the development and delivery flow.

Tip: Why adopt DevSecOps?

Mainly because this approach decentralizes security, making it one more element of the workflow instead of something exclusive to the security department. This way, secure projects are developed, and security ends up being one more element of the organization culture through the DevSecOps methodology.

According to a survey carried out by GitLab, 30% of users claim to be part of a team focused on the security of the applications they develop, but 45% of developers still consider that security tests are carried out in a phase too late in the life cycle.

Security testing

Security testing in code is an essential element of a DevSecOps tool because it helps determine application security flaws at the code level, before they can be exploited by an attacker. So, it is important to analyze all the dependencies that are being used in the application and check them for vulnerabilities that arise from the lack of security patches.

Security testing is often called **intrusion testing** or **penetration testing**. This testing can be carried out in two modes: white box or black box. It is aimed at breaking the security measures of a system.

- **White box testing** allows **static analysis**, checking the internal functioning of the applications, and having all the necessary knowledge through source code and architecture.

- **Black box testing** focuses on examining the functionality of the application without the knowledge of its internal structure using **dynamic analysis**. The test cases of this approach focus on exploiting the interaction with the application from the outside (APIs, databases, files, protocols, input data, and so on) to break the application's security measures.

Specific teams of attackers or adversaries called **Red Team** and teams of defenders called **Blue Team** are often employed to organize and optimize security tests on an ongoing basis. Red team members explicitly put themselves in the role of an adversary or attacker and operate independently and continuously. Members of the blue team focus on monitoring and defending a system against these attacks.

The main advantage of using white box testing is that it saves development time and costs by identifying vulnerabilities during development. This way, developers can spend time developing and innovating, rather than correcting bugs in applications deployed in production.

You can scan your source code for known vulnerabilities if you are using GitLab as your CI/CD continuous deployment and integration application. GitLab performs a comparison between the source and target branches and displays the information directly when merging between the two branches.

> **Tip: Security testing with GitLab**
>
> If you are working with GitLab, this tool supports both static and dynamic analysis and automatically includes extensive security analysis every time a commit or pull request is performed. This includes static and dynamic security testing, along with dependency and container analysis.
>
> - **GitLab secure:** https://docs.gitlab.com/ee/user/application_security/
> - **Static analysis:** https://docs.gitlab.com/ee/user/application_security/sast/
> - **Dynamic analysis:** https://docs.gitlab.com/ee/user/application_security/dast/
> - **Dependency analysis:** https://docs.gitlab.com/ee/user/application_security/dependency_scanning/
> - **Container analysis:** https://docs.gitlab.com/ee/user/application_security/container_scanning/

Security code review

A security code review is an activity that consists of analyzing the software's source code to find errors and security problems. This activity can be carried out both in traditional and agile development processes. It allows us to identify problems like common programming errors, incorrect use of security tools provided by frameworks, insecure use of cryptography primitives, and incomplete development of a requirement, among others.

In agile methodologies, it is usually convenient to perform a code review every time a change is made. These reviews can be carried out by the developer who made the change as well as by another person. At the same time, it improves the code quality by verifying that it complies with guides and good coding practices, whether they are specific to each language or to the organization.

Various types of reviews can be performed on the code in order to detect security problems like peer reviews, code audits, and automated code reviews.

Continuous integration and continuous delivery

DevOps manages principles that are part of the collaborative structure and are used throughout the development and deployment of applications. The following are the principles in which DevOps operates:

- Continuous integration
- Continuous delivery
- Continuous deployment

Software integration raises problems that are known to those involved in software development—new code is written that implements a new feature and integrates with the rest of the project by performing unit and integration tests.

In order to avoid errors at the end of the development phase, many teams are committed to applying continuous integration, with which we can implement changes directly in the project every day, and if possible, several times a day.

Like continuous delivery, continuous integration is a common practice, especially in the field of agile software development. The goal of this approach is to work in small steps to achieve a more effective development process and to be able to react more flexibly to changes.

Since they work with small functionalities that can be developed in hours or a few days, integration is done quickly and the developer can make their work available to the rest of the team in just a few minutes. Any errors discovered in this process can be quickly located and fixed.

Continuous Integration (CI)

Continuous integration is the way in which the software development team integrates its partial or total work, in a certain time established by the work team. It requires automation tools that are unique to the entire team of developers. These tools help integrate in continuous form parts of code that are validated by automatic tests, which makes the development team's work more efficient by allowing them to detect failures in the early stages of the development cycle.

Continuous integration originated under the extreme programming methodology and is a software development practice that requires the periodic integration of code changes into a shared repository. Several useful steps can be followed to have a continuous integration process:

- Have a code repository in which the development is centralized. Each developer works on small tasks, and the changes to the central line of the repository are included when each task is finished.

- Start a process of compilation and testing in an automated way, which proves that the changes and additions are correct and have not altered any part of the software. For this to work properly, there must be a good set of tests that can be trusted.

- Execute this process several times a day, paying attention to the reported errors, which become a priority until they disappear. With this, we can have the latest functional version of the project status on the main line, a version that is updated several times a day.

The following image shows the **continuous integration pipeline** where developers integrate their code in the repository. Every time a commit occurs, a build tool and CI integration server are in charge of executing the construction process automatically, in addition to executing the tests to verify that the uploaded code is correct from functional the point of view:

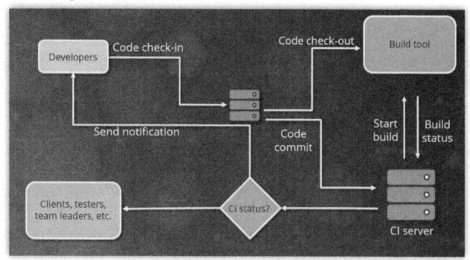

Figure 1.3: Continuous integration pipeline

The **continuous integration tools** (**CI tools**) help in repository creation, execution of tests, compilation, and version control, sometimes autonomously and sometimes in combination with other applications.

Orchestrating CI

One of the things necessary to achieve the objectives set by the DevSecOps methodology is the coordination of the work done by the team of developers. This is when the concept of continuous integration comes into play. Its main objective is to coordinate and integrate the work of the entire software development team in a main line frequently and deliver the product with these new changes as soon as possible. Jenkins is one of the leading engines for monitoring continuous integration.

Jenkins **https://jenkins.io** is probably one of the best-known continuous integration tools in the market. This software written in Java has been in constant development since 2005 and has numerous functions that assist in continuous integration, deployment, and continuous delivery. This tool can be used mainly to orchestrate processes in software development. Let's highlight its main capabilities:

- Open source and written in Java programming language
- Great support for plugins that add new functionalities
- Complements on delivery tasks and continuous deployment
- Compatible with many version control systems
- Controls via GUI (web-based), REST API and command line
- Execute manual or automatic tasks
- Distributed execution in agents

Jenkins acts by orchestrating each process and the main function is to download sources from version control, compile them, run tests, and generate reports.

Selection of continuous integration tools

In principle, continuous integration can be applied without the need for specific tools as all phases can be carried out manually, but this would require a lot of time and discipline. The appropriate tools can help facilitate work since they usually provide a server and help in the compilation of the project and version control.

Today, we can find a wide variety of tools for **Continuous Integration (CI)**. They all aim to help the developer implement this methodology, and they do it in different ways. These tools not only differ from each other in terms of their features, but there is also a great variety when it comes to licensing.

While many of them are open source and freely available, other vendors offer commercial tools. The most used tools in the market whose objective is continuous integration are:

Travis CI https://travis-ci.org. It is a continuous integration tool that works in conjunction with GitHub repositories and can be configured with a YAML file saved in the root directory of the project. This way, GitHub informs Travis CI of all the changes made in the repository and keeps the project updated every time there is a change in this file. The main features are as follows:

- Multiplatform and developed in Ruby
- Works with GitHub repository
- It is configured with a YAML file
- Free for open source projects

- Open source (MIT license)

Bamboo https://www.atlassian.com/software/bamboo is a solution developed by the Atlassian company, which also manages the Bitbucket file hosting service and allows the execution of continuous integration tasks, deployment, and release management functions. The main features are as follows:

- Multiplatform and developed in Java
- Provides a web interface and REST API
- Free for open source projects

GitLab CI is part of the popular GitLab version control system and is compatible with GitLab CI Docker. In addition to continuous integration, GitLab offers continuous deployment and delivery. As with Travis CI, the GitLab CI configuration is done with a YAML file, and pipelines can be configured and adapted to the requirements of each project.

You can get more information about this tool in the GitLab documentation at **https://about.gitlab.com/stages-devops-lifecycle/continuous-integration/**.

CircleCI (https://circleci.com) is a continuous integration tool that works with both GitHub and Bitbucket repositories. One of the main advantages offered by CircleCI is its ability to automatically run compatible builds in different environments, thanks to the use of Docker containers. The main features are as follows:

- Configuration with a YAML file
- Supports also continuous deployment
- You can deploy it on-premise or using hosting with a cloud provider
- The free tier allows deployment in a container

CruiseControl (**http://cruisecontrol.sourceforge.net/**) has probably been the oldest continuous integration tool since its launch in 2001. It has been developed ever since, by *Martin Fowler*, a pioneer in the field of continuous integration, among others. Along with a clear dashboard, developers have numerous plugins at their disposal to make their work easier. CruiseControl offers developers a control panel where they can check the build status, and its main features are:

- Cross-platform and written in Java
- Web-based dashboard
- Versions for Ruby (CruiseControl.rb) and .NET (CruiseControl.NET)
- Open source (BSD license)

Codeship (**https://www.cloudbees.com/products/codeship**) is a continuous integration tool developed by *CloudBees* with support for GitHub, BitBucket, and GitLab repositories. The tool is available in two versions: the basic version with a simple web interface, and the professional version that offers support for working with Docker containers. It offers a pre-defined CI environment and CI/CD workflows in its free version, which allow for simultaneous build testing on shared and pre-configured containers. The main features are as follows:

- Web interface in the basic version

- Configuration files in the repository in the professional version

- Support for Docker containers in the professional version

- Free tier for 100 builds per month in a test pipeline

TeamCity (https://www.jetbrains.com/teamcity) is a software that has *"gated commits"* as its main functionality, allowing the tool to verify changes in the code before integrating them into the main branch. So, only when the code is free of errors and the tests have been run correctly does it become part of the code base for the whole team. The tool automatically runs tests in the background so that the developer team can continue working on the code.

This tool emphasizes interoperability with other tools, and thanks to the pre-tested commits feature, it has the ability to check the new code before integrating it into the main line and inform in case it detects any errors. The main features are as follows:

- Cross-platform and written in Java

- Gated commits

- Free tier for 100 builds with 3 build agents

- Offers 50% discount for startups and free for open source projects

Continuous delivery (CD) - Pipelines in software development

Continuous delivery is an innovative concept of software development that is being heard more and more frequently. Thanks to this practice, the production phases that include development, quality control, and delivery are automatically repeated throughout the development process through a continuous delivery pipeline.

The main advantage is that with this methodology, software can be built under quality controls every so often in each of its development phases, allowing deliveries to be made even if the team continues to work on the development of the final product.

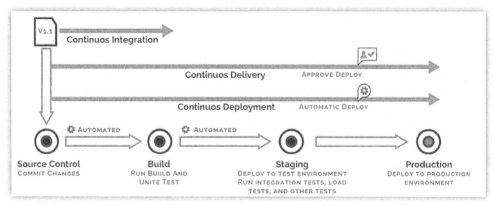

Figure 1.4: *Software delivery pipeline*

In **Continuous Delivery (CD)**, the **integrated code (IC)** is automatically tested through many environments throughout the process to reach the preproduction phase, where it is ready to be implemented definitively. The interaction between CI and CD is called CI/CD. Additionally, the pipeline provides continuous feedback, which allows us to improve the software immediately after each modification to the source code.

Advantages of continuous delivery

Software development worked differently earlier—the final product was only delivered if all functionalities were fully developed, worked perfectly, and no major flaws were detected when quality tests were performed. So, the developer had to release patches or updates every so often. Thanks to continuous delivery, the customer receives the product at an earlier stage of development, wherein it has not yet been completed.

This pre-delivery usually includes the structural functionality of the software so that the customer can test it in a real environment. This way, the client themselves (or the software tester) play an important role in the quality control process.

Thanks to the feedback received, the developer can improve the functionalities of the product in the development phase. Additionally, they receive valuable information that gives them a clear idea about what functionality they should develop next.

In this way, the three areas that include development, quality control, and production are not replaced by a single process but are constantly interconnected. When working with multiple clients, it is impossible to achieve something like this if we do not have automated processes. This is where continuous delivery intervenes as it is responsible for automating the entire process.

Thanks to continuous delivery, we can check the processes and improvements implemented on the software in real time to get feedback. If a change generates unwanted side effects, we can detect them quickly and take the necessary actions early in development. This point is an important improvement because it facilitates, for example, the detection of bugs within the code.

Continuous Integration (CI) versus Continuous Delivery (CD)

The term continuous integration often appears in the same context as that of continuous delivery. However, an important difference affects the scope of both terms. We are referring to the automation of the testing process when we talk about continuous integration, so the pipeline is a shared component with continuous delivery. Continuous delivery is a broader term as it encompasses the software delivery process as an automated process.

This way, continuous delivery complements the continuous integration model and involves the end user as they deliver the product and simultaneously run the relevant tests. The following table compares the two concepts:

Continuous Integration (CI)	Continuous Delivery (CD)
Automated testing process that thoroughly reviews each modification made to the source code.	It covers more than the testing process and includes the delivery process. New features and modifications made to the code automatically reach the end user.
The team has to run automated tests each time a new feature is added or an enhancement or code change occurs.	The tests have to be really effective on CD because the results are delivered directly to the end user.
It requires a dedicated and continuous integration server to monitor and run automated tests.	Installation on the target system must also be as automated as possible, which places greater demands on the server.
Developers have to merge code modifications frequently and continuously.	Developers have to maintain good communication with the customer and be able to clearly explain how the software works.
It requires a relatively high use of resources if the quality of the product is to be guaranteed at the time of delivery.	The effort is even greater in the case of CD, but the product can be delivered much earlier after having undergone "*real*" tests.

The development is more efficient, but it needs to be paused more often due to manual releases.	It enables continuous development because the release process is highly automated.

Table 1.1: Comparison between CI and CD

Next, we will review the main DevSecOps tools and resources that can help an organization evolve to a security-based methodology, helping develop its own security program in DevOps.

DevSecOps tools

When implementing DevSecOps, it is important to emphasize the principles and values rather than the use of tools. The people involved in the development process, and the people in charge of the product must understand the risks and vulnerabilities to which they are exposed if measures are not taken to avoid them.

This collection of tools is useful for establishing a DevSecOps platform. We have divided the tools into several categories that will help you with the different DevSecOps tasks and processes:

- Static Analysis Security Testing (SAST)
- Dynamic Analysis Security Testing (DAST)
- Dependency analysis
- Infrastructure as code security
- Secrets management
- Vulnerability management
- Vulnerability assessment

This list of DevSecOps tools and resources is dynamic and will likely change as the DevSecOps ecosystem matures and the community learns and improves how DevSecOps is implemented and adopted. In this list, we will only find initiatives that provide free or open source capabilities that help with the mission of creating a good DevSecOps environment.

> **Tip: Periodic Table of DevOps Tools**
>
> A good reference for knowing all the available tools is this periodic table of DevOps tools made by digital.ai (https://digital.ai/periodic-table-of-devops-tools), which has become a guide of reference tools or a source of information to discover new ones.

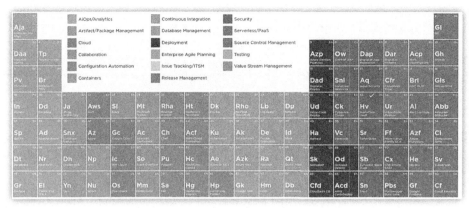

Figure 1.5: Periodic table of DevOps tools

Static Analysis Security Testing (SAST)

Tools in the SAST category are known as **white box testing tools**, where information about the system being tested is known, including the architecture and access to the source code. These tools allow you to examine the source code in a static way with the aim of detecting and reporting weaknesses that could become security vulnerabilities.

Using automated tools to perform security code controls can help us detect the main vulnerabilities we can find in applications like **SQL injection** and **Cross-site scripting**. The purpose of these tools is to verify OWASP top 10 compliance, dynamically scan the running application for vulnerabilities, and promote software security culture among developers.

For example, we can use the *Bandit* tool, which performs an in-depth analysis of the code and provides a comprehensive report for all the vulnerabilities identified in the code, for *Python-based applications*. From there, the decision is made to continue or stop the pipeline, depending on the number and severity of the vulnerabilities, with the aim of fixing them before continuing.

Other tools like *SonarQube* can be used for continuous quality inspection of software with support for multiple languages and *checkmarx* as a complete set of software security solutions providing security testing for static and dynamic applications.

These tools are flexible and easily integrated into the development cycle, providing feedback even while the code is being written. Since they do not require the code to be executed to identify security problems, we can integrate them into the development environments of each developer. This is also known as **Integrated Development Environment (IDE)**.

Bugs can be caught quickly this way, and development teams can work on mitigations early. This leads to improvements in code integrity and enables developers to write more secure code.

For example, *SonarQube* incorporates within its quality rules more than 600 expressions for the analysis of vulnerabilities like XSS, SQL Injection, and CSFR, which include the ability to identify vulnerabilities from the OWASP Top 10, SANS Top 25, and the CWE list.

Here's a list of open source tools that can be used for SAST:

- *Bandit* **https://github.com/PyCQA/bandit**
- *FindSecBugs* **https://find-sec-bugs.github.io**
- *LGTM* **https://lgtm.com**
- *SonarQube* **https://www.sonarqube.org**
- *Flawfinder* **https://dwheeler.com/flawfinder**
- *Checkmarx* **https://www.checkmarx.com**

SAST solutions analyze the code of a developed application, following a series of rules that look for patterns and flows in the source code without the need to compile it, according to standards like **Common Weakness Enumeration (CWE)**.

This type of solutions can be easily integrated into continuous integration systems, allowing you to monitor the code and detect the vulnerabilities related to input validation, race conditions, or the incorrect use of pointers and references that could cause a buffer overflow.

For example, LGTM is a tool that allows us to analyze the GitHub public repositories for the execution of static code analysis and vulnerability analysis. Here are some of its main features:

- Supports many programming languages like Java, TypeScript/JavaScript, Python, C/C ++ and C #
- Analyzes the content of projects whose source code is stored in public repositories hosted on BitBucket, GitHub, and GitLab
- Analyzes each revision of a certain project that contains vulnerabilities

We could do a search for the security rules defined by language. For example, we can use the search string *"language: Python security"* if we are interested in searching for security rules in Python.

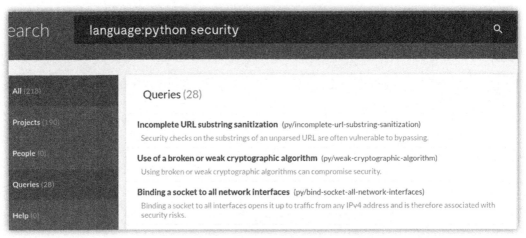

Figure 1.6: LGTM Python security rules

At this point, projects are evaluated based on code quality and provide information on the impact of each commit. When a commit is performed, it is analyzed against a set of rules depending on the language, each of which corresponds to a particular aspect of the best programming practices for that language. The result is data that shows trends in productivity and quality for a given project.

Finding problems with the code and fixing them in the branch we are working on is useful before the code merges with the main repository. If you own or manage a repository parsed by LGTM, you can enable automated code review every time a branch is merged. We can activate the code review mode every time we make a pull request to do this.

Tip: Source code analysis tools

In the following links, you can check many tools for source code analysis categorized by programming language:

- https://samate.nist.gov/index.php/Source_Code_Security_Analyzers.html

- https://owasp.org/www-community/Source_Code_Analysis_Tools

Software quality control aims to identify security problems in the source code. This control can be performed both in the pre-commit phase by integrating it into the IDE, and in the continuous integration phase by integrating it into the pipeline. This control is carried out through the **Static Analysis Security Testing (SAST)** and **Dynamic Analysis Security Testing (DAST)** testing tools, whose objective is to examine the source code to find possible vulnerabilities.

Dynamic Analysis Security Testing (DAST)

In the development of web applications, each time a new version or update is created, the security team's support is necessary to execute on-demand and manual security evaluations with DAST tools to identify vulnerabilities. This ensures the deployment of applications in accordance with the organization's secure software development methodology.

DAST, unlike **static tests (SAST)**, focuses on finding vulnerabilities in real-time, that is, while the application is running. The objective of DAST testing is to detect vulnerabilities not detected in the previous phases.

Web application scanners are an important part of vulnerability assessment and security testing. Most of them have access via API or CLI, which can be used to initiate analysis in the target applications. Here are some of the main open source tools for dynamic analysis security testing:

- **OWASP ZAP** - https://owasp.org/www-project-zap/
- **Arachni Scanner** - http://www.arachni-scanner.com/
- **Nikto** - https://cirt.net/Nikto2

OWASP Zed Proxy Attack - ZAP is one of the most widely used security scanners by security professionals to identify vulnerabilities in code and server configuration. Automatic vulnerability analysis is performed on the web application, based on the OWASP Top 10 list, through OWASP's *Zed Attack Proxy* tool.

With this tool you can perform a security scan in the QA/staging environment and solve the most critical configurations at the security level, such as the revelation of sensitive information or the use of HTTP headers in an insecure way.

Dependency analysis

In general, libraries and dependencies developed by third parties provide us essential functionalities for our application. In the majority of developments, an application can base half of the development on third-party libraries.

In today's software development environment, much of the work is done collaboratively, and in open source communities it is normal to run into security issues and the risks associated with these issues.

So, we can find vulnerabilities that do not originate in our development but in an imported library that we did not know was vulnerable if a static analysis of the complete code is carried out.

For this reason, it is important to use a dependency analysis tool, which, as a general rule, analyzes the dependency managers used by our software for compilation, such as a `pom.xml` in Maven and `requirements.txt` in Python. These tools have the capacity to query vulnerability databases like NIST in search of known vulnerabilities for a specific version of a library.

Tools like *OWASP Dependency Check* could be used for applications developed in Java and .NET. These tools can be run before creating the builds to detect if any vulnerable software is being used in the application.

Other tools include *npm-check* that allows you to check npm update packages, *hakiri* that monitors Ruby apps for dependency and code security vulnerabilities, and *FBInfer* that detects bugs in Java and C/C++/Objective-C code. All these tools can detect vulnerable code and identify outdated library dependencies.

- **Dependency Check- https://owasp.org/www-project-dependency-check**
- **SonaType (Free for Open Source projects)- https://ossindex.sonatype.org/**
- **Snyk (Free for Open Source) - https://snyk.io/**
- **Bunder Audit - https://github.com/rubysec/bundler-audit**
- **Rubysec - https://rubysec.com/**
- **Retire JS - https://github.com/RetireJS/retire.js**
- **NPM check - https://www.npmjs.com/package/npm-check**
- **Hakiri- https://hakiri.io**
- **FBInfer- https://fbinfer.com**

Tip: Learn with vulnerable applications

Here's a list of vulnerable applications that can be implemented to know the main security risks that we can find in the applications. These same applications can be protected by fixing the vulnerabilities to learn how to prevent attackers from exploiting some of the vulnerabilities.

- https://github.com/owasp/nodegoat
- https://github.com/OWASP/OWASPWebGoatPHP
- https://github.com/WebGoat/WebGoat
- https://github.com/OWASP/WebGoat.NET

The purpose of dependency control is to control and minimize vulnerabilities from third-party frameworks or libraries. To do this, we could integrate the OWASP Dependency-Check plugin into the pipeline, the purpose of which is to identify the dependencies of the projects and check for any known vulnerability.

Dependency Check currently supports the Java and .NET languages, along with providing experimental support for Ruby, Node.js, and Python and limited support for C/C ++.

Infrastructure as Code security

Infrastructure as Code (IaC) implies that your server configuration is stored in a source code repository with the application source. In this way, automation tools like Ansible, Chef, or Puppet will take the configuration artifact (usually written in a simple or scripting language like YAML or Ruby) and apply each task to the system where we have to automate the configuration process.

Container solutions like Docker are very popular even though they build the infrastructure using just a few lines of code. For example, *"Docker Hub"* is a public repository of Docker images from where you can download the images to generate the containers.

However, these Docker images can be exposed as they contain different vulnerabilities. At this point, it is important to run specific tools to analyze container images before deploying them in the infrastructure.

Within the Docker ecosystem, we find solutions that offer the possibility of scanning the images. For example, *Clair* scans the base Docker images and offers a report with the main vulnerabilities of an image, performing a preliminary analysis of the dependencies and packages that this image downloads.

Anchore Engine is another interesting tool. It is an open source policy-based compliance that provides a centralized service to inspect, analyze, and certify container images and allows developers to obtain detailed analysis on Docker images and define security policies to be applied during image analysis.

Here are some of the main open source tools for security in Infrastructure as Code:

- **Clair** - **https:**//github.com/coreos/clair
- **Anchore Engine** - https://github.com/anchore/anchore-engine
- **Dagda** - https://github.com/eliasgranderubio/dagda
- **Open-Scap** - https://www.open-scap.org/getting-started
- **Dockscan** - https://github.com/kost/dockscan
- **Inspec** - https://community.chef.io/tools/chef-inspec/

Secrets management

Due to automation processes, storing credentials in configuration files and environment variables to access services is a common practice used by developers and administrators. However, storing credentials in files or settings can expose credentials with sensitive information.

This can be avoided by using different tools that aim to search files for sensitive information before committing or pushing it to the repository.

To support the security of the code at the level of credentials, secret keys, and confidential data, it would be important to be able to use tools that automate the process of managing these keys.

The following tools allow us to store these credentials in separate environments, where we can store and retrieve the credentials from a specific environment and use them programmatically from our code. Here are a few open source tools available for secrets management:

- **Hashicorp Vault** - https://www.vaultproject.io/
- **Torus** - https://tor.us/
- **Keywhiz** - https://square.github.io/keywhiz/
- **EnvKey** - https://www.envkey.com/
- **Confidant** - https://github.com/lyft/confidant
- **AWS Secrets Manager** - https://aws.amazon.com/secrets-manager/
- **Transcrypt** -https://github.com/elasticdog/transcrypt
- **BlackBoxr** -https://github.com/StackExchange/blackbox
- **Git Secrets** -https://github.com/awslabs/git-secrets
- **Git leaks** -https://github.com/zricethezav/gitleaks
- **BlueBracket**-https://blubracket.com

These tools allow you to check sensitive information (such as AWS keys, access tokens, and SSH keys) leaked through public source code repositories due to accidental commits.

Vulnerability management

In addition to performing the security validations of the code itself, we must detect the vulnerabilities in dependencies used by the application. The tools that create the DevSecOps pipeline can generate many vulnerabilities, and each has its own format.

This makes it difficult to manage all the data, let alone monitor and fix vulnerabilities. So, vulnerability management solutions are essential in the DevSecOps process, enabling all the data to be managed, examined, and monitored and the vulnerabilities fixed. The following are some of the main open source tools available for vulnerability management:

- **ArcherySec** - https://github.com/archerysec/archerysec
- **DefectDojo** - https://www.defectdojo.org/
- **JackHammer** - https://github.com/olacabs/jackhammer

Tip: Discovering Vulnerabilities

It is recommended to query the list of existing CVE vulnerabilities in third-party libraries and applications for more details about the vulnerabilities that we find in the applications. The list and description of the vulnerabilities can be found at https://www.cvedetails.com, and a detailed description is available at https://nvd.nist.gov.

Vulnerability assessment

A common practice is to perform vulnerability assessments on production systems to identify running services and the associated vulnerabilities.

For example, if we execute a vulnerability assessment tool in the machine where Docker is installed and then run the scan, it will give us a good overview of the services that are actually running.

This can be done with various solutions, such as OpenVas, that can be integrated into the CI/CD pipeline. Here are a few open source tools for vulnerability assessment:

- **OpenVAS - http://openvas.org/**
- **Docker Bench - https://github.com/docker/docker-bench-security**

Alerts and monitoring

It is convenient to monitor the applications once they are deployed in production in a secure and automated way. This allows us to ensure that the systems are working correctly and that their performance is adequate.

This process can be automated, and is known as continuous monitoring. It consists of configuring and deploying monitoring tools in an automated way that ensure that the systems behave as expected. This allows you to quickly detect and respond to potential security issues.

These tools can also detect performance or code problems, exceptions, and **Denial of Service (DoS)** attacks or brute force attacks. For this, it is necessary to have tools that provide traceability about the system's events and activities. In turn, they can store information that is useful in the face of a potential security or regulatory compliance incident.

Production applications always face new threats from unforeseen and unknown agents. Having an intrusion prevention and monitoring solution active can mitigate them. *"ModSecurity WAF (Web Application Firewall)"* is an open source solution of this type. It detects when one of the 10 main OWASP vulnerabilities, such as SQL injection or cross-site scripting, is attacked.

- **ModSecurity WAF** - https://github.com/SpiderLabs/ModSecurity

Regarding *monitoring*, there must be something transversal to all development teams with the target for getting feedback about the results of developments. In this category, we can highlight applications like *Nagios* **https://www.nagios.com/** and *Zabbix* **https://www.zabbix.com/**, which are classic monitoring tools that have evolved while adapting to the philosophy of DevOps work teams, competing to become the standard for infrastructure monitoring. Both are free and open source and written mainly in C.

From the open source point of view, solutions like *Prometheus* **https://prometheus.io/** are becoming more relevant. Additionally, it allows the visualization of metrics stored in its database as time series with *Grafana* **https://grafana.com/**. They are open source solutions and written in Golang.

Tip: DevSecOps Labs

These labs are hands-on learning opportunities to develop skills in DevSecOps:

- `https://pentesterlab.com/exercises/`
- `https://www.vulnhub.com/`
- `https://github.com/devsecops/bootcamp`
- `https://github.com/devsecops/awesome-devsecops`
- `https://www.katacoda.com/hackingtechnology/scenarios/snyk-scan`

Conclusion

In this chapter, we focused on how DevSecOps can operate in an environment. That said, only the tools and techniques are not always enough since the DevSecOps methodology requires a cultural change that promotes a *"default security"* way of working to minimize risks.

In a world where we need to develop quickly to adapt the business to changes and customer demands, organizations that have adopted DevOps within the development cycle must also implement appropriate security measures to detect and correct vulnerabilities in a more agile way.

Finally, it is important to note that DevSecOps represents the evolution of the existing DevOps practices. Ultimately, it should help improve quality and reduce risk in relation to the product and the organization.

There is no point in being the first to come out with a new product if it is discovered to have security flaws later. This is the reason why DevSecOps can be the key and the best way to manage security in automated processes, with the aim of creating security experts in each area and increasing the collaboration with the security team.

In the next chapter, we will review the main container platforms that provide infrastructure for both development and operations teams.

Points to remember

- **DevSecOps** is a philosophy that integrates the DevOps security process, generating a natural response to the bottlenecks that originate in the traditional security patterns that exist in continuous delivery developments. This philosophy focuses on the cooperation between development, operations, and security. It seeks to integrate the work of all teams in each part of the process, creating a synchronized and automated progress in activities.

- **Security testing** is usually the most widespread security measure and involves carrying out specific security tests in addition to software quality assurance tests (unit, integration, functional, performance, and so on).

Multiple choice questions

1. Which tools have the capacity to perform an in-depth analysis of the code and provide a comprehensive report for all the vulnerabilities that have been identified in the code?

   a. Bandit and SonarQube

   b. SonarQube and OWASP ZAP

   c. Snyk and Anchore engine

   d. Clair and NPM check

2. Which tools have the capacity to identify vulnerabilities using dynamic analysis to ensure the deployment of applications in accordance with the organization's secure software development methodology?

    a. Snyk and SonarQube

    b. SonarQube and OWASP ZAP

    c. Clair and NPM check

    d. Nikto and OWASP ZAP

Answers

1	a
2	d

Questions

1. What is the difference between continuous integration and continuous delivery?

2. What are the main components used by DevSecOps methodology?

3. What are the main techniques for security testing?

Key terms

- **DevSecOps**: Acronym that defines the unification of development, security, and operations

- **Pipeline**: It is a concept that allows automating the software development process

- **Continuous integration**: Consists of making automatic integrations of a project as often as possible to detect errors when compiling and executing the tests of an entire project

- **Continuous delivery**: Continuous delivery is an extension of continuous integration, wherein the software delivery process is automated to allow easy and reliable deployments at any time

- **SAST - Static Application Security Testing**: Also known as *"white box test"*, it allows developers to find security vulnerabilities in the application source code

- **DAST - Dynamic Application Security Testing**: Also known as a *"black box"* test, it allows you to find vulnerabilities and weaknesses in the security of a running application, typically web applications

- **IAST - Interactive Application Security Testing**: It is a combination of static and dynamic analysis techniques (SAST + DAST) generating a global analysis of the entire system

CHAPTER 2
Container Platforms

In this chapter, we will review main containers platforms that provide infrastructure for both the development and operations teams, like Docker and Kubernetes. We will also review other alternatives like Podman for containers. This chapter will introduce you to the main technologies that will be used throughout the book.

Containers have helped streamline the process of moving applications through development, testing, and production, while Docker and Kubernetes have helped reinvent the way applications are built and deployed—as collections of microservices rather than with monolithic approaches.

Structure

We will cover the following topics in this chapter:

- Docker containers
- Podman
- Container Orchestration
- Kubernetes
- Kubernetes alternatives

Objective

After studying this chapter, you should be able to understand the concept of Docker containers, learn about other container platforms like Podman, and get familiar with container orchestration and container orchestration platforms like Kubernetes and alternatives.

Docker containers

DevOps aims to improve the quality of the new software versions and accelerate the development, delivery, and implementation, thanks to the effective cooperation of all those involved and continued automation. Automated DevOps tasks include automated build processes, static and dynamic code analysis, and module, integration, system, and performance testing.

The core spine of DevOps is still the reflections on **Continuous Integration (CI)** and **Continuous Delivery (CD)**, two central fields of automatic deployment of applications.

Docker offers integration options for consolidated CI/CD tools like Jenkins or Travis and allows you to automatically load your images from the Docker Hub repository or version control repositories like GitHub, GitLab or Bitbucket. This is how the container platform represents a base for DevOps workflows, in which developers can create new components for applications in common and run them in any testing environment.

With containerized platforms, developers can own the applications and their dependencies to frameworks and components, enabling them to reduce the dependency on IT operations teams.

What is Docker?

Docker is a container platform to quickly develop, deploy, and manage applications, and it packages software into standardized units called **containers** that include everything necessary for the software to run, including libraries, system tools, and code.

With Docker, you can deploy and quickly adjust the scale of applications in any environment with the certainty of knowing that your code will run the same, from the development to the production environment and both in the cloud and on-premise.

A remarkable feature of this container is the *Docker Hub* **http://hub.docker.com**, a repository where Docker users can share the images they have created with other users. For Linux users, installing one of these containers is as easy as downloading an application from the package manager. The download from the Docker Hub is done through commands and runs on the system itself.

Docker uses the *LibContainer* module to manage the Linux Kernel functions and a group of isolation technologies like *Namespaces, Control Groups, AppArmor, security profiles, network interfaces* and rules for the firewall necessary for the operation of the containers.

Containers versus virtual machines

To contextualize this new paradigm defined by Docker in which applications run inside completely independent containers, we must compare it with other virtualization paradigms, such as virtual machines.

Containers are a multi-level abstraction above the hardware abstraction of virtual machines and abstract the application layer by packing code and dependencies in one container.

Virtual machines allow the abstraction of physical hardware, while the hypervisor allows multiple virtual machines to run on a single computer. Each virtual machine includes a full copy of an operating system, application, binaries, and the required libraries.

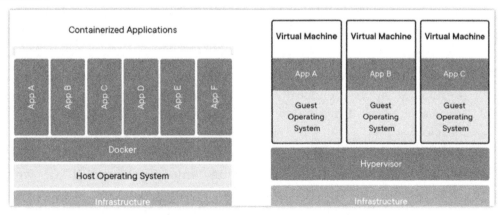

Figure 2.1: *Containers vs virtual machines*

Docker features for container management

With the use of containers, resources can be isolated and services restricted. Additionally, processes are given the ability to have an almost completely private vision of the operating system with its own process space identifier, the structure of the file system, and the network interfaces.

Multiple containers share the same core, but each container can be restricted to using a defined amount of resources such as CPU, memory, and I/O. These are some of the main features that Docker offers:

- It takes better advantage of the hardware and only needs the minimum file system for the services to work

- The containers are self-managed (although they can depend on other containers), so they don't need anything more than the image of the container for the services offered to work

- A Docker image can be understood as an operating system with dependencies for supporting installed applications; the container is created from an image

- Docker images are portable between different platforms, with the only requirement being that Docker is installed and the service is running in the host system

- The project offers us a repository of images like GitHub code repository; this service is called **Docker Hub Registry** and allows you to create, share, and use the images created by us or other providers

Virtualizing with Docker offers us a series of advantages, including the following:

- **Portability**: All containers are portable, so we can take them to any other Docker device without having to reconfigure anything. Docker allows you to run your application locally on any operating system, on any on-premise server, or even in a cloud provider like Google Cloud or Amazon Web Services.

- **Performance**: Containers have better performance than traditional virtualization, since they are based on **Linux Containers** (**LXC**), which runs directly on the kernel of the host machine, avoiding the traditional virtualization layer based on a hypervisor that penalizes performance.

- **Self-management**: Docker is responsible for everything, so the containers should only have what is necessary for the application to work; for example, the libraries, files, and configurations necessary for executing the application in a specific environment.

Docker architecture

Docker uses a client-server architecture where the client part communicates with the daemon so that it is in charge of building, executing, and distributing the containers. Client and server are able to run both on the same host and on different platforms since communication between them is done using a REST API over UNIX sockets or a network interface.

The following screenshot shows the different elements of the Docker architecture:

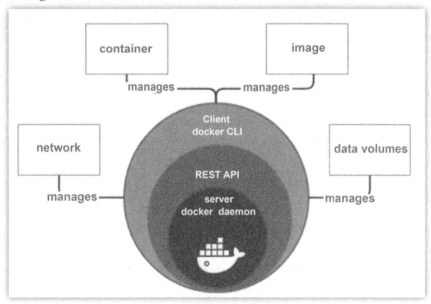

Figure 2.2: Docker architecture

A Docker container system consists mainly of the following elements:

- **Docker engine (Daemon)**: It is a process that runs on any Linux distribution and exposes an external API for the management of images and containers. This process is responsible for creating images, uploading and downloading from a Docker Registry, and executing and managing containers.

- **Docker Client**: The Docker Client allows us to manage the Docker Engine and can be configured to work with a local or remote Docker Engine, allowing us to manage both our local development environment and our production environment.

- **Docker Image**: Template used to create the container for the application that we want to deploy.

- **Docker registry**: It has the repositories where the images are stored, both public and private access. The purpose of this component is to store the images generated by the Docker Engine and distribute our applications.

- **Docker Containers**: These have the folders where everything necessary (libraries, dependencies, binaries, and so on) is stored so that the application can be executed. The Docker tool offers the ability to package and run an application in an isolated environment called a container.

The logic of operation is that the command line interface, depending on the requests it receives from the client, uses the REST API to communicate with the daemon. The Docker daemon process is responsible for creating and managing objects like images, containers, network, and volumes.

Docker engine

The heart of any Docker project is the Docker engine, which is an open source client-server application available to all users in the current version on all established platforms.

The components that make up the basic architecture of this engine are: a daemon with server functions, application programming interface (**API**) based on **Representational State Transfer** (**REST**), and the terminal of the operating system **Command-Line Interface** (**CLI**) as an interface of the user (client). Docker bases its operation on a client-server architecture with the main components defined by:

- **Docker daemon**: Docker engine uses a daemon process as a server that works in the background of the host system and allows central control of the Docker engine. It is also responsible for creating and managing all images, containers, or networks.

- **REST API**: Specifies a series of interfaces that allows other applications to interact with the Docker daemon.

- **CLI**: Docker uses the terminal of the operating system as a client program, which interacts with the daemon through the REST API and allows users to control it through scripts or commands.

Docker allows you to execute and manage software containers directly from the terminal. The **docker** command and instructions like build (create), pull (download) or run (execute) can be used to communicate with the daemon, enabling both client and server to be in the same system.

Depending on the type of connection to be established, communication between client and server occurs either through the REST API, UNIX socket, or a network interface.

The **docker run** command starts the Docker daemon to search the image in your host and starts a container with the name **hello-world**. If Docker has been installed correctly, you should receive an output like the one shown in the following image:

```
$ docker run hello-world
Unable to find image 'hello-world:latest' locally
latest: Pulling from library/hello-world
0e03bdcc26d7: Pull complete
Digest: sha256:95ddb6c31407e84e91a986b004aee40975cb0bda14b5949f6faac5d2deadb4b9
Status: Downloaded newer image for hello-world:latest

Hello from Docker!
This message shows that your installation appears to be working correctly.

To generate this message, Docker took the following steps:
 1. The Docker client contacted the Docker daemon.
 2. The Docker daemon pulled the "hello-world" image from the Docker Hub.
    (amd64)
 3. The Docker daemon created a new container from that image which runs the
    executable that produces the output you are currently reading.
 4. The Docker daemon streamed that output to the Docker client, which sent it
    to your terminal.

To try something more ambitious, you can run an Ubuntu container with:
 $ docker run -it ubuntu bash

Share images, automate workflows, and more with a free Docker ID:
 https://hub.docker.com/

For more examples and ideas, visit:
 https://docs.docker.com/get-started/
```

Figure 2.3: Docker hello-world execution

The container is started after downloading the image successfully and receiving the *"Downloaded newer image for hello-world: latest"* message. It includes a simple **hello-world** script. You can share images, automate workflows, and do a lot more with a free Docker ID subscription in **https://hub.docker.com**.

You can refer to the Docker user guide at **https://docs.docker.com/get-started/ overview** for more examples.

Docker client

The Docker client uses the remote API of the Docker Engine and can be configured to talk with a local or remote Docker Engine, allowing us to manage both our local development environment and our production servers. The following are the most common Docker commands:

- **docker info**: Gives information about the number of containers and images that the current machine is managing as well as the plugins currently installed.
- **docker images**: Lists information of the images that are available on the machine (name, ID, space it occupies, and the time elapsed since it was created).

- **docker build**: Creates an image from the Docker file of the current directory.
- **docker pull <image>: <version>**: Downloads the indicated image version to the current machine. If the download version is not indicated, all available versions are downloaded.
- **docker push <image>: <version>**: Uploads the version of the indicated image to a Docker Registry, allowing its distribution to other machines.
- **docker rmi <image>: <version>**: Deletes an image on the current machine.
- **docker run <image>: <version>**: Creates a container from an image. This command allows a multitude of parameters, which are updated for each version of the Docker Engine. So, it is best to refer to the official page for its documentation.
- **docker ps**: Shows the containers that are running on the machine. With the **-a** flag, it also shows the containers that are stopped.
- **docker inspect container**: Shows detailed information of a container in JSON format. You can access a particular field with the **docker inspect -f '{{.Name}}' container** command.
- **docker stop <container>**: For the execution of a container.
- **docker start <container>**: Resumes the execution of a container.
- **docker rm <container>**: Deletes a container. You can execute the **docker rm -fv $ (docker ps -aq)** command to delete all the containers of a machine.
- **docker logs <container>**: Shows the logs of a container.
- **docker stats <container>**: Shows the execution statistics of a container, such as the memory used, the CPU, and the disk.
- **docker exec <container> <command>**: Executes a command in a container. It is useful to debug containers in execution with the command **docker exec -it container bash**.
- **docker volume ls**: Lists the existing volumes on the machine. Run **docker volume –help** for a complete list of commands related to volumes.
- **docker network ls**: Lists the existing networks on the machine. Run the **docker network –help** command for a complete list of commands related to networks.
- **docker cp**: Copies files between the host and a container.

The Docker command line will connect to this daemon, which will keep the Docker status and so on. Each of the commands will also be executed as superuser, by having to contact this daemon using a protected socket. From there, we can create a container by downloading it from the official repository.

```
$ docker pull nginx
```

```
$ docker pull nginx
Using default tag: latest
latest: Pulling from library/nginx
45b42c59be33: Pull complete
8acc495f1d91: Pull complete
ec3bd7de90d7: Pull complete
19e2441aeeab: Pull complete
f5a38c5f8d4e: Pull complete
83500d851118: Pull complete
Digest: sha256:f3693fe50d5b1df1ecd315d54813a77afd56b0245a404055a946574deb6b34fc
Status: Downloaded newer image for nginx:latest
$ docker images
REPOSITORY          TAG               IMAGE ID          CREATED         SIZE
nginx               latest            35c43ace9216      3 days ago      133MB
hello-world         latest            bf756fb1ae65      13 months ago   13.3kB
```

Figure 2.4: Executing the docker pull command

The **pull** command downloads a basic Nginx container and installs it. Many images are created and can be shared on the Docker website, in the style of Python libraries or Debian packages. You can search all the images of a certain type, like Ubuntu, or search for the most popular images.

You can start executing the commands once downloaded. We are executing a **nginx** container using the following command, with the **-t** option indicating that a terminal is being created and the **-i** option that allows the execution of the command interactively.

```
$ docker run -i -t nginx /bin/bash
```

```
$ docker run -i -t nginx /bin/bash
root@808298c388a0:/# ls -l
total 72
drwxr-xr-x   2 root root 4096 Feb  8 00:00 bin
drwxr-xr-x   2 root root 4096 Jan 30 17:37 boot
drwxr-xr-x   5 root root  360 Feb 20 21:57 dev
drwxr-xr-x   2 root root 4096 Feb 17 19:20 docker-entrypoint.d
-rwxrwxrwx   4 root root 1202 Feb 17 19:20 docker-entrypoint.sh
drwxr-xr-x   1 root root 4096 Feb 20 21:57 etc
drwxr-xr-x   2 root root 4096 Jan 30 17:37 home
drwxr-xr-x   8 root root 4096 Feb 17 19:20 lib
drwxr-xr-x   2 root root 4096 Feb  8 00:00 lib64
```

Figure 2.5: Executing nginx container with docker

In the previous instruction, we are executing the **/bin/bash** command for getting a terminal shell inside the container.

Tip: Testing and training Docker in the cloud

In the https://labs.play-with-docker.com URL, we have a service that allows you to run Docker containers in the cloud.

Play with Docker http://training.play-with-docker.com is an online environment that allows you to run Docker commands without having a Docker installed on your machine.

This environment gives the experience of having an Alpine Linux virtual machine in the browser, where you can build and run Docker containers and even create clusters in the Docker Swarm mode. Play with Docker also includes a training site composed of a set of laboratories with practices from basic to advanced levels.

Containerd

In recent years, the adoption of Docker in projects has led it to become the standard platform for building, shipping, and running distributed applications, covering functional areas from infrastructure to orchestration.

In this way, Docker offers developers with tools to be more productive and containerd is the core container runtime that provides the primitives to use container-based solutions like Linux containers, Docker, or Podman.

Containerd **https://containerd.io/** aims to offer the primitives and core functions that will allow you to manage containers on Linux and Windows operating systems. Furthermore, the main advantage is that Docker and AWS ECS, Microsoft AKS, or Kubernetes will be able to use containerd. These are some of the main characteristics:

- Execution and supervision of containers
- Image distribution
- Network interface management
- Local storage
- Native plumbing API

The goal of containerd is to divide the Docker platform into a modular architecture of decoupled components. We can see the containerd architecture in the GitHub repository:

- https://github.com/docker-archive/containerd/blob/master/design/architecture.md

> **Tip: Open Container Initiative**
> - The Open Container Initiative https://opencontainers.org aims to create industry standards around container formats and execution environments. This initiative comes from Docker and other industry leaders and is coordinated by the Linux Foundation. It currently has two specifications: the Runtime Specification and the Image Specification.
> - It's basically about all this container stuff being completely transparent to you, regardless of whether you're using Docker, Podman, or any other container-based system. This means the instructions have to be basically the same.

Podman

Podman **https://podman.io** is a native, open source tool for Linux that does not use any daemons or background processes. It has been thought and designed to facilitate the search, execution, construction, sharing, and deployment of applications using the Open Containers Initiative (OCI) container and image technology.

The key innovation that Podman brings with it is that it doesn't need a daemon process for controlling the instances for each of the containers. This provides the opportunity to access the various virtualized applications without root privileges.

Podman is the container engine that allows us to lift these containers in a similar way to Docker but with some fundamental differences:

- **Root-less**: It allows us to lift containers without having root privileges. Thanks to Podman's modular architecture, it is not necessary to execute our containers as root, which is an advantage as we can execute our containers with different users who have different privileges. This happens without the risk of someone who has access to the container service executing containers as root user.
- **Daemon-less**: Podman does not need to raise a single daemon of many services to work. Rather, it is something similar to the microservices architecture and executes the necessary services for each container.
- **Pods**: Podman coined the term pod as we know it with Kubernetes so that we could lift pods from one or more containers and isolate them from other pods.
- **Command line**: The commands are equivalent to those of Docker, and there are no differences.

Tip: Podman security

- From the security point of view, what Podman does when running as a non-root user is create a directory in the user's home directory and store all the information about the images and containers that this user has there. For example, if we execute the Podman images command with our non-root user, it will show only the images that this user has created or downloaded.

Podman design and main functions

In addition to giving up a central daemon, a prominent feature of Podman is the so-called **pods**. Inspired by the concept of Kubernetes pods, these pods are the fusion of multiple containers in a common Linux namespace that share specific resources. A wide variety of virtualized applications can be combined this way.

As we have already mentioned, we can run the containers on the main computer as a regular user without root privileges, although the processes are run by root within a container. Podman does this by resorting to the Linux kernel user namespaces, which assign special privileges and a user ID to processes. The fact that the containers actually run as an administrator gives the Podman virtualized environment a high standard of security.

Podman is capable of running containers in exactly the same way as Docker, but it is also capable of running Pods. The fundamental difference is that a Pod can contain more than one container. The idea is to have a main container accompanied by one or more "*sidecars containers*" running in the same Pod as the main container. This way, the containers within the same Pod cooperate with each other to execute a service.

Podman has some characteristics that make it really interesting:

- It has a syntax equivalent to Docker, so you don't need to learn a new set of instructions to manage your images and containers with Podman.
- Containers can be run as root or as a user without administrator rights.
- Podman manages the entire container ecosystem, including pods, containers, images, volumes, and all using the `libpod` library.
- Podman only works on Linux platforms, although it supports different image formats, including OCI and Docker.
- You don't need a daemon or background application running permanently.
- Unlike Docker where containers are run as root users, containers under Podman's control can be run by root or by an unprivileged user.

- You can mount a podman-compose, and we can use it as docker-compose **https://github.com/containers/podman-compose**.

- It also allows us to generate a Kubernetes manifest through the running Pod, that is, we can automatically generate the YAML file that we can use in Kubernetes using the `$ podman generate kube pod_name > file.yaml` command.

Tip: Integration with Python

- A series of Python libraries have been developed to be able to implement integrations and communicate with the remote Podman API.

- For example, there is an application called Pypodman `https://github.com/containers/python-pypodman` developed in Python, which is capable of running everything that Podman runs locally and remotely and has the ability to communicate with the Podman API.

Podman commands

This container software is similar to Docker in many ways and uses the same command line interpreter, making it easy to use the same Docker commands in Podman. You can get the commands you can use in the following URL:

- **Podman commands: http://docs.podman.io/en/latest/Commands.html**

For example, we can use the following command to run a container based on the NGINX server:

```
$ podman run -d -p 80:80 --name nginx nginx:latest
```

```
$ podman run -d -p 80:80 --name nginx nginx:latest
Trying to pull docker.io/library/nginx:latest...
Getting image source signatures
Copying blob sha256:45b42c59be334ecda0daaa139b2f7d310e45c564c5f12263b1b8e68ec9e810ed
 25.84 MB / 25.84 MB [==================================================] 3s
Copying blob sha256:8acc495f1d914a74439c21bf43c4319672e0f4ba51f9cfafa042a1051ef52671
 25.34 MB / 25.34 MB [==================================================] 2s
Copying blob sha256:ec3bd7de90d781b1d3e3a55fc40b1ec332b591360fb62dd10b8f28799c2297c1
 599 B / 599 B [==================================================] 0s
Copying blob sha256:19e2441aeeab2ac2e850795573c62b9aad2c302e126a34ed370ad46ab91e6218
 894 B / 894 B [==================================================] 0s
Copying blob sha256:f5a38c5f8d4e817a6d0fdc705abc21677c15ad68ab177500e4e34b70e02a201b
 666 B / 666 B [==================================================] 0s
Copying blob sha256:83500d85111837bbc4a04125fd930f68067e4de851a56d89bd2e03cc3bf7e8ca
 1.38 KB / 1.38 KB [==================================================] 0s
Copying config sha256:35c43ace9216212c0f0e546a65eec93fa9fc8e96b25880ee222b7ed2ca1d2151
 7.55 KB / 7.55 KB [==================================================] 0s
Writing manifest to image destination
Storing signatures
186b83ed9bb4f2abcb537baa4b8d17084db3450f1f99f6a22bc7de8855ea1b32
```

Figure 2.6: Executing nginx container with Podman

With the following command, we can see the containers we have running:

```
$ podman ps
CONTAINER ID  IMAGE                COMMAND                    CREATED AT
STATUS              PORTS                                        NAMES
186b83ed9bb4      docker.io/nginx:latest       /docker-entrypoint.sh
nginx -g daemon off;   2021-02-20 22:49:02 +0000 UTC   Up 2 minutes
ago    0.0.0.0:80->80/udp, 0.0.0.0:80->80/tcp   nginx
```

The configuration of a container can be outputted via inspect, and the output is compatible with the Docker API. We can use the inspect command to see details about the container:

```
$ podman inspect <container_id or container name>
```

```
$ podman inspect nginx
[
    {
        "ID": "186b83ed9bb4f2abcb537baa4b8d17084db3450f1f99f6a22bc7de8855ea1b32",
        "Created": "2021-02-20T22:49:02.523824021Z",
        "Path": "/docker-entrypoint.sh",
        "Args": [
            "nginx",
            "-g",
            "daemon off;"
        ],
        "State": {
            "OciVersion": "1.0.0",
            "Status": "running",
            "Running": true,
            "Paused": false,
            "Restarting": false,
            "OOMKilled": false,
            "Dead": false,
            "Pid": 1931,
            "ExitCode": 0,
            "Error": "",
            "StartedAt": "2021-02-20T22:49:02.871173192Z",
            "FinishedAt": "0001-01-01T00:00:00Z"
        },
        "Image": "35c43ace9216212c0f0e546a65eec93fa9fc8e96b25880ee222b7ed2ca1d2151",
        "ImageName": "docker.io/nginx:latest",
```

Figure 2.7: Inspecting nginx container with Podman

In addition to being able to download an image from both public and private repositories, Podman allows you to search for the image you need (the package that contains your application), download it to your computer or the infrastructure where you work, and install it.

```
$ podman search python
```

```
$ podman search python
INDEX            NAME                                      DESCRIPTION                                    STARS   OFFIC
IAL   AUTOMATED
docker.io        docker.io/library/python                  Python is an interpreted, interactive, objec... 5871    [OK]

docker.io        docker.io/circleci/python                 Python is an interpreted, interactive, objec... 42

docker.io        docker.io/nikolaik/python-nodejs          Python with Node.js                            65
    [OK]
docker.io        docker.io/bitnami/python                  Bitnami Python Docker Image                    10
    [OK]
docker.io        docker.io/joyzoursky/python-chromedriver  Python with Chromedriver, for running automa... 57
    [OK]
docker.io        docker.io/library/pypy                    PyPy is a fast, compliant alternative implem... 263     [OK]

docker.io        docker.io/centos/python-35-centos7        Platform for building and running Python 3.5... 39

docker.io        docker.io/centos/python-27-centos7        Platform for building and running Python 2.7... 17

docker.io        docker.io/d3fk/python_in_bottle           Simple python:alpine completed by Bottle+Req... 5
    [OK]
docker.io        docker.io/arm32v7/python                  Python is an interpreted, interactive, objec... 56

docker.io        docker.io/centos/python-36-centos7        Platform for building and running Python 3.6... 31

docker.io        docker.io/arm64v8/python                  Python is an interpreted, interactive, objec... 24
```

Figure 2.8: Searching Python images with Podman

If you want to run any of the previous images, you just have to execute the following command to launch a Python container based shell.

```
$ podman run -it docker.io/library/python sh
```

Once you have a shell, the security of the container can be tested with the fool using amicontained—**https://github.com/jessfraz/amicontained**.

```
$ wget -O amicontained https://github.com/jessfraz/amicontained/
releases/download/v0.3.0/amicontained-linux-amd64;        chmod      +x
amicontained; ./amicontained
```

Figure 2.9: Testing security of Python container with Podman

In addition, we access it through **sh**, and we can check the operating system version inside the Python container with the following command when entering the container:

```
# cat /etc/os-release
PRETTY_NAME="Debian GNU/Linux 10 (buster)"
NAME="Debian GNU/Linux"
VERSION_ID="10"
VERSION="10 (buster)"
VERSION_CODENAME=buster
ID=debian
HOME_URL="https://www.debian.org/"
SUPPORT_URL="https://www.debian.org/support"
BUG_REPORT_URL="https://bugs.debian.org/"
```

Tip: Testing Podman

- You can get the instructions to install podman in your operating system at https://podman.io/getting-started/installation.

- As we're running a compatible service, we can just set an alias to replace the Docker CLI and have the same experience. If you know Docker, you can use Podman just by making an alias, that is, by executing this instruction on Linux: $ alias docker=podman.

- Podman provides the ability to run containers via the LibPod project. LibPod provides a library for applications looking to use the Container Pod concept popularized by Kubernetes. With Podman, we can use the same runtime for running containers locally.

- In the following lab we can launch containers using Podman and Libpod: https://www.katacoda.com/courses/containers-without-docker/running-containers-with-podman.

Container orchestration

- Working with containers has completely changed the way people think about software development, deployment, and maintenance. Containers are so light and flexible that they have given rise to new architectures of applications. This new approach consists of packaging the different services that are part of an application into separate containers, and then deploying those containers through a cluster of physical or virtual machines.

When development is simple, its administration does not require large resources. That said, the need for container orchestration appears as our project grows. Container orchestration is a tool that automates the implementation, administration, scaling, creation of networks, and the availability of applications based on this technology.

But nowadays, applications are complex and the trend with new architectures oriented toward microservices is to have at least one container for the front-end, one or more for the service interface, and another for the database.

All this gives rise to the need for container orchestration, that is, having a tool or system that automates the deployment, management, scaling, interconnection, and availability of our container-based applications. A **container orchestrator** is responsible for the following tasks:

- Deployment and raised automatic container-based services
- Self-scaling and load balancing
- Control of the *"health"* of each container
- Secrets management in parameters and configurations

Docker compose

Docker compose **https://docs.docker.com/compose/gettingstarted/** allows you to connect several containers and execute them with a single command. Implemented in the Python scripting language, its fundamental component is a central control file based on the YAML markup language. This file's syntax is similar to open source software Vagrant files used in the creation and provisioning of virtual machines.

Docker compose allows you to define a series of containers and the relationships between them at the level of a YML file with a very intuitive format. Given this YML file, it is responsible for orchestrating the creation of the containers in the correct order. It is also capable of detecting the definitions that have changed from one YML file to another and relaunching only the services that have changed.

You can define as many software containers as you want in the `docker-compose.yml` file, including all the dependencies and their interrelationships. The scheme followed to manage the multi-container applications does not differ from the one needed to manage simple containers. With the `docker-compose` command, the corresponding subcommand manages the entire life cycle of the application.

Here's an example using `docker-compose.yml` where we are starting an `nginx` container configuring path volumes, ports, and some environment variables:

```
web:
  image: nginx
  volumes:
    - ./templates:/etc/nginx/templates
  ports:
    - "8080:80"
  environment:
    - NGINX_HOST=domain.com
    - NGINX_PORT=80
```

Another characteristic of Docker compose is that it provides an **integrated scaling mechanism** through the definition of how many containers are to be started for a given service.

Kubernetes

Kubernetes **https://kubernetes.io**, also known as K8S, is the most popular container orchestration engine on the market. It is an open source orchestrator for applications executing in software containers, automating the deployment, scalability, and management of distributed applications.

The reception of Kubernetes was so great that the project was adopted by the community at the head of the **Cloud Native Computing Foundation** (CNCF) **https://www.cncf.io**, an organization created as part of the Linux Foundation. With this foundation, the project is developed with the support of many organizations and thousands of members of the open source community.

Kubernetes groups the containers in logical fragments called *"Pods"*, which represent the basic units of the manager that can be distributed in the cluster by the scheduler Kubernetes process. A pod represents a set of containers that share storage and a single IP address.

Kubernetes architecture

Kubernetes follows a master-slave architecture where each role has different tasks. The **master** controls and schedules all the activities of the cluster, while the **workers** are nodes where the containers are executed. The ease of having multiple orchestrated containers makes Kubernetes a perfect complement for microservices-based applications.

The master acts as a central control level (control plane) in the cluster and is composed of four basic elements that allow coordination within the cluster and distribute tasks:

- **API server**: In a Kubernetes cluster, all automations are launched in an API server by means of a REST API. This server acts as the central management point in the cluster.

- **etcd**: It's an open source key value store and can be considered a Kubernetes cluster's memory. It has been developed especially for distributed systems and storing configuration data.

- **Scheduler**: The role of the scheduler is to distribute the pods in the cluster, for which it finds out how many resources a Pod needs and adjusts them with the resources available to each node in the cluster.

- **Controller Manager**: This is a service of the Kubernetes master that manages the status of the cluster and executes routine tasks, directing the orchestration. The main function is to ensure that the cluster state corresponds to the state that was previously defined as the objective.

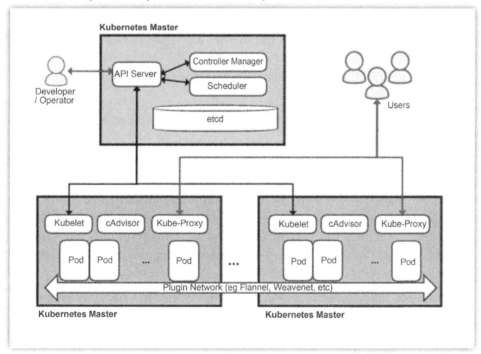

Figure 2.10: Kubernetes architecture

While the master is responsible for the orchestration, the distributed pods in the cluster are run on different nodes called workers. To do this, each node needs to run a container engine compatible with Containerd like Docker or Podman. In addition to the container engine, the Kubernetes nodes include these components:

- **kubelet**: An agent is designated with this name; running in each node, it directs and manages it. This process maintains the communication and ensures that the information is sent to the worker nodes. The agent receives the requests and supervises their execution in each node.

- **kube-proxy**: This proxy service is executed in each Kubernetes node to serve the requests that come from the worker nodes and provide services to the users of containerized applications.

Kubernetes key terms

The advantages of using containers to run and group software applications have already been mentioned. However, in a production environment, managing running containers is important to minimize the downtime of a service. This is where Kubernetes kicks in to automatically start a new one if a container fails. Here are some of the capabilities that Kubernetes can provide:

- **Service discovery and load balancing**: Kubernetes can expose a container using its own domain name or IP address. It is also capable of balancing the workload and distributing the traffic in a way that the deployment is stable.

- **Storage orchestration**: Kubernetes allows you to automatically mount a storage system of your choice, such as local storages and public cloud computing providers.

- **Automatic deployments and rollbacks**: You can describe the desired state for your deployed containers using Kubernetes, and you can change the current state to the desired state. For example, you can automate Kubernetes to create new containers for deployment, remove existing containers, and adopt all of its resources into the new container. In addition, Kubernetes restarts the containers that fail and replaces the ones not responding within the cluster.

- **Resource management**: Kubernetes allows you to specify how much CPU and memory (RAM) each container needs. Kubernetes can make better decisions to manage container resources when containers have specified resource requests.

- **Secret and configuration management**: Kubernetes allows you to store and manage information related to the configuration of the containers as well as the most sensitive information, like passwords, keys, and tokens. This sensitive information and the configuration parameters can be updated without the need to reconstruct the container images and without the need to open the sensitive information.

These are some terms that we should understand when we dive deeper into Kubernetes:

- **Cluster**: These are physical or virtual resources and storage resources used by Kubernetes where the pods are deployed, managed, and replicated.
- **Pod https://kubernetes.io/docs/concepts/workloads/pods/pod**: Pods are the smallest unit that can include one or more containers. In many cases, a Pod is composed of a single container, but its ability to accommodate several containers very close to each other is a powerful feature of Kubernetes.
- **Replication controller**: A replication controller is a Kubernetes mechanism that ensures that a Pod has raised a certain number of replicas. For example, the replication controller raises more replicas if we need more, kills them if we need less, and raises new replicas to keep the number defined if any of them fails and dies.
- **Services**: Services define how to access a group of Pods and allow access to containers with a unique **Domain Name Server (DNS)** and IP address.
- **Labels**: Labels are used to organize and select a group of objects in pairs of type key: value.

A Pod can contain one or more containers running, and it is the unit that Kubernetes manages. There are several **advantages** that Kubernetes brings to the management of containers as Pods:

- **Multiple nodes**: Kubernetes can implement a set of pods on multiple nodes instead of simply deploying a container on a single host. Essentially, a node provides the environment where a container is executing.
- **Replication**: Kubernetes can act as a replication driver for a pod. This means you can set the number of replicas you need for a specific pod.
- **Services**: A service in the Kubernetes context implies that you can assign a service name (ID) to a specific IP address and port and then assign a pod to provide that service. Kubernetes internally tracks the location of that service using the IP address to redirect requests to another pod that is executing another service.

You must understand the following concepts before you begin configuring Kubernetes:

- **Kubernetes driver**: A Kubernetes controller acts as a node from which pods, replication controllers, and services of a Kubernetes environment are deployed and managed. To create a Kubernetes driver, you must configure and run the `systemd`, `kube-api-server`, `kube-controller-manager` and `kube-scheduler` services.

- **Kubernetes nodes**: A Kubernetes node provides the environment in which containers are executed. To run a machine as a Kubernetes node, it must be configured to run a container engine, `kube-proxy` and `kubelet` services. These services must be executed on each node of the Kubernetes cluster.

- **Kubectl command**: Kubernetes management is done on the master node using the `kubectl` command. With `kubectl`, we can create, obtain, describe, or eliminate any resources that Kubernetes manages, like pods, replication controllers, and services.

- **Resource files (YAML or JSON)**: These are the formats that Kubernetes can manage to create a pod, a replication controller, a service, or another resource.

Tip: Installing and testing Kubernetes

- You can use minikube https://github.com/kubernetes/minikube if you want to install Kubernetes in your local machine.

- We can also install and deploy a Kubernetes cluster with kubeadm https://kubernetes.io/docs/setup/independent/create-cluster-kubeadm.

Kubernetes cloud provider solutions

Kubernetes is currently open-source and is used as the basis for the majority of container orchestration services. If we want to have all the advantages of Kubernetes, we have all these alternatives with a cloud provider:

- **Google Kubernetes engine https://cloud.google.com/kubernetes-engine** is a service managed and offered by Google. It is responsible for managing the instances, monitoring, logging, and updating Kubernetes to the latest available version.

- **Amazon Elastic Kubernetes Service https://aws.amazon.com/eks** is a service offered by Amazon as a managed Kubernetes service. Amazon also provides its own container orchestration system called Amazon Elastic Container Service **https://aws.amazon.com/ecs/**.

- **Azure Kubernetes Service** has its own service based on Kubernetes, which it has called AKS **https://azure.microsoft.com/en-us/services/kubernetes-service/** .

- **IBM** also offers a managed Kubernetes service called IBM Cloud Kubernetes Service **https://www.ibm.com/cloud/kubernetes-service** in its cloud.

- **Red Hat OpenShift https://www.openshift.com** proposes a complete platform of containers integrating Docker, Kubernetes as native technologies of execution and container orchestration with a series of special functions to manage permissions, storage, application life cycle, and other functions of the enterprise base in Red Hat Enterprise Linux.

- **CloudFoundry https://www.cloudfoundry.org/** offers Kubernetes in its container runtime.

- **Kops https://github.com/kubernetes/kops** is used to create and manage Kubernetes clusters in production and with high availability.

- **k0s https://github.com/k0sproject/k0s** is a Kubernetes distribution with many options preconfigured to make building a Kubernetes cluster a matter of just copying an executable to every host and running it.

Kubernetes offers solutions to most problems of a distributed deployment, such as horizontal scaling, auto scaling, monitoring the status of the cluster and each service, discovery and balancing of services, secret and configuration management, network level abstractions, deployments and automated rollbacks, and storage volume management.

In addition to using a newer version of Kubernetes, these tools provide a new container runtime called **CRI-O** as the default runtime container. CRI-O **https://cri-o.io** is the new container runtime designed for Kubernetes, which allows executing any container image that follows the **Open Container Initiative** (**OCI**) standard and is compatible with container images like Docker and Podman.

Kubernetes makes it easy to deploy pre-configured applications with Helm charts. **Helm https://helm.sh** is essentially a package manager for Kubernetes, and its function is to save time in the installation and configuration of packages. For example, many software applications must run on Kubernetes as a group of interdependent containers, and this is where helm provides a mechanism that describes how an application or service can run as a group of containers within Kubernetes.

Tip: Kubernetes learning scenarios

You can find interactive learning scenarios that provide you with a pre-configured Kubernetes instance accessible from your browser without any downloads or configuration at https://www.katacoda.com/courses/kubernetes. You can use this service to experiment, learn, and see how we can help solve real-world problems.

Figure 2.11: Kubernetes learning scenarios

Kubernetes alternatives

We can find other alternatives in the market with similar characteristics for all types of applications, from small environments to large infrastructures through various levels of complexity. For example, Nomad is a solution that has a much simpler architecture that requires other external pieces to add load balancing, service, or service discovery functionalities.

Docker Swarm

Swarm **https://docs.docker.com/engine/swarm** is the solution proposed by Docker to solve tasks related to orchestrating and planning containers through many servers. Swarm comes bundled with the Docker engine from version 1.12.0 and offers many advanced integrated features, like service discovery, load balancing, scaling, and security.

Swarm follows Docker's philosophy of focusing on the simplicity and experience of the developer, and we could say that it's easier to use than other solutions like Kubernetes. This solution it's not as powerful and not adopted by many companies, cloud providers, or by the community.

The main elements of the Swarm architecture are as follows:

- **Swarm master**: Is responsible for the entire cluster and manages the resources of several Docker hosts. In this model, services are orchestrated instead of running container commands.

- **Swarm worker nodes**: Each node of the cluster must be accessible by the master. Each node executes an agent so that it registers the Docker daemon referenced, monitors, and updates the backend with the node state. Nodes can be distributed on premises or in a public cloud provider.

- **Swarm discovery**: By default, Swarm uses a discovery service based on Docker Hub, using a token to discover the nodes that are part of a cluster. It also supports other discovery services like etcd **https://etcd.io**, Consul **https://www.consul.io**, and Zookeeper **https://zookeeper.apache.org**.

- **Swarm strategy**: Swarm has multiple strategies for the classification of nodes. When a new container is executed, the Swarm decides to locate it in the node with the highest-ranking calculated for its chosen strategy.

- **Swarm networking**: It is fully compatible with the new overlay network model of Docker.

At the base of this software is a master-slave architecture: When tasks need to be distributed in the Swarm, users transfer a so-called service to the manager node that acts as a master node in the cluster. The master node is responsible for planning the containers in the cluster and acts as the primary interface when accessing Swarm resources.

Each Docker cluster consists of at least one master node (also called administrator or manager) and as many slave nodes (called work or workers) as necessary. While the Swarm master is responsible for managing the cluster and delegating tasks, a slave is responsible for executing the units of work (tasks or tasks). In addition, container applications are distributed in services in the selected Docker accounts.

Thanks to its flexibility, it allows us to easily add new nodes, making scalability simple and fast. In addition, it provides high availability since the services can be easily replicated.

Tip: Swarm in practice

Docker Swarm is still used in development, while Kubernetes is used more often for production environments by large providers.

In the following labs, you will deploy a simple application to a single host and learn how that works. Then, you will configure a Docker Swarm mode and learn to deploy the same simple application across multiple hosts. You will then see how to scale the application and move the workload across different hosts.

- In the https://training.play-with-docker.com/swarm-stack-intro lab, you can create a Docker Swarm cluster with two nodes running an application.

- In the https://training.play-with-docker.com/ops-s1-swarm-intro lab, you will begin to explore running multiple services as a single stack with Docker Swarm.

- In the https://training.play-with-docker.com/orchestration-hol lab, you will play around with the container orchestration features of Docker.

In this section, we have analyzed Docker Swarm as a Docker native clusters management tool. For its original design, it is more a scheduler than a tool that manages the life cycle of our applications. From the point of view of filtering, tags, and the scheduler, we have seen that it offers many options and is very flexible.

Nomad

Nomad **https://www.nomadproject.io** is a workload orchestrator to handle different types of applications, including containers and microservices-based applications. This solution is compatible with Docker containers and other technologies, and it can also be used on various operating systems, such as Linux, Windows, BSD, and MacOSX.

Nomad is handled with two types of modes—the client and the server—similar to what we have in Docker Swarm. The client is in charge of performing the tasks, while the server is in charge of managing the nodes.

The recommendation is to install between 3 and 5 servers, which will be in charge of managing the deployments and monitoring, and as many clients as required to host these deployments in the cluster.

Nomad does not include discovery functionality to resolve the locations where each application has been deployed, but it integrates easily with consul **https://www. consul.io** for this function. Neither offers load balancing functions to send requests to the nodes where the application is deployed but it integrates very well with Nginx or HAProxy with automatic configuration based on consul.

Rancher - Kubernetes as a service

Rancher **https://rancher.com/**, more than an alternative to Kubernetes, is a different and easier way to use it.

It allows adding extra value in the areas of operations and cluster administration, intuitive workload management, and business support. It defines itself as a full Kubernetes distribution and supports other Kubernetes distributions, including RKE **https://rancher.com/products/rke/** and K3s **https://k3s.io/**.

Conclusion

In the next chapter, we will review how to manage containers and Docker images. Nowadays, container technologies in general and Docker in particular are becoming an indispensable technology. They are being used not only to deploy applications in production but also to create replicable development environments among all members of a team and ensure that the applications are going to execute the same in all environments (development, testing, and production).

By understanding how the building blocks fit together, with Kubernetes, you can design systems that take full advantage of the platform's capabilities to run and manage your workloads at scale.

For example, if the architecture is to be mounted on a public cloud like AWS, Google Cloud, or Azure, usually it's recommended using Kubernetes as it is a complete solution and is fully managed.

In this way, you can have a complete container orchestration system with auto-discovery, load balancing, volume management, network abstraction, secret and configuration management, and so on without difficult administration.

On the other hand, when the architecture is to be mounted on the client's own servers, it may not be worth the installation, configuration, and maintenance of a Kubernetes cluster. A simpler solution based on Docker Swarm or Nomad could be enough.

Points to remember

- Today, we can find multiple container technologies like Docker, **Linux Containers** (**LXC**), and Podman, with Docker being the most used.

- Docker is an open source project, which has provided the community with a new approach to the concept of virtualization at a technological level. It allows you to deploy and run applications within software containers, making use of a single host operating system. To do this, Docker uses the resource isolation features provided by the Linux kernel, such as namespaces and cgroups.

- Kubernetes is an open-source container orchestrator with which we can scale our applications, make automated deployments, and achieve a cluster with N nodes capable of deploying our distributed application.

- A Kubernetes cluster is made up of different nodes, which, in turn, are made up of pods that offer services. A node corresponds to a real or virtual machine that contains all the services necessary to run the pods that it contains.

- A pod represents a process that is running within the cluster and can be made up of one or more running containers.

- Although Kubernetes continues to be the main container orchestrator and has been adopted by Google cloud services, AWS, Azure, and other technologies built on Kubernetes with different technological add-ons and platform maintenance support services have been emerging. An example would be Red Hat's Openshift, which stands out over Kubernetes for its ease of use, reduced user security responsibilities, and its own networking system.

Multiple choice questions

1. What are the main components of a Kubernetes worker node?
   a. Controller Manager, Scheduler, and etcd
   b. Kubelet and Kube-proxy
   c. Replication Controller, Controller Manager, and Scheduler
   d. Pod, Kubelet and Replication Controller

2. What are the main components of a Kubernetes master node?
   a. Kubelet and Kube-proxy
   b. Replication Controller, Controller Manager, and Scheduler
   c. Controller Manager, Scheduler, and etcd
   d. Pod, Kubelet and Replication Controller

Answers

1	b
2	c

Questions

1. What is the difference between Docker and Podman?

2. Which are the main features of a Kubernetes master node for maintaining high availability in the cluster?

3. What are the main advantages of using Kubernetes over other orchestrator tools like Docker Swarm or Podman?

Key terms

- **Docker containers** allow the software to run in self-contained mini-environments that are isolated from the rest of the system.

- **Podman** is Red Hat's alternative to Docker containers. The strength of this technology is based on the optimization of resources since each container that Podman executes corresponds to a single service on the host machine.

- **Kubernetes** is a solution focused more on Docker containers and offering a complete system of orchestration with auto-discovery, load balancing, volume management, networking, secret management, configuration, etc.

## CHAPTER 3

Managing Containers and Docker Images

Introduction

This chapter covers how Docker manages images and containers, explores the main commands used for generating our images from Dockerfile, and walks us through how we can optimize our Docker images, minimizing their size and, in turn, reducing the attack surface.

A container is considered a running image, and Docker adds a layer on the image in a read/write mode when the image is in execution. Docker automatically removes the read/write layer when the container stops or is deleted, leaving the image in its original state. This allows you to reuse the same image in several environments.

Structure

We will cover the following topics in this chapter:

- Managing Docker images
- Dockerfile commands
- Managing Docker containers
- Inspecting Docker containers
- Optimizing Docker images

Objectives

After studying this unit, you will understand the concept of managing Docker containers and images. You will also learn about Dockerfile commands and best practices for optimizing and get a hang of inspecting Docker containers and optimizing Docker images.

Managing Docker images

Docker images are read-only templates that we can use as a basis for launching containers. This means what we do in the container only persists in that container, and we do not make these modifications in the image. We must create a custom image for our future containers if we want to have one.

Introducing Docker images

If we download an image using the **docker pull** command and then save it, we can see that an image is a set of directories and files with a specific structure, where each folder refers to one of the layers in the image. Within each layer, there are some files to reference the said layer and a compressed file with the file system that will form the image.

We can make backup copies of images. The process is carried out using the '**save**' option, which will pack the content and generate a file with a "**tar**" extension.

The following command can be used to download Ubuntu image and save it in a tar file as a backup:

```
$ docker pull ubuntu
$ docker save ubuntu -o ubuntu.tar
$ docker save ubuntu > backup_ubuntu.tar
```

Figure 3.1: Executing pull and save commands

When an image is extracted and constructed so that it can be usable, we are unzipping the content of each layer in order from the last one, which corresponds to the base image. This generates a file system whose content is built or modified incrementally with each layer.

The last layer of a Docker image is mounted in *read/write* mode and differentiates one container from another or any container from its base image. All the structures made on a container add new data or modify the existing data in the last layer. The writing layer is also deleted when a container is removed, but the base image remains unchanged.

An image is a permanently stored instance of a container. The **docker images** command shows you the images on your system. You can assign multiple aliases (including names and tags) to the same image whenever it is useful.

```
$ docker images
```

```
$ docker images
REPOSITORY          TAG           IMAGE ID        CREATED        SIZE
ubuntu              latest        4dd97cefde62    10 days ago    72.9MB
ubuntu              <none>        16508e5c265d    2 years ago    84.1MB
redis               latest        4e8db158f18d    2 years ago    83.4MB
weaveworks/scope    1.9.1         4b07159e407b    2 years ago    68MB
alpine              latest        11cd0b38bc3c    2 years ago    4.41MB
nginx               1.11-alpine   bedece1f06cc    3 years ago    54.3MB
```

Figure 3.2: Executing the docker images command

Here are some of the main commands we can perform on a container:

- **docker ps**: Allows you to see containers in execution
- **docker ps -a**: Allows you to see saved containers that are no longer in execution
- **docker [start|stop] <id_container>**: Let you start and stop the container execution

Docker layers

Docker layers are like Git confirmations and store the difference between the previous and current version of the image. And like Git commits, they are useful if you share them with other repositories.

Layers use space, and the more layers you have, the thicker the final image will be. Git repositories are similar in this regard. Git stores all changes between commits, so the size of your repository increases with the number of layers.

When you request an image from a repository, it downloads only the layers that you don't have downloaded to your machine locally. It is much more efficient to share images this way.

We can see the layers of an image with the following command. In this example, we are getting layers from Ubuntu image:

```
$ docker image history <image_name>: <version>
$ docker image history ubuntu:latest
```

```
$ docker image history ubuntu:latest
IMAGE            CREATED          CREATED BY                                       SIZE
4dd97cefde62     10 days ago      /bin/sh -c #(nop)  CMD ["/bin/bash"]             0B
<missing>        10 days ago      /bin/sh -c mkdir -p /run/systemd && echo 'do…    7B
<missing>        10 days ago      /bin/sh -c [ -z "$(apt-get indextargets)" ]      0B
<missing>        10 days ago      /bin/sh -c set -xe   && echo '#!/bin/sh' > /…    811B
<missing>        10 days ago      /bin/sh -c #(nop) ADD file:c77338d21e6d1587d…    72.9MB
```

Figure 3.3: Docker layers in Ubuntu image

Tip: Obtaining Docker images information using microbadger service

Another way to get the layers of an image is through the microbadger online service that shows the contents of Docker's public images, including metadata and information about the layers that make up the images. https://github.com/microscaling/microbadger

---

The following image shows the information of Ubuntu image using microbadger service: **https://microbadger.com/images/ubuntu**

Figure 3.4: Metadata from Ubuntu image using the microbadger service

Image tags

Image tags allow you to identify the versions of the images; images are listed with their associated tags. We can see the tags available for Ubuntu operating system on the Ubuntu Docker hub page at **https://hub.docker.com/_/ubuntu**:

- **18.04, bionic-20210222, bionic**
- **20.04, focal-20210217, focal, latest**
- **20.10, groovy-20210225, groovy, rolling**
- **21.04, hirsute-20210119, hirsute, devel**
- **14.04, trusty-20191217, trusty**
- **16.04, xenial-20210114, xenial**

We can download a specific tag image with the **docker pull** command. We are downloading a specific version for Ubuntu operating system with the following command:

```
$ docker image pull ubuntu:18.04
$ docker image pull ubuntu:21.04
```

```
$ docker image pull ubuntu:18.04
18.04: Pulling from library/ubuntu
92dc2a97ff99: Pull complete
be13a9d27eb8: Pull complete
c8299583700a: Pull complete
Digest: sha256:4bc3ae6596938cb0d9e5ac51a1152ec9dcac2a1c50829c74abd9c4361e321b26
Status: Downloaded newer image for ubuntu:18.04
$ docker image pull ubuntu:21.04
21.04: Pulling from library/ubuntu
486d08009c1b: Pull complete
31e228808914: Pull complete
7316b1e8087c: Pull complete
Digest: sha256:2fc51f401cb873bfec33022d065efacbaf868b2e23f4dd76d7230d129258e255
Status: Downloaded newer image for ubuntu:21.04
$ docker images
REPOSITORY          TAG             IMAGE ID        CREATED          SIZE
ubuntu              18.04           329ed837d508    10 days ago      63.3MB
ubuntu              21.04           1fc773f9e714    7 weeks ago      80.7MB
redis               latest          4760dc956b2d    3 years ago      107MB
ubuntu              latest          f975c5035748    3 years ago      112MB
```

Figure 3.5: Tags when pulling Ubuntu image from docker hub

Design considerations for Docker Images

An image is made up of layers mounted one on top of the other. All layers in the image are read-only when a new container is created from an image, and a read-write layer is added above them.

The original layered organization and *copy-on-write strategy* promote some of the best practices for creating and sharing Docker images:

- **Minimalist images**: Docker images get benefits from the point of view of stability, security, and loading time while smaller. You can always install tools in a container if you need to solve problems related to development.

- **Choosing a base image**: The base image can contain many layers and add many capacities. Official images for many distributions, programming languages, databases, and runtime environments are available in the Docker Hub repository at **https://hub.docker.com/**.

Dockerfile commands

One of the nice things about containers built using the automated build approach is that Docker Hub will show you the Dockerfile used to build the container, which provides some level of transparency over what you're downloading.

We can see the Dockerfile that is using the Ubuntu base image at **https:// github.com/tianon/docker-brew-ubuntu-core/blob/d8b441737e0291a5c 1c99f817ff1ba9ab6ccac11/focal/Dockerfile**.

Images are created using a series of commands called **instructions**. The instructions are placed in the Dockerfile file, which is basically a text file that contains a collection of changes in the root file system and the corresponding execution parameters for use within a container.

The result will be the final image. Each instruction creates a new layer in the image, which then becomes the parent of the layer created by the next instruction.

What is a Dockerfile?

A DockerFile is a text document that contains all the commands we want to execute on the command line to build an image. This image will be created using the **docker build** command that will follow the instructions.

The Docker engine executes the instructions one by one independently during the construction of the image. A layer is created for each instruction that allows them to be reused if they are cached, significantly speeding up the construction process.

For example, an instruction that requires an image of the registry in the cloud would suppose a great workload if we need to download it in each execution. Cached data is used for this, so the image will be used directly if it has been downloaded in a previous run. Every time the cached data is used, a text is displayed in the console so that the user is aware of it.

Building images from Dockerfile

The **docker build** command builds an image following the instructions of a Dockerfile that can be found in the current directory or a repository.

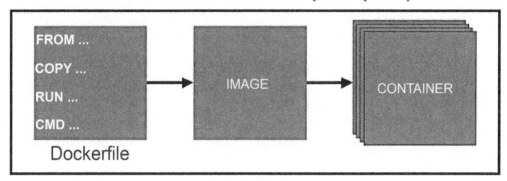

Figure 3.6: *Building process from a Dockerfile*

It is important to note that **docker build** sends the entire context of the current directory to the daemon, so it is a good practice to put the Dockerfile in a clean directory and add the necessary files to that directory if necessary.

The syntax for the command is:

```
$ docker build [options] [Dockerfile_path]
```

```
$ docker build --help

Usage:  docker build [OPTIONS] PATH | URL | -

Build an image from a Dockerfile

Options:
      --add-host list            Add a custom host-to-IP mapping (host:ip)
      --build-arg list           Set build-time variables
      --cache-from strings       Images to consider as cache sources
      --cgroup-parent string     Optional parent cgroup for the container
      --compress                 Compress the build context using gzip
      --cpu-period int           Limit the CPU CFS (Completely Fair Scheduler) period
      --cpu-quota int            Limit the CPU CFS (Completely Fair Scheduler) quota
  -c, --cpu-shares int           CPU shares (relative weight)
      --cpuset-cpus string       CPUs in which to allow execution (0-3, 0,1)
      --cpuset-mems string       MEMs in which to allow execution (0-3, 0,1)
      --disable-content-trust    Skip image verification (default true)
  -f, --file string              Name of the Dockerfile (Default is 'PATH/Dockerfile')
      --force-rm                 Always remove intermediate containers
      --iidfile string           Write the image ID to the file
```

Figure 3.7: *Docker build options command*

The most commonly used options are as follows:

- **-t, name [: tag]**: Creates an image with the specified name and label from the instructions in the file.

- **-no-cache**: Allows us to generate a new image by omitting the cache we will use. By default, Docker caches recently executed instructions. If we run a **docker build** several times, Docker will check if the file contains the same instructions and will not generate a new image if so.

- **-pull**: Docker will only download the image specified in the FROM expression. We can use this option to force you to download the new version of the image.

The build command can be run from the same directory where the Dockerfile is located or from another as long as the build file is referenced using the **-f (--file)** command, followed by the path to the file. We can also assign labels to the images to have them located with the **-t (--tag)** command, leaving the final syntax of the form:

```
$ docker build --file <Dockerfile_path> --tag <repository>:<tag>
```

The preceding command means that the image created in the Dockerfile will be built in the indicated path, and it will add a specific name given by the repository and the tag.

Dockerfiles always start with the definition of a base image using the **FROM** instruction. The main instructions that can be used in a Dockerfile are as follows:

- **FROM <image>**: Allows us to establish the base image of our container and initializes the construction of a new image based on the specified image.

- **RUN <command>**: Allows you to execute a command in the context of the image.

- **CMD <command>**: Allows establishing the command that the container executes on startup.

- **EXPOSE <port>**: Allows you to define ports where the container is listening to connections at runtime.

- **ENV**: Used to define environment variables with the *key = value* format.

- **COPY <source destination>**: Allows you to copy files and directories to the file system of the container.

- **ADD**: This instruction copies new files, directories, and remote files from URLs and adds them to the container's file system.

- **WORKDIR**: Establishes the working directory.

- **VOLUME <path>**: Allows you to use the location of our Docker host in the container to store data permanently. Container volumes are always accessible on the Docker host at **/var/lib/docker/volumes/**.

- **USER**: Allows configuring the user with which the instructions will be executed.
- **MAINTAINER**: Establishes the author of the Dockerfile.
- **ENTRYPOINT**: Allows you to configure a container as executable, usually with the process that we want it to expose.

For a complete list of available instructions, you can check the official documentation at **https://docs.docker.com/engine/reference/builder/**.

The **COPY**, **ADD**, and **RUN** instructions add a new layer to your image. The following Dockerfile example creates two layers, where each layer executes the **RUN** command.

```
FROM ubuntu
RUN apt-get update
RUN apt-get install vim
```

Combining several **RUN** instructions in a single line so that we only have one layer is a good practice.

```
FROM ubuntu
RUN apt-get update && apt-get install vim
```

Here are some of the instructions found in this file:

- **FROM instruction**: The **FROM** instruction sets the base image for the following instructions. The image can be any local or public image. If the image is not found locally, the Docker compilation command will try to download the image from the public record. The tag or **tag** command is optional, so the latest tag is assumed by default if it is not specified.

  - FROM <image>: <tag | label>
- **RUN instruction**: The **RUN** instruction will execute any command in a new layer at the top of the current image and confirm this image. The generated image will be used for the next instruction in the Docker file. The **RUN** instruction has two forms:

  - RUN <command>
  - RUN ["executable", "arg1", "arg2" ...]

The **RUN** instruction is only interpreted and used when the **docker build** command is used for creating an image. The purpose of the **RUN** instructions is to execute commands that modify the image in some way.

For example, you can install software packages or create a configuration file that becomes part of the image. In this example, a file is created at the time of compilation and viewed with the **RUN** command:

```
FROM ubuntu:latest
MAINTAINER maintainer
RUN echo "This container was built on $(date)." > /tmp/built.txt
ENTRYPOINT ["cat","/tmp/built.txt"]
```

The command reads the current date and time and sends it to the **/tmp/build.txt** file when the Docker compilation is executed. The command was executed at compile time, so the exact same date is displayed each time you use a **docker run** command:

```
$ docker build -t ubuntu_image .

$ docker run ubuntu_image
```

```
$ docker build -t ubuntu_image .
Sending build context to Docker daemon  3.072kB
Step 1/4 : FROM ubuntu:latest
 ---> 16508e5c265d
Step 2/4 : MAINTAINER maintainer
 ---> Running in 4689d54842bd
Removing intermediate container 4689d54842bd
 ---> 506274fd770b
Step 3/4 : RUN echo "This container was built on $(date)." > /tmp/built.txt
 ---> Running in dbb5339fdd6f
Removing intermediate container dbb5339fdd6f
 ---> a66dffbc50f0
Step 4/4 : ENTRYPOINT ["cat","/tmp/built.txt"]
 ---> Running in 43f2917b4092
Removing intermediate container 43f2917b4092
 ---> a8cc522a75e6
Successfully built a8cc522a75e6
Successfully tagged ubuntu_image:latest
$ docker run ubuntu_image
This container was built on Sun Mar 14 20:45:04 UTC 2021.
```

Figure 3.8: Executing docker build and docker run with Ubuntu image

In the following example, we are creating a Docker image for the redis server using the latest version of Ubuntu 18.04 as the base image. This can be the content of our Dockerfile:

```
FROM ubuntu:18.04

RUN apt-get update && \
apt-get install -y redis-server && \
apt-get clean

EXPOSE 6379

CMD ["redis-server", "--protected-mode no"]
```

- The **RUN** instruction updates the apt index, installs the "**redis-server**" package, and clears the apt cache. The commands used in the instructions are the same as what you would use to install redis on the Ubuntu server.
- The **EXPOSE** statement defines the port on which the redis server is listening.
- The **CMD** instruction allows you to set the default command that will be executed when the container is executed.

The next step is to build the image. Run the following command from the directory where the Dockerfile is located:

```
$ docker build -t myredis .
```

```
$ docker build -t myredis .
Sending build context to Docker daemon  3.072kB
Step 1/4 : FROM ubuntu:18.04
18.04: Pulling from library/ubuntu
92dc2a97ff99: Pull complete
be13a9d27eb8: Pull complete
c8299583700a: Pull complete
Digest: sha256:4bc3ae6596938cb0d9e5ac51a1152ec9dcac2a1c50829c74abd9c4361e321b26
Status: Downloaded newer image for ubuntu:18.04
 ---> 329ed837d508
Step 2/4 : RUN apt-get update && apt-get install -y redis-server && apt-get clean
 ---> Running in 943cdd2390af
Get:1 http://archive.ubuntu.com/ubuntu bionic InRelease [242 kB]
Get:2 http://archive.ubuntu.com/ubuntu bionic-updates InRelease [88.7 kB]
Get:3 http://archive.ubuntu.com/ubuntu bionic-backports InRelease [74.6 kB]
Get:4 http://security.ubuntu.com/ubuntu bionic-security InRelease [88.7 kB]
Get:5 http://archive.ubuntu.com/ubuntu bionic/multiverse amd64 Packages [186 kB]
Get:6 http://archive.ubuntu.com/ubuntu bionic/restricted amd64 Packages [13.5 kB]
Get:7 http://archive.ubuntu.com/ubuntu bionic/main amd64 Packages [1344 kB]
Get:8 http://archive.ubuntu.com/ubuntu bionic/universe amd64 Packages [11.3 MB]
Get:9 http://archive.ubuntu.com/ubuntu bionic-updates/multiverse amd64 Packages [31.4 kB]
Get:10 http://archive.ubuntu.com/ubuntu bionic-updates/main amd64 Packages [2394 kB]
```

Figure 3.9: Executing docker build with redis image

Now that the image has been created, we can run a container by executing the following command:

```
$ docker run -d -p 6379:6379 --name redis myredis
```

The **-d** option tells Docker to run the container in detached mode, the option **-p 6379: 6379** will post the image to port 6379 on the docker host, and the **--name redis** option specifies the name of the container. The last parameter is the name of the image used to run the container:

```
$ docker ps
CONTAINER ID          IMAGE              COMMAND                       CREATED
STATUS                PORTS                       NAMES
617f62174be8          myredis            "redis-server '--pro…"    23
minutes ago           Up 23 minutes      0.0.0.0:6379->6379/tcp    redis
```

Once we have created the container and have it running in the background with **-d** option, we can connect using the **exec** command, which executes a process inside the container:

```
$ docker exec -it redis /bin/bash
root@617f62174be8:/# redis-cli
127.0.0.1:6379> ping
PONG
127.0.0.1:6379> set mykey value
OK
127.0.0.1:6379> get mykey
"value"
```

In the preceding output, we can see how we are accessing the redis container and executing the **redis-cli** command to verify that we have the redis service running on port 6379.

We will continue explaining some of the most important guidelines that must be followed to optimize the time it takes to create the image, its security, and its size as much as possible.

Best practices writing DockerFiles

Docker exposes a section of good practices for writing Dockerfiles. Here are some best practices to create optimized Docker images:

- **Command order matters**: Due to the way the cache works when building an image, Docker is able to detect if the command we want to execute has been executed before and reuse the result from the cache to make it faster. So, it is recommended to order the commands according to how frequently they have to be changed.

- **Run only one process per container**: Following the practice of a single process per container allows us to make decoupled applications and reuse containers more easily. Plus, they are easier to scale and result in more decoupled systems. This also allows us to use container links or other container networking techniques.

- **Reduce the size of your images**: A Docker image should only contain what is strictly necessary to run your application. You should avoid installing packages just because they can be useful for debugging a container in order to reduce complexity, dependencies, image size, and build time of an image. As an example, do not include text editors in your images. Another practical option is the use of small base images, for example, using alpine.

- **Build the images in multiple stages**: Using multistage builds will make our final image less heavy and probably more secure. When we create an image, we can generate intermediate images that we use for a specific purpose (such as generating an artifact) and that end up being eliminated and are not part of the final image.

- **Minimize the number of layers of our images using the image cache**: Docker uses Union Filesystems to store images. This means each image is made from a base image plus a collection of differences that add the required changes. Each difference represents an additional layer in an image, which has a direct impact on how we write our Dockerfile and the directives we use.

- **Group the commands by layers**: In a Dockerfile, each command represents a layer of the final image. So, it is important to bring together the layers that share the same logic to improve the use of the cache and make the Dockerfile more maintainable.

```
FROM ubuntu
RUN apt update && apt install openjdk-8-jdk vim -y
```

- **User without privileges**: It is good practice to modify the image's end user in a Dockerfile to someone with just the right privileges to fulfil the image's purpose. This will make our image more secure and prevent an admin user in the container from gaining access to the host. To do this, it is best to add a new user and a group and give it the permissions you need.

```
FROM ubuntu
RUN groupadd -r usergroup && useradd -r -g user usergroup
ENTRYPOINT ["sh", "myScript.sh"]
COPY ./myScript.sh /myScript.sh
RUN chown user /myScript.sh
USER
```

We should avoid executing commands as root inside the container. This is a vital security measure, and it prevents a hypothetical attacker, for example, from using **apt-get** to install new packages. In this case, a user is being created to perform the operations that must build the image.

Tip: Dockerfile best practices in Docker documentation

Writing a Dockerfile may seem like something simple, but it is important to follow certain recommendations that will make our building process run faster and ensure that the resulting image is smaller and more secure. You can find more tips and best practices in the Docker documentation:

- `https://docs.docker.com/develop/develop-images/dockerfile_best-practices`
- `https://docs.docker.com/engine/reference/builder`

Managing Docker containers

The Docker Hub at **https://hub.docker.com** provides you and your organization with a place to host and deliver images. You can configure the Docker Hub repositories in two ways: *Repositories*, which allow us to upload and update the images whenever we want from the Docker daemon and automatic images that allow us to configure a GitHub, and BitBucket account that triggers the reconstruction of an image when any changes are made to the repository.

Searching and executing a Docker image

Docker images can be an easy way to experiment without installing and configuring anything on your host machine if you want to try out a new software application or are looking for a new one that serves a particular purpose.

We can perform a search with the following command if you are interested in trying Python:

```
$ docker search python
```

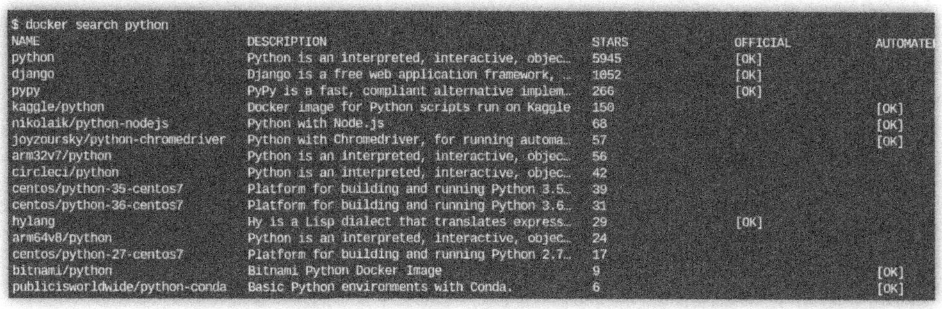

Figure 3.10: *Executing docker search Python command*

Another way we can search for an image is through the DockerHub interface:

Figure 3.11: *Searching Python application in DockerHub*

Once we have downloaded the Python image, we will launch a container based on that image and interact with the command line of that container with the **docker run** command.

```
$ docker run [options] [image] [commands] [arguments]
```

We must specify an image that we will use as a base while launching the container when executing the **docker run** command. Another point is that the options can replace almost all the default values configured in the execution. We have several *configuration parameters* when starting a container:

- -i allows you to establish a connection with the *"standard input"*

- **-t** manages a *"pseudo TTY"*
- **-d** runs the container in *"background"* mode
- **-a** associates standard input or output to the open session
- **-cpus** is the number of CPUs assigned
- **-ip** assigns an IP address
- **-mac-address** assigns a special mac address to the container
- **-m** sets a memory limit for that container (usually a few megabytes)
- **-name** assigns a name to the container
- **-p** publishes container ports in the assigned network
- **-rm** stopping the container will be automatically deleted
- **–tmpfs** mounts a directory in tmpfs mode (temporary to be deleted, no persistence)
- **-v** mounts a directory in the container with persistence; it can be a real computer folder or a Docker volume

We can execute the run command using the **-t** and **-i** flags for executing the image. The **-t** flag creates a terminal device, and the **-i** flag specifies that terminal session is interactive:

```
$ docker run -t -i python /bin/bash
```

```
$ docker run -t -i python /bin/bash
Unable to find image 'python:latest' locally
latest: Pulling from library/python
e22122b926a1: Pull complete
f29e09ae8373: Pull complete
e319e3daef68: Pull complete
e499244fe254: Pull complete
5a6ebed20e89: Pull complete
56b703a5a371: Pull complete
4dd0a64393b6: Pull complete
1d2280ee5e8b: Pull complete
8b6ce844793f: Pull complete
Digest: sha256:168fd55b03929f88cd3e1e05b9ebe8f9cc1c095af8b53a8c0cd50da04a8c3a40
Status: Downloaded newer image for python:latest
root@1b0b9149b7e5:/# python
Python 3.9.2 (default, Mar 12 2021, 18:54:15)
[GCC 8.3.0] on linux
Type "help", "copyright", "credits" or "license" for more information.
```

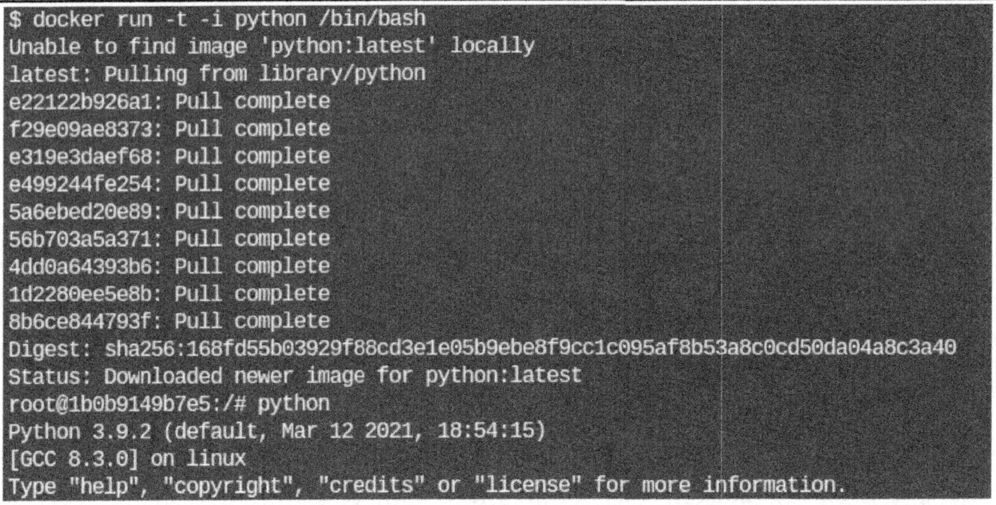

Figure 3.12: Executing Python container

With the previous command, we are interacting with the container for checking the Python version.

Executing a container in background mode

You can use the **--detach** or **-d** option to execute a container in background mode. The **-d** option allows you to indicate that it runs in the background (usually as a service daemon process).

```
$ docker container run --detach -ti --name mypython python:latest
/bin/bash
```

```
$ docker container run --detach -ti --name mypython python:latest /bin/bash
b29847c3d9147ed4e355a177287692eb517066b2cd2a7bb173d35d4636711332
$ docker ps
CONTAINER ID      IMAGE           COMMAND          CREATED          STATUS          PORTS          NAMES
b29847c3d914      python:latest   "/bin/bash"      11 seconds ago   Up 7 seconds                   mypython
$ docker ps
CONTAINER ID      IMAGE           COMMAND          CREATED          STATUS          PORTS          NAMES
b29847c3d914      python:latest   "/bin/bash"      19 seconds ago   Up 16 seconds                  mypython
$ docker exec -it mypython /bin/bash
root@b29847c3d914:/# python
Python 3.9.2 (default, Mar 12 2021, 18:54:15)
```

Figure 3.13: Executing Python container in detached mode

Inspecting Docker containers

Docker commands give you access to information about images and containers, but you want to get more information about the metadata of these objects sometimes.

The **docker inspect** command gives access to the metadata of a Docker image in JSON format. The syntax of the command is as follows:

```
$ docker inspect [OPTIONS] CONTAINER|IMAGE|TASK [CONTAINER
|IMAGE|TASK...]
```

You can run the **docker inspect** command in any container or Docker image.

```
$ docker inspect python
[
    {
        "Id": "sha256:2c31ca135cf9ec96774d56c80d4c91870588f56a5b64c2e4aed95cb344715b93",
        "RepoTags": [
            "python:latest"
        ],
        "RepoDigests": [
            "python@sha256:168fd55b03929f88cd3e1e05b9ebe8f9cc1c095af8b53a8c0cd50da04a8c3a40"
        ],
        "Parent": "",
        "Comment": "",
        "Created": "2021-03-12T18:55:32.014074727Z",
        "Container": "a247b311805915be68f8714ac2d287d6ebf65155daf4ff524604476ea487fba3",
        "ContainerConfig": {
            "Hostname": "a247b3118059",
```

Figure 3.14: Inspecting Python image

Tip: Inspect command options

Docker inspect command provides a series of options that allow you to identify specific attributes with the --format option. For example, you can verify the IP address configured for your container.

https://docs.docker.com/engine/reference/commandline/inspect

You can inspect images and containers by name or ID. We are using the **docker inspect** command *to obtain environment variables in the python container* in the following command.

```
$ docker inspect --format '{{.ContainerConfig.Env}}' <container_
id|container_name>
$ docker inspect --format '{{.ContainerConfig.Env}}' python
[PATH=/usr/local/bin:/usr/local/sbin:/usr/local/
bin:/usr/sbin:/usr/bin:/sbin:/bin LANG=C.UTF-8 GPG_
KEY=E3FF2839C048B25C084DEBE9B26995E310250568 PYTHON_
VERSION=3.9.2 PYTHON_PIP_VERSION=21.0.1 PYTHON_
GET_PIP_URL=https://github.com/pypa/get-pip/raw/
b60e2320d9e8d02348525bd74e871e466afdf77c/get-pip.py PYTHON_GET_
PIP_SHA256=c3b81e5d06371e135fb3156dc7d8fd6270735088428c4a9a5ec1
f342e2024565]
```

We can check the packages installed in a Docker container. For example, we can use the **dpkg -l** command to check the packages installed in a Docker container. We first need to find the ID of the container that is running.

```
$ docker exec <container_id | container_name> dpkg -l
$ docker exec mypython dpkg -l
```

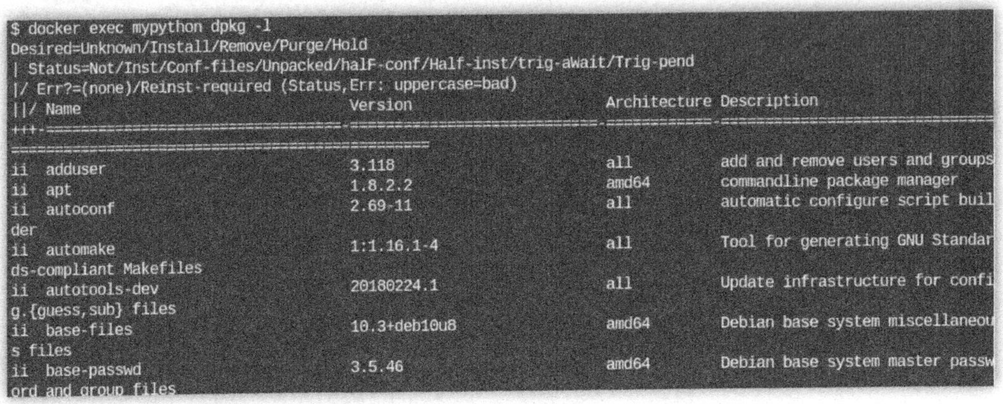

```
$ docker exec mypython dpkg -l
Desired=Unknown/Install/Remove/Purge/Hold
| Status=Not/Inst/Conf-files/Unpacked/halF-conf/Half-inst/trig-aWait/Trig-pend
|/ Err?=(none)/Reinst-required (Status,Err: uppercase=bad)
||/ Name                           Version                  Architecture Description
+++-==============================-========================-============-=========================
==========================================
ii  adduser                        3.118                    all          add and remove users and groups
ii  apt                            1.8.2.2                  amd64        commandline package manager
ii  autoconf                       2.69-11                  all          automatic configure script buil
der
ii  automake                       1:1.16.1-4               all          Tool for generating GNU Standar
ds-compliant Makefiles
ii  autotools-dev                  20180224.1               all          Update infrastructure for confi
g.{guess,sub} files
ii  base-files                     10.3+deb10u8             amd64        Debian base system miscellaneou
s files
ii  base-passwd                    3.5.46                   amd64        Debian base system master passw
ord and group files
```

Figure 3.15: Inspecting packages in docker container

Optimizing Docker images

Optimizing space and reducing container size is essential to create efficient container environments. If we think that Docker is designed to be able to mount a big number of containers, both space and speed are key factors in a development environment and production.

One way to optimize images is to use as few layers as possible. For example, the following set of instructions generates four layers, one for each **RUN** instruction.

```
# RUN apt-get update -y
# RUN apt-get install -y curl
# RUN apt-get install -y postgresql
# RUN apt-get install -y postgresql-client
```

During construction, Docker tends to reuse the layers of an image of a previous construction whenever possible, ignoring a step that could be costly. We can consider these use cases:

- **Place the Dockerfile instructions that could change in the final part of the file**
  Docker can reuse the previous layers this way.

- **Group instructions in the same layer**

  We can group similar instructions, for example, the **apt-get** command, which usually requires an update of repositories and previous packages. The same command with one **RUN** instruction only generates one layer in the following example:

```
RUN apt-get update -y && \
apt-get install -y curl postgresql postgresql-client
```

Docker's cache

The construction of a Docker image from a Dockerfile can be an expensive process since it can involve the installation of a large number of libraries. At the same time, it is a repetitive process because successive builds of the same Dockerfile are similar to each other. This is why Docker introduces the concept of cache to optimize the image building process.

Each time an image is reconstructed from a Dockerfile, Docker checks if the current instruction has been executed correctly and so, has the results of the instruction available in cache. If the results are correct and are cached, Docker uses the instruction's cached data by default and reuses it with the new compilation.

Starting with the base image that is already cached, the following instruction is compared to all the derived images from that base image to see if one of them was created using the exact same instructions; the cache is invalidated if not.

For the **ADD** and **COPY** instructions, the contents of the files in the image are examined and a checksum is calculated for each file. During the cache search, the checksum is compared against the checksums of the images already created. The cache is invalidated if something changes.

The following statements in the Dockerfile will generate new images and will not use the cache once it is invalidated. Note the following aspects about the Docker cache:

- *The Docker cache is local*, that is, all Dockerfile instructions will be executed if you're building a Dockerfile for the first time on a given machine, even if the image has already been built in a Docker Registry.
- The cache is invalidated if an instruction has changed and you cannot use the cache, and the following Dockerfile instructions will be executed without using the cache.
- The behavior of the **ADD** and **COPY** instructions is different in terms of the behavior of the cache. Although these instructions do not change, they invalidate the cache if the content of the files being copied has been modified.
- Finally, you can use the **--no-cache = true** flag if, for some reason, you want to *build without using the cache*.

When creating our image from the Dockerfile, there is an interesting feature that we can use to reconstruct the image using the Docker cache *so that a certain layer associated with a command is only rebuilt if the command has changed*. The cache will be invalidated in these situations:

- When the **docker build** command is executed with the **--no cache** flag
- When a command that can be cached is provided, such as the **apt-get** update
- When the first **ADD** instruction invalidates the cache for all the following instructions in the Docker file if the context content has changed
- For example, we can use the **--no-cache** flag to force a complete reconstruction of the image without using the cache.

Building an application with NodeJS

In this example, we will develop an application with NodeJS that will be served by a web server that will run in a Docker container. In Docker, we also have the option of joining multiple layers in a structure called **multi-stage**. In this example, we will build a Node.js container with an express-based application **https://www.npmjs. com/package/express**.

index.js

```
const express = require('express')
const app = express()
app.get('/', (req, res) => res.send('Hello World!'))
app.listen(3000, () => {
console.log(`Example app listening on port 3000!`)
})
```

package.json

```
{"name": "hello-world-nodejs",
"main": "index.js",
"dependencies": {
"express": "^4.17.1"
},
"scripts": {
"start": "node index.js"
}}
```

We are using a node base image in this example, and we will package this application with the following Dockerfile, where we will execute the **npm install** command from the **package.json** and **index.js** files:

```
FROM node:latest
EXPOSE 3000
WORKDIR /app
COPY package.json index.js ./
RUN npm install
CMD ["npm", "start"]
```

Next, we will create our image from the directory where we have saved the Dockerfile. We can *build the image* with the following **docker build** command:

```
$ docker build -t node-app .
```

After creating the image, we can execute the following command for creating the container with the application running on port 3000:

```
$ docker ps
CONTAINER ID        IMAGE               COMMAND                 CREATED
STATUS              PORTS                       NAMES
9147096a3e66        node-app            "docker-entrypoint.s…"
22 seconds ago      Up 20 seconds       0.0.0.0:3000->3000/tcp
angry_keller
$ docker exec -it 9147096a3e66 bash
root@9147096a3e66:/app# ls
index.js  node_modules  package-lock.json  package.json
root@9147096a3e66:/app# node index.js
Example app listening on port 3000!
```

In the previous command, we are interacting with the node-app container using the container ID. Finally, we will execute index.js with the node server command. Additionally, this container has an IP address with which we can interact with the container.

Tip: Docker history command

In the previous Dockerfile, we can find COPY and RUN commands that generate two additional layers for the base image. The resulting image has five new layers, one for each statement in its Dockerfile file. We can see the different layers with the docker history command.

- https://docs.docker.com/engine/reference/commandline/history/

```
$ docker history node-app
```

```
$ docker history node-app
IMAGE            CREATED          CREATED BY                                    SIZE
c3d715290cb2     4 minutes ago    /bin/sh -c #(nop)  CMD ["npm" "start"]        0B
405d15d48444     4 minutes ago    /bin/sh -c npm install                        4.64MB
da92698b553b     4 minutes ago    /bin/sh -c #(nop) COPY multi:907b0319fb52308…  326B
4d1ac85f7943     4 minutes ago    /bin/sh -c #(nop) WORKDIR /app                0B
32ddd4f35238     4 minutes ago    /bin/sh -c #(nop)  EXPOSE 3000                0B
56bc674036dc     3 days ago       /bin/sh -c #(nop)  CMD ["node"]               0B
<missing>        3 days ago       /bin/sh -c #(nop)  ENTRYPOINT ["docker-entry…  0B
<missing>        3 days ago       /bin/sh -c #(nop) COPY file:238737301d473041…  116B
<missing>        3 days ago       /bin/sh -c set -ex  && for key in      6A010…  7.76MB
<missing>        3 days ago       /bin/sh -c #(nop)  ENV YARN_VERSION=1.22.5     0B
<missing>        3 days ago       /bin/sh -c ARCH= && dpkgArch="$(dpkg --print…  93.8MB
<missing>        3 days ago       /bin/sh -c #(nop)  ENV NODE_VERSION=15.11.0    0B
<missing>        3 days ago       /bin/sh -c groupadd --gid 1000 node   && use…  333kB
<missing>        3 days ago       /bin/sh -c set -ex;  apt-get update;  apt-ge…  561MB
```

Figure 3.16: Layers from node-app using the docker history command

Reducing image size with multistage

Now, let's test the construction of the Dockerfile through multiple stages. We will use the same DockerFile, but now we will rewrite it with multi-stage mode. The main difference is that we are using the **FROM node:latest** instruction twice in this case:

```
FROM node:latest as build
WORKDIR /app
COPY package.json index.js ./
RUN npm install


FROM node:latest
COPY --from=build /app /
EXPOSE 3000
CMD ["index.js"]
```

The first section of the Dockerfile creates three layers. The layers are fused and copied in the second and last stage. Two more layers are added above the image for a total of three layers. When executing the build and history commands, we can see how the image generated with multi-stage is smaller.

Tip: Multi Stage build

You can refer to the Docker documentation about multistage-build at https://docs.docker.com/develop/develop-images/multistage-build for more information.

When using multistage build, we are using the image generated in the previous step to optimize the construction of the second one. For this task we can use the from = build instruction.

```
$ docker build -t node-multi-stage
```

We can verify the size of the image using node-multi-stage with the following command:

```
$ docker images | grep node-
node-multi-stage    latest          eebccd4812cf        54 seconds
ago        938MB
node-app            latest          c3d715290cb2        19 minutes
ago        941MB
```

Reducing image size with alpine Linux

Image size plays an essential role in creating a good Dockerfile. Using smaller images will result in faster deployments and less attack surface, so a best practice when creating images in Docker is to make them as small as possible.

Alpine Linux-based images **https://hub.docker.com/_/alpine** have the capacity to produce the smallest images to run applications with minimal resources at the memory and disk space level. At this point, images based on this distribution are much faster to download and configure.

In our Node application, the distribution of alpine-Linux lets us reduce the size of the image using the following Dockerfile:

```
FROM node:15 as build
WORKDIR /app
COPY package.json index.js ./
RUN npm install


FROM node:15-alpine
COPY --from=build /app /
EXPOSE 3000
CMD ["npm", "start"]
```

In the construction of the second image, we are using the alpine version for the node image:

```
$ docker build -t node-alpine .
```

We can use the following command to verify the size of the image using node-alpine:

```
$ docker images | grep node-
node-alpine         latest          0b166f9aba49        6 seconds
ago         114MB
node-multi-stage    latest          eebccd4812cf        33 minutes
ago         938MB
node-app            latest          c3d715290cb2        About
an hour ago    941MB
```

In the previous output, we can see that the image size has been reduced from 938MB with multistage to 114MB with alpine Linux.

Distroless Docker images

Distroless images contain only the application and its dependencies at runtime. They do not contain package management applications or programs that we normally find in a standard Linux distribution.

We can execute the following commands to see the size differences between these images and the official images of each platform based on Alpine:

```
$ docker pull gcr.io/distroless/python3
$ docker pull python
```

This will let us see the size difference between the Python official image (885MB) and another based in Python distroless image (49.6MB).

```
$ docker images
REPOSITORY                      TAG             IMAGE  ID
CREATED             SIZE
python                  latest          2c31ca135cf9        3 days
ago         885MB
gcr.io/distroless/python3    latest      c2596fdf7d32        51
years ago    49.6MB
```

As you can see, there is a significant difference in size between the two images. This saves us disk space and network traffic, and it also improves security. Not having libraries or services that we do not need reduces security risks and unnecessary alerts from image scanners for obsolete or vulnerable versions.

Tip: Distroless images from Google Container Tools project

The Google Container Tools project hosts a series of Docker images oriented to specific programming languages without an operating system. So, they do not contain any distribution, and all the images contain the files needed to run the application.

We can find the source code of the project in the GitHub repository at https://github.com/GoogleCloudPlatform/distroless. Here are some of the images currently available:

- `gcr.io/distroless/python2.7`
- `gcr.io/distroless/python3`
- `gcr.io/distroless/nodejs`
- `gcr.io/distroless/java`

In the following URL, you can see an example of the construction of our Dockerfile for an application based on Python 3 using a distroless approach:

`https://github.com/GoogleContainerTools/distroless/tree/master/examples/python3`

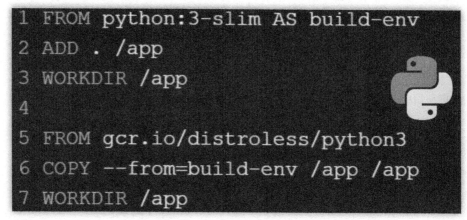

```
1 FROM python:3-slim AS build-env
2 ADD . /app
3 WORKDIR /app
4
5 FROM gcr.io/distroless/python3
6 COPY --from=build-env /app /app
7 WORKDIR /app
```

Figure 3.17: Dockerfile example using Python 3 distroless image

Distroless is a simplified version of the original operating system, so there are no additional binaries and we can't run a **bash** or **sh** to get a shell.

The fact that these images do not contain a shell is not of great importance, unless we need to jump into the container to debug or inspect something. There are the same images with the debug tag, including busybox, for this.

For example, we can use the `gcr.io/distroless/python3:debug` image if we need to debug a container based on a Python application, and we can enter by writing the entry point once we have created the container. Consider this example:

```
$ docker run -it --rm --entrypoint sh gcr.io/distroless/python3:debug
```

```
$ docker run -it --rm --entrypoint sh gcr.io/distroless/python3:debug
Unable to find image 'gcr.io/distroless/python3:debug' locally
debug: Pulling from distroless/python3
9e4425256ce4: Already exists
8d239582974e: Already exists
a704ebe6fabe: Pull complete
e708be98c58f: Pull complete
6035c9448ae3: Pull complete
Digest: sha256:72684cdc6e9405189ad24356248950f5480b02db35ab59dfee9f849769feec33
Status: Downloaded newer image for gcr.io/distroless/python3:debug
# python
Python 3.5.3 (default, Nov 18 2020, 21:09:16)
[GCC 6.3.0 20170516] on linux
Type "help", "copyright", "credits" or "license" for more information.
>>>
```

Figure 3.18: Executing Python interpreter with distroless image

This way, we have improved both the size of the image and its security. An attacker will not be able to access a shell to execute commands even if it manages to exploit the application and gains access to the container. It will *only have access to the binaries that have the image installed.* Now, we can conclude that less binaries mean smaller image sizes and greater security.

Conclusion

Docker images are based on a layered file system that offers many advantages for use cases that containers are designed for, like being lightweight and sharing common parts that many containers can deploy and run on the same machine economically.

From the security point of view, attack vectors and network traffic are reduced if we get smaller and specialized images focusing on only one function or application. This, in turn, lowers the risk.

This also drastically reduces system updates and so, the complete maintenance of all mounted architecture. And this is where images without a system or *"Distroless Images"* play an important role from the security point of view.

In the next chapter, we will review the main points for starting with Docker security, analyzing topics like Docker Content Trust and Docker Registry.

Points to remember

- A Docker image represents the state of an operating system, including its dependencies, where each layer is mounted on top of another. All layers are mounted in read-only mode, except the last layer, which is mounted in **read/write** mode.

- Dockerfiles are scripts containing successively declared commands and instructions that will be executed in the order given by Docker to automatically create a Docker image.

- The **docker build** command will follow the instructions in the Dockerfile for building the image.

- Google Distroless Docker Images are base images that only contain the dependencies necessary to run your application and eliminate all the other elements, reducing the attack surface of our containers.

Multiple choice questions

1. Which Dockerfile instruction allows us to establish the base image of our container?

   a. FROM <image>

   b. CMD <image>

   c. RUN <image>

   d. COPY <image>

2. Which Dockerfile instruction allows us to establish the command that the container executes on startup?

   a. FROM <command>

   b. COPY <command>

   c. RUN <command>

   d. CMD <command>

Answers

1	a
2	D

Questions

1. What are the best practices for creating and sharing Docker images?

2. Which command allows you to see the different layers inside a Docker image?

3. What are the main advantages of using Distroless images?

Key terms

- A Docker image corresponds to the information needed to start a container, and it basically consists of a file system and other metadata, like the commands to be executed, the environment variables, the container volumes, and the ports used by our container.

- The Dockerfile allows you to build an image, and this image can be uploaded to a registry so that it can be downloaded to the servers you use to deploy your application.

- Docker has a feature called multi-stage, which is useful for reducing the size of images as it allows you to use different images at each stage.

CHAPTER 4
Getting Started with Docker Security

Introduction

This chapter covers topics like security best practices and other aspects like Docker capabilities, which containers leverage in order to provide more features, such as the privileged container.

While Docker provides a central registry to store public images, you may not want your images to be accessible to the world. You must use a private registry in this case. Now, we will review **Docker Content Trust** and **Docker Registry**, which provide a secure way to upload our images in **Docker Hub** platform and other registries like Quay and Harbor.

Structure

We will cover the following topics in this chapter:

- Docker security principles and best practices
- Docker capabilities
- Docker Content Trust
- Docker Registry

Objectives

After studying this unit, you should understand Docker security principles and security best practices, Docker capabilities and Docker Content Trust, and Docker Registry and other registries like Quay and Harbor.

Docker security principles and best practices

From the security point of view, Docker containers use the resources of the host machine but have their own runtime environment.

This means a container cannot access other containers or the underlying operating system (except the storage volumes to which you give access), and it will communicate with other networks and containers with the specific network configuration that you want to grant.

The most significant advantage of container-based virtualization is that applications with different requirements can run isolated from each other without having to assume the overhead of a separate guest system. At this point, container technology takes advantage of two basic functions of the Linux kernel: *the control groups (Cgroups) and the kernel namespaces.*

- **Namespaces** provide isolation for processes and mount points, so processes that run in a container cannot interact with or see processes that run in another container. The isolation of the mounting points implies that they cannot interact with the mounting points in another container.

- **Control groups (Cgroups)** are a feature of the Linux kernel that facilitates the limitation of the use of resources at the level of CPU and memory that a container can use. This ensures that each container gets only the resources it really needs.

The development team behind Docker is also aware of security problems, considering them an obstacle to the consolidation of this technology in production systems.

Along with the fundamental isolation techniques of the Linux kernel, the latest versions of the Docker engine support technologies like *AppArmor*, *SELinux* and *Seccomp*:

- **AppArmor** allows you to regulate permissions and access of the containers in the filesystem

- **SELinux** provides a system of rules that allows you to implement access controls to the kernel resources

- **Secure Computing Mode (Seccomp)** monitors kernel system calls

Docker also uses the so-called *"Linux capabilities"* that limits the capabilities the container can use.

Docker daemon attack surface

While Docker facilitates virtualization work, we may forget the security implications of the execution of Docker containers sometimes. From a security point of view, we must keep in mind that Docker requires root privileges for working in normal conditions.

The Docker daemon is responsible for creating and managing containers, which includes creating filesystems, assigning IP addresses, routing packets, process management, and tasks that require administrator privileges. So, it is essential to start the daemon as a user administrator.

> **Tip: Securing Docker daemon**
>
> Docker Daemon is the main process that manages the life cycle of containers and needs root privileges to run. Unfortunately, Docker daemon executes with root privileges, so it also presents an attack vector.
>
> You can refer to the official documentation at https://docs.docker.com/engine/security for more information.
>
> It is recommended to ensure that only trusted clients have access if you want to expose the Docker daemon to the outside of your network and use the remote API. A simple way is to secure Docker with SSL and certificates using HTTPS. You can find ways to configure this at https://docs.docker.com/articles/https.

Starting new containers, stopping, and reconfiguring on running containers are some of the main actions we can perform on the containers.

One of Docker's ultimate goals is to be able to run even the Daemon as a non-root user, without affecting its functionality, and delegate operations that require root privileges to a dedicated thread with elevated privileges.

Security best practices

The following list summarizes the best security practices when executing Docker containers:

- It is advisable to run the daemon Docker process on a dedicated server isolated from other virtual machines

- Special care must be taken to link certain Docker host directories as volumes because a container can gain full read and write access and perform critical operations on these directories

- From the point of view of security in communications, the best option is to use SSL-based authentication

- Avoid running processes with root privileges inside the containers

- We can study the option of enabling specific security profiles, such as *AppArmor* and *SELinux*, on the Docker host

- All containers share the host Docker Kernel, so it is important to have the kernel updated with the latest security patches

The following best practices can help create services improving container security:

- One application per container using a microservice-oriented approach.

- Do not run containers as root, and disable SETUID permissions.

- Use the **-cap-drop** and **-cap-add** flags to remove and add capabilities in the container.

- It is advisable not to use environment variables or run containers in privileged mode if you are going to share secrets.

- You must have Docker updated to the latest version to ensure that all security issues have been solved and also to provide the latest features that Docker is incorporating in the core.

- Kernel is one of the most vulnerable components in container management as it is shared among all containers. So, special care should be taken to keep the Linux Kernel with the latest update.

We will analyze some best practices in further detail in the following points. First, we will check the default user within a container.

Execution with non-root user

By default, *containers run with root privileges*. We see that *root is the default user* if we execute the following commands. We are executing Ubuntu container for checking root user in the following command:

```
$ docker run -v /bin:/host/bin -it --rm ubuntu sh
#whoami
#id
```

With the execution of the previous commands, we can check the user that the container is using by default:

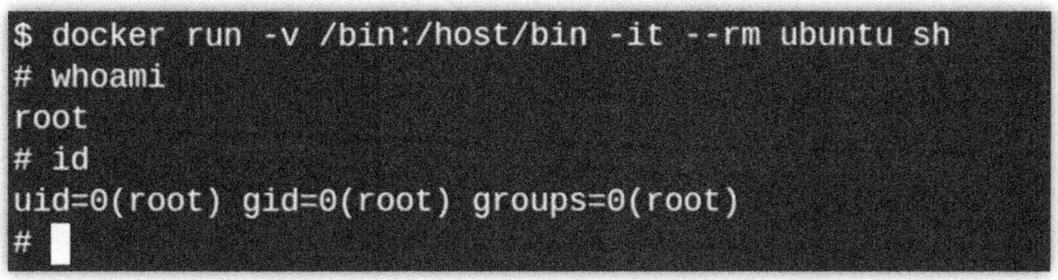

```
$ docker run -v /bin:/host/bin -it --rm ubuntu sh
# whoami
root
# id
uid=0(root) gid=0(root) groups=0(root)
#
```

Figure 4.1: Executing Docker container with default root user

The containers are executed by default with the root user, so root privileges are available within the container. From a security point of view, it is important to configure the namespaces to limit access to the container at this point. While the container engine must be run with the root user, it is not a good practice for the containers to do so, and it is necessary to create a user for each running container.

The security solution is to indicate the user who wants to be able to execute the creation of the image in the Dockerfile. You can add the user inside the Dockerfile with the following commands:

```
RUN useradd <options>
USER <user>
```

We can include the information about the user in the *Dockerfile* with the following commands:

```
FROM python:latest
RUN useradd -s /bin/bash unix_user
USER unix_user
ENTRYPOINT ["bin/bash"]
```

We can build the image with the following command:

```
$ docker image build -t python_image .
```

When executing the container with the (-i) interactive option, we see how the user corresponds to the one we have declared in the Dockerfile:

```
$ docker run -ti python_image
```

In the following output, we can see the content from the **/etc/passwd** file after executing the preceding command:

```
unix_user:x:1000:1000::/home/unix_user:/bin/bash
unix_user@5f4833b156fb:/$
unix_user@5f4833b156fb:/$ whoami
unix_user
unix_user@5f4833b156fb:/$ id
uid=1000(unix_user) gid=1000(unix_user) groups=1000(unix_user)
```

In this way, the **whoami** command returns the user created with the Dockerfile, and we see how the user is added inside the container when inspecting the file **etc/passwd**.

Start containers in read-only mode

Best practice recommendations for Linux systems administrations include the application of the principle of minimum privilege. For this, flags like *read-only* can be applied when executing a container.

Limiting the use of the filesystem can prevent a potential attacker writing and executing scripts inside the container. We can use the **docker run** command with the read-only flag to do this:

```
$ docker run -it --read-only python sh
# touch file
touch: cannot touch 'file': Read-only filesystem
```

In the preceding output, we can see that we get the *"cannot touch file: Read-only filesystem"* message if we try to create a file when executing the container with this flag.

The main disadvantage of using the read-only option is that most applications need to write files in directories such as **/ tmp** and will not work in a read-only environment. In these cases, we can use folders and files in which the application needs write access and use volumes to mount only those files.

A volume can be provided to make persistent changes if the container needs to write to the filesystem. It is recommended to use Docker volumes in the case of temporary files.

A **volume** is a directory that is separate from the root filesystem of the container, is managed directly by the daemon docker process, and can be shared between containers.

In the following example, we are running a **mysql container** and configuring it as read-only, with exception of the **/var/lib/mysql** and **/tmp** directories.

It means that these directories are the only location where data can be written into the container. You won't be allowed to write anything in any other location inside the container. We can run the **mysql container** in combination with other parameters like **MYSQL_ROOT_PASSWORD** and define a volume with the **-v** flag to do this:

```
$ docker run --name mysql --read-only -v /var/lib/mysql -v /tmp -d
-e MYSQL_ROOT_PASSWORD=password mysql
```

The following output shows that we get an error when trying to create a file inside the mysql container with read-only mode:

```
$ docker ps
CONTAINER ID         IMAGE              COMMAND                    CREATED
STATUS               PORTS                    NAMES
aea913f35c28         mysql              "docker-entrypoint.s…"   9 seconds
ago        Up 7 seconds          3306/tcp, 33060/tcp    mysql
$ docker exec mysql touch /opt/file
touch: cannot touch '/opt/file': Read-only filesystem
```

We get the *"Read-only filesystem"* error message when executing the container and trying to write a file outside the **/tmp** directory. We can use the: ro flag, indicating that the volume is read-only, when working with volumes with Docker containers:

```
$ docker run -v $(pwd):/pwd:ro debian touch /pwd/x
Unable to find image 'debian:latest' locally
latest: Pulling from library/debian
e22122b926a1: Already exists
Digest: sha256:9d4ab94af82b2567c272c7f47f
a1204cd9b40914704213f1c257c44042f82aac
Status: Downloaded newer image for debian:latest
touch: cannot touch '/pwd/x': Read-only filesystem
```

At this point, we have reviewed how to start a container and mount a volume in read-only mode.

Disable the setuid and setgid permissions

The Set User ID (**setuid**) and Set Group ID (**setgid**) bits are special permissions that are used to access directories and files in the operating system by users who do not have root permissions.

The main problem with these bits is that they can be exploited by attackers. At this point, the best practice is to disable the SETUID permissions in the Dockerfile.

The setuid and setgid permissions are deleted during the image construction phase using the Dockerfile with the following command:

```
RUN find / -perm +6000 -type f -exec chmod a-s {} ; || true
```

The preceding command performs a search for executables and withdraws any setuid and setgid permission from any user.

We can also disable the **setuid** and **setgid** bits when you start a Docker container with the following command:

```
$ docker run -d --cap-drop SETGID --cap-drop SETUID <container_name>
```

With the previous command, you have disabled the setuid and setgid capabilities when running a specific Docker container.

Verifying images with Docker Content Trust

The **DOCKER_CONTENT_TRUST** environment variable allows you to verify that the images you download from a Docker registry like Docker Hub are trusted and signed. You need to export this variable with the following command to enable this feature:

```
$ export DOCKER_CONTENT_TRUST=1
```

Use the following command to download an image from the DockerHub repository and verify the image hash:

```
$ docker pull someimage@sha256:a25306f3850e1bd44541976aa7b5fd0a29be
```

The preceding command checks the SHA256 hash of the filesystem manifest, where a manifest is a metadata file that describes the content of a Docker image.

The manifest file contains a list of all the image layers identified by the hash, so you can securely download and trust all layers, , even over untrusted channels like HTTP, if you can verify that the manifest has not been modified.

Resource limitation

By default, all containers share host machine resources equitably. This means that there is no preference between containers when it comes to consuming resources like CPU and memory from the Docker host.

One of the problems that may arise is determining which containers in the system may be affecting the stability of the entire infrastructure, preventing its normal operation. A possible solution to resource problems that may arise is to limit the use of CPU and memory for each of the containers.

The **docker run** command has different configuration parameters that allow both to limit the use of resources:

```
$ docker run [OPTIONS] [IMAGE] [COMMAND] [ARG]
```

The following command shows information about the options available related with CPU, devices, and memory:

```
$ docker run --help | grep 'cpu\|device\|memory'
```

The following screenshot shows the options available for limiting the use of CPU, devices, and memory when running a container:

```
$ docker run --help | grep 'cpu\|device\|memory'
      --blkio-weight-device list        Block IO weight (relative
                                         device weight) (default [])
      --cpu-period int                   Limit CPU CFS (Completely
      --cpu-quota int                    Limit CPU CFS (Completely
      --cpu-rt-period int                Limit CPU real-time period
      --cpu-rt-runtime int               Limit CPU real-time runtime
  -c, --cpu-shares int                   CPU shares (relative weight)
      --cpus decimal                     Number of CPUs
      --cpuset-cpus string               CPUs in which to allow
      --cpuset-mems string               MEMs in which to allow
      --device list                      Add a host device to the
      --device-cgroup-rule list          Add a rule to the cgroup
                                         allowed devices list
      --device-read-bps list             Limit read rate (bytes per
                                         second) from a device
      --device-read-iops list            Limit read rate (IO per
                                         second) from a device
      --device-write-bps list            Limit write rate (bytes per
```

Figure 4.2: Command options for limiting resources in containers

At this point, we have reviewed the different options available for adjusting performance needs, such as CPU, devices, and memory.

Just like different privileges can be added, by default, the ideal in terms of security is to apply as less as possible. In other words, do not provide permissions until it is shown that they are necessary to execute the different functionalities required.

Docker capabilities

Docker capabilities allow us to manage the permissions that a process can use to access the kernel and segregate root user privileges to limit actions that can be accessed with privileges.

Tip: Linux capabilities

Linux capabilities provide a tool to design a more advanced security strategy with different privilege levels.

You can check the man pages for Linux capabilities at http://man7.org/linux/man-pages/man7/capabilities.7.html.

We already know that, by default, when we execute a Docker container, it runs as root. We all know that this practice is not a good idea, especially services that receive requests either from users or from other sources.

It is also important to note that a container does not have the same privileges as the root user of the Docker host even if it is run as root. This is because Docker containers run with a limited number of capabilities by default. These include the following:

- **CAP_SYSLOG**: For modifying the behavior of the Kernel log
- **CAP_NET_ADMIN**: For modifying the network configuration
- **CAP_SYS_MODULE**: For managing Kernel modules
- **CAP_SYS_RAWIO**: For modifying the Kernel memory
- **CAP_SYS_NICE**: For modifying the priority of the processes
- **CAP_SYS_TIME**: For modifying the system clock
- **CAP_SYS_TTY_CONFIG**: For configuring tty devices
- **CAP_AUDIT_CONTROL**: For configuring the audit subsystem

Thanks to this granularity, capabilities are a useful method to execute privileged tasks with minimal permissions. This way, the capabilities are used in virtualization environments like Linux or Docker containers, where they play a fundamental role in the **management of security contexts**.

The main advantage is to avoid granting a process elevated privileges when you actually need only certain permissions for a specific operation. This table lists some Linux capabilities with a description:

Capability Key	Capability Description
CAP_AUDIT_CONTROL	Enable and disable kernel auditing; change auditing filter rules; retrieve auditing status and filtering rules.
CAP_AUDIT_WRITE	Write records to the kernel auditing log.
CAP_NET_RAW	Use RAW and PACKET sockets; bind to any address for transparent proxying.
CAP_CHOWN	Make arbitrary changes to file UIDs and GIDs.
CAP_MAC_ADMIN	Allow MAC configuration or state changes. Implemented for the Smack **Linux Security Module (LSM)**.
CAP_NET_ADMIN	Perform various network-related operations.
CAP_NET_BIND_SERVICE	Bind a socket to Internet domain privileged ports (port numbers less than 1024).

Table 4.1: Linux capabilities

The Linux kernel prefixes all capability constants with the "**CAP_**" prefix. For example, **CAP_CHOWN** makes changes in bits UIDs and GIDs to change the owner of a file.

Listing all capabilities

The Linux **libcap** packages incorporate commands and binaries for listing and managing capabilities:

- **getcap**: Allows listing the capabilities of a file
- **setcap**: Allows assigning and deleting the capabilities of a file
- **getpcaps**: Allows listing the capabilities of a process
- **capsh**: Provides a command line interface for testing and exploring capabilities

We can check the capabilities by starting a container, connecting to a shell, and listing the capabilities. The following commands will deploy an Ubuntu image and install the **libcap2-bin** package, which contains utilities to check capabilities:

```
$ docker run -it ubuntu
root@e1773474e22c:/# apt update
Get:1 http://security.ubuntu.com/ubuntu bionic-security InRelease
[88.7 kB]
Get:2 http://archive.ubuntu.com/ubuntu bionic InRelease [242 kB]
Get:3 http://archive.ubuntu.com/ubuntu bionic-updates InRelease
[88.7 kB]
Get:4 http://archive.ubuntu.com/ubuntu bionic-backports InRelease
[74.6 kB]
Get:5 http://security.ubuntu.com/ubuntu bionic-security/universe
Sources [346 kB]
Get:6 http://security.ubuntu.com/ubuntu bionic-security/universe
amd64 Packages [1398 kB]
...
root@e1773474e22c:/# apt install -y libcap2-bin
Reading package lists... Done
Building dependency tree
Reading state information... Done
The following additional packages will be installed:
  libcap2 libpam-cap
The following NEW packages will be installed:
  libcap2 libcap2-bin libpam-cap
....
Setting up libcap2-bin (1:2.25-1.2) ...
root@e1773474e22c:/# grep Cap /proc/$BASHPID/status
CapInh: 00000000a80425fb
CapPrm: 00000000a80425fb
CapEff: 00000000a80425fb
CapBnd: 00000000a80425fb
CapAmb: 0000000000000000
root@e1773474e22c:/# capsh --decode=00000000a80425fb
0x00000000a80425fb=cap_chown,cap_dac_override,cap_fowner,cap_
fsetid,cap_kill,cap_setgid,cap_setuid,cap_setpcap,cap_net_bind_
service,cap_net_raw,cap_sys_chroot,cap_mknod,cap_audit_write,cap_
setfcap
```

At this point, we have reviewed the different capabilities activated by default in a Docker container.

Add and drop capabilities

Docker provides the following commands to provide or remove Linux permissions to different containers. Here, we can apply add or remove privileges through cap-add and cap-drop flags:

```
$ docker run --cap-add = {capability}
$ docker run --cap-drop = {capability}
```

We can add a specific capability with the following command:

```
$ docker run --rm -it --cap-add $CAP ubuntu sh
```

We can use the following command to drop capabilities from the root account of a container:

```
$ docker run --rm -it --cap-drop $CAP ubuntu sh
```

We can use the following command to drop all capabilities and then explicitly add individual capabilities to the root account of a container:

```
$ docker run --rm -it --cap-drop ALL --cap-add $CAP ubuntu sh
```

For example, we can delete the chown capability inside a container and then try to add a user. The action of adding a user will fail because this operation needs the **CAP_CHOWN** capability. In the following command, we can see the action of changing the ownership of a file or directory inside an Ubuntu container:

```
$ docker run --cap-add=ALL --cap-drop=CHOWN -ti ubuntu sh
# useradd test
useradd: failure while writing changes to /etc/shadow
# chown test /usr/share
chown: changing ownership of '/usr/share': Operation not permitted
# id
uid=0(root) gid=0(root) groups=0(root)
```

When executing the preceding command, we can see that the action of changing the ownership of a file or directory will fail, and it will show a *"Operation not permitted"* message. As we can see, we do not have the permission to change the owner of a file even as a root user as we have disabled the capability corresponding to the change of the owner.

Docker containers start with a reduced capacity set. Docker enables these capabilities by default: `chown`, `dac_override`, `fowner`, `kill`, `setgid`, `setuid`, `setpcap`, `net_bind_service`, `net_raw`, `sys_chroot`, `mknod`, `setfcap`, and `audit_write`.

We can also remove all the capabilities that are enabled in Docker by default and check that the container stops working. With the following command, we are starting a bash shell without the capabilities that are enabled by default:

```
$ docker run -ti --cap-drop=CHOWN --cap-drop=DAC_OVERRIDE
--cap-drop=FSETID    --cap-drop=FOWNER    --cap-drop=KILL    --cap-drop=MKNOD
--cap-drop=NET_RAW --cap-drop=SETGID --cap-drop=SETUID
--cap-drop=SETFCAP --cap-drop=SETPCAP --cap-drop=NET_BIND_SERVICE
--cap-drop=SYS_CHROOT --cap-drop=AUDIT_WRITE ubuntu /bin/bash
```

It is also recommended to drop the setuid and setgid capabilities from containers that will be running on your hosts. The Linux kernel is responsible for managing the uid and gid space, and kernel-level syscalls are used to determine if the requested privileges should be granted.

In the following command, we are dropping the setuid and setgid capabilities when you are executing a Docker container:

```
$ docker run -it --cap-drop SETGID --cap-drop SETUID python sh
# cat /proc/self/status
Name:    cat
Umask:   0022
State:   R (running)
Tgid:    6
Ngid:    0
Pid:     6
PPid:    1
TracerPid:      0
Uid:     0       0       0       0
Gid:     0       0       0       0
...
```

If we try to get the capabilities inside the container, we can see that uid and gid bits are equal to 0. For example, a possible attacker who finds a vulnerability within the container cannot not obtain a shell with root privileges if uid and gid bits are eliminated.

The best practice at this point is to eliminate all capacities and add only those we need in our container with the **cap-drop** and **--cap-add** flags.

Disabling ping command in a container

We can use the following command that disables the **NET_RAW** capability in the Python container for disabling ping in a container:

```
$ docker run -it --cap-drop NET_RAW python sh
```

In the following example, we are removing the **NET_RAW** capability of the container, so we cannot execute the ping command:

```
$ docker run -it --cap-drop NET_RAW python sh
Unable to find image 'python:latest' locally
latest: Pulling from library/python
e22122b926a1: Pull complete
f29e09ae8373: Pull complete
e319e3daef68: Pull complete
e499244fe254: Pull complete
5a6ebed20e89: Pull complete
56b703a5a371: Pull complete
4dd0a64393b6: Pull complete
1d2280ee5e8b: Pull complete
8b6ce844793f: Pull complete
Digest: sha256:168fd55b03929f88cd3e1e05b9ebe8f9cc1c095af8b53a8c0cd50da04
c3a40
Status: Downloaded newer image for python:latest
# ping 8.8.8.8
ping: socket: Operation not permitted
```

Figure 4.3: Disabling ping in Python container

In the preceding command, we have disabled the use of **RAW** and **PACKET** sockets. If we try to execute the ping command inside the container, it will return the *"ping:Lacking privilege for raw socket"* message.

We can eliminate all the capacities of a container as a good security practice. Docker provides the **ALL** option to refer to all the capacities. The following command shows the result for dropping all capabilities in the Python container:

```
$ docker run -it --cap-drop=all python sh
# ping 8.8.8.8
ping: socket: Operation not permitted
# apt update
E: setgroups 65534 failed - setgroups (1: Operation not permitted)
E: setegid 65534 failed - setegid (1: Operation not permitted)
E: seteuid 100 failed - seteuid (1: Operation not permitted)
E: setgroups 0 failed - setgroups (1: Operation not permitted)
...
```

Ideally, you would run the container as a user without any capabilities, and if necessary, add only the capabilities needed to run the container. If we use **docker-compose**, we can indicate it as follows:

```
version: "1.0"
services:
  my_service:
    ...
    cap_drop:
      - ALL
    cap_add:
      - NET_ADMIN
      - SYS_ADMIN
    ...
```

If we are using Kubernetes, it can be defined within the security context when we define the pod:

```
apiVersion: v1
kind: Pod
metadata:
name: capabilities_k8s
spec:
containers:
- name: capabilities_k8s
    image: my_image
    securityContext:
```

```
capabilities:
    drop:
        - ALL
    add:
        - NET_ADMIN
        - SYS_TIME
```

Adding capability for managing network

Sometimes we need to add capabilities for managing and configuring the network. We can use the **--cap-add=NET_ADMIN** flag for this task. The following command is used to add the **net_admin** capability inside Python container:

```
$ docker run -ti --cap-add=NET_ADMIN python sh -c "ip link set eth0 down"
```

We can disable the network interface executing the **link set eth0 down** command by adding this capability. The following screenshot depicts the result of executing the preceding command:

```
$ docker run -ti --cap-add=NET_ADMIN python sh
# ip link
1: lo: <LOOPBACK,UP,LOWER_UP> mtu 65536 qdisc noqueue state UNKNOWN mode DEFAULT group default qlen 1
000
    link/loopback 00:00:00:00:00:00 brd 00:00:00:00:00:00
8: eth0@if9: <BROADCAST,MULTICAST,UP,LOWER_UP> mtu 1500 qdisc noqueue state UP mode DEFAULT group def
ault
    link/ether 02:42:ac:12:00:02 brd ff:ff:ff:ff:ff:ff link-netnsid 0
# ip link set eth0 down
# ip link
1: lo: <LOOPBACK,UP,LOWER_UP> mtu 65536 qdisc noqueue state UNKNOWN mode DEFAULT group default qlen 1
000
    link/loopback 00:00:00:00:00:00 brd 00:00:00:00:00:00
8: eth0@if9: <BROADCAST,MULTICAST> mtu 1500 qdisc noqueue state DOWN mode DEFAULT group default
    link/ether 02:42:ac:12:00:02 brd ff:ff:ff:ff:ff:ff link-netnsid 0
# ping 8.8.8.8
connect: Network is unreachable
```

Figure 4.4: Enabling capability for managing network

CAP_NET_RAW is another capability related to the network. From the security point of view, this capability has several implications related to the sending of packages. This is because it allows any package to be generated, and impersonation attacks can be made to perform MITM attacks from a container.

Execution of privileged containers

Sometimes you need your container to have special Kernel capabilities that would normally be denied. This can include mounting a USB drive, modifying network settings, or creating a new Unix device.

The following command can be used to change the container's MAC address in the eth0 interface:

```
$ docker run --rm -ti ubuntu /bin/bash
root@b328e3449da8:/# ip link ls
1: lo: <LOOPBACK,UP,LOWER_UP> mtu 65536 qdisc noqueue state ...
link/loopback 00:00:00:00:00:00 brd 00:00:00:00:00:00
9: eth0: <BROADCAST,UP,LOWER_UP> mtu 1500 qdisc noqueue state ...
link/ether 02:42:0a:00:00:04 brd ff:ff:ff:ff:ff:ff
root@b328e3449da8:/# ip link set eth0 address 02:0a:03:0b:04:0c
RTNETLINK answers: Operation not permitted
```

We can see that this operation is not allowed since the Linux Kernel blocks it in the container. However, if we need this functionality for executing our container, we can do it with the **--privileged = true** option.

The following command is used to execute Ubuntu container with full privileges:

```
$ docker run -ti --rm --privileged=true ubuntu /bin/bash
```

We can see how the MAC address has been modified correctly with this option:

```
root@88d9d17dc13c:/# ip link ls
1: lo: <LOOPBACK,UP,LOWER_UP> mtu 65536 qdisc noqueue state ...
link/loopback 00:00:00:00:00:00 brd 00:00:00:00:00:00
9: eth0: <BROADCAST,UP,LOWER_UP> mtu 1500 qdisc noqueue state ...
link/ether 02:42:0a:00:00:04 brd ff:ff:ff:ff:ff:ff
root@88d9d17dc13c:/# ip link set eth0 address 02:0a:03:0b:04:0c
root@88d9d17dc13c:/# ip link ls
1: lo: <LOOPBACK,UP,LOWER_UP> mtu 65536 qdisc noqueue state ...
link/loopback 00:00:00:00:00:00 brd 00:00:00:00:00:00
9: eth0: <BROADCAST,UP,LOWER_UP> mtu 1500 qdisc noqueue state ...
link/ether 02:0a:03:0b:04:0c brd ff:ff:ff:ff:ff:ff
```

With privileged access within the container, we will provide more capabilities to perform operations normally performed by root. As we can see, the privileged container can access much more hardware than the container that is not privileged.

The problem with using the **--privileged=true** flag is that it gives your container a lot of privileges, and in most cases, you probably only need one or two Kernel capabilities to perform the necessary operations.

Docker Content Trust

Docker Content Trust (DCT) is a mechanism that allows developers to sign their content, completing the reliable distribution mechanism.

When a user downloads an image from a repository, this mechanism allows you to check the image signature, receiving a certificate that includes the public key that lets you verify the image origin.

This option is disabled by default, and we need to define the **DOCKER_CONTENT_TRUST** environment variable or run Docker Engine with the **--disable-content-trust** = **false** option to enable it.

```
$ export DOCKER_CONTENT_TRUST=1
```

The following screenshot shows the result of pulling Python Docker image with Docker content trust enabled:

```
$ export DOCKER_CONTENT_TRUST=1
$ docker pull python
Using default tag: latest
Pull (1 of 1): python:latest@sha256:797aee34488c660ebaf5b88e622fdd458e65bb3c2500d4
8f9fbb3711e8688a1e
sha256:797aee34488c660ebaf5b88e622fdd458e65bb3c2500d48f9fbb3711e8688a1e: Pulling f
rom library/python
756975cb9c7e: Pull complete
d77915b4e630: Pull complete
5f37a0a41b6b: Pull complete
96b2c1e36db5: Pull complete
c495e8de12d2: Pull complete
33382189822a: Pull complete
414ebfa5f45b: Pull complete
dd860911922e: Pull complete
b434dcf770b1: Pull complete
Digest: sha256:797aee34488c660ebaf5b88e622fdd458e65bb3c2500d48f9fbb3711e8688a1e
Status: Downloaded newer image for python@sha256:797aee34488c660ebaf5b88e622fdd458
e65bb3c2500d48f9fbb3711e8688a1e
```

Figure 4.5: Downloading Python image with Docker Content Trust

Docker Content Trust can protect against certain attack scenarios, including the following:

- **Protection of malicious code in images**: For example, this mechanism protects you if a possible attacker wants to make a modification in an official image to introduce malicious code.

- **Protection against repeated attacks**: The security mechanism of Docker Content Trust allows you to maintain the integrity of the image through the use of timestamps.

- **Protection against key commitments**: This mechanism creates a new key if a key is compromised, and we can create a new version of the image with this new key.

We can verify a Docker image using the Docker trust command. For example, we can *verify images signatures from the python image* with the following command:

```
$ docker trust inspect --pretty python:latest


Signatures for python:latest


SIGNED TAG        DIGEST                                      SIGNERS
latest                                  797aee    34488c660ebaf
5b88e622fdd458e65bb3c2500d48f9fbb3711e8688a1e    (Repo Admin)


Administrative keys for python:latest


    Repository   Key:                abdd8255df05a14ddc919bc43ee
34692725ece7f57769381b964587f3e4decac
         Root      Key:                              a1bbec
595228fa5fbab2016f6918bbf16a572df61457c9580355002096bb58e1
```

When an image is downloaded, the Docker client will return a string representing the image's hash. This hash is the one with which the image will be validated when performing a pull.

We'll get the following error message if the hash with which we are downloading the image does not match the original:

```
$ docker pull python@sha256:11111111111111111111111111111111111
11111111
invalid checksum digest length
```

Docker will verify that the hash matches with the original image each time an image is attempted to be downloaded like this. Any update of the image will result in the generation of a new hash.

When enabling Docker Content Trust, the Docker engine will only download the images that have been signed and will deny the execution of the images whose signatures do not match.

Notary as a tool for managing images

Docker Notary **https://docs.docker.com/notary/** is a tool that allows you to securely publish and manage images. Some of Notary's objectives are to improve confidence in the images we download, either from a public or private repository, delegate trust between users, and securely distribute over different repositories.

Notary consists of server and client parts. The client part is installed on the local machine and handles the storage of the keys locally, and it also handles communication with the Notary server. You can check the GitHub repository at **https://github.com/docker/notary** for more information on how to compile and configure the Notary server.

From the server point of view, you can find official precompiled binaries for many operating systems in the GitHub repository at **https://github.com/theupdateframework/notary/releases**.

These are the steps we can follow to deploy your notary server:

- Use the `docker-compose` file that we find inside the repository at **https://github.com/theupdateframework/notary.git**

```
docker-compose build

docker-compose up -d
```

- Run the following commands to connect the notary server to the Docker client:

```
export DOCKER_CONTENT_TRUST = 1

export DOCKER_CONTENT_TRUST_SERVER = https://notary_server:4443
```

The first environment variable allows you to enable and disable Docker Content Trust verification. If enabled, the integrity of the image will be verified, relying on this verification on the Docker Notary server indicated in the second environment variable that allows you to define the URL where the Notary server is located.

Docker Registry

Docker provides a software distribution mechanism, also known as *"Registry"*, which facilitates the discovery and distribution of Docker images. The concept of registry is fundamental as it provides a set of utilities to package, send, store, and discover new images. The best known Docker Registry is the Docker Hub.

What is a registry?

A registry is one of the key pieces when creating our Docker environments as soon as we start creating our own images. Having a registry in our own infrastructure saves us bandwidth and gives us better access/download time.

The idea behind Docker Registry is that developers can extract the image from the registry to create other containers and deploy them either in the public cloud or in an organization's private servers.

The Docker registry works almost like Git. Each image, also known as a repository, is a succession of layers. *Every time we build our image locally, the Docker Registry only stores the difference from the previous version*, making the image creation and distribution process much more efficient.

Public Docker registries

Docker Hub **https://hub.docker.com/** is the main image registry service that is offered as a Software as a Service platform with several usage plans.

The main problem with the official Docker Hub image repository is that it has quite a few limitations regarding the number of images that we can upload and download, which means the number of pushes and pulls is limited to a certain number during a period of time.

An option to avoid being aware of this limitation is to set up our own internal Docker Registry in our organization. This option is viable, especially since our users are doing builds continuously and have a CI/CD system that depends on a registry for downloading the images.

We have other options for using public registries like *Quay* **https://quay.io/** and *Harbor* **https://goharbor.io/**. These registries allow you to open an account, authenticate, and bring images from this registry simply by registering a user.

The *Gitlab* registry **https://docs.gitlab.com/ee/user/packages/package_registry** is also an excellent option to host our images, especially if we manage our projects directly on this platform.

If you are familiar with Amazon web services, you can use services like Amazon Elastic Container Registry **https://aws.amazon.com/ecr** as a managed container registry that makes it easy to store, manage, share, and deploy your container images and artifacts anywhere.

Creating Docker registry

Docker Registry is an open source project that can be installed on any server to create your own registry and upload your images privately. This project aims to have an alternative to the Docker Hub to track the images hosted on your own server.

You can run and deploy a Docker registry on your own server in several ways to store and distribute your own Docker images. For Linux distributions that include a Docker registration package (such as Fedora and Red Hat Enterprise Linux), you can install the package and start the service.

You can also use the following image available in the Docker hub at `http://hub.docker.com/_/registry`, which contains an implementation of the Docker Registry HTTP API V2. Here are the *steps to set up a private Docker registry* on your own server:

1. We are executing a registry container in detached mode with port 5000 exposed with the following command:

```
$ docker run -d -p 5000:5000 --restart=always --name registry
registry:2
```

The following screenshot illustrates the result of executing the previous command:

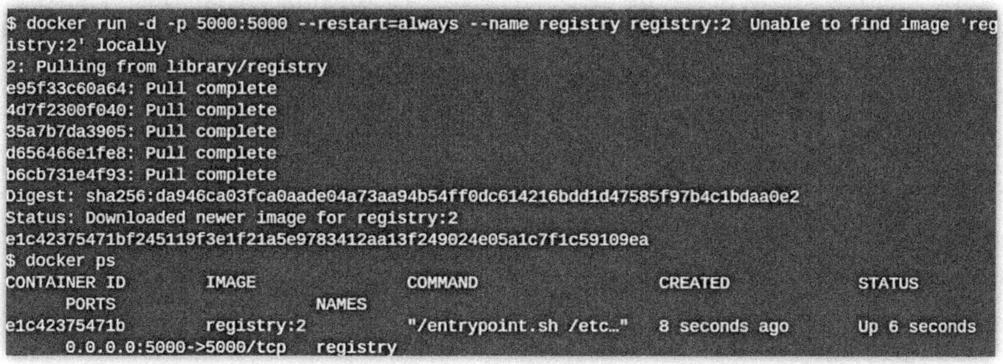

```
$ docker run -d -p 5000:5000 --restart=always --name registry registry:2  Unable to find image 'reg
istry:2' locally
2: Pulling from library/registry
e95f33c60a64: Pull complete
4d7f2300f040: Pull complete
35a7b7da3905: Pull complete
d656466e1fe8: Pull complete
b6cb731e4f93: Pull complete
Digest: sha256:da946ca03fca0aade04a73aa94b54ff0dc614216bdd1d47585f97b4c1bdaa0e2
Status: Downloaded newer image for registry:2
e1c42375471bf245119f3e1f21a5e9783412aa13f249024e05a1c7f1c59109ea
$ docker ps
CONTAINER ID        IMAGE               COMMAND                  CREATED             STATUS
      PORTS                    NAMES
e1c42375471b        registry:2          "/entrypoint.sh /etc…"   8 seconds ago       Up 6 seconds
      0.0.0.0:5000->5000/tcp   registry
```

Figure 4.6: *Downloading docker image for creating local registry*

The preceding command starts a registry container in TCP port 5000. You can upload and download images in the private repository for testing this container. For example, you can download the hello world image available in the Docker Hub Registry.

```
$ docker run --name myhello hello-world
```

2. We must now tag the hello world Docker image. We can use the **`docker tag`** command to name the Docker image:

```
$ docker tag hello-world localhost:5000/hello-me:latest
$ docker images
REPOSITORY              TAG             IMAGE ID            CREATED
SIZE
hello-world             latest          d1165f221234        2 weeks
ago          13.3kB
localhost:5000/hello-me   latest        d1165f221234        2 weeks
ago          13.3kB
registry                2               5c4008a25e05        3 weeks
ago          26.2MB
```

3. The next step is to push the image in the registry. We can execute the following command to save the **hello-world** image in the local Docker registry:

```
$ docker push localhost:5000/hello-me:latest
The push refers to repository [localhost:5000/hello-me]
f22b99068db9: Pushed
latest:          digest:          sha256:1b26826f602946860c
279fce658f31050cff2c596583af237d971f4629b57792 size: 525
```

4. Then, we have to ensure that you can obtain the image from the registry. We must first delete the current image with the Docker **rm** command and then retrieve it from your local registry:

```
$ sudo docker rm myhello
$ sudo docker rmi hello-world localhost:5000/hello-me:latest
$ sudo docker pull localhost:5000/hello-me:latest
```

The following screenshot depicts the result of executing the above-mentioned commands:

```
$ docker rm myhello
myhello
$ docker rmi hello-world localhost:5000/hello-me:latest
Untagged: hello-world:latest
Untagged: hello-world@sha256:308866a43596e83578c7dfa15e27a73011bdd402185a84c5cd7f32a88b501a24
Untagged: localhost:5000/hello-me:latest
Untagged: localhost:5000/hello-me@sha256:1b26826f602946860c279fce658f31050cff2c596583af237d971f4629
b57792
Deleted: sha256:d1165f2212346b2bab48cb01c1e39ee8ad1be46b87873d9ca7a4e434980a7726
Deleted: sha256:f22b99068db93900abe17f7f5e09ec775c2826ecfe9db961fea68293744144bd
$ docker pull localhost:5000/hello-me:latest
latest: Pulling from hello-me
b8dfde127a29: Pull complete
Digest: sha256:1b26826f602946860c279fce658f31050cff2c596583af237d971f4629b57792
Status: Downloaded newer image for localhost:5000/hello-me:latest
```

Figure 4.7: Deleting hello world docker image and pulling from local registry

5. Finally, we can verify that the image has been downloaded to our host Docker, and we can execute the image:

```
$ docker images
$ docker run -it localhost:5000/hello-me
```

The following screenshot shows the result of executing the preceding commands:

```
$ docker images
REPOSITORY                TAG        IMAGE ID         CREATED        SIZE
localhost:5000/hello-me   latest     d1165f221234     2 weeks ago    13.3kB
registry                  2          5c4008a25e05     3 weeks ago    26.2MB
redis                     latest     4760dc956b2d     3 years ago    107MB
ubuntu                    latest     f975c5035748     3 years ago    112MB
alpine                    latest     3fd9065eaf02     3 years ago    4.14MB
$ docker run -it localhost:5000/hello-me

Hello from Docker!
This message shows that your installation appears to be working correctly.

To generate this message, Docker took the following steps:
 1. The Docker client contacted the Docker daemon.
 2. The Docker daemon pulled the "hello-world" image from the Docker Hub.
    (amd64)
```

Figure 4.8: *Checking docker images and running docker image from localhost*

In summary, setting up a private Docker registry offers developers the capacity to send and extract images without using the public Docker registry.

Quay.io image repository

Quay.io image repository **https://docs.quay.io** is a container registry with features similar to those of the Docker Hub repository.

This registry is compatible with most container environments and orchestration platforms, and it is also available as a hosted or local service. Additionally, it supports the last version of the Docker Registry HTTP API protocol used to distribute container images.

We can use the quay registry to download an image just like when using Docker hub:

```
$ docker pull quay.io/bitnami/elasticsearch
Using default tag: latest
latest: Pulling from bitnami/elasticsearch
133717132a92: Pull complete
dbd9fadba36e: Pull complete
6b44c2d792e7: Pull complete
```

```
2f1d15f1de50: Pull complete
d9caf900187c: Pull complete
b444f54a2494: Pull complete
7410684254f7: Pull complete
f5de5c0b3731: Pull complete
6ff0318ae752: Pull complete
6f51a6553225: Pull complete
Digest: sha256:533ac49a17131fa9e14edbccd77
cc8fca36ce11566808885a1c307d2ccee3bd4
Status: Downloaded newer image for quay.io/bitnami/
elasticsearch:latest
quay.io/bitnami/elasticsearch:latest
```

Execute the following command to log in to Quay.io:

```
$ docker login quay.io
Username: myusername
Password: mypassword
```

Quay provides a visual interface for creating a repository. Click on the + icon in the upper-right corner and select '**New repository**'. The following screenshot shows the quay.io page for creating a new repository:

Figure 4.9: Quay.io page for creating a new repository

We can use many options for create a repository:

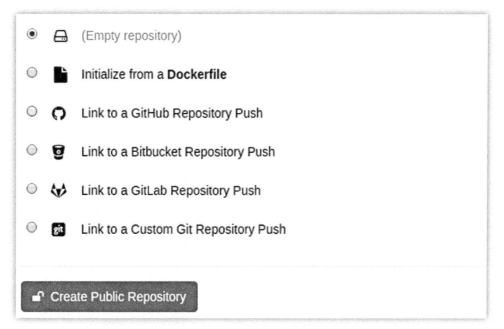

Figure 4.10: Quay.io options for creating a new repository

Quay also provides an interface to assign several labels to the same image. A new tag can be added to a tagged image by clicking on the icon next to the tag and selecting **Add New Tag**. Quay.io will confirm the action of adding a new label to the image. The following screenshot shows actions related to tags:

Figure 4.11: Actions related to tags

One of the interesting features of this repository is that we can enable the Docker Content Trust.

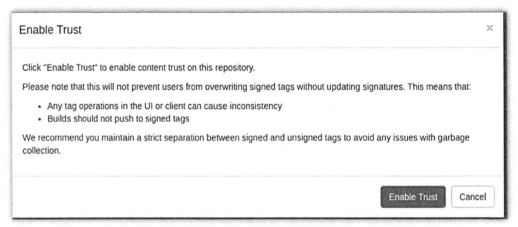

Figure 4.12: Enable Docker Content Trust in Quay

Repository tags and Docker Content Trust can make a signed tag point to a different image than the actual tag. So, it is important to have a separation between tags that are signed and tags that are not.

Harbor repository

Harbor **https://goharbor.io** is an image repository for Docker and Kubernetes that applies features like vulnerability analysis, content signing and validation, multi-tenant, and access through API and web interface.

> **Tip: Testing Harbor repository**
>
> Harbor allows us to create secure repositories for our organization, with the possibility of managing access and integrating it with Kubernetes securely and efficiently.
>
> Visit https://www.katacoda.com/courses/harbor for an example for deploying a harbor registry.

Harbor is released as an installer that includes default configuration and installation scripts. You can download and extract the installer with the following command:

```
$ curl -LO https://storage.googleapis.com/harbor-releases/harbor-
online-installer-v1.5.2.tgz;  tar  -xvf  harbor-online-installer-
v1.5.2.tgz; cd harbor
```

```
$ curl -LO https://storage.googleapis.com/harbor-releases/harbor-online-installer-v1.5.2.tgz; tar -xvf harbor-onl
ine-installer-v1.5.2.tgz; cd harbor/
  % Total    % Received % Xferd  Average Speed   Time    Time     Time  Current
                                 Dload  Upload   Total   Spent    Left  Speed
  0     0    0     0    0     0      0        0 --:--:-- --:--:-- --:--:--     0curl -LO https://storage.googleapis
.com/harbor-releases/harbor-online-installer-v1.5.2.tgz; tar -xvf harbor-online-installer-v1.5.2.tgz; cd harbor/
100  225k  100  225k    0     0    434k       0 --:--:-- --:--:-- --:--:--   434k
harbor/common/templates/
harbor/common/templates/ui/
harbor/common/templates/ui/env
harbor/common/templates/ui/app.conf
harbor/common/templates/ui/private_key.pem
harbor/common/templates/log/
harbor/common/templates/log/logrotate.conf
harbor/common/templates/nginx/
harbor/common/templates/nginx/notary.upstream.conf
harbor/common/templates/nginx/nginx.https.conf
harbor/common/templates/nginx/nginx.http.conf
harbor/common/templates/nginx/notary.server.conf
harbor/common/templates/adminserver/
harbor/common/templates/adminserver/env
harbor/common/templates/notary/
```

Figure 4.13: Extracting harbor installer

The IP address or URL for the registry needs to be configured in the **harbor.cfg** file to configure Harbor:

```
$ cat harbor.cfg
## Configuration file of Harbor

#This attribute is for migrator to detect the version of the .cfg file, DO NOT MODIFY!
_version = 1.5.0
#The IP address or hostname to access admin UI and registry service.
#DO NOT use localhost or 127.0.0.1, because Harbor needs to be accessed by external clients.
hostname = 172.17.0.35

#The protocol for accessing the UI and token/notification service, by default it is http.
#It can be set to https if ssl is enabled on nginx.
ui_url_protocol = http

#Maximum number of job workers in job service
max_job_workers = 50

#Determine whether or not to generate certificate for the registry's token.
#If the value is on, the prepare script creates new root cert and private key
#for generating token to access the registry. If the value is off the default key/cert will be used.
#This flag also controls the creation of the notary signer's cert.
customize_crt = on

#The path of cert and key files for nginx, they are applied only the protocol is set to https
```

Figure 4.14: Harbor configuration file

Run the installation script with the following command to deploy:

```
$ ./install.sh
```

```
Creating harbor-log ... done
Creating harbor-db          ... done
Creating harbor-adminserver ... done
Creating registry           ... done
Creating redis              ... done
Creating harbor-ui          ... done
Creating harbor-jobservice  ... done
Creating nginx              ... done

✔ ----Harbor has been installed and started successfully.----

Now you should be able to visit the admin portal at http://172.17.0.35.
For more details, please visit https://github.com/vmware/harbor .
```

Figure 4.15: Harbor installation process

Once installed, we can access the admin portal using the IP address configured in the **harbor.cfg** config file. The admin portal provides a web interface for creating a project:

Figure 4.16: Creating a project with Harbor web interface

Once we have created a project, images can be pushed into the registry with the following commands:

< Projects

project *Project Admin*

Repositories   Members   Replication   Labels   Logs   Configuration

PUSH IMAGE ∨

Push Image ⓘ

Tag an image for this project:
docker tag SOURCE_IMAGE[:TAG] 172.17.0.35/project/IMAGE

Push an image to this project:
docker push 172.17.0.35/project/IMAGE[:TAG]

Figure 4.17: Commands for uploading an image into repository

The following command tags the existing Ubuntu docker image with the IP address of the registry and the project name:

```
$ docker tag ubuntu <ip_address>/project/Ubuntu
```

This image can now be pushed to the registry with the following command:

```
$ docker push <ip_address>/project/ubuntu
The push refers to repository [ip_address/project-a/ubuntu]
cc9d18e90faa: Pushed
0c2689e3f920: Pushed
47dde53750b4: Pushed
latest:         digest:           sha256:1d7b639619bdca2d008eca2d
5293e3c43ff84cbee597ff76de3b7a7de3e84956 size: 943
```

Now, we have the image available within the Harbor registry:

Figure 4.18: Ubuntu image inside Harbor registry

At this point, we have seen how we can deploy our own registry using the official Docker registry or the registry provided by Harbor.

The use of a registry helps us improve the security and integrity of our images, but we do not depend on public repositories like Docker hub, where images are not always completely secure.

Conclusion

Docker containers present unique security challenges, so you must keep some Docker security concerns in mind. First, running containers and applications with Docker means running the Docker daemon, which requires root privileges. Other concerns include container flexibility, which makes it easy to run multiple instances of containers. These containers can be in different levels of security patches.

Like any other technology, Docker is not exempt from possible security problems. So, it is best to apply good practices and audit our infrastructure frequently for vulnerabilities to minimize these issues.

In the next chapter, we will review the security state in the Docker host and tools for testing the security.

Points to remember

- Namespaces is a kernel feature that provides isolation at different levels between processes. This allows each container to have its own **Process Identifiers (PIDs)**, its own private IP address, or its own user space.

- Control groups is a feature that provides control over the sharing of resources such as CPU and memory, and it is used as a mechanism to manage these resources, limiting their use.

- It is a good practice to start the container in read-only mode. If the container needs to write to the filesystem, a volume can be provided to further make the changes persistent after the container is stopped. Use the `docker run` command with the read-only `docker run -d --read-only python` flag to do this.

- We can use the Docker trust command to check who has signed the images: `docker trust inspect --pretty <image>:<tag>`. In this way, we can avoid impersonation of images and ensure secure image downloading.

- Quay and Harbor projects provide tools for compiling, storing, and distributing container and application images as well as a web-based interface for managing the registry.

Multiple choice questions

1. Which environment variable allows the verification of images you download from Docker Hub of a Docker registry?

   a. DOCKER_CONTENT_TRUST_SERVER=1

   b. DOCKER_TRUST_CONTENT=1

   c. DOCKER_TRUST_SERVER=1

   d. DOCKER_CONTENT_TRUST=1

2. Which Linux capability allows us to manage and configure the network?

   a. NET_RAW

   b. NET_ADMIN

    c. NET_CONFIGURE

    d. NET_MANAGE

Answers

1	d
2	b

Questions

1. What is responsible for creating and managing containers, including creating filesystems, assigning IP addresses, routing packets, process management, and other tasks that require administrator privileges?

2. Which directory is separate from the root filesystem of the container, is managed directly by the daemon Docker process, and can be shared between containers?

3. Which bits are special permissions that are used to access directories and files in the operating system by users who do not have root permissions?

Key terms

- Docker containers offer a degree of isolation that cannot be achieved with virtual machines. From a security point of view, containers provide encapsulated instances of a common Linux kernel.

- Docker uses a series of isolation techniques to protect applications from each other. The most important are the central functions of the Linux kernel, such as cgroups and namespaces.

- The distribution of system resources (memory, CPU, and bandwidth) takes place by means of a cgroup mechanism, which guarantees that each container can only consume the quota reserved for it.

- Docker Capabilities allow us to manage permissions to access the Linux kernel features and segregate root user privileges to limit actions that can be accessed with privileges.

- Docker Content Trust offers the ability to sign images sent and received to and from remote Docker registries like the Docker hub repository or our private registry.

- When pulling a tagged image when Docker Content Trust is enabled, the Docker client contacts the trusted server to obtain the latest signed version of the image it requested, verifying the content signature and then downloading the signed image.

- Notary allows secure image downloading by making it easier for people to publish and verify Docker images.

- Quay and Harbor are Docker registries that can be used to store, build, and deploy container images, which comprise the system libraries, system tools, and other platform configurations that applications need to run on a containerized platform.

CHAPTER 5
Docker Host Security

Analyzing the security of the Docker host is important since most attacks take advantage of a kernel vulnerability or occur because some package has not been updated. At this point, we will review some tools for auditing the security of the Docker Host.

This chapter covers topics like Docker daemon and *AppArmor* and *Seccomp* profiles, which provide kernel-enhancement features to limit system calls. Also, we will review tools like Docker bench security and Lynis, which follow security best practices in the Docker environment, and some of the important recommendations that can be followed during auditing and Docker deployment in a production environment.

Structure

We will cover the following topics in this chapter:

- Docker daemon security
- Apparmor and Seccomp profiles
- Docker bench security
- Auditing Docker host with Lynis

Objectives

After studying this chapter, you will understand Docker daemon security, the *Apparmor* and *Seccomp* profiles, and Docker bench security. You will also learn about auditing Docker hosts with Lynis.

Docker daemon security

The most important element of the Docker architecture is the Docker daemon process that guarantees communication between containers, and the traffic is protected by HTTPS protocol.

Docker works primarily as a client that communicates with a daemon process called **dockerd**. This process with root privileges is a socket located in the path **/var/run/docker.sock**. At this point, it is important to note that Docker socket exposure can result in privilege escalation.

You must check the access permissions by the users when using the **/var/run/docker.sock** socket. In particular, only the root user has to write permissions, and the Docker group does not contain users who can compromise the container.

We are creating a new container inside another container on the Docker host with the following command. We are using the **/var/run/docker.sock** process that must be mounted as a volume:

```
$ docker run -it -v /var/run/docker.sock:/var/run/docker.sock
debian /bin/bash
```

We can mount root user from the Docker host with the following commands:

```
$ docker run -it -v /:/host debian /bin/bash
$ chroot /host
$ /bin/bash
```

This way, we see how the Docker container starts a new mount point in the **/host** container. The second container connects to **/host**, and you can check how effectively it is using the root user. This way, we have checked that we have root access in the host from any process.

The following screenshot shows the output of the preceding commands:

```
$ docker run -it -v /:/host debian /bin/bash
root@1672b6149298:/# chroot /host
# whoami
root
# /bin/bash
$ whoami
root
$ 
```

Figure 5.1: Mounting root inside Docker

As we have seen, the Docker daemon runs with root permissions, so it is important to limit users who have control over the Docker daemon. We can give a series of recommendations on how we should configure access to the directories and files to the Docker daemon.

The following table lists the default permissions of each file that is part of the Docker daemon:

File/folder	User:group	Permissions
docker.service	root:root	644(rw-r--r--)
/etc/docker	root:root	755(rwxr-xr-x)
/etc/default/docker	root:root	644(rw-r--r--)
Docker registration certificate	root:root	444(r--r--r--)

Table. 5.1: Docker permissions by file/folder

At this point, we have reviewed the Docker daemon security and the default permissions for each service this process is using at low level.

Auditing files and directories

The Docker daemon runs with root privileges, so all directories and files should be constantly audited to know all the activities and operations that are running. We can use the Linux audit daemon framework to audit all events that take place on the host Docker. It has the following features:

- Audit processes and file modification
- Monitor system calls

- Detecting intrusions
- Register commands by users

The Linux Audit daemon is a framework that allows auditing events on Linux systems and is configured using two files: one for the daemon itself (**auditd.conf**) and one for the rules used by the *auditctl* tool (**audit.rules**):

- **auditd.conf**: This file configures the Linux audit daemon (auditd) and focuses on where and how events should be traced. It also defines how to behave when the disk is full, the rotation of the log file, and the number of logs to keep. The default settings will be appropriate for most systems.
- **audit.rules**: This file configures which events should be audited.

For example, we can monitor the file located in the path **/etc/passwd**. We use the following command to indicate to the audit framework which directory or file we want to observe using the path option:

```
$ auditctl -a exit,always -F path=/etc/passwd -F perm=wa
```

We have to add new rules in the **/etc/audit/rules.d/audit.rules** file to correctly configure the audit daemon. Next, we will add the necessary rules to be able to audit the directories:

```
-w /usr/bin/docker -k docker
-w /var/lib/docker -k docker
-w /etc/docker -k docker
-w /usr/lib/systemd/system/docker.service -k docker
-w /usr/lib/systemd/system/docker.socket -k docker
-w /etc/default/docker -k docker
-w /etc/docker/daemon.js -k docker
-w /usr/bin/docker-containerd -k docker
-w /usr/bin/docker.runc -k docker
```

We need to restart the audit daemon using the following command once the rules have been added:

```
$ sudo service auditd restart
```

The logs generated during the audit can be found in the path **/var/log/audit/audit.log** if you want to review them.

Next, we will introduce SELinux, which enables an additional layer of isolation.

Kernel Linux security and SELinux

Security-Enhanced Linux (**SELinux**) is a Linux kernel security module that provides different security controls like access controls, integrity controls, and **Role-Based Access Control** (**RBAC**). In addition, it provides privacy policies between the Docker host and containerized applications.

On Red Hat Enterprise Linux, SELinux is enabled by default and in enforcing mode. You can confirm this by inspecting the output of **sestatus** on the system:

```
$ sestatus
SELinux status:                 enabled
SELinuxfs mount:                /sys/fs/selinux
SELinux root directory:         /etc/selinux
Loaded policy name:             targeted
Current mode:                   enforcing
Mode from config file:          enforcing
Policy MLS status:              enabled
Policy deny_unknown status:     allowed
Memory protection checking:     actual (secure)
Max kernel policy version:      32
```

We can install it in Debian-based distributions using the following command:

```
$ sudo apt-get install selinux
```

You can also install the relevant SELinux policy creation tools to use SELinux. For example, you can run the following command to install SELinux policies if you have a distribution with the yum package manager:

```
$ yum -y install selinux-policy-devel
```

These tools are **Mandatory Access Control** (**MAC**) tools that impose security rules in Linux to ensure that apart from the normal read-write-execute rules that apply to files and processes, more precise rules can be applied to them at the kernel level.

For example, a MySQL process can only afford to write files under specific directories, such as **/var/lib/mysql**. The equivalent standard for Debian-based systems is *AppArmor*.

Apparmor and Seccomp profiles

AppArmor enables the administrator to assign each running process a secure profile and define filesystem access, network capacities, and execution rules. Basically, it provides protection for external and internal threats, enabling system administrators to associate a secure profile with each application, which restricts that application's capabilities.

You can find more information in the *AppArmor* official documentation at **https://gitlab.com/apparmor/apparmor/-/wikis/home**.

AppArmor is enabled by default in Debian-based distributions. You can check this property using the following command:

```
$ docker info
```

The following screenshot shows the output of the preceding command:

```
Runtimes: runc io.containerd.runc.v2 io.containerd.runtime.v1.linux
Default Runtime: runc
Init Binary: docker-init
containerd version: 05f951a3781f4f2c1911b05e61c160e9c30eaa8e
runc version: 12644e614e25b05da6fd08a38ffa0cfe1903fdec
init version: de40ad0
Security Options:
 apparmor
 seccomp
  Profile: default
Kernel Version: 4.4.0-193-generic
Operating System: Ubuntu 16.04.7 LTS
OSType: linux
Architecture: x86_64
CPUs: 2
Total Memory: 1.461GiB
```

Figure. 5.2: Execution of docker info

Tip: Docker info command

With the docker info command, we can obtain information about the use of CPU, memory and other information related to the kernel, operating system, and the directory where Docker is installed.

In the security options, we can see that AppArmor is enabled by default. We can simplify the checking process with the following command:

```
$ docker info | grep apparmor
Security Options: apparmor seccomp
```

We can also use **docker inspect** to check if the property is enabled on our containers:

```
$ docker ps -q | xargs docker inspect --format '{{ .Id }}:
AppArmorProfile={{ .AppArmorProfile}}'
b4949a7cce2024e7efada0d2a2001a8037b0474ac7e9d94e55bbb225c64ad5a2:
AppArmorProfile=docker-default
```

By default, Docker uses the AppArmor Docker-default profile that is located in the **/etc/apparmor.d/docker/** path.

You can find more information about it in the AppArmor documentation at **https://docs.docker.com/engine/security/apparmor/#understand-the-policies**.

Installing AppArmor on Ubuntu distributions

We can find the AppAmor-profiles package within the repository of the different versions of Ubuntu:

- https://packages.ubuntu.com/bionic/apparmor-profiles

We can execute the following command on Ubuntu terminal for execution:

```
$ sudo apt-get install apparmor-profiles
```

Some directories are common once you have installed AppArmor:
- **/etc/apparmor/**: This folder contains the files that configure the daemon
- **/etc/apparmor.d/**: This folder contains the ruleset files that limit an application's access to the rest of the system

Applications commonly used to configure and customize AppArmor include:
- **/usr/sbin/aa-enforce**: This enables a profile or set of rules
- **/usr/sbin/aa-logprof**: This enables registration for a profile, and you must enable the profile with the **aa-enforce** command to use this command
- **/usr/sbin/aa-complain**: This enables the profile for registration
- **/usr/sbin/aa-genprof**: This generates custom profiles
- **/usr/sbin/aa-notify**: This returns users and processes that have been denied access to an application
- **usr/sbin/aa-status**: This informs you about active profiles; AppArmor considers each profile active to create a policy for the system, also available as **/usr/sbin/apparmor_status**

At this point, we have reviewed the installation of AppArmor and the folder structure to check the default configuration.

AppArmor Docker-default profile

From the security point of view, AppArmor proactively protects the operating system and applications against external or internal threats and even zero-day attacks by applying a specific set of rules for each application.

Docker automatically generates and loads a default profile for containers called docker-default. In Docker versions 1.13.0 and later, the Docker binary generates this profile and then loads it into the kernel.

In Docker versions prior to 1.13.0, this profile is generated in /etc/apparmor.d/ docker instead. Security policies fully define what system resources individual applications can access and with what privileges.

The docker-default profile is the default for running containers and provides broad application compatibility. The profile is generated using the following template available in this repository:

- https://github.com/moby/moby/blob/master/profiles/apparmor/ template.go

When you run a container, it uses the docker-default policy unless you override it with the security-opt option. For example, the following instruction explicitly indicates the default policy:

```
$ docker run --rm -it --security-opt apparmor=docker-default hello-
world
```

We can check the status of AppArmor in the Docker host and determine whether the Docker containers are running with an AppArmor profile. We can execute the **apparmor_status** command to do this.

```
$ apparmor_status
apparmor module is loaded.
49 profiles are loaded.
12 profiles are in enforce mode.
   /sbin/dhclient
   /usr/lib/NetworkManager/nm-dhcp-client.action
   /usr/lib/NetworkManager/nm-dhcp-helper
  /usr/lib/chromium-browser/chromium-browser//browser_java
  /usr/lib/chromium-browser/chromium-browser//browser_openjdk
  /usr/lib/snapd/snap-confine
  /usr/lib/snapd/snap-confine//mount-namespace-capture-helper
   /usr/sbin/ntpd
   /usr/sbin/tcpdump
  docker-default
```

```
37 profiles are in complain mode.
   /usr/lib/chromium-browser/chromium-browser
    /usr/lib/chromium-browser/chromium-browser//chromium_browser_
sandbox
   /usr/lib/chromium-browser/chromium-browser//lsb_release
   /usr/lib/chromium-browser/chromium-browser//xdgsettings
   /usr/lib/dovecot/anvil
   /usr/lib/dovecot/auth
   /usr/lib/dovecot/config
   /usr/lib/dovecot/deliver
   /usr/lib/dovecot/dict
   /usr/lib/dovecot/dovecot-auth
   /usr/lib/dovecot/dovecot-lda
   /usr/lib/dovecot/dovecot-lda///usr/sbin/sendmail
   /usr/lib/dovecot/imap
   /usr/lib/dovecot/imap-login
   /usr/lib/dovecot/lmtp
   /usr/lib/dovecot/log
   /usr/lib/dovecot/managesieve
   /usr/lib/dovecot/managesieve-login
   /usr/lib/dovecot/pop3
   /usr/lib/dovecot/pop3-login
   /usr/lib/dovecot/ssl-params
   /usr/sbin/avahi-daemon
   /usr/sbin/dnsmasq
   /usr/sbin/dnsmasq//libvirt_leaseshelper
   /usr/sbin/dovecot
   /usr/sbin/identd
   /usr/sbin/mdnsd
   /usr/sbin/nmbd
   /usr/sbin/nscd
   /usr/sbin/smbd
   /usr/sbin/smbldap-useradd
   /usr/sbin/smbldap-useradd///etc/init.d/nscd
   /usr/{sbin/traceroute,bin/traceroute.db}
   /{usr/,}bin/ping
   klogd
   syslog-ng
   syslogd
```

```
4 processes have profiles defined.
4 processes are in enforce mode.
   /sbin/dhclient (757)
   /usr/sbin/ntpd (819)
   docker-default (6112)
   docker-default (6168)
0 processes are in complain mode.
0 processes are unconfined but have a profile defined
```

Keep in mind that Docker-default is now displayed in application mode procedures as well. The values in parentheses are the container process's PID, available in the Docker host's PID namespace.

Tip: Executing apparmor with new profiles

We can use the following command to load a new profile in AppArmor for using with containers:

```
$ apparmor_parser -r -W /path/to/your_profile
```

Later, we can execute the custom profile with the --security-opt option, as follows:

```
$ docker run --rm -it --security-opt apparmor=your_profile hello-world
```

We can find documentation on how to create these profiles in the project repository - https://gitlab.com/apparmor/apparmor/wikis/QuickProfileLanguage.

Run container without AppArmor profile

We have some options to run the container by disabling the AppArmor profile or enable Docker using the default profile:

- We can use the **--security-opt apparmor = docker-default** option to execute a container with an AppArmor profile.

- We can use the **--security-opt apparmor = unconfined** option to execute a container without AppArmor profile.

- We can execute the **apparmor_status** command to verify that the new container is not running with an AppArmor profile.

```
$ apparmor_status
apparmor module is loaded.
<SNIP>
1 processes are in enforce mode.
/sbin/dhclient (610)
0 processes are in complain mode.
0 processes are unconfined but have a profile defined.
```

When executing the preceding command, we can see that there are no instances of the **docker-default** profile in the processes that appear in the enforce section.

Run container with Seccomp profile

Each of the processes that we execute on the operating system have the option of interacting with the kernel through system calls. The processes can ask the kernel to perform some task, such as modifying a file, creating a new process, changing the permissions to a directory, or using an **Application Programming Interface (API)**, by which the kernel gives access to its services.

Many of the system calls are accessible to every process in the user area, but a large part are not used for the entire life of the process. At this point, Seccomp is a tool that allows you to limit the exposure of the kernel to system calls by an application. Combined with other tools that the system offers us, like capabilities and namespaces among others, we have a set designed to secure applications.

You can find more information about Seccomp in the Linux man-pages documentation:

*   https://man7.org/linux/man-pages/man2/seccomp.2.html

Seccomp is a sandboxing facility in the Linux kernel that acts like a firewall for system calls (syscalls). It uses **Berkeley Packet Filter (BPF)** rules to filter syscalls and control how they are handled.

These filters can significantly limit container access to the Docker Host's Linux kernel, especially for simple containers/applications. The following commands show you how to check if seccomp is enabled in your system's kernel:

```
$ docker info | grep seccomp
Security Options: apparmor seccomp
```

We can also check from the Linux command line:

```
$ grep SECCOMP /boot/config-$(uname -r)
CONFIG_HAVE_ARCH_SECCOMP_FILTER=y
CONFIG_SECCOMP_FILTER=y
CONFIG_SECCOMP=y
```

Docker uses seccomp in filter mode and has its own JSON-based DSL that allows you to define profiles that compile down to seccomp filters. A container gets the default seccomp profile when you run it, unless you override this by passing the **--security-opt** flag to the **docker run** command.

We can create the following file that allows us to define the system calls that we want to block. We are blocking the **chmod** and **chown** syscalls in this example.

```
$ touch profile_policy.json
```

```
{
  "defaultAction": "SCMP_ACT_ALLOW",
  "syscalls": [
    {
      "name": "chmod",
      "action": "SCMP_ACT_ERRNO"
    },
    {
      "name": "chown",
      "action": "SCMP_ACT_ERRNO"
    }
  ]
}
```

Then, we can execute the container based on the alpine distribution, passing the **profile_policy.json** policy file as a parameter.

The following example command starts an interactive container based on the Alpine image and starts a shell process. It also applies the seccomp profile described by **profile_policy.json** to it.

```
$ docker run --rm -it --security-opt seccomp:profile_policy.json
alpine sh
```

We can verify that the **chmod** and **chown** commands cannot be used inside the container, and we get the **Operation not permitted** error when executing them:

```
/ # chown root:root bin
chown: bin: Operation not permitted
/ # chmod +x /etc/resolv.conf
chmod: /etc/resolv.conf: Operation not permitted
```

Our container attempted to execute **chmod**, so the call failed and threw the **Operation not permitted** error. This is because our seccomp profile blocked it.

We can extend our seccomp profile to list all the calls we want to allow or disallow. This lets us block potential attack vectors or close vulnerabilities without changing our application.

Deny all syscalls

Docker seccomp profiles operate using a whitelist approach that specifies allowed syscalls. Only syscalls on the whitelist are permitted.

The following profile has an empty syscall whitelist, meaning all syscalls will be blocked.

```
$ touch deny_sys_calls.json
```

```
{
  "defaultAction": "SCMP_ACT_ALLOW",
  "architectures": [
              "SCMP_ARCH_X86_64",
              "SCMP_ARCH_X86",
              "SCMP_ARCH_X32"
     ],
  "syscalls": [
  ]
}
```

Note that there are no syscalls in the whitelist, which means no syscalls will be allowed from containers started with this profile.

Docker supports many security-related technologies. Other security-related technologies may interfere with your testing of seccomp profiles, so the best way to test the effect of seccomp profiles is to add all capabilities and disable AppArmor. In this way, we can trust the behavior observed in the following step is only due to changes in the seccomp configuration.

We will add all capabilities and effectively disable AppArmor in the following command so that you know that only your seccomp profile is preventing the syscalls:

```
$ docker run --rm -it --cap-add ALL --security-opt apparmor=unconfined
--security-opt seccomp=deny_sys_calls.json alpine sh
docker: Error response from daemon: cannot start a stopped process:
unknown.
ERRO[0001] error waiting for container: context canceled
```

In this scenario, Docker doesn't actually have enough syscalls to start the container, and it returns an error because it can't start the Docker daemon process.

At this point, we have removed capabilities and AppArmor from interfering and started a new container with a seccomp profile that had no syscalls in its whitelist. You saw how this prevented all syscalls from within the container.

Run a container with no seccomp profile

Unless you specify a different profile, Docker will apply the default seccomp profile to all new containers. In this section, you will see how to force a new container to run without a seccomp profile. You can use the unconfined value to run a container without the default seccomp profile.

For this task, you can start a new container with the **--security-opt seccomp= unconfined** flag so that no seccomp profile is applied to it:

```
$ docker run --rm -it --cap-add SYS_PTRACE --security-opt
seccomp=unconfined benhall/strace-ubuntu
Unable to find image 'benhall/strace-ubuntu:latest' locally
latest: Pulling from benhall/strace-ubuntu
Image docker.io/benhall/strace-ubuntu:latest uses outdated
schema1 manifest format. Please upgrade to a schema2 image for
better future compatibility. More information at https://docs.
docker.com/registry/spec/deprecated-schema-v1/
6d28225f8d96: Pull complete
166102ec41af: Pull complete
d09bfba2bd6a: Pull complete
c80dad39a6c0: Pull complete
a3ed95caeb02: Pull complete
b668194b0fb4: Pull complete
Digest: sha256:edbf5bff42c0858def0393e69b9e1538bb3433f0793e4c
74501f3590a4aad454
Status: Downloaded newer image for benhall/strace-ubuntu:latest
```

You can execute the following **strace** command from your Docker Host to see a list of the syscalls used by the `whoami` command:

```
root@b5250d6addad:/# strace -c -f -S name whoami 2>&1 1>/dev/null
| tail -n +3 | head -n -2 | awk '{print $(NF)}'
access
arch_prctl
brk
close
connect
execve
fstat
geteuid
ioctl
lseek
mmap
mprotect
munmap
open
read
socket
write
```

Here, we are using strace to get a list of all system calls made by the whoami program.

The preceding output shows the syscalls that will need to be enabled for a container running the whoami command to work, in addition to the syscalls required to start a container.

Write a seccomp profile

We can write Docker seccomp profiles from scratch, and you can also edit the existing profiles. In this section, you will learn about the syntax and behavior of Docker seccomp profiles.

The layout of a Docker seccomp profile looks like this:

```
{
    "defaultAction": "SCMP_ACT_ERRNO",
    "architectures": [
        "SCMP_ARCH_X86_64",
        "SCMP_ARCH_X86",
        "SCMP_ARCH_X32"
    ],
    "syscalls": [
        {
            "name": "accept",
            "action": "SCMP_ACT_ALLOW",
            "args": []
        },
        {
            "name": "accept4",
            "action": "SCMP_ACT_ALLOW",
            "args": []
        },
        ...
    ]
}
```

The following table lists the possible actions in order of precedence. Higher actions overrule lower actions.

Action	Description
SCMP_ACT_KILL	Kill with an exit status of 0x80 + 31 (SIGSYS) = 159
SCMP_ACT_TRAP	Send a SIGSYS signal without executing the system call
SCMP_ACT_ERRNO	Set errno without executing the system call
SCMP_ACT_TRACE	Invoke a ptracer to make a decision or set errno to -ENOSYS
SCMP_ACT_ALLOW	Allow

Table. 5.2: Seccomp actions

The most important actions for Docker users are **SCMP_ACT_ERRNO** and **SCMP_ACT_ALLOW**. Profiles can contain more granular filters based on the value of the arguments to the system call.

```
{
    ...
    "syscalls": [
        {
            "name": "accept",
            "action": "SCMP_ACT_ALLOW",
            "args": [
                {
                    "index": 0,
                    "op": "SCMP_CMP_MASKED_EQ",
                    "value": 2080505856,
                    "valueTwo": 0
                }
            ]
        }
    ]
}
```

- index is the index of the system call argument
- op is the operation to perform on the argument. It can be one of the following:
  - **SCMP_CMP_NE** - not equal
  - **SCMP_CMP_LT** - less than
  - **SCMP_CMP_LE** - less than or equal to
  - **SCMP_CMP_EQ** - equal to
  - **SCMP_CMP_GE** - greater than
  - **SCMP_CMP_GT** - greater or equal to
  - **SCMP_CMP_MASKED_EQ** - masked equal: true if (value & arg == valueTwo)
- value is a parameter for the operation
- valueTwo is used only for **SCMP_CMP_MASKED_EQ**

In this section, you learned the format and syntax of Docker seccomp profiles. You also learned the order of preference for actions and how to determine the syscalls needed by an individual program.

> **Tip: Default Seccomp profile**
>
> The default seccomp profile can be found at https://github.com/moby/moby/blob/master/profiles/seccomp/default.json.
>
> This profile is a whitelist that blocks access to system calls by default and then to specific system calls. The profile works by defining a defaultAction SCMP_ACT_ERRNO, overriding that action only for specific system calls. The profile also defines a specific list of system calls that are allowed.

Security in-depth

Security in-depth allows multiple lines of security to work together to provide improved overall capabilities from the security point of view. With the following command, we can start an Ubuntu container with Seccomp disabled by default:

```
$ docker container run --rm -it --cap-add SYS_ADMIN --security-opt
seccomp=unconfined ubuntu sh
```

To verify that AppArmor is working, we can try to create two directories and group them with the mount command and the bind option:

```
# mkdir mydir1; mkdir mydir2; mount --bind mydir1 mydir2
mount: /mydir2: bind /mydir1 failed
```

The operation returns permission denied because the AppArmor profile denied the operation. We can start a new container without an AppArmor profile and retry the same operation to confirm that the default AppArmor profile is the one that denied the operation:

```
$ docker container run --rm -it --cap-add SYS_ADMIN --security-opt
seccomp=unconfined --security-opt apparmor=unconfined ubuntu sh
# mkdir dir1; mkdir dir2; mount --bind dir1 dir2
# ls -l
total 56
lrwxrwxrwx    1 root      7 Apr  1 01:23 bin -> usr/bin
drwxr-xr-x    2 root 4096 Apr 15  2020 boot
drwxr-xr-x    5 root  360 Apr  5 18:58 dev
drwxr-xr-x    2 root 4096 Apr  5 18:58 dir1
drwxr-xr-x    2 root 4096 Apr  5 18:58 dir2
drwxr-xr-x    1 root 4096 Apr  5 18:58 etc
drwxr-xr-x    2 root 4096 Apr 15  2020 home
```

This shows that the procedure in the first scenario was denied by the default AppArmor profile.

> **Tip: Apparmor & Seccomp practice labs**
>
> You can use the following labs to practice the concepts we reviewed in this section:
>
> - https://dockerlabs.collabnix.com/advanced/security/apparmor/
>
> - https://dockerlabs.collabnix.com/advanced/security/seccomp/
>
> - https://training.play-with-docker.com/security-seccomp
>
> - https://www.katacoda.com/courses/docker-security/intro-to-seccomp

Reducing the container attack surface

Reducing the attack surface is a fundamental principle of security. For example, container security depends on the Kernel and Docker daemon that is accessed through system calls. At this point, Docker has made significant improvements in the ability to call Seccomp profiles. These profiles only disable certain calls by default, but there are others that are available, leaving a large number of syscalls that can be invoked without any restriction.

Another example is the ability to link the Docker daemon process with the Unix Docker access group or the TCP port that allows containers to communicate with each other.

The ultimate goal in security is to obtain a balance between the container's isolation and the communication needs between them. This implies taking measures to limit the number of containers that are accessible to groups and to control the degree to which the containers interact with each other.

Docker bench security

Docker bench security is a useful tool to test the security of your Docker containers. The objective is to perform the Docker CIS checks against a container, and a report is generated that tells you if that container is potentially insecure at the level of permissions and access to resources.

The tool mainly focuses on best practices in areas like file permissions and registry settings. The following links are the Docker CIS benchmark guides:

- https://www.cisecurity.org/cis-benchmarks/
- https://www.cisecurity.org/benchmark/docker/

Docker bench security is a shell script that looks for common best practice patterns around the implementation of Docker containers in production. It is a set of bash scripts, which must be run as a root user on any machine with Docker installed, and the tool will produce a report with all the checks.

From the Docker host and Docker daemon settings point of view, this is the best tool you can use to check these best practices. The source code is available in the GitHub repository at **https://github.com/docker/docker-bench-security**.

The tool will inspect the following components:

- Host configuration
- The Daemon Docker configuration
- Docker daemon configuration files
- Image container and compilation files
- Runtime container
- Docker security operations

We can execute the tool through an image that we can find in the Docker Hub, copying the following command in our Docker host:

```
https://hub.docker.com/r/docker/docker-bench-security
```

We can execute the following command to start the Docker bench security for analyzing the Docker host with a default configuration:

```
$ docker run -it --net host --pid host --cap-add audit_control \
-v /var/lib:/var/lib \
-v /var/run/docker.sock:/var/run/docker.sock \
-v /usr/lib/systemd:/usr/lib/systemd \
-v /etc:/etc --label docker_bench_security \
docker/docker-bench-security
```

The following screenshot shows the output of the preceding command:

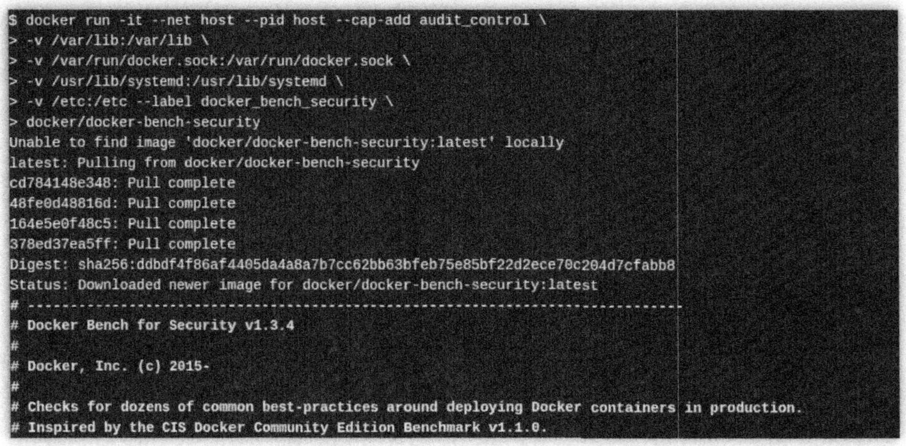

Figure 5.3: *Executing Docker bench security*

Docker bench security execution

Docker bench executes in a container with high privileges and runs a set of tests against all the containers in the Docker host. Here are some of the configuration checks executed by Docker bench:

- **Host configuration**: This section checks the security over the host Docker configuration.

- **Daemon Docker configuration**: This section offers recommendations about the security of the Docker daemon. Everything in this section affects the configuration of the Docker Daemon as well as each running container.

- **Docker daemon configuration files**: This section shows information about the configuration files used by the daemon Docker. This ranges from permissions to properties. Sometimes, these areas may contain information that you do not want others to know, which could be in a plain text format.

- **Daemon Docker configuration**: This section shows information about the Docker daemon configuration and can detect containers that are running on the same Docker host and checking the access to each other's network traffic. By default, all containers that run on the same Docker host have access to each other's network traffic.

The following screenshot shows the output of Docker bench security in the `Host configuration` section:

```
[INFO] 1 - Host Configuration
[PASS] 1.1  - Ensure a separate partition for containers has been created
[NOTE] 1.2  - Ensure the container host has been Hardened
[INFO] 1.3  - Ensure Docker is up to date
[INFO]       * Using 20.10.0, verify is it up to date as deemed necessary
[INFO]       * Your operating system vendor may provide support and security maintenance for Docker
[INFO] 1.4  - Ensure only trusted users are allowed to control Docker daemon
[WARN] 1.5  - Ensure auditing is configured for the Docker daemon
[WARN] 1.6  - Ensure auditing is configured for Docker files and directories - /var/lib/docker
[WARN] 1.7  - Ensure auditing is configured for Docker files and directories - /etc/docker
[INFO] 1.8  - Ensure auditing is configured for Docker files and directories - docker.service
[INFO]       * File not found
[INFO] 1.9  - Ensure auditing is configured for Docker files and directories - docker.socket
[INFO]       * File not found
[INFO] 1.10 - Ensure auditing is configured for Docker files and directories - /etc/default/docker
[INFO]       * File not found
[WARN] 1.11 - Ensure auditing is configured for Docker files and directories - /etc/docker/daemon.json
[INFO] 1.12 - Ensure auditing is configured for Docker files and directories - /usr/bin/docker-containerd
[INFO]       * File not found
[INFO] 1.13 - Ensure auditing is configured for Docker files and directories - /usr/bin/docker-runc
[INFO]       * File not found
```

Figure 5.4: Checking host configuration with Docker bench security

Here, we can see that checks marked with a warning must be reviewed at the host configuration level:

```
[WARN] 1.5 - Ensure auditing is configured for the Docker daemon
[WARN] 1.6 - Ensure auditing is configured for Docker files and
directories
/var/lib/docker
[WARN] 1.7 - Ensure auditing is configured for Docker files and
directories
/etc/docker
[WARN] 1.11 - Ensure auditing is configured for Docker files and
directories  /etc/docker/daemon.json
```

The following screenshot shows the output of Docker bench security in the Docker daemon configuration section:

```
[INFO] 2 - Docker daemon configuration
[WARN] 2.1  - Ensure network traffic is restricted between containers on the default bridge
[PASS] 2.2  - Ensure the logging level is set to 'info'
[PASS] 2.3  - Ensure Docker is allowed to make changes to iptables
[WARN] 2.4  - Ensure insecure registries are not used
[PASS] 2.5  - Ensure aufs storage driver is not used
[INFO] 2.6  - Ensure TLS authentication for Docker daemon is configured
[INFO]      * Docker daemon not listening on TCP
[INFO] 2.7  - Ensure the default ulimit is configured appropriately
[INFO]      * Default ulimit doesn't appear to be set
[WARN] 2.8  - Enable user namespace support
[PASS] 2.9  - Ensure the default cgroup usage has been confirmed
[PASS] 2.10 - Ensure base device size is not changed until needed
[WARN] 2.11 - Ensure that authorization for Docker client commands is enabled
[WARN] 2.12 - Ensure centralized and remote logging is configured
[INFO] 2.13 - Ensure operations on legacy registry (v1) are Disabled (Deprecated)
[WARN] 2.14 - Ensure live restore is Enabled
[WARN] 2.15 - Ensure Userland Proxy is Disabled
[PASS] 2.16 - Ensure daemon-wide custom seccomp profile is applied, if needed
[WARN] 2.17 - Ensure experimental features are avoided in production
[WARN] 2.18 - Ensure containers are restricted from acquiring new privileges
```

Figure 5.5: Checking Docker daemon configuration with Docker bench security

Docker daemon configuration checks the file permissions related to the Docker daemon, such as **docker.service** and **docker.socket**. Basically, it verifies that these files can only be run with root permissions.

The following screenshot illustrates the output of Docker bench security in the **Container Images and Build Files** section:

```
[INFO] 4 - Container Images and Build File
[INFO] 4.1  - Ensure a user for the container has been created
[INFO]       * No containers running
[NOTE] 4.2  - Ensure that containers use trusted base images
[NOTE] 4.3  - Ensure unnecessary packages are not installed in the container
[NOTE] 4.4  - Ensure images are scanned and rebuilt to include security patches
[WARN] 4.5  - Ensure Content trust for Docker is Enabled
[WARN] 4.6  - Ensure HEALTHCHECK instructions have been added to the container image
[WARN]       * No Healthcheck found: [alpine:latest]
[WARN]       * No Healthcheck found: [benhall/strace-ubuntu:latest]
[INFO] 4.7  - Ensure update instructions are not use alone in the Dockerfile
[INFO]       * Update instruction found: [benhall/strace-ubuntu:latest]
[NOTE] 4.8  - Ensure setuid and setgid permissions are removed in the images
[INFO] 4.9  - Ensure COPY is used instead of ADD in Dockerfile
[INFO]       * ADD in image history: [alpine:latest]
[INFO]       * ADD in image history: [docker/docker-bench-security:latest]
[INFO]       * ADD in image history: [benhall/strace-ubuntu:latest]
[NOTE] 4.10  - Ensure secrets are not stored in Dockerfiles
[NOTE] 4.11  - Ensure verified packages are only Installed
```

Figure 5.6: Checking Container Images and Build Files

The preceding section checks whether Docker Content Trust is enabled in the Docker host. Execute the following command to solve this warning:

```
$ export DOCKER_CONTENT_TRUST=1
```

The following screenshot depicts the output of Docker bench security in the **Container Runtime** section:

```
[INFO] 5 - Container Runtime
[PASS] 5.1  - Ensure AppArmor Profile is Enabled
[WARN] 5.2  - Ensure SELinux security options are set, if applicable
[WARN]       * No SecurityOptions Found: elegant_agnesi
[PASS] 5.3  - Ensure Linux Kernel Capabilities are restricted within containers
[PASS] 5.4  - Ensure privileged containers are not used
[PASS] 5.5  - Ensure sensitive host system directories are not mounted on containers
[PASS] 5.6  - Ensure ssh is not run within containers
[PASS] 5.7  - Ensure privileged ports are not mapped within containers
[NOTE] 5.8  - Ensure only needed ports are open on the container
[PASS] 5.9  - Ensure the host's network namespace is not shared
[WARN] 5.10  - Ensure memory usage for container is limited
[WARN]       * Container running without memory restrictions: elegant_agnesi
[WARN] 5.11  - Ensure CPU priority is set appropriately on the container
[WARN]       * Container running without CPU restrictions: elegant_agnesi
[WARN] 5.12  - Ensure the container's root filesystem is mounted as read only
[WARN]       * Container running with root FS mounted R/W: elegant_agnesi
[PASS] 5.13  - Ensure incoming container traffic is binded to a specific host interface
[WARN] 5.14  - Ensure 'on-failure' container restart policy is set to '5'
[WARN]       * MaximumRetryCount is not set to 5: elegant_agnesi
[PASS] 5.15  - Ensure the host's process namespace is not shared
```

Figure 5.7: Checking Container Runtime

To solve the most critical warnings, we can execute the container limiting resources at the memory and CPU levels, add read-only permissions, and use a non-root user for this container.

The following command executes a Python container using the **--read-only** flag, limiting memory and CPU resources:

```
$ docker container run --detach -ti -u 1000 --read-only -m 256mb
--security-opt=no-new-privileges --cpu-shares=500 --pids-limit=1
python /bin/bash
```

If we execute **docker bench** with the new runtime configuration, we can see how it passes configuration checking in the cases related with privileges, read only, and CPU and memory usage.

```
[INFO] 5 - Container Runtime
[PASS] 5.1  - Ensure AppArmor Profile is Enabled
[PASS] 5.2  - Ensure SELinux security options are set, if applicable
[PASS] 5.3  - Ensure Linux Kernel Capabilities are restricted within containers
[PASS] 5.4  - Ensure privileged containers are not used
[PASS] 5.5  - Ensure sensitive host system directories are not mounted on containers
[PASS] 5.6  - Ensure ssh is not run within containers
[PASS] 5.7  - Ensure privileged ports are not mapped within containers
[NOTE] 5.8  - Ensure only needed ports are open on the container
[PASS] 5.9  - Ensure the host's network namespace is not shared
[PASS] 5.10 - Ensure memory usage for container is limited
[PASS] 5.11 - Ensure CPU priority is set appropriately on the container
[PASS] 5.12 - Ensure the container's root filesystem is mounted as read only
[PASS] 5.13 - Ensure incoming container traffic is binded to a specific host interface
```

Figure 5.8: Checking Container Runtime with read-only flag

Thanks to this tool and the generated report, we have access to almost 100 security recommendations to always keep in mind before using Docker in production.

At this point, we have reviewed the execution of the Docker bench security tool for checking the security configuration in the Docker host, showing the output of the report in specific sections.

Auditing Docker host with Lynis

Lynis is an open-source security audit tool for evaluating the security of Linux and UNIX-based systems. Lynis executes directly on the Docker host so that it has access to the Linux kernel. We can find the source code and the installation in the following repositories:

- https://cisofy.com/lynis/
- https://github.com/CISOfy/Lynis
- https://cisofy.com/documentation/lynis/get-started/#installation%20manual

Once installed, the audit system command performs the following checks:

- Check the operating system
- Perform a search for available tools and utilities
- Check for any Lynis update
- Perform tests with the enabled add-ons
- Perform safety tests by category
- Security scanning status report

Here are some of the main options it offers for auditing:

```
Usage: lynis command [options]


  Command:


    audit
        audit system                  : Perform local security scan
            audit system remote <host>    : Remote security scan
            audit dockerfile <file>    : Analyze Dockerfile
```

The following command checks the configuration and security of your Docker host:

```
$ lynis audit system
```

1. In the first phase, it checks configurations related with boot, services, and kernel:

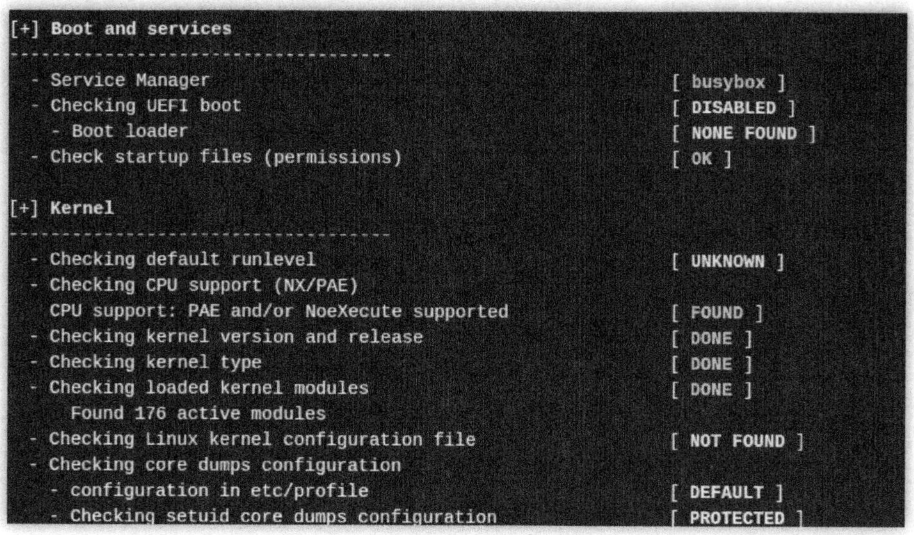

Figure 5.9: *Checking boot, services, and kernel in Docker host*

2. Next, it checks configurations related to users, groups, and authentication:

```
[+] Users, Groups and Authentication
----------------------------------
  - Administrator accounts                             [ OK ]
  - Unique UIDs                                        [ OK ]
  - Unique group IDs                                   [ OK ]
  - Unique group names                                 [ OK ]
  - Password hashing methods                           [ SUGGESTION ]
  - Query system users (non daemons)                   [ DONE ]
  - NIS+ authentication support                        [ NOT ENABLED ]
  - NIS authentication support                         [ NOT ENABLED ]
  - Sudoers file                                       [ NOT FOUND ]
  - PAM password strength tools                        [ SUGGESTION ]
  - PAM configuration file (pam.conf)                  [ NOT FOUND ]
  - PAM configuration files (pam.d)                    [ NOT FOUND ]
  - PAM modules                                        [ NOT FOUND ]
  - LDAP module in PAM                                 [ NOT FOUND ]
  - Accounts without expire date                       [ OK ]
  - Accounts without password                          [ OK ]
  - Locked accounts                                    [ OK ]
  - Checking expired passwords                         [ OK ]
```

Figure 5.10: Checking users, groups, and authentication

3. Third, it checks configurations related to shells and filesystems:

```
[+] Shells
----------------------------------
  - Checking shells from /etc/shells
    Result: found 3 shells (valid shells: 3).
    - Session timeout settings/tools                   [ NONE ]
  - Checking default umask values
    - Checking default umask in /etc/profile           [ WEAK ]

[+] File systems
----------------------------------
  - Checking mount points
    - Checking /home mount point                       [ SUGGESTION ]
    - Checking /tmp mount point                        [ SUGGESTION ]
    - Checking /var mount point                        [ SUGGESTION ]
  - Query swap partitions (fstab)                      [ NONE ]
  - Testing swap partitions                            [ OK ]
  - Testing /proc mount (hidepid)                      [ SUGGESTION ]
  - Checking for old files in /tmp                     [ OK ]
  - Checking /tmp sticky bit                           [ OK ]
  - Checking /var/tmp sticky bit                       [ OK ]
```

Figure 5.11: Checking configurations related to shells and filesystems

4. Finally, it checks configurations related to Docker containers and security frameworks like AppArmor and SELinux:

```
[+] Containers
------------------------------------
    - Docker
        - Docker daemon                              [ RUNNING ]
          - Docker info output (warnings)            [ 4 ]
        - Containers
          - Total containers                         [ 0 ]
      - File permissions                             [ OK ]

[+] Security frameworks
------------------------------------
    - Checking presence AppArmor                     [ NOT FOUND ]
    - Checking presence SELinux                      [ NOT FOUND ]
    - Checking presence TOMOYO Linux                 [ NOT FOUND ]
    - Checking presence grsecurity                   [ NOT FOUND ]
    - Checking for implemented MAC framework         [ NONE ]
```

Figure 5.12: *Checking configurations related to Docker containers and security frameworks*

At this point, we have reviewed the execution of the Lynis security tool for checking the security configuration in the Docker host.

Tip: Auditing a Dockerfile

We can use Lynis for testing and auditing content related to DockerFile security.

```
$ lynis audit dockerfile <file>
```

We can find the script used to analyze the Dockerfile in the GitHub repository at

https://github.com/CISOfy/lynis/blob/master/include/helper_audit_dockerfile.

Conclusion

The host machine can be defined as the most important part of the Docker environment. The ultimate goal is to minimize the attack vectors that can be produced on the Docker host. All the containers that run on the same Docker host share the same execution kernel, so it makes sense to spend time securing the core.

For this task, we can find tools like Docker bench security and Lynis that define a series of guidelines and configuration best practices. This way, the audit and internal security teams will be aware of these guidelines in order to perform the corresponding compliance and security testing.

In the next chapter, we will review some open source tools, like *Clair* with *quay. io* repository and Anchore, for scanning and discovering vulnerabilities in Docker images.

Points to remember

- *SELinux* is a tool created by the **National Security Agency (NSA)** of the United States to protect systems in general and is integrated into the Linux Kernel.

- *AppArmor* is a Linux security module that allows you to implement security at the process level. Security profiles developed specifically through AppArmor can allow functions like folder access, network access, and permissions to read, write, or execute files.

- *SecComp* defines which system calls should and should not be allowed to be executed by a container. These system calls are defined in a JSON file that is applied when a container starts.

Multiple choice questions

1. Which Linux kernel security module provides security controls among which we can highlight access controls, integrity controls, and RBAC?

   a. Security-Enhanced Linux (SELinux)

   b. Apparmor

   c. Seccomp

   d. SecLinux

2. Which tool provides protection for external and internal threats, enabling system administrators to associate a secure profile with each application that restricts that application's capabilities?

   a. SecLinux

   b. Security-Enhanced Linux (SELinux)

   c. Apparmor

   d. Seccomp

Answers

1	a
2	c

Questions

1. What are the best practices for reducing the container attack surface from a security point of view?

2. Which tool allows us to test the security of our Docker containers and focuses on best practices in areas like file permissions and registry settings?

3. Which open source security audit tool is used to evaluate the security of Linux- and Unix-based systems?

Key terms

- **AppArmor** allows you to limit what an application can do through a set of rules.

- **Seccomp** is an isolated space installation in the Linux Kernel that acts as a firewall that allows you to limit system calls (syscalls).

- **Docker Bench for Security** is a script that performs different tests, checking best security practices in a productive environment where we deploy our containers either on our own servers or in the cloud. This script can help with testing for Docker content trust features and access control issues.

CHAPTER 6
Docker Images Security

In addition to ensuring that your container is properly configured from a security point of view, you must ensure that all image layers in a container are free from known vulnerabilities. This is done through tools that perform a static scan of images in the Docker repositories. In this chapter, you will learn best practices for building container images securely.

We will review some open source tools, such as *Clair* and *Anchore*, to discover vulnerabilities in container images by learning static analysis tools that analyze the different layers that compose an image. As a result, developers will be able to detect vulnerabilities in container applications before uploading them to production.

Structure

We will cover the following topics in this chapter:

- Docker Hub repository and security scanning process
- Open source tools for vulnerability analysis
- Scanning Docker images with *Clair* and *Quay*
- Scanning Docker images with *Anchore* Engine

Objectives

After studying this chapter, you will learn about Docker hub repository and security scanning process. You will also explore open source tools for vulnerability analysis, learn about Clair scanner and Quay repository, and understand Anchore engine and Anchor CLIP for vulnerability analysis.

Docker Hub repository and security scanning process

Docker Hub `https://hub.docker.com/` is a repository of Docker images in which any user can create an image and upload it in the repository to share it with the community.

There are two types of images within this repository, depending on their origin. First of all, we have official images that are maintained by the main suppliers, such as *Apache*, *Ngnix*, *MongoDB*, *Ubuntu*, and *Alpine*.

On the other hand, we can find images created by users that have been customized and adapted according to their needs for the project.

Docker security scanning

Docker security scanning is a service available in Docker Hub for private repositories that compares a container's contents layer by layer by inspecting the binary packages in that container against the **Common Vulnerabilities and Exposures (CVE)** database. This scanning tool's effectiveness depends on:

- **Static analysis depth and integrity**: The scanner discovers the image's inner layers and the nature of those layers.
- **Vulnerability feeds quality**: It indicates coverage and how much the vulnerability lists need to be updated.

We will continue with the Docker security scanning process that allows you to start a review process of images in Docker Hub repositories.

Docker security scanning process

Docker security scanning is the tool that integrates directly with the official Docker Hub repository and allows you to automatically review images found in public and private repositories.

This service is available for Docker Hub public and private repositories, in Docker cloud and on-premise versions, being a paid service in all cases.

When a new image is uploaded to the Docker Hub or Docker cloud, it launches a process that extracts that image and sends it to the scanning service that scans composite layers by analyzing each of the binaries with the CVE database.

Periodically, Docker analyzes the images uploaded in the Docker hub and provides us with a result of the different found vulnerabilities as well as the level of criticality for each vulnerability.

The level of criticality depends on the score assigned to the CVE code by the **Common Vulnerability Score System** (**CVSS**). They may be classified as follows, based on the score given to the vulnerability:

- **High**: Vulnerability has a score within the range [8-10]
- **Medium**: Vulnerability has a score within the range [4-7.9]
- **Low**: Vulnerability has a score within the range [0.0-3.9]

The scan process can be easily integrated into continuous integration and continuous delivery workflows so that scanning can be started automatically every time a developer completes a new container.

Today, most DevOps teams generally only discover a new vulnerability with high criticality level by consulting the CVE database. At this point, the main problem is that lower criticality vulnerabilities may not even be discovered but could be exploited by potential attackers.

Within the Docker ecosystem, the Dockerfile file describes dependencies and what will be installed in the container so that the application can run on it. When running within a continuous integration environment, it will automatically generate and publish in the Docker registry, including that container's software dependencies.

In conclusion, it is a good tool that Docker provides to know a little about the state of health in terms of security for public and private images.

Open source tools for vulnerability analysis

In recent times, threat actors have devised complex techniques for exploiting vulnerabilities in Docker containers and images. While hackers try to find more sophisticated attack methods, cybersecurity analysts and researchers are working to prevent these attacks, looking for a way to protect these resources from potential risks.

The software unification process (DevOps) requires the establishment of functional image scanning and validation mechanisms, comprehensively protecting these processes.

The following is a list of recommendations to guarantee the control of the source code and the deployment in different environments. We can include tools that allow you to automate and organize the source code, like these:

- **Source code control**: Source code control should be a common practice in DevOps security and operations to ensure quality while contributing to unit and integration testing. The main tools for source code control are GitHub `https://github.com/`, GitLab `https://about.gitlab.com/`, and Bitbucket `https://bitbucket.org/`.

- **CI/CD tools**: Development teams use construction tools that are an essential part of their automated compilation processes through CI/CD tools like Bamboo `https://www.atlassian.com/software/bamboo` and Jenkins `https://www.jenkins.io/`.

- **JFrog Xray** `https://jfrog.com/xray`: This is a security tool for container and image analysis. This solution allows you to scan any dependencies for security vulnerabilities and policy compliance issues. JFrog XRay proactively identifies security vulnerabilities that could impact our environment, and it integrates natively with JFrog Artifactory.

Next, we will review the different open source tools or solutions that can be used to perform static vulnerability analysis in Docker images. Tools like Clair, Dagda, and Anchore can automatically check for image vulnerabilities and send notifications via email and look for security fixes when a vulnerability is detected.

Clair security scanning

Clair `https://github.com/quay/clair` is an open-source project for static vulnerability analysis in container-based applications. Layers can be shared among many containers, so introspection is important to create a package inventory and compare it with known CVEs.

This tool provides a container vulnerability analysis service, which works through an API that analyzes each container layer looking for existing vulnerabilities. This tool can report the list of known vulnerabilities that affect each container and notify users.

The methodology for using this tool is by command line. Clair is the security engine that uses Quay registry `https://quay.io/repository/` internally. It basically extracts all the layers of the image and notifies the vulnerabilities found, storing the information in a database.

Dagda

Dagda is an open source tool developed in Python to perform the static analysis of known vulnerabilities in Docker images/containers. It also helps you monitor running Docker containers for detecting anomalous activities.

Dagda retrieves information about the software installed in your Docker image, such as operating system packages, library dependencies, and modules and matches it against a vulnerability database.

This database is created by collating vulnerability data from sources like NVD, SecurityFocus BID & Exploit-DB into a MongoDB database that stores static analysis scans performed on the Docker images. The project can be found in the GitHub repository at https://github.com/eliasgranderubio/dagda.

Dagda supports multiple Docker base Linux images, including:
- Red Hat/CentOS/Fedora
- Debian/Ubuntu
- OpenSUSE
- Alpine Linux

Dagda internally uses OWASP dependency check and Retire.js to analyze packages and dependencies in many languages, such as Java, Python, NodeJS, JS, Ruby, and PHP, identifying known vulnerabilities in Docker images.

The following image illustrates the Dagda architecture:

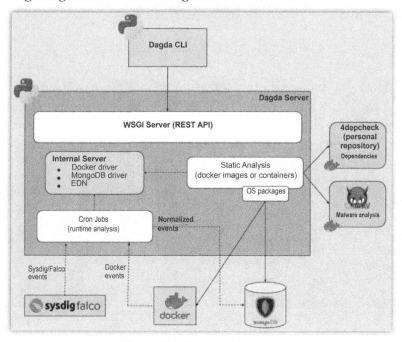

Figure 6.1: Dagda architecture

Dagda executes *ClamAV* to search for malware or detect Trojanized images, and it integrates with *Sysdig Falco* as a tool to detect runtime anomalies and monitor containers on Unix environments at the level of image monitoring.

Sysdig Falco `https://falco.org/` is a tool that can be installed as an agent on each Docker host. It operates internally, analyzing system calls and kernel filters against the rules stored in a database for identifying attacks or anomalous calls inside the containers and in the Docker host.

The following screenshot shows the options of the Dagda Python script:

```
usage: usage: dagda.py [--version] [--help] <command> [args]

Dagda Commands:
  check              perform the analysis of known vulnerabilities in
                     docker images/containers
  docker             list all docker images/containers
  history            retrieve the analysis history for the docker images
  monitor            perform the monitoring of anomalous activities in
                     running docker containers
  start              start the Dagda server
  vuln               perform operations over your personal CVE, BID &
                     ExploitDB database

Optional Arguments:
  -h, --help         show this help message and exit
  -v, --version      show the version message and exit
```

Figure 6.2: Dagda Python script options

We can initialize the vulnerability database and indicate if we want to filter by a specific CVE code with the **vuln** option. The following screenshot shows the options for checking vulnerabilities in a Docker image:

```
$ python3 dagda.py vuln --help
usage: dagda.py vuln [-h] [--init] [--init_status]
                     [--bid BID] [--bid_info BID] [--cve CVE] [--cve_info CVE]
                     [--exploit_db EXPLOIT_DB] [--exploit_db_info EXPLOIT_DB]
                     [--rhba RHBA] [--rhba_info RHBA] [--rhsa RHSA] [--rhsa_info RHSA]
                     [--product PRODUCT] [--product_version PRODUCT_VERSION]

Your personal CVE, BID, RHBA, RHSA & ExploitDB database.

Optional Arguments:
  -h, --help         show this help message and exit
  --init             initializes your local database with all CVEs provided
                     by NIST publications, all BugTraqs Ids (BIDs)
                     downloaded from the "http://www.securityfocus.com/"
                     pages (See my "bidDB_downloader" project for details
                     [https://github.com/eliasgranderubio/bidDB_downloader]
                     for details), all RHSAs (Red Hat Security Advisories)
                     and RHBAs (Red Hat Bug Advisories) provided by Red Hat
                     publications, and all exploits from Offensive Security
                     Exploit Database. If this argument is present, all
                     CVEs, BIDs, RHBAs, RHSAs and exploits of your local
```

Figure. 6.3: Dagda options for checking vulnerabilities in an image

The first thing that should be done is to run the script with the **--init** option to initialize the database with updated information about database vulnerabilities like CVE, exploit database, and Red Hat security advisories.

OWASP dependency check

OWASP dependency check **https://owasp.org/www-project-dependency-check/** is an analysis tool that lets you scan Docker images layer by layer, allowing you to analyze several languages such as Java, Python, Node.js, JavaScript, Ruby, and PHP.

Internally, it performs a scan about the **pom.xml** and manifest files in the case of Java projects and JAR files. In the case of JavaScript projects, the target is to analyze the **package.json** file and the NPM dependencies. This information is compared with the NVD and CVE database.

This project can be found within the OWASP project and can be installed as a command-line tool or as a maven plugin to integrate it into projects like another library. We can generate a report with the vulnerabilities detected if we analyze a project. We can see an example report at **https://jeremylong.github.io/DependencyCheck/general/SampleReport.html**.

The tool is also available as a Docker image in the public Docker hub repository at **https://hub.docker.com/r/deepfenceio/deepfence_depcheck**.

```
$ docker pull deepfenceio/deepfence_depcheck
```

We can see the options and commands offered if we check the Docker image with the **-h** parameter:

```
$ docker run -ti -v /var/run/docker.sock:/var/run/docker.sock -v /
var/lib/docker/:/fenced/mnt/host/var/lib/docker/:rw -v /:/fenced/mnt/
host/:ro -v /home/sandman/db:/tmp:rw deepfenceio/deepfence_depcheck -h
usage: /usr/local/bin/start_services.sh options
    OPTIONS:
        -h      Show this message
        -i      Container image name accessible locally [Must, de-
                fault host]
        -p      Proxy ip:port if localhost is not connected to
                internet (http://proxy.server.com:8080) [Optional,
                default none]
        -t      Scantype{java|nodejs|js|python|ruby|php|all}[Must,
                default all]
        -u      Only database Update {true|false} [Optional, default
                false]
        -j      JSON pretty print {true|false} [Optional, default false]
```

We can also see execution examples for the Deepfence Docker image:

Examples:

Build initial database:

$ docker run -ti -v /var/run/docker.sock:/var/run/docker.sock -v /var/lib/docker/:/fenced/mnt/host/var/lib/docker/:rw

-v /:/fenced/mnt/host/:ro -v /home/user/db:/tmp:rw deepfenceio/deepfence_depcheck -u true

Subsequent runs without updating db for every run.

With proxy:

```
$ docker run -ti -v /var/run/docker.sock:/var/run/docker.sock -v
/var/lib/docker/:/fenced/mnt/host/var/lib/docker/:rw

-v /:/fenced/mnt/host/:ro -v /home/user/db:/tmp:rw
deepfenceio/deepfence_depcheck -i deepfence_java -t all -p
http://205.147.101.100:8003
```

Without proxy, assuming localhost can talk to the world:

```
$ docker run -ti -v /var/run/docker.sock:/var/run/docker.sock -v
/var/lib/docker/:/fenced/mnt/host/var/lib/docker/:rw

-v /:/fenced/mnt/host/:ro -v /home/user/db:/tmp:rw deepfenceio/
deepfence_depcheck -i deepfence_java -t java

Update the db first and then perform scan:

$ docker run -ti -v /var/run/docker.sock:/var/run/docker.sock -v
/var/lib/docker/:/fenced/mnt/host/var/lib/docker/:rw

-v /:/fenced/mnt/host/:ro -v /home/user/db:/tmp:rw deepfenceio/
deepfence_depcheck -i deepfence_java -t java -u true
```

The first step before analyzing our images is to build the initial vulnerability database. The following command will initialize the database with data recovered from public database vulnerability:

```
$ docker run -ti -v /var/run/docker.sock:/var/run/docker.sock
-v /var/lib/docker/:/fenced/mnt/host/var/lib/docker/:rw -v /:/
fenced/mnt/host/:ro -v /home/user/db:/tmp:rw deepfenceio/
deepfence_depcheck -u true
```

To analyze a specific image, for example, we can download the **deepfenceio/fis-java-openshift** image from the Docker hub repository at **https://hub.docker.com/r/deepfenceio/fis-java-openshift**.

```
$ docker pull deepfenceio/fis-java-openshift
```

We can pass the **-t** all parameter to analyze a specific image:

```
$ docker run -ti -v /var/run/docker.sock:/var/run/docker.sock -v /
var/lib/docker/:/fenced/mnt/host/var/lib/docker/:rw -v /:/fenced/
mnt/host/:ro -v   /home/sandman/db:/tmp:rw deepfenceio/deepfence_
depcheck -t all  -j true


[INFO] OWASP Dependency Check is building initial database
[INFO] Retirejs is building initial database
{
 "cve_id": "CVE-2012-6708",
  "cve_type": "js",
 "cve_container_image": "f1b590cfaa8a",
  "cve_severity": "medium",
  "cve_caused_by_package": "jquery-1.7.1",
      "cve_container_layer":   "analyze-local-host-f1b590cfaa8a-
eth0-172.18.0.2",
  "cve_fixed_in": "Unknown",
   "cve_link": "[http://bugs.jquery.com/ticket/11290 https://nvd.
nist.gov/vuln/detail/CVE-2012-6708   http://research.insecurelabs.
org/jquery/test/]",
  "cve_description": "Selector interpreted as HTML",
  "cve_cvss_score": "0.00",
  "cve_attack_vector": "Unknown"
}
{
  "cve_id": "CVE-2015-9251",
  "cve_type": "js",
  "cve_container_image": "f1b590cfaa8a",
  "cve_severity": "medium",
```

```
    "cve_caused_by_package": "jquery-1.7.1",
  "cve_container_layer": "analyze-local-host-f1b590cfaa8a-
  eth0-172.18.0.2",
    "cve_fixed_in": "Unknown",
    "cve_link":        "[https://github.com/jquery/jquery/issues/2432
    http://blog.jquery.com/2016/01/08/jquery-2-2-and-1-12-released/
    https://nvd.nist.gov/vuln/detail/CVE-2015-9251  http://research.
    insecurelabs.org/jquery/test/]",
    "cve_description": "3rd party CORS request may execute",
    "cve_cvss_score": "0.00",
    "cve_attack_vector": "Unknown"
}
{
  "cve_id": "CVE-2019-11358",
    "cve_type": "js",
  "cve_container_image": "f1b590cfaa8a",
    "cve_severity": "medium",
    "cve_caused_by_package": "jquery-1.7.1",
        "cve_container_layer":     "analyze-local-host-f1b590cfaa8a-
eth0-172.18.0.2",
    "cve_fixed_in": "Unknown",
    "cve_link": "[https://blog.jquery.com/2019/04/10/
jquery-3-4-0-released/ https://nvd.nist.gov/vuln/
detail/CVE-2019-11358 https://github.com/jquery/jquery/
commit/753d591aea698e57d6db58c9f722cd0808619b1b]",
    "cve_description": "jQuery before 3.4.0, as used in Drupal,
Backdrop CMS, and other products, mishandles jQuery.extend(true,
{}, ...) because of Object.prototype pollution",
    "cve_cvss_score": "0.00",
    "cve_attack_vector": "Unknown"
}
```

The output of the preceding command shows how it has detected some vulnerabilities for the image that we are analyzing, along with the corresponding CVE codes and the packages and versions that are vulnerable. At this point, we have reviewed the OWASP dependency check script for checking vulnerabilities in Docker images.

Trivy

Trivy **https://github.com/aquasecurity/trivy** is an open source tool that focuses on detecting vulnerabilities in packages at the operating system level and dependency files of different languages.

Trivy provides installers for most Linux and macOS systems. We can use the following commands to install Trivy in a Debian based distribution:

```
$ sudo apt-get -y install wget apt-transport-https gnupg lsb-release
$ wget -qO - https://aquasecurity.github.io/trivy-repo/deb/public.
key | sudo  apt-key add
$ echo  deb  https://aquasecurity.github.io/trivy-repo/deb $(lsb_
release -sc) main | sudo tee -a /etc/apt/sources.list.d/trivy.list
$ sudo apt-get update
$ sudo apt-get -y install trivy
```

Once installed, we can see the options it offers with the **-h** option:

```
$ trivy -h
NAME:
   trivy - A simple and comprehensive vulnerability scanner for
   containers


USAGE:
   trivy [global options] command [command options] target


VERSION:
   0.16.0
COMMANDS:
   image, i           scan an image
   filesystem, fs     scan local filesystem
   repository, repo   scan remote repository
   client, c          client mode
   server, s          server mode
   help, h            Shows a list of commands or help for one command
```

```
GLOBAL OPTIONS:
   --quiet, -q          suppress progress bar and log output (default:
                        false) [$TRIVY_QUIET]
   --debug, -d          debug mode (default: false) [$TRIVY_DEBUG]
   --cache-dir value    cache directory (default: "/root/.cache/
                        trivy") [$TRIVY_CACHE_DIR]
   --help, -h           show help (default: false)
   --version, -v        print the version (default: fal
```

We can analyze both local and remote images with the following command:

```
$ trivy image ubuntu:18.04
```

When analyzing the image, we see the vulnerabilities that have been detected and the information related to the vulnerable packages and libraries, organized by level of criticality:

```
ubuntu:18.04 (ubuntu 18.04)
===========================
Total: 47 (UNKNOWN: 0, LOW: 40, MEDIUM: 7, HIGH: 0, CRITICAL: 0)

+--------------+------------------+----------+--------------------+---------------+--------------------------------------+
|   LIBRARY    | VULNERABILITY ID | SEVERITY | INSTALLED VERSION  | FIXED VERSION |                TITLE                 |
+--------------+------------------+----------+--------------------+---------------+--------------------------------------+
| bash         | CVE-2019-18276   | LOW      | 4.4.18-2ubuntu1.2  |               | bash: when effective UID is not      |
|              |                  |          |                    |               | equal to its real UID the...         |
|              |                  |          |                    |               | -->avd.aquasec.com/nvd/cve-2019-18276|
+--------------+------------------+          +--------------------+---------------+--------------------------------------+
| coreutils    | CVE-2016-2781    |          | 8.28-1ubuntu1      |               | coreutils: Non-privileged            |
|              |                  |          |                    |               | session can escape to the            |
|              |                  |          |                    |               | parent session in chroot             |
|              |                  |          |                    |               | -->avd.aquasec.com/nvd/cve-2016-2781 |
+--------------+------------------+----------+--------------------+---------------+--------------------------------------+
| gcc-8-base   | CVE-2020-13844   | MEDIUM   | 8.4.0-1ubuntu1~18.04 |             | kernel: ARM straight-line            |
|              |                  |          |                    |               | speculation vulnerability            |
|              |                  |          |                    |               | -->avd.aquasec.com/nvd/cve-2020-13844|
+--------------+------------------+----------+--------------------+---------------+--------------------------------------+
| gpgv         | CVE-2019-13050   | LOW      | 2.2.4-1ubuntu1.4   |               | GnuPG: interaction between the       |
|              |                  |          |                    |               | sks-keyserver code and GnuPG         |
|              |                  |          |                    |               | allows for a Certificate...          |
|              |                  |          |                    |               | -->avd.aquasec.com/nvd/cve-2019-13050|
```

Figure 6.4: Analyzing Ubuntu image with Trivy

We obtain more information for each vulnerability in the form of metadata:

- **Library**: Package where the vulnerability has been identified
- **Vulnerability ID**: Vulnerability identifier according to the CVE standard
- **Severity**: There is a classification with five severity levels, depending on the score assigned by the **Common Vulnerability Scoring System** (**CVSS**):
    - **Critical (score 9.0-10.0)**: Bug that an unauthenticated attacker could easily exploit and compromise the system without user interaction
    - **High (score 7.0-8.9)**: Bugs that could easily compromise the confidentiality, integrity, or availability of resources

- **Medium (score 4.0-6.9)**: Bugs that, although are more difficult to exploit, may continue to compromise the confidentiality, integrity, or availability of resources in certain circumstances
  - **Low (score 0.1-3.9)**: Vulnerabilities that are considered to be exploited in unlikely circumstances or would have minimal consequences
- **Installed version**: Version installed on the analyzed image
- **Fixed version**: Version in which the issue is solved; it is pending resolution if the fixed version is not reported.
- **Title**: Vulnerability description

Tip: Executing Trivy from Docker container

We can also use the following Docker image from aquasec repository in Docker Hub:

`https://hub.docker.com/r/aquasec/trivy`

We can analyze Ubuntu image with this image using the following command:

```
$ docker run --rm -v /var/run/docker.sock:/var/run/docker.sock -v /
tmp/trivycache:/root/.cache/ aquasec/trivy ubuntu:18.04
```

The vulnerability database is hosted on GitHub, so we can avoid downloading this database in each analysis operation using the **--cache-dir** parameter:

```
$ trivy --cache-dir .cache/trivy image ubuntu:18.04
```

At this point, we have reviewed Trivy for checking vulnerabilities in Docker images.

Scanning Docker images with Clair and Quay

Clair provides a JSON API that extracts all layers of the image and can be executed to inspect container images, for example, as part of continuous integration and continuous delivery process.

We can install Clair through the Docker Compose tool and the repository **https://github.com/quay/clair#docker-compose**. These are the commands for installing it in your local machine:

```
$ https://raw.githubusercontent.com/coreos/
clair/05cbf328aa6b00a167124dbdbec229e348d97c04/contrib/compose/
docker-compose.yml
```

This is the content of **docker-compose.yml**, where we can see the services of Postgres and Clair:

```
version: '2'
services:
  postgres:
    container_name: clair_postgres
    image: postgres:latest
    restart: unless-stopped
    environment:
      POSTGRES_PASSWORD: password

  clair:
    container_name: clair_clair
    image: quay.io/coreos/clair-git:latest
    restart: unless-stopped
    depends_on:
      - postgres
    ports:
      - "6060-6061:6060-6061"
    links:
      - postgres
    volumes:
      - /tmp:/tmp
      - ./clair_config:/config
    command: [-config, /config/config.yaml]
```

The Clair configuration defines how images should be scanned. You can download it with the following command:

```
$ mkdir clair_config && curl -L https://raw.githubusercontent.com/
coreos/clair/master/config.yaml.sample -o clair_config/config.yaml
```

Next, we need to update the Clair configuration, setting the version of Clair to the last stable release and the default database password:

```
$ sed 's/clair-git:latest/clair:v2.0.1/' -i docker-compose.yml && \
    sed 's/host=localhost/host=postgres password=password/' -i
clair_config/config.yaml
```

Clair requires a Postgres instance to store the CVE data and its service that will scan Docker images for vulnerabilities:

```
$ docker-compose up -d postgres
```

Next, we can download and load the CVE details for Clair to use:

```
curl -LO https://gist.githubusercontent.com/
BenHall/34ae4e6129d81f871e353c63b6a869a7/
raw/5818fba954b0b00352d07771fabab6b9daba5510/clair.sql

docker run -it \
    -v $(pwd):/sql/ \
    --network "${USER}_default" \
    --link clair_postgres:clair_postgres \
    postgres:latest \
        bash -c "PGPASSWORD=password psql -h clair_postgres -U
        postgres < /sql/clair.sql"
```

Finally, we can use the following command to start the **clair** container service:

```
$ docker-compose up -d clair
```

We have two containers running when executing the previous **docker-compose** commands: one corresponding to the Postgres database listening on port 5432 and another corresponding to the image analyzer listening on port 6061:

```
$ docker ps

CONTAINER ID          IMAGE                           COMMAND
CREATED               STATUS                          PORTS
NAMES

fd827a709f1e               quay.io/coreos/clair:v2.0.1    "/clair -con-
fig /con…"    8 minutes ago              Restarting (1) 37 seconds ago
clair_clair

01779e11a91e            postgres:latest                  "docker-entry-
point.s…"    21 minutes ago       Up 21 minutes                  5432/
tcp          clair_postgres
```

We can now send Docker Images to scan and return which vulnerabilities it contains. To scan all the layers from a Docker image we can use tools like Klar **https://github. com/optiopay/klar**. This tool allows analyzing images stored in a private or public Docker registry for security vulnerabilities using Clair container service.

We can use the following command to download the latest release from GitHub:

```
$ curl -L https://github.com/optiopay/klar/releases/download/
v1.5/klar-1.5-linux-amd64 -o /usr/local/bin/klar && chmod +x $_
```

We can use the following command to analyze vulnerabilities in a Docker image, where **CLAIR_ADDR** is the server address where Clair has been hosted:

```
$ CLAIR_ADDR=<clair_server> klar <Docker_image>
```

At this point, we have reviewed the execution of Clair using Docker compose and how we can detect vulnerabilities in a specific Docker image. Next, we will review the Quay.io image repository for static image analysis.

Quay.io image repository

Quay registry **https://quay.io/repository/** provides static image analysis with the objective of finding obsolete and vulnerable packages in binaries.

With this service we can see information related to the image scan, including packages with vulnerabilities that have been detected in each of the layers. The following screenshot shows the packages with vulnerabilities:

Figure 6.5: Packages with vulnerabilities detected by Quay security scanner

The following screenshot depicts the CVE vulnerabilities detected by Quay security scanner in a specific Docker image:

Figure 6.6: CVE vulnerabilities detected by Quay security scanner

For each vulnerability, it shows the CVE number, the level of criticality, the package with vulnerability, a version that contains the vulnerability, and the version that could fix the security issue.

If we go into the details, we can see the metrics for calculating the final score and the criticality level:

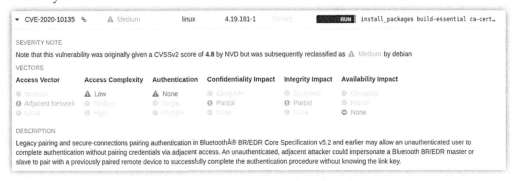

Figure 6.7: Metrics for specific vulnerability

Here, we can see that each vulnerability defines a series of metrics that will give the final score and the level of criticality. The increase in the impact of integrity increases the vulnerability score. Here are some of the main metrics:

- **Access complexity**: This metric measures the complexity of the attack required to exploit the vulnerability once an attacker has accessed the target system.

- **Authentication**: This metric measures the strength or complexity of the authentication process; for example, whether an attacker is required to provide credentials before they can execute an exploit. The fewer authentication instances required, the higher the vulnerability score.

- **Confidentiality impact**: Confidentiality refers to limiting access and disclosure of information to authorized users as well as preventing access or disclosure to unauthorized persons. Increasing the impact of confidentiality increases the vulnerability score.

- **Integrity impact**: This metric measures the impact on the integrity of a successfully exploited vulnerability. The increase in the impact of integrity increases the vulnerability score.

Analyzing Docker images with Anchore

Anchore is an open source tool that inspects, analyzes, and certifies Docker images. This analysis is done against a proprietary database (Postgres) formed by the collection of information on vulnerabilities and security problems (CVE) from operating system distributions. It also collects the same information from the logs of popular packages like Node.JS, NPM, and Ruby.

Anchore can download any image from a registry compatible with Docker V2. And with the result of the analysis, it generates a report with the details of the image, a list of artifacts (npm, gem, Python, and Java), a list of operating system packages, the list of image files, and a list of vulnerabilities.

The following table lists the different origins of the data source that Anchore uses internally for identifying vulnerabilities:

Driver	Feed Type	External Data Source
alpine	Vulnerabilities	`https://github.com/alpinelinux/alpine-secdb/archive/master.tar.gz`
CentOS	Vulnerabilities	`https://www.redhat.com/security/data/oval/com.redhat.rhsa-all.xml.bz2`
Debian	Vulnerabilities	`https://security-tracker.debian.org/tracker/data/json` `https://salsa.debian.org/security-tracker-team/security-tracker/raw/master/data/DSA/list`

Oracle	Vulnerabilities	`https://linux.oracle.com/` `security/oval/com.oracle.elsa-` `all.xml.bz2`
Ubuntu	Vulnerabilities	`https://launchpad.net/ubuntu-` `cve-tracker`
Gem	Packages	`https://s3-us-west-2.amazonaws.` `com/rubygems-dumps`
Npm	Packages	`https://replicate.npmjs.com`
NVD	nvd	`https://nvd.nist.gov/vuln/data-` `feeds`

Table. 6.1: Data sources for identifying vulnerabilities

Anchore engine architecture consists of five components that can be implemented in a single container or in a Kubernetes cluster:

- **Anchore Engine CLI**: It is the main command line interface provided by the Anchore suite to be able to rule the solution. It is mainly responsible for interpreting and sending the commands passed to the Anchore Engine API.

- **Anchore Engine API**: This service allows you to orchestrate the entire solution. It is also used to analyze images and obtain policy evaluations and govern the solution completely.

- **Anchore Policy Engine**: The policy engine is responsible for scanning for vulnerabilities in the artifacts found in the image and providing a quick assessment of the policies on that data.

- **Anchore Engine Analyzer**: This component is responsible for the downloading of images and their analysis.

- **Anchore Engine Database**: Anchore is built around a PostgreSQL database that contains tables for all the necessary services that are communicated through API calls.

Basically, Anchore Engine allows developers to perform a detailed analysis of images, executing queries, generating reports, and defining policies that can be used in the CI/CD cycle.

The open source version is highly customizable and reusable for different jobs, from CD/CI tasks to inspection and debugging tasks. Here are some of the things it allows:

- Extract packages and components from Docker images
- Scan images for known vulnerabilities

Anchore engine is provided as a Docker image that can be with other orchestration platforms like Kubernetes, Docker Swarm, or Rancher. We will continue with Anchore engine installation using Docker compose.

Deploying Anchore engine

The easiest way to deploy Anchore engine is through the **docker-compose.yaml** file we can find in the **scripts/docker-compose** folder in the GitHub project.

- https://github.com/anchore/anchore-engine/blob/master/docker-compose-dev.yaml

You can use the following command to download the latest version of **anchore-engine**:

```
$ git clone https://github.com/anchore/anchore-engine
$ cd anchore-engine
```

The first step is to download the configuration files (**docker-compose.yaml** and **config.yaml**) from the GitHub project.

```
$ curl https://raw.githubusercontent.com/anchore/anchore-engine/master/docker-compose-dev.yaml > docker-compose.yaml


$ curl https://raw.githubusercontent.com/anchore/anchore-engine/master/conf/default_config.yaml > config.yaml
```

The **config.yaml** file is a configuration file with the basic configuration the Anchore Engine requires to run. It has several parameters, including defaults, log level, listening port, username, and password, that you can adjust to meet specific requirements.

We can execute the following **docker-compose** command using the same path where we have downloaded the **docker-compose.yaml** file to start Anchore Engine:

```
$ docker-compose up –d
```

The preceding command will extract the Anchore image and automatically create the Anchore engine and database. Once completed, the command will start the Anchore engine.

The following screenshot shows the output of the previous command:

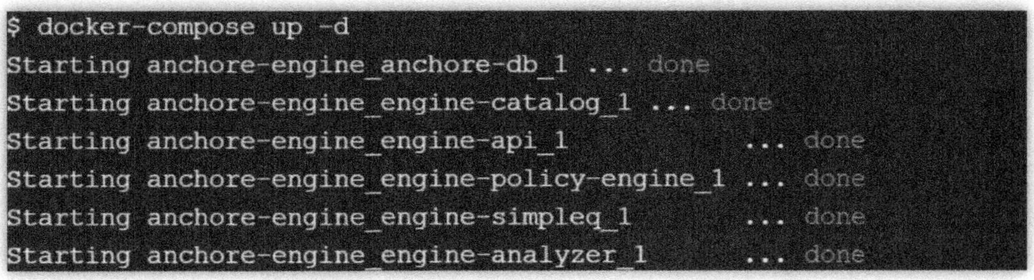

Figure 6.8: Starting Anchore engine containers

In the preceding output, we can see different Anchore engine containers and services related with database, catalog, API, and policies. The following output shows us Anchore engine containers in execution:

```
$ docker ps

CONTAINER ID          IMAGE                                   COMMAND
CREATED               STATUS                                    PORTS
NAMES
b53cdc41207b          anchore/anchore-engine-dev:latest   "/docker-
entrypoint.…"  29 seconds ago    Up 26 seconds (health: starting)
8228/tcp                   root_queue_1
dd1dd2205777          anchore/anchore-engine-dev:latest   "/docker-
entrypoint.…"  29 seconds ago    Up 26 seconds (health: starting)
8228/tcp                   root_policy-engine_1
829970e315e6          anchore/anchore-engine-dev:latest   "/docker-
entrypoint.…"  29 seconds ago    Up 27 seconds (health: starting)
8228/tcp                   root_analyzer_1
c90621d6c9b9          anchore/anchore-engine-dev:latest   "/docker-
entrypoint.…"  29 seconds ago    Up 27 seconds (health: starting)
0.0.0.0:8228->8228/tcp    root_api_1
b6e925075210          anchore/anchore-engine-dev:latest   "/docker-
entrypoint.…"  30 seconds ago    Up 29 seconds (health: starting)
8228/tcp                   root_catalog_1
23b7f4ee8f55          postgres:9                              "docker-
entrypoint.s…"  31 seconds ago    Up 30 seconds             5432/
tcp                   root_db_1
```

We can also verify that the containers are running with the **docker-compose** command:

```
$ docker-compose ps

          Name               Command              State              Ports
--------------------------------------------------------------------------------
root_analyzer_1           /docker-             Up (healthy)   8228/tcp
                          entrypoint.sh anch
                          ...
root_api_1                   /docker-                         Up (healthy)
0.0.0.0:8228->8228/t
                          entrypoint.sh anch                              cp
                          ...
root_catalog_1            /docker-             Up (healthy)   8228/tcp
                          entrypoint.sh anch
                          ...
root_db_1                 docker-entrypoint.sh  Up             5432/tcp
                          postgres
root_policy-engine_1      /docker-             Up (healthy)   8228/tcp
                          entrypoint.sh anch
                          ...
root_queue_1              /docker-             Up (healthy)   8228/tcp
                          entrypoint.sh anch
```

After installing and starting Anchore engine, you can scan the images using the *AnchoreCLI* tool. However, you must first install the AnchoreCLI command line utility, as shown here.

The installation of AnchoreCLI can be done in several ways. The most direct way is through the **pip install** command or through the source code:

```
$ pip install anchorecli
$ git clone https://github.com/anchore/anchore-cli
$ cd anchore-cli
$ pip install --user –upgrade .
$ python setup.py install
```

AnchoreCLI can communicate with Anchore engine to analyze the images that we have locally on the Docker host. It provides a command-line interface at the top of the REST API of the Anchore engine for this task.

```
$ docker-compose exec api anchore-cli
```

The following screenshot shows the options of the **anchore-cli** command:

```
$ docker-compose exec api anchore-cli
Usage: anchore-cli [OPTIONS] COMMAND [ARGS]...

Options:
  --config TEXT          Set the location of the anchore-cli yaml configuration
                         file
  --debug                Debug output to stderr
  --u TEXT               Username (or use environment variable ANCHORE_CLI_USER)
  --p TEXT               Password (or use environment variable ANCHORE_CLI_PASS)
  --url TEXT             Service URL (or use environment variable
                         ANCHORE_CLI_URL)
  --hub-url TEXT         Anchore Hub URL (or use environment variable
                         ANCHORE_CLI_HUB_URL)
  --api-version TEXT     Explicitly specify the API version to skip checking.
                         Useful when swagger endpoint is inaccessible
  --insecure             Skip SSL cert checks (or use environment variable
                         ANCHORE_CLI_SSL_VERIFY=<y/n>)
  --json                 Output raw API JSON
  --as-account TEXT      Set account context for the command to another account
                         than the one the user belongs to. Subject to authz
```

Figure 6.9: Anchore cli command options

The following output shows the commands supported by anchore-cli:

Commands:	
account	**Account operations**
analysis-archive	**Archive operations**
enterprise	**Enterprise Anchore operations**
evaluate	**Policy evaluation operations**
event	**Event operations**
help	
image	**Image operations**
policy	**Policy operations**
query	**Query operations**
registry	**Registry operations**
repo	**Repository operations**
subscription	**Subscription operations**
system	**System operations**

For example, you can run the following command to get the status of the Anchore Engine services:

```
$ docker-compose exec api anchore-cli system status

Service catalog (anchore-quickstart, http://catalog:8228): up
Service apiext (anchore-quickstart, http://api:8228): up
Service simplequeue (anchore-quickstart, http://queue:8228): up
Service analyzer (anchore-quickstart, http://analyzer:8228): up
Service policy_engine (anchore-quickstart, http://policy-
engine:8228): up

Engine DB Version: 0.0.14
Engine Code Version: 0.9.3
```

The first time you execute Anchore Engine, it will take some time for the vulnerability data to get synced into the engine. You can check the status of your feed sync with the following command:

```
$ docker-compose exec api anchore-cli system feeds list
```

The preceding command allows you to check the status of the Anchore database, where the solution stores the latest vulnerabilities depending on the type of image.

For the best experience, wait until the core vulnerability data feeds have completed before proceeding. We can use the following command to check the options available for analyzing a Docker image:

$ `docker-compose exec api anchore-cli image`
Usage: `anchore-cli image [OPTIONS] COMMAND [ARGS]...`
Options:
  `-h, --help` **Show this message and exit.**
Commands:

`add`   Add an image

`content`   Get contents of image

`del`   Delete an image

`get`   Get an image

`import`   Import an image from anchore scanner export

`list`   List all images

`metadata` Get metadata about an image

`vuln`   Get image vulnerabilities

`wait`   Wait for an image to analyze

These are the commands that can be most useful for analyzing Docker images:

```
# Add an image to Anchore to analyze
$ anchore-cli image add <image_name>


# Display image content
$ anchore-cli image content <image_name> os


# Analyze image content
$ anchore-cli image content <image_name> files


# Evaluate based on policy compliance
$ anchore-cli evaluate check <image_name> os
```

To start analyzing images, we must first add the images to the engine. We are adding the latest Debian docker image with the following command:

```
$ docker-compose exec api anchore-cli image add docker.io/library/debi-
an:latest
Image    Digest:   sha256:fa335fed387465ccc369958d7908e1975e7d65677f7f-
3050d862161754ebcf90
Parent     Digest:     sha256:ba4a437377a0c450ac9bb634c3754a17b1f814ce-
6fa3157c0dc9eef431b29d1f
Analysis Status: not_analyzed
Image Type: docker
Analyzed At: None
Image ID: 0d587dfbc4f4800bfe9ab08662e8396ffc37060c493f8ef24b-
          2823fef3320df6
Dockerfile Mode: None
Distro: None
Distro Version: None
Size: None
Architecture: None
Layer Count: None

Full Tag: docker.io/library/debian:latest
```

The analysis begins automatically after adding these images to the Anchore engine, without user intervention. You can check the progress and view the list of uploaded images, along with their analysis status.

```
$ docker-compose exec api anchore-cli image list
Full Tag           Image Digest                      Analysis Status
docker.io/library/debian:latest
                   sha256:fa335fed387465ccc369958d7908e1975e7d65677
                   f7f  3050d862161754ebcf90            analyzed
docker.io/library/openjdk:14-jdk-alpine3.10    sha256:7c29ddf86e7
fc5ea5fe01e1ad3e3439422fc50dc2c568b00d6bd79bdb026bfdf      analyzed
```

Depending on the number of images that we are analyzing, they will be analyzed according to their size and those that have completed their analysis, those that are in process and the images that are in the queue pending analysis will be shown in the output.

We can check the results of vulnerability scans, policy checks, and other issues that the Anchore engine has identified after the scan is complete.

The following command will return the packages installed inside the debian image:

```
$ docker-compose exec api anchore-cli image content docker.io/
library/debian:latest os
```

We can execute the following command to check the results of the vulnerability analysis in the **debian:latest** image:

```
$ docker-compose exec api anchore-cli image vuln docker.io/library/
debian:latest all
```

```
$ docker-compose exec api anchore-cli image vuln docker.io/library/debian:latest all            Vulnerabili
y ID       Package                        Severity       Fix       CVE Refs       Vulnerabili
y URL                                          Type     Feed Group     Package Path

CVE-2011-3389            libgnutls30-3.6.7-4+deb10u6    Medium        None
https://security-tracker.debian.org/tracker/CVE-2011-3389         dpkg      debian:10        pkgdb

CVE-2005-2541            tar-1.30+dfsg-6                Negligible    None
https://security-tracker.debian.org/tracker/CVE-2005-2541         dpkg      debian:10        pkgdb

CVE-2007-5686            login-1:4.5-1.1                Negligible    None
https://security-tracker.debian.org/tracker/CVE-2007-5686         dpkg      debian:10        pkgdb

CVE-2007-5686            passwd-1:4.5-1.1               Negligible    None
https://security-tracker.debian.org/tracker/CVE-2007-5686         dpkg      debian:10        pkgdb

CVE-2010-4051            libc-bin-2.28-10               Negligible    None
https://security-tracker.debian.org/tracker/CVE-2010-4051         dpkg      debian:10        pkgdb
```

Figure 6.10: Checking vulnerabilities in the debian image

The report shows the CVE identifier, the vulnerable package, the severity, and whether or not there is a fix.

The following command will get metadata from the Docker image:

```
$ docker-compose exec api anchore-cli image metadata docker.io/
library/debian:latest manifest
Image Digest: sha256:fa335fed387465ccc369958d7908e1975e7d65677f7f-
3050d862161754ebcf90
Metadata: {"schemaVersion": 2, "mediaType": "application/vnd.dock-
er.distribution.manifest.v2+json", "config": {"mediaType": "appli-
cation/vnd.docker.container.image.v1+json", "size": 1463, "di-
gest":   "sha256:0d587dfbc4f4800bfe9ab08662e8396ffc37060c493f8ef24
b2823fef3320df6"}, "layers": [{"mediaType": "application/vnd.
docker.image. rootfs.diff.tar.gzip", "size": 50432971, "digest":
"sha256:bd8f6a7501ccbe80b95c82519      ed6fd4f7236a41e0ae59ba4a8d-
f76af24629efc"}]}
Metadata Type: manifest
```

We can also check the policies for the debian: latest image with the following command:

```
$ docker-compose exec api anchore-cli evaluate check  docker.io/
library/debian:latest --detail
Image Digest: sha256:fa335fed387465ccc
369958d7908e1975e7d65677f7f3050d862161754ebcf90
Full Tag: docker.io/library/debian:latest
Image ID: 0d587dfbc4f4800bfe9ab08662e8396
ffc37060c493f8ef24b2823fef3320df6
Status: pass
Last Eval: 2021-04-24T18:27:41Z
Policy ID: 2c53a13c-1765-11e8-82ef-23527761d060
Final Action: warn
Final Action Reason: policy_evaluation


Gate              Trigger       Detail                    Status
dockerfile             instruction       Dockerfile directive
'HEALTHCHECK' not found, matching condition 'not_exists' check
warn
vulnerabilities        package           MEDIUM Vulnerability
found in os package type (dpkg) - libgnutls30 (CVE-2011-3389 -
https://security-tracker.debian.org/tracker/CVE-2011-3389)     warn
```

The evaluation shows general information about the image and the result, which is successful in this case by having the status pass. This implies that the image has passed the evaluation against Anchore's default policy.

In addition to the status, it shows that there are things to improve. It includes a warning in the final action, indicating that the warning was launched by the evaluated policy, and it also shows where the problem is so that it can be solved for the next time.

Policies for image evaluation

In addition to providing information about an image, Anchore can perform an image evaluation based on user-defined policies.

A policy is made up of a set of rules used to evaluate a container image. These rules may include checks for security vulnerabilities, image black and white lists, configuration file content, presence of credentials in the image, exposed ports, or other user-defined checks. These policies can be applied globally or customized for specific images or categories of applications.

Bundles (packages) are the unit of definition and evaluation of policies in Anchore. A user can have several bundles of policies, but only one is used for the evaluation of an image. This can be the one that is active in the Anchore engine when performing the analysis or the one indicated in the inline scan.

A bundle contains zero or more policies. The policies of a package define the checks to be performed against an image and the actions to be recommended if the checks find a match.

A policy bundle is a JSON document composed of the following:

- **Policies**: Rules and actions
- **Whitelisting**: Rule exclusions to unmatch some policy
- **Mappings**: Determine which policies and whitelists should be applied to a specific image at the time of evaluation so that we can apply more or less rules according to the image
- **Image Whitelist**: Images that will automatically pass the assessment, regardless of whether they comply with policies
- **Image Blacklist**: Replace specific images to statically set the end result to a bug, regardless of the outcome of the policy evaluation

Anchore has a policy activated by default to be able to run the image analysis without having to do any extra configuration. This policy checks that there are no high or critical vulnerabilities. If there are any, it marks them in the logs and causes the continuous integration to fail if the analysis is running in one phase. Medium or low vulnerabilities are flagged with a warning, but these will not cause the continuous integration to fail.

The following command allows you to list the policies that Anchore has downloaded and which of them can be applied. Note that only one of them can be active at a time at the engine level.

```
$ docker-compose exec api anchore-cli policy list
Policy ID              Active      Created              Updated
2c53a13c-1765-11e8-82ef-23527761d060                   True
2021-04-24T19:21:58Z
```

The '**2c53a13c-1765-11e8-82ef-23527761d060**' policy corresponds to the default policy used by Anchore. We can get more information about a policy using the following command:

```
$ docker-compose exec api anchore-cli policy get 2c53a13c-1765-
11e8-82ef-23527761d060

Policy ID: 2c53a13c-1765-11e8-82ef-23527761d060

Active: True

Source: true

Created: 2021-04-24T19:21:58Z

Updated: 2021-04-24T19:21:58Z
```

With the aim of maintaining order within a policy, Anchore separates each of the sections in which it can perform analysis by categories. You can use the following command to show the different categories or gates allowed within a policy:

```
$ docker-compose exec api anchore-cli policy describe
```

```
$ docker-compose exec api anchore-cli policy describe
+----------------+------------------------------------------------------------+
| Gate           | Description                                                |
+----------------+------------------------------------------------------------+
| always         | Triggers that fire unconditionally if present in policy,   |
|                | useful for things like testing and blacklisting.           |
+----------------+------------------------------------------------------------+
| dockerfile     | Checks against the content of a dockerfile if provided, or |
|                | a guessed dockerfile based on docker layer history if the  |
|                | dockerfile is not provided.                                |
+----------------+------------------------------------------------------------+
| files          | Checks against files in the analyzed image including file  |
|                | content, file names, and filesystem attributes.            |
+----------------+------------------------------------------------------------+
| licenses       | License checks against found software licenses in the      |
|                | container image                                            |
+----------------+------------------------------------------------------------+
| malware        | Checks for malware scan findings in the image              |
```

Figure 6.11: Checking categories within a policy

There are different triggers within each policy gate, and they are the evaluations that will capture the result of the analysis of a rule. The following command shows the triggers that exist within the vulnerability gate:

```
$ docker-compose exec api anchore-cli policy describe
--gate=vulnerabilities
```

In this section, we have reviewed Anchore engine for analyzing each Docker image based on data and policy enforcement, following these phases for each analysis:

a. Gets and extracts the content of the image, without executing it

b. Analyzes the content, extracting and classifying as much metadata as possible

c. Saves the result of the previous analysis in the database

d. Evaluates policies against the scan result, including vulnerability matches in artifacts discovered in the image

e. Updates the data used for the vulnerability and policy assessment and updates the results of the image analysis by applying the new data if there is any change to the data

Conclusion

In this chapter, we reviewed some open source tools to discover vulnerabilities in Docker images. It is important to analyze possible vulnerabilities layer by layer to minimize the exposure of our images before deploying in a productive environment. This is because these vulnerabilities could cause an attacker to take control of the application.

In the next chapter, we will review topics like Docker container threats and system attacks that can impact Docker applications, and we will discuss the main vulnerabilities we can find in Docker images.

Points to remember

- Trivy is a vulnerability scanner for detecting errors in packages of multiple operating systems and application dependencies.

- Clair is an open source project for Docker application and container vulnerability scanning. It can be considered an analysis engine powered by an API that performs layer-by-layer checking to detect security issues in containers. It also automatically monitors all containers for exploitable vulnerabilities, sending notifications in real-time.

- Anchore Image Scanner is an image analysis tool that identifies a wide range of vulnerabilities and policy issues in Docker images. After testing it with docker-compose, Anchore's greatest utility is to use it as part of a continuous integration phase that runs with every change to a Docker image to check for new vulnerabilities or fixes that already exist.

- Policies can be described as a set of rules and checks that allow Anchore to obtain an assessment of a Docker image with regard to the compliance of the image with respect to the policy.

Multiple choice questions

1. Which Anchore command allows you to check the status of the Anchore database, where the solution stores the latest vulnerabilities depending on the type of image?

   a. $ anchore-cli system feeds status

   b. $ anchore-cli system images list

   c. $ anchore-cli system feeds list

   d. $ anchore-cli system images status

2. Which Anchore command allows you to start analyzing images?

   a. $ anchore-cli image <Docker image>

   b. $ anchore-cli image analyze <Docker image>

   c. $ anchore-cli system add <Docker image>

   d. $ anchore-cli image add <Docker image>

Answer

1	C
2	D

Questions

1. What enables Clair to analyze each layer of the container and look for existing vulnerabilities in Debian, Ubuntu, and CentOS databases?

2. Which Docker registry provides static image analysis with the objective of finding obsolete and vulnerable libraries in binaries?

3. Which are the main components of Anchore engine architecture?

Key terms

- Scanning for vulnerabilities in Docker containers and images is a practice that strengthens application security, establishing the necessary mechanisms to prevent cyberattacks.

- Anchore is available as a Docker image that can be run independently with docker-compose on your local machine, with orchestration platforms like Kubernetes or as part of continuous integration on Gitlab CI, Jenkins, Travis CI, etc.

- The vulnerability database allows scanners such as Anchore to make a comparison in the analysis phase between the different packages that make up the Docker image, with their respective versions, and the existing vulnerabilities for that versions.

## CHAPTER 7

Auditing and Analyzing Vulnerabilities in Docker Containers

From a security point of view, it is important to have knowledge about Docker container threats and system attacks, which can impact Docker applications. These threats and attacks are also applicable to specific Docker container versions of the applications.

In this chapter, you will learn about the main Docker container threats, the main vulnerabilities we can find in Docker images, and some services and tools for getting information about these vulnerabilities. As a result, developers will have the capacity to obtain details about vulnerabilities in container applications.

We will review examples of attacks and exploits that could target running containers. We will also look at specific CVE in Docker images and how we can get details about specific vulnerabilities with Vulners API.

Structure

We will discuss the following topics in this chapter:

- Understanding Docker containers threats and attacks
- Analyzing vulnerabilities in Docker images
- CVE in Docker images
- Getting CVE details with Vulners API

Objectives

After studying this chapter, you will learn about Docker containers threats and attacks, analyzing vulnerabilities in Docker images, and CVE in Docker images. You will also learn about obtaining CVE details with Vulners API.

Docker containers threats and attacks

Nowadays, it is critical to ensure that the images you are running are up-to-date and do not contain software versions with known vulnerabilities. Here are some of the common attacks and threats that containers might suffer:

- **Direct attacks on the kernel** taking advantage of a vulnerability that has not been patched.
- **Denial of Service (DoS) attacks**: The main problem is that the container may monopolize the access to certain resources, such as CPU and memory, resulting in a denial of service.
- **Use of trojanized images**: If an attacker gets someone to execute a trojanized image with malicious code, both the Docker host and the data exposed by it are at risk.

We can see the main vulnerabilities and container attacks related to Docker, organized by category, at:

- `https://www.cvedetails.com/vendor/13534/Docker.html`

The following screenshot shows the main Docker vulnerabilities organized by category:

Docker : Vulnerability Statistics

Products (5)   Vulnerabilities (27)   Search for products of Docker   CVSS Scores Report   Possible matches for this vendor   Related Metasploit Modules

Vulnerability Feeds & Widgets

Vulnerability Trends Over Time

Year	# of Vulnerabilities	DoS	Code Execution	Overflow	Memory Corruption	Sql Injection	XSS	Directory Traversal	Http Response Splitting	Bypass something	Gain Information	Gain Privileges	CSRF	File Inclusion	# of exploits
2014	6		2							1		1			
2015	4										1	1			
2016	2									1		1			
2017	6	3													
2018	2														
2019	7		1					1		1		1			
Total	27	3	3					1		3	1	4			
% Of All		11.1	11.1	0.0	0.0	0.0	0.0	3.7	0.0	11.1	3.7	14.8	0.0	0.0	

Figure 7.1: Docker vulnerabilities organized by category

The following image depicts the main Docker attacks organized by year and type:

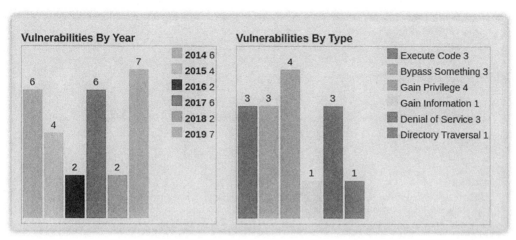

Figure 7.2: Common attacks in Docker containers

The containers will always share the kernel in the Docker host, so the container can exploit any vulnerability in the kernel interface to compromise the Docker host, unless it uses seccomp or apparmor to limit calls between the container and the host. Here are some of the *threats inside the containers*:

- **Denial of Service (DoS)** and **Distributed Denial of Service (DDoS)** attacks
- Containers that attempt to download additional malware or scan internal systems for vulnerabilities or confidential data
- A container that is forced to use system resources in an attempt to block other containers
- The *Dirty Cow* exploits in the Linux kernel allows root privilege escalation on a host or container
- Ransomware attacks on insecure server containers by *MongoDB* and *ElasticSearch* containers
- Buffer overflow vulnerability in specific programming language libraries that allow the execution of malicious code; for example, vulnerabilities such as buffer overflow based on the glibc stack can give control to hackers through man-in-the-middle attacks
- SQL injection attacks allow you to take control of a database container in order to steal data

For example, this type of CVE related to a vulnerability in the **glibc** library is common in some Docker images.

Figure 7.3: CVE related to a vulnerability in the glibc library

We can also check if there is an exploit available for this CVE:

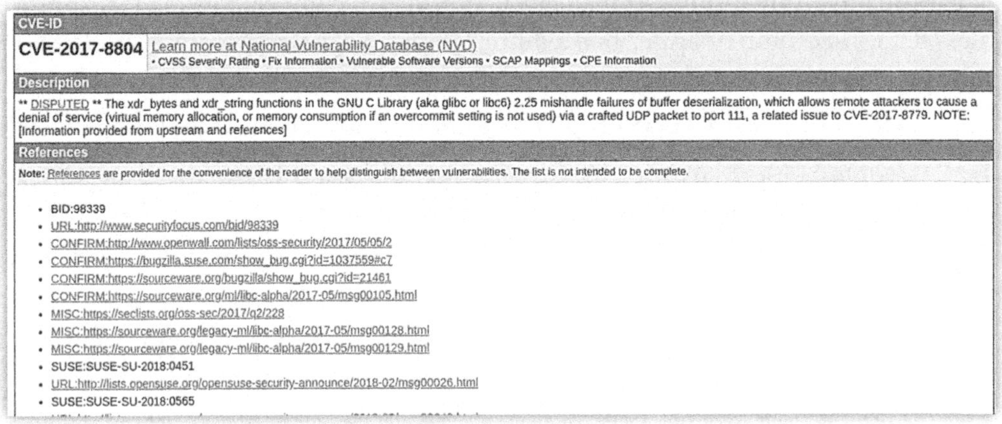

Figure 7.4: Details for CVE-2017-8804 vulnerability

You can find more information about this vulnerability at **https://cve.mitre.org/cgi-bin/cvename.cgi?name=CVE-2017-8804**.

Most vulnerabilities associated with CVE are associated with one or more vulnerabilities. For example, CVE-2015-1781, which is a vulnerability related to a buffer overflow that can be abused in DNS servers and leads to denial of service or arbitrary code execution, may fall into three categories: denial of service, execution code, and buffer overflow.

Buffer overflow is a common vulnerability in web servers that occurs when an application tries to place more data in a buffer that was designed to store. In the case of a buffer overflow, a programmer creates a buffer in the code but does not place restrictions on it. The data must go somewhere, which means adjacent buffers in this case. When data overflows in buffers, the result may be corrupt or overwritten data.

One of the most critical CVEs in Docker discovered in 2019 is **CVE-2019-5736**. This CVE allows attackers to overwrite the host runc binary and, consequently, obtain host root access.

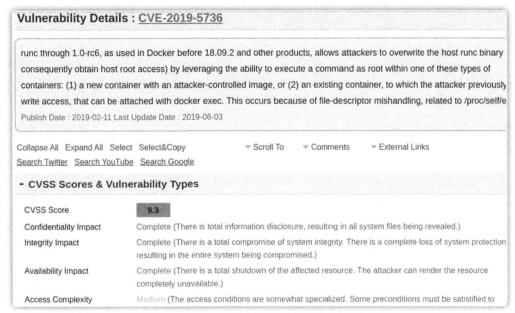

Figure 7.5: CVE-2019-5736 details

This vulnerability was discovered in runc, the utility to run containers of the open container's initiative by which it is possible to obtain root permissions on the host machine.

Only one malicious container that will overwrite the binary runc of the host machine is necessary for the exploitation of this vulnerability. The attack is not blocked by AppArmor's default policy, just like SELinux on systems like Fedora. However, the attack is blocked using the enforcing mode with a correct configuration of namespaces. You can find more information about this vulnerability at **https://www.cvedetails.com/cve/CVE-2019-5736/**.

In this case, the **Common Vulnerability Scoring System** (**CVSS**) is being used to measure and compare threats. The common vulnerability scoring system is based on factors like the attack vector, complexity of the attack, privileges, user interaction, scope, integrity, and the availability of the data at the time of the attack.

For obtaining the level of criticality of vulnerabilities, we can also use metrics like the access vector, the access complexity, authentication, the confidentiality, and the integrity impact. Next, we will look at these metrics in detail:

- **Access vector**: This metric reflects how the vulnerability is exploited. A vulnerability exploitable with network access means the vulnerable software is bound to the network stack, and the attacker does not require local network access. Such vulnerability is often called **exploitable remotely**. An example of a network attack is an RPC buffer overflow.

- **Access complexity**: This metric measures the complexity of the attack required to exploit the vulnerability once an attacker gains access to the target system. For example, consider a buffer overflow in internet service. The attacker could initiate an exploitation process once the target system is located.

- **Authentication**: This metric analyzes the number of times an attacker must authenticate on a target to exploit a vulnerability. It measures that an attacker is required to provide credentials before the vulnerability occurs. The fewer authentication instances required, the higher the vulnerability score.

- **Confidentiality impact**: This metric measures the impact of the confidentiality of a successfully exploited vulnerability. Confidentiality refers to limiting access and disclosure of information to authorized users as well as preventing access by unauthorized persons. The greater the impact of confidentiality, the higher the vulnerability score.

- **Integrity impact**: This metric measures the impact on the integrity of a successfully exploited vulnerability. The greater the impact on integrity, the higher the vulnerability score. For example, if an attacker can modify any file in the target system, at this point, we have a very high score.

Dirty Cow Exploit (CVE-2016-5195)

DirtyCow (CVE-2016-5195) is a privilege escalation vulnerability in the Linux kernel, and it allows any existing user without privileges to perform an elevation of administration privileges.

Change on Write (COW) is a technique used to reduce objects duplication in memory in UNIX systems. When using the race condition, the user with minimal privileges will modify the read-only objects, which should not occur in ideal cases.

The vulnerability used in Dirty Cow is one that exploits the contents of the memory while the kernel is executing system calls to perform actions in the same memory address space.

The vulnerability opens a file that only the root user with read-only permissions has access to and tries to write some content to the file. This is usually denied by the privilege hierarchy, but the exploit allows opening the file in a read-only segment in memory.

The following screenshot shows the versions that are vulnerable, along with the version that would solve the bug:

Name	CVE-2016-5195
Description	Race condition in mm/gup.c in the Linux kernel 2.x through 4.x before 4.8.3 allows local users to gain privileges by leveraging incorrect handling of a copy-on-write (COW) feature to write to a read-only memory mapping, as exploited in the wild in October 2016, aka "Dirty COW."
Source	CVE (at NVD; CERT, LWN, oss-sec, fulldisc, bugtraq, EDB, Metasploit, Red Hat, Ubuntu, Gentoo, SUSE bugzilla/CVE, Mageia, GitHub code/issues, web search, more)
References	DLA-670-1, DSA-3696-1
NVD severity	high

Vulnerable and fixed packages

The table below lists information on source packages.

Source Package	Release	Version	Status
linux (PTS)	stretch	4.9.228-1	fixed
	stretch (security)	4.9.258-1	fixed
	buster	4.19.181-1	fixed
	buster (security)	4.19.171-2	fixed
	bullseye, sid	5.10.28-1	fixed

Figure 7.6: Linux versions affected by DirtyCow

You can find more information at **https://security-tracker.debian.org/tracker/CVE-2016-5195**.

You can find some proofs of concept that allow simulating the behavior of this exploit in the following GitHub repositories:

- `https://github.com/scumjr/dirtycow-vdso`
- `https://github.com/gebl/dirtycow-docker-vdso`
- `https://github.com/dirtycow/dirtycow.github.io/wiki/PoCs`

Link	Usage	Description	Family
dirtyc0w.c	`./dirtyc0w file content`	Read-only write	/proc/self/mem
cowroot.c	`./cowroot`	SUID-based root	/proc/self/mem
dirtycow-mem.c	`./dirtycow-mem`	libc-based root	/proc/self/mem
pokemon.c	`./d file content`	Read-only write	PTRACE_POKEDATA
dirtycow.cr	`dirtycow --target --string --offset`	Read-only write	/proc/self/mem
dirtyc0w.c	`./dirtycow file content`	Read-only write (Android)	/proc/self/mem
dirtycow.rb	`use exploit/linux/local/dirtycow` and run	SUID-based root	/proc/self/mem
0xdeadbeef.c	`./0xdeadbeef`	vDSO-based root	PTRACE_POKEDATA
naughtyc0w.c	`./c0w suid`	SUID-based root	/proc/self/mem
c0w.c	`./c0w`	SUID-based root	PTRACE_POKEDATA
dirty_pass[...].c	`./dirty_passwd_adjust_cow`	/etc/passwd based root	/proc/self/mem

Figure 7.7: Exploit files for DirtyCow

The following repository contains the Dockerfile and the scripts to run it:

- **https://github.com/Alpha-Cybersecurity/dirtyc0w-docker**

This is the content of the Dockerfile we can find in the repository mentioned earlier:

```
FROM ubuntu:12.04


RUN apt-get update

RUN apt-get install -y build-essential


RUN mkdir /dirtycow

COPY dirtyc0w.c /dirtycow/dirtyc0w.c


RUN groupadd -r dcow && useradd --no-log-init -r -g dcow

RUN echo 'dcow:pass' | chpasswd


RUN chown -R dcow:dcow /dirtycow


USER dcow


WORKDIR /dirtycow


RUN gcc -pthread dirtyc0w.c -o dirtyc0w
```

In the previous Dockerfile, we can see that the Dirty COW environment is based on the Ubuntu image. GCC compiler and build-essential packages are prerequisites for the compilation of Dirty COW exploit.

These are the commands we can use for building and executing the Dirty COW container with root privileges:

```
$ docker build -t dirtycow .

$ docker run --privileged --security-opt seccomp=unconfined --secu-
  rity-opt apparmor=unconfined -it dirtycow bash
```

The following screenshot shows the execution of Dirty COW exploit:

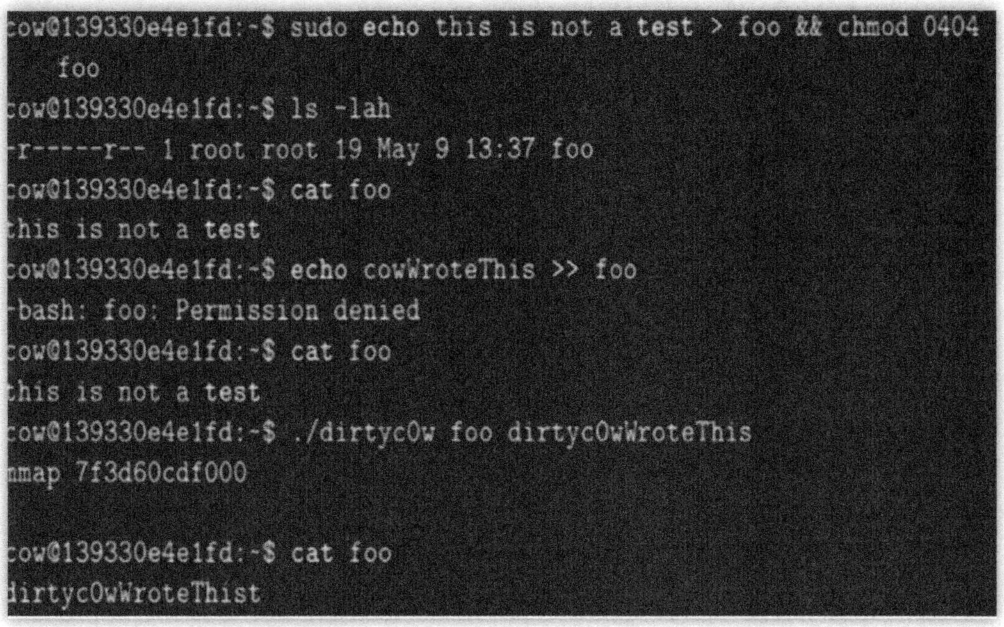

```
cow@139330e4e1fd:~$ sudo echo this is not a test > foo && chmod 0404
   foo
cow@139330e4e1fd:~$ ls -lah
-r-----r-- 1 root root 19 May 9 13:37 foo
cow@139330e4e1fd:~$ cat foo
this is not a test
cow@139330e4e1fd:~$ echo cowWroteThis >> foo
-bash: foo: Permission denied
cow@139330e4e1fd:~$ cat foo
this is not a test
cow@139330e4e1fd:~$ ./dirtyc0w foo dirtyc0wWroteThis
mmap 7f3d60cdf000

cow@139330e4e1fd:~$ cat foo
dirtyc0wWroteThist
```

Figure 7.8: Executing DirtyCow proof of concept

The Dirty COW exploit demonstrates how to write in files as a root user. In this output, we can see that a file is created in read only mode, and we try to write in the file using the Dirty COW binary or exploit.

The vulnerability occurs when opening a file that the root user only has read-only permissions to and writing some content to the file. This is usually rejected by the privilege hierarchy, but the exploit has the capacity to open the file in a read-only memory segment and override the information.

Preventing DirtyCow exploit with apparmor

AppArmor is a security feature that is part of the Linux kernel and is a tool to restrict the capabilities of an application during runtime. If we execute the DirtyCow container with AppArmor enabled, we can cause the exploit to have no effect by establishing restrictions on which applications within the container have permission to read, write, and execute.

```
$ docker run --security-opt apparmor:docker-default -it dcow bash
```

The following screenshot shows the execution of Dirty COW exploit with apparmor enabled:

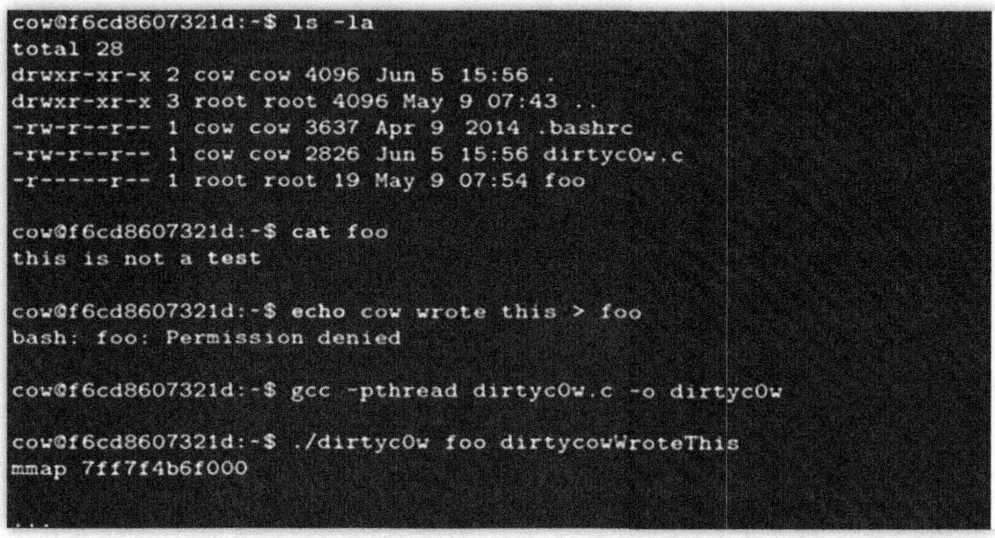

```
cow@f6cd8607321d:~$ ls -la
total 28
drwxr-xr-x 2 cow  cow  4096 Jun 5 15:56 .
drwxr-xr-x 3 root root 4096 May 9 07:43 ..
-rw-r--r-- 1 cow  cow  3637 Apr 9 2014 .bashrc
-rw-r--r-- 1 cow  cow  2826 Jun 5 15:56 dirtyc0w.c
-r-----r-- 1 root root   19 May 9 07:54 foo

cow@f6cd8607321d:~$ cat foo
this is not a test

cow@f6cd8607321d:~$ echo cow wrote this > foo
bash: foo: Permission denied

cow@f6cd8607321d:~$ gcc -pthread dirtyc0w.c -o dirtyc0w

cow@f6cd8607321d:~$ ./dirtyc0w foo dirtycowWroteThis
mmap 7ff7f4b6f000
```

Figure 7.9: Executing DirtyCow with apparmor enabled

Here, we can see that the Dirty COW exploit was stopped using the default apparmor profile. Another possibility is to run containers in read-only mode since the execution of the containers as read-only can prevent an attacker from making changes in the system.

Vulnerability jack in the box (CVE-2018-8115)

This is a remote code execution vulnerability that affects Docker for Windows. This vulnerability is related to the compatibility of Windows Compute Service Shim published and maintained by Microsoft. This service uses a file path as input that would allow an attacker to delete and replace files on the host's file system, which can be the origin of remote code execution.

The vulnerability is due to the fact that the file path in that function is not validated correctly and the destination file can be written to an arbitrary location on the victim's host. The good news is that Docker patched this vulnerability in the Docker CE 18.03.1 and Docker CE 17.05.0-rc1 versions.

Additionally, we can find open source tools that allow you to check images to see if they contain this vulnerability. To do this, the tool downloads an image from the registry, obtains the image layers, and performs a verification of the .tar file for each layer. The script can be found in the following repository:

- `https://github.com/aquasecurity/scan-cve-2018-8115`

Basically, it is a Python script that will connect to the Docker Hub Registry **https:// registry.hub.docker.com** and verify that an image, in any of its layers, has any access level path related to the filesystem that may exploit this vulnerability.

Most vulnerable packages

We will conclude this section by analyzing packages that contain vulnerabilities more frequently in Docker images. The following table shows 10 packages that contain most of the vulnerabilities in the images:

Rank	Package name (Percentage of impacted images)			
	Official	Official :latest	Community	Community :latest
1	glibc (89.81%)	glibc (81.91%)	glibc (84.24%)	glibc (84.82%)
2	util-linux (89.55%)	util-linux (81.91%)	openssl (78.32%)	openssl (78.51%)
3	shadow (89.55%)	shadow (81.91%)	util-linux (77.01%)	util-linux (77.24%)
4	perl (87.29%)	audit (77.66%)	shadow (77.01%)	shadow (77.24%)
5	apt (83.82%)	perl (73.40%)	perl (74.07%)	perl (73.05%)
6	openssl (83.79%)	tar (72.34%)	pam (70.92%)	pam (70.53%)
7	tar (83.58%)	apt (70.21%)	pcre3 (66.54%)	audit (67.10%)
8	openldap (76.85%)	openssl (67.02%)	audit (65.48%)	pcre3 (65.59%)
9	krb5 (76.06%)	systemd (67.02%)	krb5 (64.99%)	dpkg (64.36%)
10	audit (73.51%)	gcc (65.96%)	libidn (64.54%)	libidn (62.93%)

Figure 7.10: Most vulnerable packages

Here, we can see that the **glibc** library contains the most vulnerabilities in the different versions of the images.

In this section, we reviewed some topics like Docker container threats and examples of container attacks like Dirty COW.

Analyzing vulnerabilities in Docker images

An audit process ensures that all containers are based on updated containers and both hosts and containers are configured securely. Here are some of the main features we can validate in an audit process:

- **Isolation and minimum privilege**: The containers are executed with the minimum resources and privileges for their execution. For this, it is important to limit both the memory and the use of CPU and network functions.
- **Limiting memory and CPU**: Limiting the amount of memory available to a container will prevent attackers from consuming all the memory on the host and killing other services. Limiting the use of CPU and the network can prevent attackers from executing denial of service attacks.

- **Access controls**: Linux security modules, such as AppArmor or SELinux, can be used to enforce access controls and limit system calls.

Specific considerations in an audit process:

- Checking that images and packages are updated with the last version.
- Using base file systems in read-only mode will make it easy to find problems.
- Our images should take up as little space as possible. The larger the images, the more difficult the audit will be.
- The kernel of the machine where th e Docker server is running should always be updated since it is the shared point between all the containers running on the same server.

The NVD database, which is managed by the U.S. government, contains the latest vulnerabilities discovered related to the Docker ecosystem.

`https://nvd.nist.gov/vuln/search/results?form_type=Basic&results_type=overview&query=docker&search_type=all`

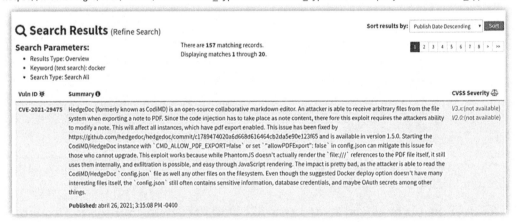

Figure 7.11: National vulnerability database

We can obtain the details of each vulnerability, along with information on how to reproduce and fix this vulnerability.

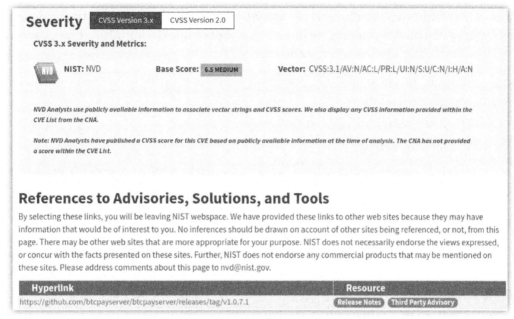

Figure 7.12: *Vulnerability details in NVD*

Security vulnerability classification

MITRE **https://www.mitre.org/** is an agency that provides and maintains a **Common Vulnerabilities and Exposures (CVE)** list of vulnerabilities contained in operating systems and servers. The NVD database, managed by the U.S. government, details the effects for each vulnerability, including its affected code and possible solutions.

NVD assigns a score of 0 to 10 to each vulnerability. Scores of 7-10 are graded as highly critical vulnerability, scores of 4-6 scores as moderate vulnerability, and 0-4 as low vulnerability.

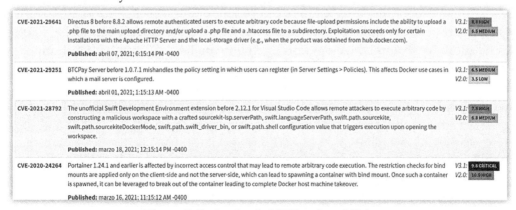

Figure 7.13: *Scoring in NVD vulnerabilities*

This classification considers several factors, including the complexity needed to exploit a system and vulnerability impact. Lower complexity implies a higher score, and greater impact implies a higher score.

Some examples of vulnerabilities classified by level criticality that we can find in Docker images are as follows:

- **High criticality vulnerabilities**:
  - **ShellShock**

    This vulnerability allows an attacker to remotely connect a malicious executable to a variable that is executed when the Bash interpreter is invoked.

  - **Heartbleed http://heartbleed.com**

    This is a critical vulnerability in the *OpenSSL* cryptographic software library and allows an attacker to protect information that is normally sent in encrypted form using the SSL/TLS protocol.

- **Medium criticality vulnerabilities**:
  - **Poodle (OpenSSL) https://www.acunetix.com/blog/web-security-zone/what-is-poodle-attack/**

- **Low criticality vulnerabilities**:
  - **Buffer Overflow**: GCC memory allocations can cause a buffer overflow when accessing memory areas that have not been assigned.

To obtain the latest known vulnerabilities of NVD, a script developed in Python is available in the following GitHub repository:

- `https://github.com/linxack/nvdparser`

The classification of a vulnerability is often subjective, and organizations usually classify them depending on specific configurations or the score given by certain Linux distributions. For example, we can take a reference to the score assigned by a given distribution. For example, we can find the following list for Ubuntu distribution:

- `https://ubuntu.com/security/cve`

Red hat organization also manages its own CVE database available at `https://access.redhat.com/security/security-updates/#/cve`.

Figure 7.14: Red Hat CVE database

Next, we will review a vulnerability that we can find in Alpine Docker images.

Alpine image vulnerability (CVE-2019-5021)

This vulnerability was discovered in the alpine Linux image for versions 3.3, 3.4, 3.5. These versions contain an empty password for the root user. In addition to exploiting the vulnerability, you need to have the Linux-pam authentication package or the shadow package installed on Linux.

- `https://launchpad.net/ubuntu/+source/shadow`
- `https://cve.mitre.org/cgi-bin/cvename.cgi?name=CVE-2019-5021`

The following screenshot shows the details of this vulnerability:

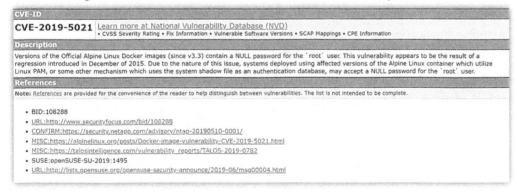

Figure 7.15: Alpine image vulnerability

The following GitHub repository has the script affected for this vulnerability:

https://git.alpinelinux.org/aports/commit/?id=7a2566ec8260ceacae 81088ebe2ffe6526c3809e

We can use the following command to check if version 3.4 is vulnerable since the root user is enabled:

```
$ docker run docker.io/alpine:3.4 cat /etc/shadow | head -n1
```

The following screenshot shows the output of the preceding command:

Figure 7.16: Docker container running version vulnerable

The solution to this problem is to disable root login with the following instruction:

```
RUN sed -i -e 's / ^ root::/ root:!: /' / etc/shadow
```

Here, the character! means the root user cannot log in. We can use the following command to check whether the latest version is vulnerable since the root user is disabled:

```
$ docker run docker.io/alpine:latest cat /etc/shadow | head -n1
```

The following screenshot shows the output of the preceding command:

Figure 7.17: Docker container running version not vulnerable

In this section, we reviewed a specific vulnerability in alpine Docker images and the mitigation for this vulnerability.

CVE in Docker images

We can find CVEs that are directly related to Docker security incidents or issues. Visit **https://www.saucs.com/cve?vendor=docker** to learn more about Docker CVEs or see a list of current Docker CVEs.

We can find CVE vulnerabilities that are directly related to incidents or security issues in Docker in the mentioned URL:

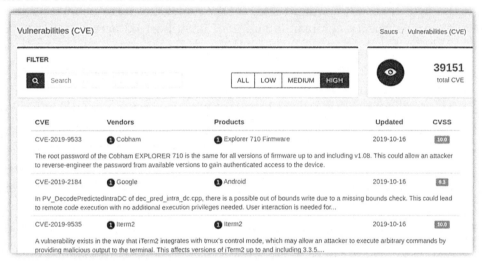

Figure 7.18: Docker CVE database

We can see the details for a specific CVE:

Figure 7.19: CVE details (1)

This list will be updated every time a CVE is detected for a specific version of Docker. As an entity handling and publishing CVEs, MITRE correlates every CVE with the program that is affected by this vulnerability.

When a new vulnerability is discovered, creating a fresh CVE is a way to make it accessible to the public. This CVE includes all the information about the vulnerability as well as an identifier unique for each security vulnerability identified.

Some of the CVEs that we can find within a Docker image are:

- **CVE-2014-6271 https://www.saucs.com/cve/CVE-2014-6271** : Shellshock is a family of security issues in the bash on Unix systems. Many web server implementations use bash to process requests, allowing an attacker to execute arbitrary commands and gain unauthorized access to a computer system.

- **CVE-2014-5282 https://www.saucs.com/cve/CVE-2014-5282** : Docker prior to version 1.3 does not correctly validate image identifiers, allowing remote attackers to redirect to another image by loading untrusted images via 'docker load'.

- **CVE-2014-5280 https://www.saucs.com/cve/CVE-2014-5280** : Boot2docker 1.2 and earlier allows attackers to conduct **Cross-Site Request Forgery (CSRF)** attacks by leveraging Docker daemons enabling TCP connections without TLS authentication.

- **CVE-2014-5279 https://www.saucs.com/cve/CVE-2014-5279** : The Docker daemon managed by boot2docker 1.2 and earlier improperly enables unauthenticated TCP connections by default, which makes it easier for remote attackers to gain privileges or execute arbitrary code from children containers.

- **CVE-2016-6515 https://www.saucs.com/cve/CVE-2016-6515** : Versions prior to 7.3 of OpenSSH do not limit the length of passwords for authentication on SSH servers, which allows a remote attacker to cause a denial of service over a long chain. This error resides in the source code of the `auth-passwd.c` file in the `auth_password` function. An attacker can take advantage of this problem to make the application go into an infinite loop and consume CPU resources until it causes a denial of service.

- **CVE-2014-0160 https://www.saucs.com/cve/CVE-2014-0160**: The Heartbleed error is a vulnerability in the OpenSSL cryptographic software library. This vulnerability compromises the secret keys used to identify service providers and encrypt user traffic, names, and passwords. It is thought that about 17% (half a million) of secure internet web servers certified by trusted authorities are vulnerable to attack, allowing theft of private keys, session passwords, and cookies from servers.

The vulnerability details show the score for each of the metrics that allow us to measure the level of criticality of the vulnerability:

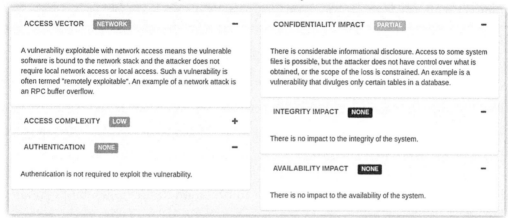

Figure 7.20: CVE details (2)

Tip: Vulnerable containers

We can find containers with latest updates about vulnerabilities at:

- `https://vulnerablecontainers.org/`

- `https://vulnerablecontainers.org/official`

In this section, we have reviewed specific CVE in Docker images. The next section covers how we can get more information about specific vulnerability and CVE details using Vulners API.

Getting CVE details with Vulners API

Vulners database (**https://vulners.com/products**) provides searches, data recovery, archiving, and vulnerability scanning API for integration purposes. It provides an API developed in Python to obtain information about the CVE by identifier, search for available public vulnerabilities, and obtain vulnerabilities by name and software version.

- `https://github.com/vulnersCom/api/blob/master/README.md`

Just run the `pip install` command to install the library:

```
$ pip install -U vulners
```

In addition, we must register on the Vulners website to obtain the *"API KEY"* that allows you to make requests.

The following Python script allows you to search in the Vulners database by specific search criteria; for example, we can search for the Shellshock vulnerability using the `search()` method.

```python
import vulners

vulners_api = vulners.Vulners(api_key="API_KEY")

Shellshock = vulners_api.search("Shellshock", limit=10)

for i, val in enumerate(Shellshock):
    for key,value in val.items():
        print(key,":",value)
```

The output of the previous script shows the information about vulnerabilities related with ShellShock:

```
bulletinFamily : scanner

cvelist : ['CVE-2014-6271']

description : The remote host is running a version of Bash that is
vulnerable to command injection via environment variable manipu-
lation. Depending on the configuration of the system, an attacker
could remotely execute arbitrary code.

modified : 2021-05-02T00:00:00

id : BASH_REMOTE_CODE_EXECUTION.NASL

href : https://www.tenable.com/plugins/nessus/77823

published : 2014-09-24T00:00:00

title : Bash Remote Code Execution (Shellshock)

…..

cvss : {'score': 10.0, 'vector': 'AV:N/AC:L/Au:N/C:C/I:C/A:C'}

vhref : https://vulners.com/nessus/SHELLSHOCK_QMAIL.NASL

lastseen : 2021-05-01T03:16:58

bulletinFamily : scanner

cvelist : ['CVE-2014-6271']
```

```
description : The remote host appears to be running SIP. SIP itself
is not

vulnerable to Shellshock; however, any Bash script that SIP runs
for

filtering or other routing tasks could potentially be affected if the

script exports an environmental variable from the content or head-
ers

of a SIP message.


A negative result from this plugin does not prove conclusively that

the remote system is not affected by Shellshock, only that any
scripts

the SIP proxy may be running do not create the conditions that are

exploitable via the Shellshock flaw.

modified : 2021-05-02T00:00:00

id : SHELLSHOCK_SIP_INVITE.NASL

href : https://www.tenable.com/plugins/nessus/78822

published : 2014-11-03T00:00:00

title : SIP Script Remote Command Execution via Shellshock

...
```

We can also obtain more information about a specific CVE. In the following code we are using the document method from the Vulners API to search for a specific CVE identifier:

```
import vulners

vulners_api = vulners.Vulners(api_key="API_KEY")

CVE_2016_6515 = vulners_api.document("CVE-2016-6515")

print(type(CVE_2016_6515))

for key,value in CVE_2016_6515.items():

        print(key,":",value)
```

In the output of the previous script, we can see information about vulnerability with **CVE-2016-6515**:

```
id : CVE-2016-6515

bulletinFamily : NVD

title : CVE-2016-6515

description : The auth_password function in auth-passwd.c in sshd
in OpenSSH before 7.3 does not limit password lengths for password
authentication, which allows remote attackers to cause a denial of
service (crypt CPU consumption) via a long string.

published : 2016-08-07T21:59:00

modified : 2018-09-11T10:29:00

cvss : {'score': 7.8, 'vector': 'AV:N/AC:L/Au:N/C:N/I:N/A:C'}

href         :        https://web.nvd.nist.gov/view/vuln/detail?vul-
nId=CVE-2016-6515

reporter : cve@mitre.org

references     :       ['http://www.securitytracker.com/id/1036487',
'https://lists.fedoraproject.org/archives/list/package-announce@
lists.fedoraproject.org/message/X2L6RW34VFNXYNVVN2CN73YAG-
J5VMTFU/',        'https://access.redhat.com/errata/RHSA-2017:2029',
'https://lists.debian.org/debian-lts-announce/2018/09/msg00010.
html', 'https://security.FreeBSD.org/advisories/FreeBSD-SA-17:06.
openssh.asc', 'https://support.hpe.com/hpsc/doc/public/display?do-
cLocale=en_US&docId=emr_na-hpesbhf03779en_us', 'http://www.securi-
tyfocus.com/bid/92212',    'https://github.com/openssh/openssh-por-
table/commit/fcd135c9df440bcd2d5870405ad3311743d78d97', 'https://
www.exploit-db.com/exploits/40888/', 'http://www.oracle.com/tech-
network/security-advisory/cpuoct2017-3236626.html', 'http://open-
wall.com/lists/oss-security/2016/08/01/2',    'http://packetstorm-
security.com/files/140070/OpenSSH-7.2-Denial-Of-Service.html',
'https://security.netapp.com/advisory/ntap-20171130-0003/']
```

The Vulners API also allows you to get the references for a specific CVE vulnerability code:

```
import vulners

vulners_api = vulners.Vulners(api_key="API_KEY")

references = vulners_api.references("CVE-2016-6515")

for key,value in references.items():
    for key,val in enumerate(value):
        for key,value in val.items():
            print(key,":",value)
```

You can get further information about the API and more examples in the GitHub repository **https://github.com/vulnersCom/api**.

In this section, we reviewed Vulner API to get more information about vulnerabilities and CVE that are common in Docker images.

Conclusion

This chapter walked the reader through the main vulnerabilities and Docker threats in Docker images and containers. As a result, developers will have the capacity to obtain details about specific CVEs in container applications.

In the next chapter we will review Docker secrets and the essential components of Docker networking, including how we can communicate with and link Docker containers.

Points to remember

- ShellShock is related to how Bash processes environment variables dictated by the operating system or by a program that calls a script. If Bash has been configured as the default shell, it can be used by hackers against servers and other Unix and Linux devices via web, SSH, telnet, or any other program that executes Bash scripts.

- It is important to keep an eye on the images we are deploying for each environment and practice defense in depth. Recommendations could be:

  a. To use containers in production, it should be verified that the application does not currently use vulnerable libraries, and vulnerability exploit does not affect the nature of the application to ensure that future updates of the application do not expose critical information.

  b. The same recommendation can be applied to Docker when using any third-party software; we should only use containers from trusted sources.

Multiple choice questions

1. Which vulnerability exploits the contents of the memory while the kernel is executing system calls to perform actions in the same memory address space?

   a. ShellShock

   b. DirtyCow

   c. Buffer overflow

   d. Heartbleed

2. Which common vulnerability in web servers occurs when an application tries to place more data in a buffer that was designed to store?

   a. ShellShock

   b. DirtyCow

   c. Buffer overflow

   d. Heartbleed

Answer

1	B
2	C

Questions

1. Which metric is used to measure and compare threats and vulnerabilities?

2. Which vulnerability affects Docker containers with root permissions discovered in a utility to run containers of the open containers initiative?

3. Which package is the most frequently used in Docker images and is one of the most vulnerable libraries?

Key terms

- **CVE** is a list of information maintained by the MITRE Corporation **https://www.mitre.org/**, whose objective is to centralize the registry of known security vulnerabilities in which each reference has a CVE-ID identification number. This number provides a standard nomenclature to uniquely identify a vulnerability, description of the vulnerability, possible solution to the security issue, or how to configure to mitigate the vulnerability and references to publications where the vulnerability has been made public.

CHAPTER 8
Managing Docker Secrets and Networking

This chapter introduces Docker secrets and the essential components of Docker networking, including how we can communicate with and link Docker containers. We will also review other concepts like port mapping, which Docker uses for exposing the TCP ports that provide services from the container to the host so that users accessing the host can access a container's services.

When creating applications with containers connected to each other, we must use Docker networks to be able to communicate with the containers. For example, you can create two containers with communication between them through a Docker network if you want to create a blog and need a database and an application server like nginx.

Structure

We will cover the following topics in this chapter:

- Introducing container secrets
- Managing secrets in Docker
- Introducing container networking
- Network managing in Docker

- Containers communication and port mapping
- Creating and managing Docker networks

Objectives

After studying this chapter, you will understand secrets in Docker and learn about container network types, network management in Docker, and container communication and port mapping. You will also learn about creating and managing Docker networks.

Introducing container secrets

Secrets management enables organizations to consistently enforce security policies within applications and ensures that only authenticated and authorized entities can access resources in applications, platforms, and cloud environments.

The following steps are typically included in a secrets management initiative. Many of these approaches and techniques are also used to protect access for those users who have the assigned privileges:

- Authenticate all access requests that use credentials and authentication tokens
- Implement the principle of least privilege
- Enforce **Role-Based Access Control (RBAC)** and regularly rotate secrets and credentials
- Automate the management of secrets and apply access policies to them
- Remove code secrets, configuration files, and other unprotected areas

Effective secrets management enables organizations to remove these secrets that we can sometimes see in configuration files and are used by CI/CD tools, while offering full audit trails, policy-based RBAC, and secrets rotation.

Docker containers need to access security sensitive data, such as usernames and passwords, SSL certificates, SSH private keys, or any other access-restricted information.

In Docker, some of this data is provided through environment variables when launching the containers. This is not a good practice because when making a list of the processes with their invocation parameters, those related to Docker will show this information, which is a possible security issue.

What is a secret?

A secret is a piece of information required for authentication, authorization, and encryption. You can use secrets to manage any sensitive information that a container needs at runtime, but you don't want to store it directly in the image.

With Docker Secrets, you can manage this information that is needed at runtime but does not want to be stored in the Docker image or in the source code repository. Some examples of sensitive information are as follows:

- Usernames and passwords
- TLS certificates and keys
- SSH keys
- The name of a database or internal server

Another use case for using secrets is to provide an abstraction layer between the container and a set of credentials. Consider a scenario where you have separate development, test, and production environments for your application.

Each of these environments can have different credentials, stored in the development, test, and production environments with the same secret name. This way, containers only need to know the name of the secret for working in all three environments.

Managing secrets in Docker

Docker secrets are provided to the containers that need them and transmitted in encrypted form to the node on which they run. Secrets are mounted on the filesystem at the **/run/secrets/<secret_name>** path in a decrypted way and can be accessed by the container service.

Until now, creating a service on swarm means having its configuration within the image, available on all hosts locally or mounted via network storage. That said, secrets can contain files, so we can use them to easily manage the configurations of the services since the information will be available on all the hosts that execute some service task.

It is common that in an image we need to use credentials and access tokens or files with information that we do not want to share. If we pass these elements to the image using commands like **COPY** or **ADD**, they will be visible in the image and anyone who has access to it will be able to see them.

So, it is important to mention that Docker secrets are only available to swarm services, not to standalone containers. That means the secrets can be pushed to containers only when containers are running as a swarm service.

At this point, we can add this information to our containers using the **docker secret** command. The main options that we can use to manage the secrets are:

```
Usage:docker secret COMMAND


Manage Docker secrets


Commands:
  create      Create a secret from a file or STDIN as content

  inspect     Display detailed information on one or more secrets

  ls          List secrets

  rm          Remove one or more secrets
```

Before we start using secrets in Docker, let's look at the downsides of not using it. Here's a **docker-compose** file with the definition of a Postgres service:

```
version: '3.1'

services:

  db:

    image: postgres

    environment:

      POSTGRES_USER: myuser

      POSTGRES_PASSWORD: mysupersecretpassword

      POSTGRES_DB: mydatabase
```

In the previous file, we provided the username, password, and database name for the Postgres service when setting the POSTGRES_USER, POSTGRES_PASSWORD, and POSTGRES_DB environment variables.

The docker secret create command allows you to read standard input where the last argument represents the file from which the secret is read.

We can use this command to create a secret for the username, password, and database by typing the following commands:

```
$ echo "myuser" | docker secret create pg_user -
$ echo "mysupersecretpassword" | docker secret create pg_password -
$ echo "mydatabase" | docker secret create pg_database -
```

Here, we used the **docker secret create** command to create secrets called **pg_user**, **pg_password**, and **pg_database**. The dash "-" at the end of the command lets Docker know that the secret data is being taken from standard input.

Now, we need to modify the file to use the secrets we have created. In the following **docker-compose**, secrets are stored in files in the container's **/run/secrets** path:

```
version: '3.1'
services:
    db:
        image: postgres
        restart: always
        environment:
            POSTGRES_USER_FILE: /run/secrets/pg_user
            POSTGRES_PASSWORD_FILE: /run/secrets/pg_password
            POSTGRES_DB_FILE: /run/secrets/pg_database
        secrets:
            - pg_password
            - pg_user
            - pg_database
secrets:
  pg_user:
    external: true
  pg_password:
    external: true
  pg_database:
    external: true
```

We can use the secrets section to define the names of the secrets using a service stack with a Docker Compose file.

This way, we have to specify new environment variables to read the secrets stored in these files. At the end of the file, we indicate that the secrets are external using **external: true**.

Setting the secret's external field to true instructs **docker-compose** to source its value from your existing Docker secrets. If external is set to true but secrets are not created, then the stack will return an error, indicating that the secret has not been created.

Docker secrets with Docker swarm scenario

In the following scenario, you will learn how to use the Docker Secrets functionality in Swarm Mode to securely manage sensitive information like certificates or passwords.

By default, Docker works as an isolated single-node. All containers are only deployed onto the engine. Swarm Mode turns it into a multi-host cluster-aware engine.

Docker has to be in *"Swarm Mode"* to use the secrets functionality. This is enabled using the following command:

```
$ docker swarm init
Swarm initialized: current node (wygyxcaiagrnlci2v8emp0uef) is now
a manager.
```

Run the following command to add a worker to this swarm manager node:

```
$          docker  swarm  join  --token  SWMTKN-1-2wy41kpais6lw5
7lvjqszc6zwx5546qytrd6bse1cr49n4ur0g-0t6ygj0celx7p5ouauph097e8
172.17.0.29:2377
```

Run '**docker swarm join-token manager**' on Swarm Manager Node and follow the instructions to add a manager to this swarm node. The next step is create a secret using **stdin** with the following command:

```
$ echo "my_secret" | docker secret create mysecret -

06rvgu3vv6evla9nt8ln6gm5e
```

You can view all secret names using the following command:

```
$ docker secret ls
ID              NAME        DRIVER      CREATED       UPDATED
06rvgu3vv6evla9nt8ln6gm5e   mysecret                  47
seconds ago        47 seconds ago
```

We can create a redis service and grant access to the secret. By default, the container can access the secret at the **/run/secrets /<secret_name>** path, and you can customize the name of the file in the container using the destination option.

```
$ docker service create --name="redis" --secret="mysecret" redis

vvophxn8cjcz0pt591ffd5v2k

overall progress: 1 out of 1 tasks

1/1: running

verify: Service converged
```

The secret appears as a file within the secrets directory:

```
$ docker exec $(docker ps --filter name=redis -q) ls -l /run/secrets

total 4

-r--r--r-- 1 root root 10 May  8 15:44 mysecret
```

We can use the following command to read the secret as a regular file from the memory disk:

```
$ docker exec $(docker ps --filter name=redis -q) cat /run/secrets/
mysecret my_secret
```

The secrets functionality is also available using Docker Compose Stacks. The viewer service has access to our Swarm Secret in the following example:

```
version: '3.1'
services:
    viewer:
        image: 'alpine'
        command: 'cat /run/secrets/mysecret'
        secrets:
            - mysecret

secrets:
    mysecret:
        external: true
```

Docker Compose Stacks are deployed using the Docker CLI. As part of the deployment, the stack will be configured with access to the secret. We can deploy the task and access the secret using the following commands:

```
$ docker stack deploy -c docker-compose.yml secrets1
Creating service secrets1_viewer


$ docker logs $(docker ps -aqn1 -f status=exited)
my_secret
```

An alternate way of creating secrets is via files. In this case, we have a **secret.crt** file that needs to be accessed from the container. First, create the **secret.txt** file, as follows:

```
$ echo "my-secret-file" > secret.txt
```

Secondly, update the **docker-compose** Stack to use the file based secret, as shown here:

```
version: '3.1'
services:
    test:
        image: 'alpine'
        command: 'cat /run/secrets/secret_file'
        secrets:
            - secret_file


secrets:
    secret_file:
        file: ./secret.txt
```

Just like earlier, we can deploy the Docker Compose Stack with the following command:

```
$ docker stack deploy -c docker-compose.yml secrets2
Creating network secrets2_default
Creating secret secrets2_secret_file
Creating service secrets2_test
```

The following command will get the log file of the last container to have exited for the newly created service:

```
$ docker logs $(docker ps -aqn1 -f name=secrets2 -f status=exited)
my-secret-file
```

> **Tip: Other secrets solutions**
>
> Vault is a tool for securely accessing secrets. A secret is anything that you want to tightly control access to, such as API keys, passwords, and certificates. Vault provides a unified interface to any secret while providing tight access control and recording a detailed audit log. You can find further details at https://github.com/hashicorp/vault and https://www.katacoda.com/courses/docker-production/vault-secrets.

Introducing container networking

Docker networking is based on Linux's network namespaces, which allows you to generate a complete communications stack for each image running within the Docker host.

When we execute a container or set of containers that form a distributed service, we can use the **--net** option to choose between these network modes.

You can use the default bridge, a different bridge, or not provide access to the network at all with this parameter. Here are examples of ways to use the **--net** option:

- **--net** = **bridge** is the default behavior and creates a new network stack for the container in the Docker bridge called docker0
- **--net** = **none** allows you to execute the container without any network connection
- **--net** = **host** means the container uses the host network stack directly from inside the container
- **--net** = **mycontainer** informs Docker to start the container with the capacity for using the container's network stack

You can execute the following command to see the options Docker provides for managing networks:

```
$ docker network

Usage:  docker network COMMAND

Manage networks

Options:

Commands:
  connect     Connect a container to a network
  create      Create a network
  disconnect  Disconnect a container from a network
  inspect     Display detailed information on one or more networks
  ls          List networks
  prune       Remove all unused networks
  rm          Remove one or more networks


Run 'docker network COMMAND --help' for more information on a
command.
```

You can use the following command to see the networks available in the Docker host:

```
$ docker network ls
```

NETWORK ID	NAME	DRIVER	SCOPE
27969551e219	bridge	bridge	local
fa054a9af353	host	host	local
f50397115ef2	none	null	local

The container does not have any communication with the **–none** network mode, and it is used when the container is not required to have access to the external or internal network. The only IP address you have enabled is loopback or localhost.

```
$ docker run --net=none -it --rm debian

Unable to find image 'debian:latest' locally

latest: Pulling from library/debian

bd8f6a7501cc: Pull complete

Digest:   sha256:ba4a437377a0c450ac9bb634c3754a17b1f814ce6fa3157c-
0dc9eef431b29d1f

Status: Downloaded newer image for debian:latest

root@6f11ae04ecf2:/# ping 127.0.0.1

PING 127.0.0.1 (127.0.0.1) 56(84) bytes of data.

64 bytes from 127.0.0.1: icmp_seq=1 ttl=64 time=0.039 ms

64 bytes from 127.0.0.1: icmp_seq=2 ttl=64 time=0.054 ms

--- 127.0.0.1 ping statistics ---

2 packets transmitted, 2 received, 0% packet loss, time 7ms

rtt min/avg/max/mdev = 0.039/0.046/0.054/0.010 ms

root@6f11ae04ecf2:/# ping google.com

ping: google.com: Temporary failure in name resolution

root@6f11ae04ecf2:/# ping -w3 google.com

ping: google.com: Temporary failure in name resolution
```

In the preceding output, you can see that your container does not have access to the external network. Docker will add the container to a networking group but without a network interface.

The following command executes a bash shell for checking network configuration:

```
$ docker run --net=none -it --rm debian:latest /bin/bash

root@abb4ed18cd14:/# ifconfig

bash: ifconfig: command not found

root@abb4ed18cd14:/# ip a

1: lo: <LOOPBACK,UP,LOWER_UP> mtu 65536 qdisc noqueue state UNKNOWN
group default qlen 1000

    link/loopback 00:00:00:00:00:00 brd 00:00:00:00:00:00

    inet 127.0.0.1/8 scope host lo

        valid_lft forever preferred_lft forever
```

When performing a Docker inspection of a container with this network mode, we can see that we have not assigned an IP address:

```
$ docker inspect <container_id> | grep -i addr

        "LinkLocalIPv6Address": "",

        "SecondaryIPAddresses": null,

        "SecondaryIPv6Addresses": null,

        "GlobalIPv6Address": "",

        "IPAddress": "",

        "MacAddress": "",

            "IPAddress": "",

            "GlobalIPv6Address": "",

            "MacAddress": "",
```

Bridge mode

The bridge mode is the default Docker network mode that allows connectivity with other interfaces in the Docker host and between the containers. When the Docker service daemon starts, it configures a virtual Ethernet device called docker0.

If we start a container based on Debian with this network mode, we can see how we have connectivity with the other containers in the Docker host and external internet connection:

```
$ docker run -it --network=bridge debian:latest /bin/bash

root@565bdff08498:/# ip a

1: lo: <LOOPBACK,UP,LOWER_UP> mtu 65536 qdisc noqueue state UNKNOWN
group default qlen 1000

    link/loopback 00:00:00:00:00:00 brd 00:00:00:00:00:00

    inet 127.0.0.1/8 scope host lo

       valid_lft forever preferred_lft forever

4: eth0@if5: <BROADCAST,MULTICAST,UP,LOWER_UP>  mtu  1500  qdisc
noqueue state UP group default

    link/ether 02:42:ac:12:00:02 brd ff:ff:ff:ff:ff:ff link-netnsid 0

    inet 172.18.0.2/24 brd 172.18.0.255 scope global eth0

       valid_lft forever preferred_lft forever
```

We can check the connectivity with external network using a simple **ping** command:

```
root@565bdff08498:/# ping google.com

PING google.com (172.217.23.110) 56(84) bytes of data.

64 bytes from mil04s23-in-f110.1e100.net (172.217.23.110): icmp_
seq=1 ttl=117 time=5.03 ms

64 bytes from mil04s23-in-f110.1e100.net (172.217.23.110): icmp_
seq=2 ttl=117 time=5.07 ms

64 bytes from mil04s23-in-f110.1e100.net (172.217.23.110): icmp_
seq=3 ttl=117 time=5.11 ms

--- google.com ping statistics ---

3 packets transmitted, 3 received, 0% packet loss, time 5ms

rtt min/avg/max/mdev = 5.029/5.068/5.106/0.031 ms
```

The output of the bridge network can be similar to the following:

```
$ docker network inspect bridge
[
    {
        "Name": "bridge",
        "Id": "27969551e2199a5837418f503adee5bc9ef3f8bb4  a6fd4d-
            251b13792e99421f6",
        "Created": "2021-05-09T16:24:55.8084154212",
        "Scope": "local",
        "Driver": "bridge",
        "EnableIPv6": false,
        "IPAM": {
            "Driver": "default",
            "Options": null,
            "Config": [
                {
                    "Subnet": "172.18.0.1/24",
                    "Gateway": "172.18.0.1"
                }
            ]
        },
        "Internal": false,
        "Attachable": false,
        "Ingress": false,
        "ConfigFrom": {
            "Network": ""
        },
        "ConfigOnly": false,
        "Containers": {},
        "Options": {
            "com.docker.network.bridge.default_bridge": "true",
            "com.docker.network.bridge.enable_icc": "true",
            "com.docker.network.bridge.enable_ip_masquerade": "true",
            "com.docker.network.bridge.host_binding_ipv4": "0.0.0.0",
```

```
            "com.docker.network.bridge.name": "docker0",
            "com.docker.network.driver.mtu": "1500"
        },
        "Labels": {}
    }
]
```

In the preceding output, we can see that bridge mode is using docker0 interface and provides an internal host network in which the containers on the same host can communicate. However, the IP addresses assigned for each container are not accessible from outside the Docker host.

For instance, we can have two containers connected to the bridge docker0 interface. With the following commands we are generating two bridge-based nginx servers with IP addresses 172.17.0.2 and 172.17.0.3:

```
$ docker run -d --name nginx-1 -p 10000:80 nginx
Unable to find image 'nginx:latest' locally
latest: Pulling from library/nginx
f7ec5a41d630: Pull complete
aa1efa14b3bf: Pull complete
b78b95af9b17: Pull complete
c7d6bca2b8dc: Pull complete
cf16cd8e71e0: Pull complete
0241c68333ef: Pull complete
Digest:        sha256:75a55d33ecc73c2a242450a9f1cc858499d468f077ea
942867e662c247b5e412
Status: Downloaded newer image for nginx:latest
637c96acee4c2274d5d18cbb182c418abf7a28edbfa67f8ec2fec45287605c69
$  docker run -d --name nginx-2 -p 10001:80 nginx
08a4ecc6ecf1eb55a39cdce94e143032148a8d004ff0e0b09fa7104513c75363
$ docker ps
```

CONTAINER ID	IMAGE	COMMAND	CREATED
STATUS	PORTS	NAMES	
08a4ecc6ecf1	nginx	"/docker-entrypoint.…" 6	
seconds ago	Up 5 seconds	0.0.0.0:10001->80/tcp nginx-2	
637c96acee4c	nginx	"/docker-entrypoint.…" 17	
seconds ago	Up 16 seconds	0.0.0.0:10000->80/tcp nginx-1	

We can check the IP address for each container using the following commands:

```
$ docker inspect <container_id> | grep -i addr

$ docker inspect 08a4ecc6ecf1 | grep -i addr
            "LinkLocalIPv6Address": "",

            "SecondaryIPAddresses": null,

            "SecondaryIPv6Addresses": null,

            "GlobalIPv6Address": "",

            "IPAddress": "172.18.0.3",

            "MacAddress": "02:42:ac:12:00:03",

                "IPAddress": "172.18.0.3",

                "GlobalIPv6Address": "",

                "MacAddress": "02:42:ac:12:00:03",

$ docker inspect 637c96acee4c | grep -i addr
            "LinkLocalIPv6Address": "",

            "SecondaryIPAddresses": null,

            "SecondaryIPv6Addresses": null,

            "GlobalIPv6Address": "",

            "IPAddress": "172.18.0.2",

            "MacAddress": "02:42:ac:12:00:02",

                "IPAddress": "172.18.0.2",

                "GlobalIPv6Address": "",

                "MacAddress": "02:42:ac:12:00:02",
```

We can see the IP address and the gateway IP address for each container when executing Docker inspect. In the following output, we can see the network configuration for the **nginx-1** container:

```
$ docker inspect <container_id_nginx-1>
```

```
"Networks": {

                "bridge": {

                        "IPAMConfig": null,

                        "Links": null,

                        "Aliases": null,

                        "NetworkID":"56f80d202b941a17615f6b2a181e9c7b-
                        bea3a263c7c56dcd4277a25376d424fe",

                        "EndpointID": "82a37df6284e4e2c67e934d-
                        935f7e5911e8013a7afd4ee1ad12225d21ec9df41",

                        "Gateway": "172.18.0.1",

                        "IPAddress": "172.18.0.2",

                        "IPPrefixLen": 24,

                        "IPv6Gateway": "",

                        "GlobalIPv6Address": "",

                        "GlobalIPv6PrefixLen": 0,

                        "MacAddress": "02:42:ac:12:00:02",

                        "DriverOpts": null

                }

        }
```

In the following output, we can see the network configuration for nginx-2 container:

```
$ docker inspect <container_id_nginx-2>
"Networks": {

                "bridge": {

                        "IPAMConfig": null,

                        "Links": null,

                        "Aliases": null,
```

"NetworkID": "56f80d202b941a17615f6b2a181e9c7b-bea3a263c7c56dcd4277a25376d424fe",

"EndpointID": "75d026150c40e241c64ccfc8a18985d-31833c939e27b5667ddbf4a7cfb92056d",

"Gateway": "172.18.0.1",

"IPAddress": "172.18.0.3",

"IPPrefixLen": 24,

"IPv6Gateway": "",

"GlobalIPv6Address": "",

"GlobalIPv6PrefixLen": 0,

"MacAddress": "02:42:ac:12:00:03",

"DriverOpts": null

    }

  }

In the preceding output, we saw that both containers share the same gateway IP address at **172.18.0.1**. Here are some of the main advantages of this mode:

- Each container runs in its own private network namespace that is separate from the Docker host
- It allows containers to run on the same Docker host without port conflicts

We have reviewed the bridge type Docker network, but sometimes we don't want to use the Docker network and directly use our host's network. We can do this using the **--net = host** argument when we deploy our container.

Host mode

In this type of network, all network interfaces defined on the Docker host will be accessible to the container, and the container shares the host's network namespace. You must execute the container with the flag **--net = host** to use the host network:

```
$ docker run -ti --net=host debian /bin/sh
```

Host mode allows us to share the namespace of the host network with the container. The following output shows network connections inside the container:

```
# ip a
1: lo: <LOOPBACK,UP,LOWER_UP> mtu 65536 qdisc noqueue state UNKNOWN
group default qlen 1000
    link/loopback 00:00:00:00:00:00 brd 00:00:00:00:00:00
    inet 127.0.0.1/8 scope host lo
        valid_lft forever preferred_lft forever
    inet6 ::1/128 scope host
        valid_lft forever preferred_lft forever
2: ens3: <BROADCAST,MULTICAST,UP,LOWER_UP> mtu 1500 qdisc fq_codel
state UP group default qlen 1000
    link/ether 02:42:ac:11:00:2f brd ff:ff:ff:ff:ff:ff
    inet 172.17.0.47/16 brd 172.17.255.255 scope global noprefixroute
    ens3
        valid_lft forever preferred_lft forever
    inet6 fe80::4471:5722:a9c5:903a/64 scope link
        valid_lft forever preferred_lft forever
3:  docker0:  <NO-CARRIER,BROADCAST,MULTICAST,UP>  mtu  1500  qdisc
noqueue state DOWN group default
    link/ether 02:42:e3:eb:3f:80 brd ff:ff:ff:ff:ff:ff
    inet 172.18.0.1/24 brd 172.18.0.255 scope global docker0
        valid_lft forever preferred_lft foreve
```

Since a container is just a process that runs on a host, the simplest option seems to connect it to the host's network namespace. The container will behave from the network point of view, just like any other process that runs on the host. So, it will use the host's IP address and the host's TCP port namespace to expose the service running inside the container.

For example, we can run an **nginx** container in host mode with the following command:

```
$ docker run -d --name nginx-1 -p 8080:80 --net=host nginx /bin/sh
```

This command executes an NGINX container web server that is listening on port 80 on the Docket host. Imagine trying to run another web server on the same host later. Unless otherwise indicated, our second container will probably try to connect on the same port. But the second container cannot be started since port 80 is now being used by our first container.

The main advantages of this mode are:

- Easy configuration to use
- It does not perform any operation on incoming traffic, so performance is not affected

We also have some disadvantages when using host mode:

- Without an additional dynamic port assignment mechanism, services can collide at the port level
- The dynamic port allocation must be managed by a container orchestration platform like Kubernetes or Docker Swarm
- Containers share the namespace of the host network, which may have security implications. Containers that are in running state will be exposed if our Docker host is exposed to some vulnerability

Network managing in Docker

As we saw in the previous section, Docker offers us three different types of networks. The bridge is the network type loaded by default by all containers, and it is a network that creates a bridge between the network interface of the container and a virtual network interface created on our computer when we install Docker.

The host mode copies the host network configuration, and we can see the same network configuration in the Docker host if we execute a container with this mode.

Docker networking

Docker uses an ethernet bridge to allow the Docker daemon to communicate with the Docker host network device. A container that connects to another container with an exposed port can communicate with the exposed port. You can assign a container port to a port on the host to make a port accessible outside the container. Now, it is important to know that you need to expose and publish the port for it to be accessed from outside the Docker host network.

For example, if you expose a port, the service in the container is only accessible from inside other Docker containers. So, this feature provides inter-container communication. The service in the container is accessible from outside the internal network if you expose and publish a port.

Here are some of the network configurations that can be established when we execute a container:

- `--dns:` A DNS server is what resolves a domain to the IP address of the server running the domain

- **`--dns-search:`** Sets up DNS search servers
- **`-h:`** This option establishes the hostname that will be added as an entry in the **`/etc/hosts`** file
- **`--link:`** Allows a container to communicate with other containers without knowing their real IP addresses
- **`--expose:`** Exposes the container port without publishing it to the Docker host
- **`--publish-all:`** Allows the publishing of all ports exposed to host interfaces
- **`--publish:`** Lets you publish the port of a container in the Docker host using the following formats:
  - ip:hostPort:containerPort
  - ip::containerPort
  - hostPort:containerPort
- **`--net:`** This option allows you to configure the network mode for the container and can contain four values:
  - **`bridge:`** This creates a network stack for the container in bridge mode
  - **`none:`** The container will be totally isolated and cannot communicate with any other container
  - **`container <name|id>:`** Uses the network stack of another container
  - **`host:`** Uses the host Docker network stack

Containers communication and port mapping

When we add a container to a network, all ports are open for machines that are within the same network and closed for an external connection by default. For example, we need not expose MySQL container ports as they are on the same network as the application container and can connect through the port without a problem. However, we won't be able to access the MYSQL port from outside the network unless we publish it.

Configuring port forwarding between containers and Docker host

Port forwarding is the easiest way to expose the services that are running in containers. There are two ways to start a container with this feature:

- **-P [--publish-all]**: When starting a container with this option, all the ports that were exposed using the EXPOSE statement will be published in the Dockerfile. This option selects a random free port on the host server where requests will be listened to.

- **-p [--publish]**: This option allows you to explicitly indicate to Docker which port should be linked to a port in a container. With this option, we must manually specify a port where we want to listen. The container will fail if that port is in use. There are three ways to use this option:
  - $ docker run -p ip:host_port: container_port
  - $ docker run -p ip::container_port
  - $ docker run -p host_port:container_port

Adding an **EXPOSE** instruction inside a Dockerfile allows you to indicate that a specific port must be exposed from the image it builds. A port exposed in a running container image allows two things to happen:

- **Linked containers**: Once you run the image, the exposed port will be available to the other container as if it were available on the same local system if you link the running container to another container.

- **Runtime exposure**: Any port identified with an **EXPOSE** statement when the image is built can easily be exposed from the same port number on the localhost. You can use the **-p** option in **docker run** on the image to assign any port exposed to it or to a different specific port on the localhost. All ports exposed from the container are assigned to random ports on the host system if you use the **-P** option in **docker run**. You can then run the **docker port** command in the resulting container to see how the ports are mapped.

From a container point of view, you can provide an IP-based web server to other containers or applications. You can expose the port used by the web server to do this. For example, an nginx server container can expose ports 80 and 443, as in the following Dockerfile:

```
FROM ubuntu:20.04

MAINTAINER Your Name <you@myapp.com>


RUN apt-get update && apt-get install -y nano htop git nginx


ADD nginx.conf /etc/nginx/nginx.conf
```

```
ADD api.myapp.conf /etc/nginx/sites-enabled/api.myapp.conf

ADD app.myapp.conf /etc/nginx/sites-enabled/app.myapp.conf

ADD Nginx-Startup.sh /etc/nginx/Nginx-Startup.sh


EXPOSE 80 443


CMD ["/bin/bash","/etc/nginx/Nginx-Startup.sh"]
```

For any practical implementation when dealing with ports, it is recommended to use port publication using the **-p** parameter to publish these ports. For example, the **nginx** container will be available on port 8080 in the Docker host if you want it on port 80. You need to execute the following command:

```
$ docker run --name docker-nginx -p 8080:80 -d nginx

9e33650715b4992dd065939ce7993635319b76c5e8fe9d48df59e4f8271af583

$ docker ps

CONTAINER ID        IMAGE           COMMAND                     CREATED
STATUS              PORTS                NAMES

9e33650715b4          nginx               "/docker-entrypoint.…"   4
seconds ago      Up 3 seconds     0.0.0.0:8080->80/tcp   docker-
nginx
```

The **-p 8080:80** option parameter indicates that port 8080 on the Docker host points to port 80 inside the container. This way, we can access port 8080 of the Docker host to display the server's welcome page:

```
$ curl docker:8080

<!DOCTYPE html>

<html>

<head>

<title>Welcome to nginx!</title>

<style>
```

```
    body {
        width: 35em;
        margin: 0 auto;
        font-family: Tahoma, Verdana, Arial, sans-serif;
    }
</style>
</head>
<body>
<h1>Welcome to nginx!</h1>
<p>If you see this page, the nginx web server is successfully in-
stalled and

working. Further configuration is required.</p>


<p>For online documentation and support please refer to
<a href="http://nginx.org/">nginx.org</a>.<br/>
Commercial support is available at
<a href="http://nginx.com/">nginx.com</a>.</p>


<p><em>Thank you for using nginx.</em></p>
</body>
</html>
```

We used port exposure, which consists of reserving a port on the Docker server to redirect requests to a specific port.

We can use the following command to verify the network configuration of this container:

```
$ docker inspect docker-nginx
```

....

```
"NetworkSettings": {

        "Bridge": "",

        "SandboxID": "f941e26014e0a24b63f695e1b4823c957caf1eb-
                      b850a2e9d0d50191e576f5123",

        "HairpinMode": false,

        "LinkLocalIPv6Address": "",

        "LinkLocalIPv6PrefixLen": 0,

        "Ports": {

            "80/tcp": [

                {

                        "HostIp": "0.0.0.0",

                        "HostPort": "8080"

                }

            ]

        },
```

....

We have performed a manual mapping here. Docker provides the `-P` flag to automatically assign a port to our application:

```
$ docker run --name docker-nginx -P -d nginx
```

```
$ docker ps
```

CONTAINER ID	IMAGE	COMMAND	CRE-
ATED	STATUS	PORTS	NAMES
073494b577dc	nginx	"/docker-entrypoint.…"	27
seconds ago	Up 25 seconds	0.0.0.0:32768->80/tcp	dock-
er-nginx			

This way, we can see how the **-P** flag automatically assigns the port with the mapping 32768:80. We can verify this port mapping configuration by inspecting **NetworkSettings**:

```
$ docker inspect docker-nginx

….

"NetworkSettings": {

        "Bridge": "",

        "SandboxID": "35f6de7fc9d60af2a5ea20a6c9d20204de8ebad6b8c-
        f983a731da37cfdc9c594",

        "HairpinMode": false,

        "LinkLocalIPv6Address": "",

        "LinkLocalIPv6PrefixLen": 0,

        "Ports": {

            "80/tcp": [

                {

                        "HostIp": "0.0.0.0",

                        "HostPort": "32768"

                }

            ]

        },

…..
```

This simple port mapping is enough for the most common use cases in Docker. We will now be able to install services or microservices as Docker containers and expose their ports to enable communication.

Creating and managing Docker networks

Docker also lets you create your own network configuration to use in your Docker containers. Docker allows us to create different virtual networks for our needs or segment different containers. This way, we can separate containers in different networks or by connecting their services to each other.

Docker network commands

A list of commands can be used with Docker networking:

```
$ docker network

Usage:  docker network COMMAND

Manage networks

Options:

Commands:
  connect       Connect a container to a network
   create          Create a network
  disconnect  Disconnect a container from a network
  inspect       Display detailed information on one or more networks
  ls                 List networks
  prune           Remove all unused networks
  rm                 Remove one or more networks

Run 'docker network COMMAND --help' for more information on a command.
```

We can execute the following command when creating the network to see all the options:

```
$ docker network create --help

Usage:  docker network create [OPTIONS] NETWORK

Create a network

Options:
    --attachable          Enable manual container attachment
```

--aux-address map	Auxiliary IPv4 or IPv6 addresses used by Network driver (default map[])
--config-from string	The network from which copying the configuration
--config-only	Create a configuration only network
-d, --driver string	Driver to manage the Network (default "bridge")
--gateway strings	IPv4 or IPv6 Gateway for the master subnet
--ingress	Create swarm routing-mesh network
--internal	Restrict external access to the network
--ip-range strings	Allocate container ip from a sub-range
--ipam-driver string	IP Address Management Driver (default "default")
--ipam-opt map	Set IPAM driver specific options (default map[])
--ipv6	Enable IPv6 networking
--label list	Set metadata on a network
-o, --opt map	Set driver specific options (default map[])
--scope string	Control the network's scope
--subnet strings	Subnet in CIDR format that represents a network segment

In the next section, we will look at how to create a network in detail.

Creating a network

A bridge network is Docker's most frequent network type. We can create our own network for the purpose we need; for example, having a subnet in a **Demilitarized Zone** (**DMZ**). We will create a bridge docker network with the following command:

Execute the following command to do this:

```
$ docker network create --subnet 10.10.1.0/24 dmz

62373bbbc2bb4f35ca04c0614f3737f1f5195e96545c8035a7a85d84e9d48a4f

$ docker network ls

NETWORK ID          NAME                DRIVER              SCOPE

8c8ec10f902b        bridge              bridge              local

62373bbbc2bb        dmz                 bridge              local

fa054a9af353        host                host                local

f50397115ef2        none                null                local
```

We can see the network configuration with the following command:

```
$ docker network inspect dmz
[
    {
        "Name": "dmz",
        "Id": "62373bbbc2bb4f35ca04c0614f3737f1f5195e-
            96545c8035a7a85d84e9d48a4f",
        "Created": "2021-05-10T17:39:19.5749642627",
        "Scope": "local",
        "Driver": "bridge",
        "EnableIPv6": false,
        "IPAM": {
            "Driver": "default",
            "Options": {},
            "Config": [
                {
                    "Subnet": "10.10.1.0/24"
                }
            ]
        },
        "Internal": false,
```

```
        "Attachable": false,
        "Ingress": false,
        "ConfigFrom": {
            "Network": ""
        },
        "ConfigOnly": false,
        "Containers": {},
        "Options": {},
        "Labels": {}
    }
]
```

We can see the subnet configuration here. Next, we will connect a container to this network.

Connecting a container to a network

In order to connect a container to a network, we must use the **--network** option to specify which network we want to connect it to, followed by the name of the network to which we want to add it.

For example, we can use the following command to run an **nginx** container and add it to the network we have just created:

```
$ docker container run -d --name docker-nginx --network dmz nginx
```

After connecting a container to a network, we can see its configuration by inspecting the configuration of the container with the following command:

```
$ docker network inspect dmz
```
……...

```
"Containers": {
        "f8aeeedaa2f72a28c1cfa891e734d81001f5b6d6d477d1290d5500a254d5a-
        f3a": {
            "Name": "docker-nginx2",
            "EndpointID": "09922e28ace9417e9c41338414a70fb-
                1d0514454a810673d14655234ac8ad405",
```

```
        "MacAddress": "02:42:0a:0a:01:02",

        "IPv4Address": "10.10.1.2/24",

        "IPv6Address": ""

    }

},
```

....

The following command is another way to connect a container to a network:

```
$ docker network connect <network_id> <container_id>
```

At this point, we have reviewed how to create new networks in Docker and connect new containers that can communicate with each other.

Linking containers

When a container node is created, it is necessary to note that these containers can be connected to each other by IP address or hostname. But if a container is restarted, new parameters are generated, such as the ID and the IP address it uses.

To solve this problem, Docker offers the functionality of linking one or more containers that allows each time one of the linked containers is restarted, the assigned IP address does not change as it is assigned by the container name.

We'll see how to establish links between containers using this linking system where one container acts as a data source and the other acts as the receiver.

The link allows a container to communicate with another container without knowing its IP address. The **--link** flag must be used when creating a container to link containers.

When using the **--link** flag, Docker adds an entry in the **/etc/hosts** file of the container, with the hostname, IP address, and the container identifier with which you are linking.

We can create an **nginx** container with the following command:

```
$ docker run -d --name docker-nginx nginx
```

Next, we can create an Ubuntu container using the link tag to connect this container with the **docker-nginx** we created earlier:

```
$ docker run -it --name ubuntu --link docker-nginx ubuntu:20.04 bash
```

After executing the preceding command, we can check how we have connectivity between Ubuntu and docker-nginx containers. The following output shows the content of the **etc/hosts** file inside the Ubuntu container:

```
root@08e201c2e992:/# cat /etc/hosts

127.0.0.1        localhost

::1      localhost ip6-localhost ip6-loopback

fe00::0 ip6-localnet

ff00::0 ip6-mcastprefix

ff02::1 ip6-allnodes

ff02::2 ip6-allrouters

172.18.0.2       docker-nginx 3ed36821081b

172.18.0.3       08e201c2e992
```

When we create a link, Docker is responsible for updating the **/etc/hosts** file to access the container on which we establish the link. If we go to the contents of the **/etc/hosts** file of the Ubuntu container, we can see the reference to the **docker-nginx** container.

In addition to modifying the **/etc/hosts** file, Docker creates some environment variables with the information of the other container (docker-nginx) in the container where we establish the link (Ubuntu). The information that Docker makes available using environment variables includes the IP address of the linked container.

For example, we can see all variables related to **docker-nginx** if we look at all the environment variables of the Ubuntu container:

```
root@08e201c2e992:/# set | grep -i nginx

DOCKER_NGINX_ENV_NGINX_VERSION=1.19.10

DOCKER_NGINX_ENV_NJS_VERSION=0.5.3

DOCKER_NGINX_ENV_PKG_RELEASE=1~buster

DOCKER_NGINX_NAME=/ubuntu/docker-nginx
```

```
DOCKER_NGINX_PORT=tcp://172.18.0.2:80

DOCKER_NGINX_PORT_80_TCP=tcp://172.18.0.2:80

DOCKER_NGINX_PORT_80_TCP_ADDR=172.18.0.2

DOCKER_NGINX_PORT_80_TCP_PORT=80

DOCKER_NGINX_PORT_80_TCP_PROTO=tcp

root@08e201c2e992:/#
```

As we see, all the information in the **docker-nginx** container is available in the Ubuntu container, so we can access and discover the services of another container using the environment variables.

In the following example, we are creating a container based on the image of Redis and linking it with a container based on Debian Linux distribution. First, we will create a redis container with the name myredis:

```
$ docker run -d --name myredis redis

fd71f0154881d63da31e72bc4448cfac30d486f7c4079615cc6f7a3cbf6597de
```

Next, we will link the **redis** and **debian** containers:

```
$ docker run --link myredis:redis debian env

Unable to find image 'debian:latest' locally

latest: Pulling from library/debian

bd8f6a7501cc: Pull complete

Digest:    sha256:ba4a437377a0c450ac9bb634c3754a17b1f814ce6fa3157c-
0dc9eef431b29d1f

Status: Downloaded newer image for debian:latest

PATH=/usr/local/sbin:/usr/local/bin:/usr/sbin:/usr/bin:/sbin:/bin

HOSTNAME=a7d271b2af8c

REDIS_PORT=tcp://172.18.0.3:6379

REDIS_PORT_6379_TCP=tcp://172.18.0.3:6379
```

```
REDIS_PORT_6379_TCP_ADDR=172.18.0.3
```

```
REDIS_PORT_6379_TCP_PORT=6379
```

```
REDIS_PORT_6379_TCP_PROTO=tcp
```

```
REDIS_NAME=/vigorous_montalcini/redis
```

```
REDIS_ENV_GOSU_VERSION=1.10
```

```
REDIS_ENV_REDIS_VERSION=4.0.8
```

```
REDIS_ENV_REDIS_DOWNLOAD_URL=http://download.redis.io/releases/
redis-4.0.8.tar.gz
```

```
REDIS_ENV_REDIS_DOWNLOAD_SHA=ff0c38b8c156319249fec61e5018cf5b5fe-
63a65b61690bec798f4c998c232ad
```

```
HOME=/root
```

In the preceding output, we can see that Docker has configured environment variables with the prefix **REDIS_PORT** inside the Debian container, which contains information on how to connect to the Redis container.

Docker has also imported environment variables from the linked container with the prefix **REDIS_ENV**. While this functionality can be very useful, it is important to keep in mind that using environment variables to store secrets such as API tokens or database passwords can increase the risk of this data being exposed in other containers.

Conclusion

In this chapter, we reviewed how networks are configured in Docker containers that should not be disconnected from other systems, whether physical, virtual, or in containers. You learned about the main types of Docker networks and how to link containers to each other by creating your own Docker network.

Thanks to the use of the Docker networks; we can create more complex applications, where each container offers a service that works autonomously and the containers can communicate with each other. This is why Docker provides commands for managing Docker networks.

Regarding working with Docker secrets, you can manage the information that is needed in the containers at runtime but that you do not want to store in the Docker image or in the application source code repository.

In the next chapter, we will review open-source tools available for Docker container monitoring, like cadvisor, dive, and sysdig Falco.

Points to remember

- Docker provides three types of networks to manage communications, both within and between containers: bridge, host, and none.
- The bridge network is used to communicate independent applications between containers, the host network is used to eliminate the network isolation of the container and use the network of the Docker host, and none allows you to disable all network functions in the container.
- By default, containers are connected to the bridge network when they are created, which means that each of them is assigned a virtual interface and private IP address. So, the traffic that passes through the main interface connects to the docker0 interface from the host.
- We can also open a specific port inside the container to the outside using the **-p** flag to expose networking through the container onto the Docker host.
- You can connect a container to an available Docker network with the **docker network connect <network_name> <container_id>** command.

Multiple choice questions

1. Which is the default Docker network mode that will allow connectivity with the other interfaces of the host machine and between the containers?

   a. Bridge mode

   b. Host mode

   c. Container mode

   d. Proxy mode

2. Which command allows you to connect a container to an available network?

   a. docker network connect <container_id> <network_name>

   b. docker connect network <network_name> <container_id>

   c. docker network connect <network_name> <container_id>

   d. docker connect network <container_id> <network_name>

Answers

1	a
2	c

Questions

1. In which type of network will all network interfaces defined on the host be accessible to the container and the container shares the host's network namespace?

2. Which flag allows you to explicitly indicate to Docker which port should be linked to a port in a container?

3. Which Dockerfile instruction allows you to indicate that a specific port must be exposed from the image it builds?

Key terms

- You can use Docker secrets to centrally manage this data and transmit it securely to only those containers that need access to it. A secret is only accessible to the services to which explicit access has been granted and only while those service tasks are running.

- The type network none removes all the network configuration from our container if we establish it. We only have available the loopback address 127.0.0.1 with no external connection.

- We can use the **EXPOSE** keyword in a Dockerfile to define a port that will be exposed from the container to the Docker host.

- For example, we can make the instance of an nginx server accessible from outside the container. To do this, we need to add the **-p (-publish)** flag when executing the container.

  a. `-p <hostport>: <container_port>`

  b. `docker run -d -p 8080:8080 nginx`

- Docker provides some commands for creating and managing our own network:

  a. `$ docker network inspect:` This command lets you know the resources used by a network as well as its configuration

  b. `$ docker network ls:` It shows a list of the networks that Docker has created

  c. `$ docker network create:` It allows you to create your own network: bridge or overlay. Containers can communicate within their network but not through networks

CHAPTER 9
Docker Container Monitoring

When you run Docker in production, one of the important things to consider is how to measure the performance of the containers. It is important to define a comprehensive strategy to monitor your Docker infrastructure with a native collection source for events, statistics, configurations, and records and provide views on the performance of the CPU, memory, and network containers.

Monitoring is an important part of the maintenance of applications for getting metrics about application behavior. This chapter introduces some of the open source tools available for Docker container monitoring, such as cAdvisor, Dive, and Falco.

Structure

We will discuss the following topics in this chapter:

- Container statistics, metrics, and events
- Monitoring with Docker stats
- Performance monitoring with cAdvisor
- Performance monitoring with Dive
- Container monitoring with Falco

Objectives

After studying this chapter, you will learn about obtaining statistics, metrics, and events from Docker containers. You will also understand cAdvisor and Dive as performance monitoring tools and learn about Falco as a container monitoring tool.

Container statistics, metrics, and events

There are several ways to control the execution of Docker containers. We can visualize the logs and observe the events and container statistics at memory usage and CPU levels. Let's see what Docker offers for us to visualize the logs that are recorded when we execute a container.

Log management

Most applications send logs to the standard output. You can see the log directly in the console if the container is running in the foreground. However, only the container identifier (ID) will be displayed on the console when running a container in background mode.

Log management is one of the most important tasks in the world of security, as it allows you to monitor what is happening inside containers. Different containers can run simultaneously in the same Docker host, and each of them can generate their own logs; so, centralized management of the logs is necessary.

There are several commands for monitoring the logs in Docker containers:

```
$ docker logs <container_id | container_name>
$ docker service logs <service | task>
```

In this case, the Docker engine collects all the standard output of containers in execution in a log file. We can visualize the execution log of a container with the following command using the container ID or name:

```
$ docker logs -f <container_id | container_name>
```

The following output shows the logs command options:

```
$ docker logs --help
```

```
Usage:  docker logs [OPTIONS] CONTAINER
```

```
Fetch the logs of a container
```

```
Options:
      --details          Show extra details provided to logs
  -f, --follow           Follow log output
      --since string     Showlogssincetimestamp(e.g.2013-01-02T13:23:37Z)
                         or relative (e.g. 42m for 42 minutes)
  -n, --tail string      Number of lines to show from the end of the
                         logs (default "all")
  -t, --timestamps       Show timestamps
      --until string     Show logs before a timestamp (e.g.
                         2013-01-02T13:23:37Z) or relative (e.g. 42m
                         for 42 minutes)
```

The way this works is that logs sent to the standard output or error output in the container are captured by the Docker daemon process and transmitted to a configurable backend, which is, by default, a JSON file for each container. The following example shows the log output of an nginx container:

```
$ sudo docker logs docker-nginx
```

/docker-entrypoint.sh: /docker-entrypoint.d/ is not empty, will attempt to perform configuration

/docker-entrypoint.sh: Looking for shell scripts in /docker-entrypoint.d/

/docker-entrypoint.sh: Launching /docker-entrypoint.d/10-listen-on-ipv6-by-default.sh

10-listen-on-ipv6-by-default.sh: info: Getting the checksum of /etc/nginx/conf.d/default.conf

10-listen-on-ipv6-by-default.sh: info: Enabled listen on IPv6 in /etc/nginx/conf.d/default.conf

/docker-entrypoint.sh: Launching   /docker-entrypoint.d/20-env-subst-on-templates.sh

/docker-entrypoint.sh: Launching /docker-entrypoint.d/30-tune-worker-processes.sh

/docker-entrypoint.sh: Configuration complete; ready for start up

The files that support container logs are located on the Docker host in the **/var /lib/ docker/containers/<container_identifier>** path. The following screenshot shows the path where logs are located for each container:

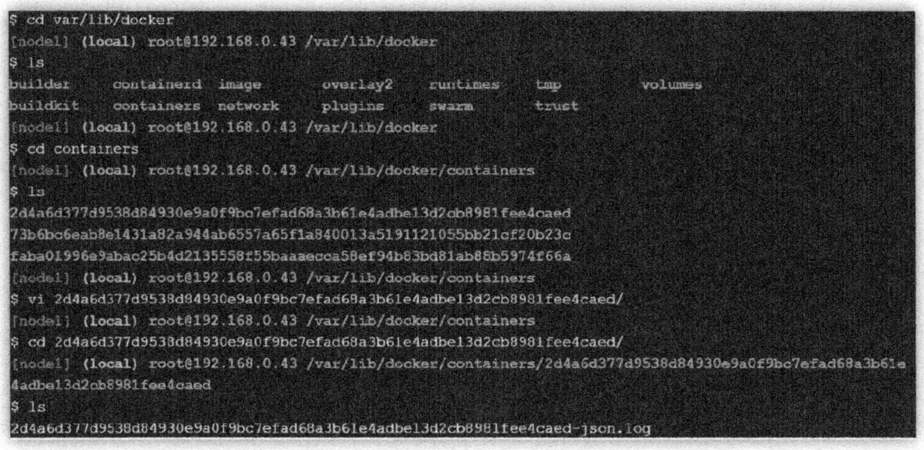

```
$ cd var/lib/docker
[node1] (local) root@192.168.0.43 /var/lib/docker
$ ls
builder    containerd  image     overlay2  runtimes  tmp      volumes
buildkit   containers  network   plugins   swarm     trust
[node1] (local) root@192.168.0.43 /var/lib/docker
$ cd containers
[node1] (local) root@192.168.0.43 /var/lib/docker/containers
$ ls
2d4a6d377d9538d84930e9a0f9bc7efad68a3b61e4adbe13d2cb8981fee4caed
73b6bc6eab8e1431a82a944ab6557a65f1a840013a5191121055bb21cf20b23c
faba01996e9abac25b4d2135558f55baaaecca58ef94b83bd81ab88b5974f66a
[node1] (local) root@192.168.0.43 /var/lib/docker/containers
$ vi 2d4a6d377d9538d84930e9a0f9bc7efad68a3b61e4adbe13d2cb8981fee4caed/
[node1] (local) root@192.168.0.43 /var/lib/docker/containers
$ cd 2d4a6d377d9538d84930e9a0f9bc7efad68a3b61e4adbe13d2cb8981fee4caed/
[node1] (local) root@192.168.0.43 /var/lib/docker/containers/2d4a6d377d9538d84930e9a0f9bc7efad68a3b61e
4adbe13d2cb8981fee4caed
$ ls
2d4a6d377d9538d84930e9a0f9bc7efad68a3b61e4adbe13d2cb8981fee4caed-json.log
```

Figure 9.1: *Path where logs are located for each container*

By default, logs are stored in a JSON file located in the **`/var/lib/docker`** path. This behavior can be changed since Docker uses the concept of registry drivers. Using different controllers lets us choose another type of storage for logging. The default driver is the JSON file, which accepts the following configuration:

```
--log-opt max-size = [0-9 +] [k|m|g]
--log-opt max-file = [0-9 +]
```

The preceding command options can be used where the standard output (STDOUT) is correctly configured. In some instances, the use of the above-mentioned commands will not be adequate because the data is not available in an appropriate format. The following steps need to be performed in such cases:

- In the case that a process is being used within a running container to handle the logs, it would not be advisable to use the **`docker logs`** command since the required information will not be displayed.
- In the case that a non-interactive process such as a web server is being executed within the container, the conventional outputs will not be enabled as it can have a service that is sending logs to a file. One solution is to make a redirection of conventional logs.

Here are the options to redirect and format the logs so that they can be used in the best possible way. These are the different drivers that Docker supports:

Driver	Description
none	The **`docker logs`** command will not show any output.
json-file	Default driver where messages are formatted in JSON format.

syslog	Logs are formatted as syslog. The syslog daemon process will have to be running.
journald	Logs are formatted as journald. `systemd-journald` is a daemon process responsible for event logging.
gelf	We can send log entries to a GELF-based server such as Graylog. **https://www.graylog.org/**, which is an open-source log management tool that supports search, analysis, and log-level alerts of events and logs.
fluentd	The main feature of **fluentd** is that it separates data sources by providing a unified log layer. It is fast and has plugins that make it a very flexible solution.
awslogs	This option writes the logs in Amazon CloudWatch service.
Logstash	Logstash is a tool that is part of the ELK stack (Elasticsearch, LogStash, Kibana) and allows us to process logs from different sources, including communication with graylog and other event monitoring systems.
splunk	Splunk provides the sending of log messages to a server that has Splunk installed using Event Http Collector. Splunk can be used as an event log analyzer in enterprise-level applications.
gcplogs	This option allows sending log entries to Google Cloud registry.

Table 9.1: Options for sending logs

You must use the **--log-driver** option when executing the **docker run** command to use any of these driver controllers. For example, we can execute the following command to store log entries in the syslog of an nginx-based container:

```
$ docker run --log-driver=syslog nginx
```

Observing logs is the most convenient way to monitor our application on the Docker host. We can also see the properties of the running containers, such as the mapped network port or the volume being mapped. Using the **docker inspect** command to display this metadata information is more efficient.

Containers stats

The **stats** command allows you to obtain statistics for one or more containers in execution in real-time. This command allows you to see the use of CPU, memory, and I/O operations at the network level. The syntax for the command is as follows:

```
$ docker stats [OPTIONS] [CONTAINER...]
```

The following output shows the **stats** command options:

```
$ docker stats --help


Usage:  docker stats [OPTIONS] [CONTAINER...]


Display a live stream of container(s) resource usage statistics


Options:
  -a, --all              Show all containers (default shows just
     running)
     --format string   Pretty-print images using a Go template
     --no-stream          Disable streaming stats and only pull
    the first result
     --no-trunc          Do not truncate output
```

The preceding command works through the Docker daemon process that obtains cgroups resource information and serves it through the APIs. By default, the command will display statistics for all running containers if no containers are specified.

```
$ docker stats

CONTAINER ID        NAME            CPU %              MEM USAGE
/ LIMIT     MEM %             NET I/O        BLOCK I/O           PIDS

4f42a4880c0d        docker-nginx        0.00%              2.047MiB /
737.6MiB   0.28%                43.5kB / 1.93kB   0B / 8.19kB           2
```

Statistics can be used to see the behavior of containers during execution. The information can be useful to verify the use of resources like memory and CPU. For example, we can use the following command to the stats if we have two containers nginx and Debian running:

```
$ docker stats <container_id_nginx> <container_id_debian>

CONTAINER CPU% MEM USO / LIMIT MEM% NET I / O

<container_id> 0.00% 7.227 MiB / 987.9 MiB 0.73% 936 B / 468 B
```

The **docker stats** command provides information about the amount of CPU a container is consuming, the amount of memory it has in use, and the limit of what it can use. You can also see the percentage of memory used to make it easier for the user to check how much free memory the container has available.

We can access stats for all containers and obtain this information in JSON format with the following command:

```
$ curl --unix-socket /var/run/docker.sock http:/v1.40/containers/json
```

```
[{"Id":"1366a6bfa068e87e890225c90f6905cb590513e3861a253e00c9fab-
cde131279","Names":["/docker-nginx"],"Image":"nginx","Image-
ID":"sha256:f0b8a9a541369db503ff3b9d4fa6de561b300f7363920c2bff-
4577c6c24c5cf6","Command":"/docker-entrypoint.sh       nginx      -g
'daemon      off;'","Created":1621709565,"Ports":[{"IP":"0.0.0.0","
PrivatePort":80,"PublicPort":8080,"Type":"tcp"}],"Labels":{"-
maintainer":"NGINX      Docker      Maintainers      <docker-maint@nginx.
com>"},"State":"running","Status":"Up 2 hours","HostConfig":{"Net-
workMode":"default"},"NetworkSettings":{"Networks":{"bridge":{"I-
PAMConfig":null,"Links":null,"Aliases":null,"NetworkID":-
"496a087cd3c860e82a9e85f3e8899bbfa8c8d928a63ab481736c5122e8216
bfd","EndpointID":"c4e72fe27c0e37e5d01d40117087a443144a3850ff-
715b8a57e373060049881d","Gateway":"172.17.0.1","IPAd-
dress":"172.17.0.2","IPPrefixLen":16,"IPv6Gateway":"","-
GlobalIPv6Address":"","GlobalIPv6PrefixLen":0,"MacAd-
dress":"02:42:ac:11:00:02","DriverOpts":null}}},"Mounts":[]}]
```

The **container/<container_id>/stats** endpoint provides the statistics in a more detailed way in JSON format. For example, can we access the stats from **nginx** container:

```
$ docker ps

CONTAINER ID         IMAGE          COMMAND                CREATED
STATUS               PORTS                 NAMES

1366a6bfa068         nginx              "/docker-entrypoint...."   3 hours
ago         Up 3 hours      0.0.0.0:8080->80/tcp   docker-nginx
```

The **nginx** container is running now, and we can access the endpoint/stats to access this information using the container identifier:

Keep in mind that the endpoint is executed by container, so we cannot obtain the statistics of all the containers of a single call using this endpoint.

```
$ curl --unix-socket /var/run/docker.sock http:/v1.40/ contain-
ers/1366a6bfa068/stats
```

{"read":"2021-05-22T21:27:06.453288688Z","pre-
read":" 0001-01-01T00:00:00Z","pids_stats":{"current":2},"blkio_stats": {"io_service_bytes_re-
cursive":[{"major":8,"minor":0,"op":"Read","value":7225344},{"major":8,"minor":0,"op":"Write","
value":8192},{"major":8,"minor":0,"op":"Sync","value":7229440},
{"major":8,"minor":0,"op":"Async","value":4096},{"major":8,"minor":0,"op": "Discard","value":0},{"major":8,"minor":0,"op":"Total","value":7233536}],"io_serviced_recursive":
[{"major":8,"minor":0,"op":"Read","value":632},{"major":8,"minor":0,"op":"Write","value":2},{"major":8,"minor":0,"op":
"Sync","value":633},{"major":8,"minor":0,"op":"Async","value":1},{"major":8,"minor":0,"op":"Discard","value":0}, {"major":8,"minor":0,"op":"Total","value":634}],"io_queue_recur-
sive":[],"io_service_time_recursive":[],"io_wait_time_recur-
sive":[],"io_merged_recursive":[],"io_time_recursive":[],"sectors_
recursive":[]},"num_procs":0,"storage_stats":{},"cpu_stats":{"cpu_
usage":{"total_usage":286473948,"percpu_usage":[27672597,189360316
,47224535,22216500,0,0,0,0],"usage_in_kernelmode":80000000,"usage_
in_usermode":210000000},"system_cpu_usage":304850400000000,"on-
line_cpus":4,"throttling_data":{"periods":0,"throttled_peri-
ods":0,"throttled_time":0}},"precpu_stats":{"cpu_usage":{"total_us-
age":0,"usage_in_kernelmode":0,"usage_in_usermode":0},"throttling_
data":{"periods":0,"throttled_periods":0,"throttled_time":0}},"mem-
ory_stats":{"usage":10969088,"max_usage":11079680,"stats":{"active_
anon":1085440,"active_file":5001216,"cache":7028736,"dirty":0,"hi-
erarchical_memory_limit":9223372036854771712,"hierarchical_memsw_
limit":0,"inactive_anon":540672,"inactive_file":1757184,"mapped_
file":1757184,"pgfault":4191,"pgmajfault":0,"pgpgin":3630,"pgpgout"
:1517,"rss":1490944,"rss_huge":0,"total_active_anon":1085440,"to-
tal_active_file":5001216,"total_cache":7028736,"total_dirty":0,"-
total_inactive_anon":540672,"total_inactive_file":1757184,"total_
mapped_file":1757184,"total_pgfault":4191,"total_pgmajfault":0,"-
total_pgpgin":3630,"total_pgpgout":1517,"total_rss":1490944,"to-
tal_rss_huge":0,"total_unevictable":0,"total_writeback":0,"un-
evictable":0,"writeback":0},"limit":8205058048},"name":"/
docker-nginx","id":"1366a6bfa068e87e890225c90f6905cb590513e3861a25
3e00c9fabcde131279","networks":{"eth0":{"rx_bytes":83925,"rx_pack-
ets":443,"rx_errors":0,"rx_dropped":0,"tx_bytes":2546,"tx_pack-
ets":14,"tx_errors":0,"tx_dropped":0}}}

{"read":"2021-05-22T21:27:07.4
```
```

Obtain metrics using docker inspect

Another way to obtain metrics is with the **docker inspect** command, where the **ps -q** option allows you to get the identifiers of all the containers in execution.

```
$ docker stats --no-stream $(docker ps -q) | sed -e "$(docker ps --for-
mat "{{.ID}} {{.Names}}" | sed -e "s/\(.*\) \(.*\)/s\/\1\/\2\t\/g;/" )"

CONTAINER ID        NAME                    CPU %               MEM USAGE /
LIMIT       MEM %                   NET I/O             BLOCK I/O           PIDS

1366a6bfa068        docker-nginx        0.00%                   2.977MiB /
7.642GiB    0.04%               256kB/2.55kB        7.23MB / 8.19kB     2
```

In this section, we reviewed the **docker stats** command to get the main statistics inside a Docker container. In the next section, we will focus on other commands to get the events generated inside a container.

Events in Docker containers

The Docker daemon process internally generates a flow of events around the container's life cycle. We can use the **docker events** command to see what life cycle events are occurring in real-time inside the container.

The sequence of events is useful for monitoring scenarios and performing additional actions, such as receiving an alert when a task ends. When running many containers in the Docker Host, it will be useful if we can see container events in real-time for monitoring and debugging purposes.

The following output shows the **events** command options:

```
$ docker events --help


Usage:docker events [OPTIONS]


Get real time events from the server


Options:
  -f, --filter filter   Filter output based on conditions provided
      --format string   Format the output using the given Go template
```

```
--since string    Show all events created since timestamp

--until string    Stream events until this timestamp
```

The event command contains the **-f**/**--filter** parameter, which allows you to filter the result if you are looking for events based in specific conditions. All events will be reported if no filter is provided. The list of possible filters includes the following:

- container **(container=<name or id>)**
- event **(event=<event action>)**
- image **(image=<tag or id>)**
- plugin (experimental) **(plugin=<name or id>)**
- label **(label=<key> or label=<key>=<value>)**
- type **(type=<container or image or volume or network or daemon>)**
- volume **(volume=<name or id>)**
- network **(network=<name or id>)**
- daemon **(daemon=<name or id>)**

We can use the **--since** or **--until** option with Docker events to filter the results for a specific timestamp:

```
--since = "Date" Show all events created from a date

--until = "Date" Show all events created up to a date
```

For example, the following command shows events from the beginning of the year 2021 until the beginning of 2022:

```
$ docker events --since '2021-01-01' --until '2022-01-01'
```

We can also obtain the events of a specific container using its identifier:

```
$ docker events --filter container=<container_id>
```

The official documentation, available at **https://docs.docker.com/engine/reference/commandline/events/**, mentions the possibilities offered by the **events** command in detail.

Other Docker container monitoring tools

We can find other monitoring tools such as *ctop* and *LazyDocker* in the Docker ecosystem.

The *ctop* (**https://ctop.sh/**) tool is developed in Golang and provides an overview of real-time metrics for multiple containers in a graphical way. The source code is available in the GitHub repository at **https://github.com/bcicen/ctop**.

You can install it by downloading the latest version and give execution permissions with the following commands:

```
$  wget  https://github.com/bcicen/ctop/releases/download/v0.7.2/
ctop-0.7.2-linux-amd64 -O /usr/local/bin/ctop
```

```
$ chmod +x /usr/local/bin/ctop
```

This tool is also available as Docker image, and you can execute it with the following command:

```
$ docker run --rm -ti \
  --name=ctop \
  --volume /var/run/docker.sock:/var/run/docker.sock:ro \
  quay.io/vektorlab/ctop:latest
```

The following screenshot shows the output of the preceding command:

Figure 9.2: Execution of the ctop command

The preceding screenshot shows the containers in execution. Other menu options for getting a single view and stopping and restarting a specific container are also available:

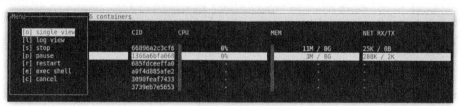

Figure 9.3: Get visualization options

We can also view logs inside the container with the log view option menu:

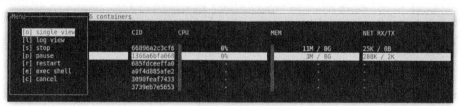

Figure 9.4: Get log details from nginx container

We can see the container details, usage of CPU, and memory if we select a single view:

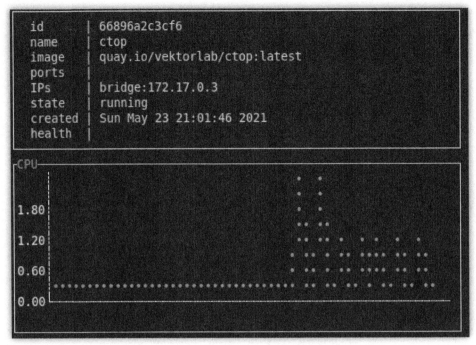

Figure 9.5: Show container details and usage of CPU

LazyDocker is a terminal user interface for both **docker** and **docker-compose**, written in Go with the **gocui** library. You can find the source code and installation instructions in the repository at https://github.com/jesseduffield/lazydocker.

You can simplify the installation and execution of this tool using the **docker-compose.yml** file in the GitHub repository at the following URL:

https://github.com/jesseduffield/lazydocker/blob/master/docker-compose.yml

```
version: '3'

services:

  lazydocker:

    build:

      context: https://github.com/jesseduffield/lazydocker.git

      args:
```

```
    BASE_IMAGE_BUILDER: golang

    GOARCH: amd64

    GOARM:

image: lazyteam/lazydocker

container_name: lazydocker

stdin_open: true

tty: true

volumes:

    - /var/run/docker.sock:/var/run/docker.sock

    - ./config:/.config/jesseduffield/lazydocker
```

We can use **docker-compose up -d** command to execute the previous file. The following screenshot shows the output of executing the preceding **docker-compose** file:

Figure 9.6: Show container details with LazyDocker

When executing LazyDocker, you can see information related to containers that are executing and the layers generated for each image.

Performance monitoring with cAdvisor

cAdvisor (**https://github.com/google/cadvisor**) is one of the most useful tools that enable container-oriented performance monitoring. Among other things, it allows monitoring the following:

- Resource isolation parameters
- Historical use of resources
- Network statistics

The tool is also available as a public image in the Docker Hub repository at **https://hub.docker.com/r/google/cadvisor**.

We must run the following command to execute cAdvisor as a Docker container:

```
$ sudo docker run \
--volume=/:/rootfs:ro \
--volume=/var/run:/var/run:ro \
--volume=/sys:/sys:ro \
--volume=/var/lib/docker/:/var/lib/docker:ro \
--volume=/dev/disk/:/dev/disk:ro \
--publish=8080:8080 \
--detach=true \
--name=cadvisor \
google/cadvisor:latest


Unable to find image 'google/cadvisor:latest' locally
latest: Pulling from google/cadvisor
ff3a5c916c92: Already exists
44a45bb65cdf: Pull complete
0bbe1a2fe2a6: Pull complete
Digest:          sha256:815386ebbe9a3490f38785ab11bda34ec8dac-
f4634af77b8912832d4f85dca04
Status: Downloaded newer image for google/cadvisor:latest
352055d5c4f5e6b03811de0d6274d34aefda031bf39e8da2a09fe1323dee93fc
$ docker ps
```

CONTAINER ID	IMAGE	COMMAND	CRE-ATED	STATUS	PORTS	NAMES
352055d5c4f5 -…"	google/cadvisor:latest About a minute ago	"/usr/bin/cadvisor Up About a minute			0.0.0.0:8080->8080/tcp	cadvisor

We can access from the browser the URL **http://localhost:8080/** after starting the **cadvisor** container.

We can use authentication using the Dockerfile available in the repository at **https:// github.com/tim545/docker-cadvisor-basicauth**.

```
FROM google/cadvisor:latest


ARG USERNAME=admin
ARG PASSWORD=Password1
ARG PORT=8080


RUN apk add --update apache2-utils \
    && rm -rf /var/cache/apk/*


RUN htpasswd -c -i -b auth.htpasswd ${USERNAME} ${PASSWORD}


EXPOSE ${PORT}
ENTRYPOINT ["/usr/bin/cadvisor", "--http_auth_file", "auth.htpass-
wd", "--http_auth_realm", "localhost"]
```

Now, we can build the Docker image. The following command builds the cadvisor container using basic authentication:

```
$ docker build --build-arg USERNAME=admin --build-arg PASSWORD=Password1
-t tim545/cadvisor-basicauth .

$ docker run \

--volume=/:/rootfs:ro \

--volume=/var/run:/var/run:rw \

--volume=/sys:/sys:ro \

--volume=/var/lib/docker/:/var/lib/docker:ro \

--publish=8080:8080 \

--detach=true \

--name=cadvisor-basicauth \

--restart=always \

tim545/cadvisor-basicauth:latest
```

This application allows graphical visualization of the use of CPU and memory. The **Docker Containers** section shows the URLs of the containers that are running on the Docker host. Clicking on any of them will show you the resource usage information for the corresponding container.

The following screenshot depicts the cAdvisor dashboard:

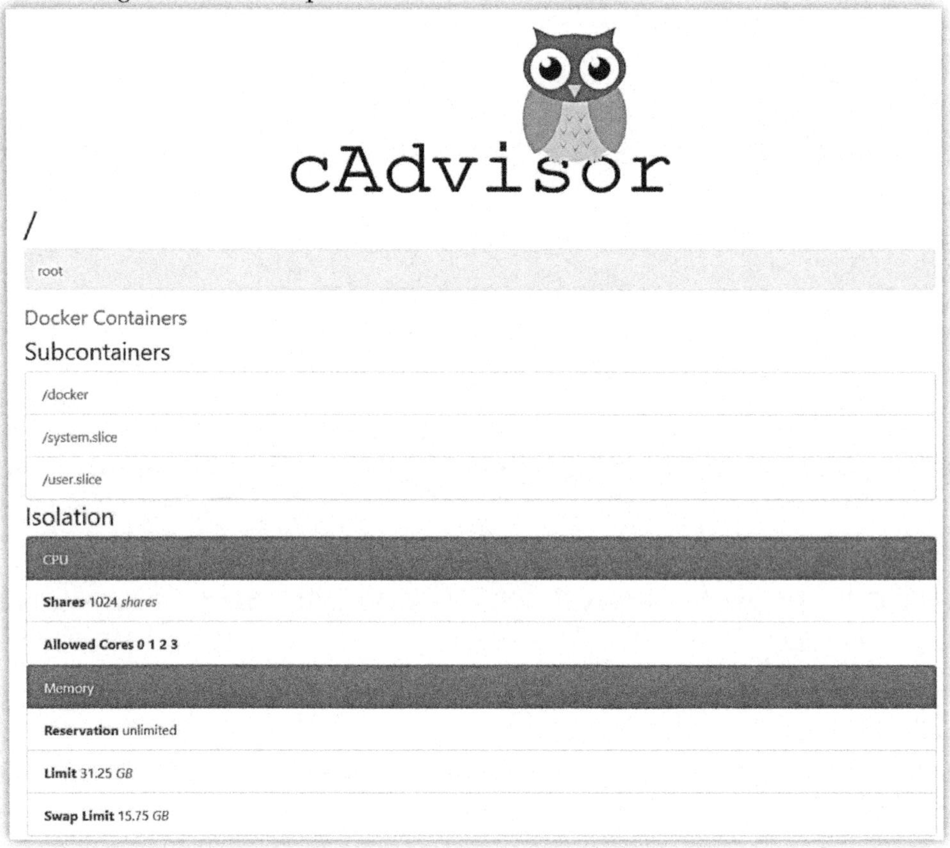

Figure 9.7: Showing information about containers in execution

cAdvisor provides an endpoint in the form of a REST API, where you can obtain all the information provided by the containers in JSON format:

```
$ curl http://localhost:8080/api/v1.3/containers
{
"name": "/",
"subcontainers": [
{
"name": "/docker"
},
{
```

```
"name": "/system.slice"
},
{
"name": "/user.slice"
}
],
….
```

The following screenshot shows processes that are running and the use of the CPU and memory:

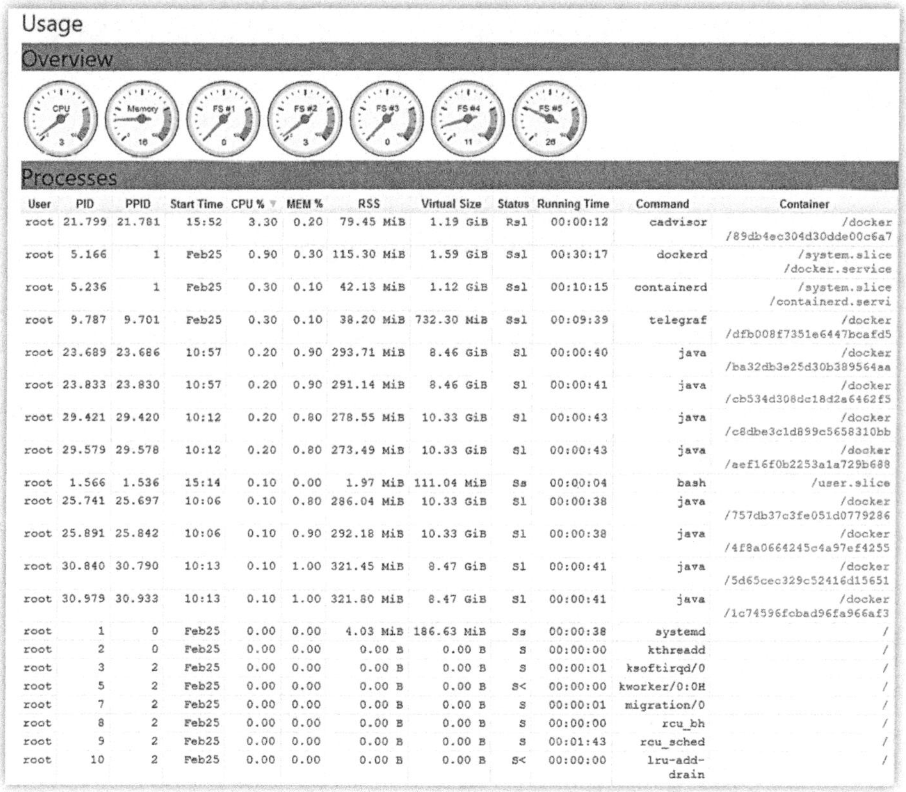

User	PID	PPID	Start Time	CPU %	MEM %	RSS	Virtual Size	Status	Running Time	Command	Container
root	21.799	21.781	15:52	3.30	0.20	79.45 MiB	1.19 GiB	Rsl	00:00:12	cadvisor	/docker /89db4ec304d30dde00c6a7
root	5.166	1	Feb25	0.90	0.30	115.30 MiB	1.59 GiB	Ssl	00:30:17	dockerd	/system.slice /docker.service
root	5.236	1	Feb25	0.30	0.10	42.13 MiB	1.12 GiB	Ssl	00:10:15	containerd	/system.slice /containerd.servi
root	9.787	9.701	Feb25	0.30	0.10	38.20 MiB	732.30 MiB	Ssl	00:09:39	telegraf	/docker /dfb008f7351e6447bcafd5
root	23.689	23.686	10:57	0.20	0.90	293.71 MiB	8.46 GiB	Sl	00:00:40	java	/docker /ba32db3e25d30b389564aa
root	23.833	23.830	10:57	0.20	0.90	291.14 MiB	8.46 GiB	Sl	00:00:41	java	/docker /cb534d308dc18d2a6462f5
root	29.421	29.420	10:12	0.20	0.80	278.55 MiB	10.33 GiB	Sl	00:00:43	java	/docker /c8dbe3c1d899c5658310bb
root	29.579	29.578	10:12	0.20	0.80	273.49 MiB	10.33 GiB	Sl	00:00:43	java	/docker /aef16f0b2253a1a729b688
root	1.566	1.536	15:14	0.10	0.00	1.97 MiB	111.04 MiB	Ss	00:00:04	bash	/user.slice
root	25.741	25.697	10:06	0.10	0.80	286.04 MiB	10.33 GiB	Sl	00:00:38	java	/docker /757db37c3fe051d0779286
root	25.891	25.842	10:06	0.10	0.90	292.18 MiB	10.33 GiB	Sl	00:00:38	java	/docker /4f8a0664245c4a97ef4255
root	30.840	30.790	10:13	0.10	1.00	321.45 MiB	8.47 GiB	Sl	00:00:41	java	/docker /5d65cec329c52416d15651
root	30.979	30.933	10:13	0.10	1.00	321.80 MiB	8.47 GiB	Sl	00:00:41	java	/docker /1c74596fcbad96fa966af3
root	1	0	Feb25	0.00	0.00	4.03 MiB	186.63 MiB	Ss	00:00:38	systemd	/
root	2	0	Feb25	0.00	0.00	0.00 B	0.00 B	S	00:00:00	kthreadd	/
root	3	2	Feb25	0.00	0.00	0.00 B	0.00 B	S	00:00:01	ksoftirqd/0	/
root	5	2	Feb25	0.00	0.00	0.00 B	0.00 B	S<	00:00:00	kworker/0:0H	/
root	7	2	Feb25	0.00	0.00	0.00 B	0.00 B	S	00:00:01	migration/0	/
root	8	2	Feb25	0.00	0.00	0.00 B	0.00 B	S	00:00:00	rcu_bh	/
root	9	2	Feb25	0.00	0.00	0.00 B	0.00 B	S	00:01:43	rcu_sched	/
root	10	2	Feb25	0.00	0.00	0.00 B	0.00 B	S<	00:00:00	lru-add-drain	/

Figure 9.8: *Showing information about processes*

We can see a containers list in the subcontainers section, and we can click on each one to get the information related to the use of total CPU usage and the CPU usage per core:

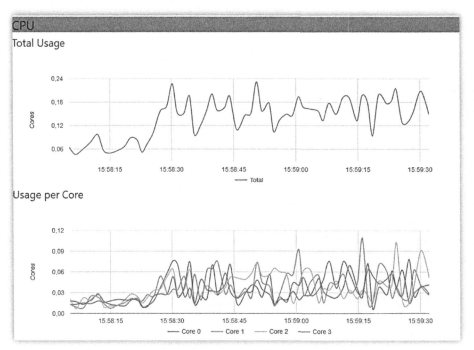

Figure 9.9: *Usage of CPU per core*

We can also get detailed information related to the usage of CPU and memory for each container:

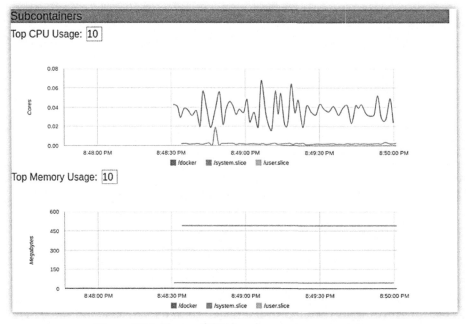

Figure 9.10: *Usage of CPU and memory per container*

Details provided by this API should be enough for many of the monitoring and CPU tasks over Docker containers.

Performance monitoring with Dive

Dive is a tool that allows you to explore the Docker images, the content of each layer image, and the sizes and percentage of image efficiency. You can find the GitHub repository at **https://github.com/wagoodman/dive**.

Here are some of the main features:

- **Show the contents of the Docker image layer by layer**: When selecting a specific layer, the content of that layer will be displayed in combination with all the previous layers.

- **Indicator of changes in each layer**: The file tree displays files that have been changed, updated, inserted, or removed.

- **Get image efficiency**: The lower left panel + displays the basic information for each layer and metrics that tell you whether your image is space-efficient. This can be due to file duplication across layers and file transfer to other layers. A percentage of punctuation and the total wasted file space are provided.

We can download the following image from the Docker hub to execute this tool:

```
$ docker pull quay.io/wagoodman/dive
```

We must use the Docker socket, along with the identifier of the image we want to analyze, for executing the container.

The following command executes the Docker container image related with this performance tool:

```
$ docker run --rm -it -v /var/run/docker.sock:/var/run/docker.sock
quay.io/wagoodman/dive:latest --help
```

```
This tool provides a way to discover and explore the contents of a
docker image. Additionally the tool estimates

the amount of wasted space and identifies the offending files from the
image.
```

```
Usage:
```

```
dive [IMAGE] [flags]

dive [command]
```

Available Commands:

   build   Builds and analyzes a docker image from a Dockerfile
(this is a thin wrapper for the `docker build` command).

   help   Help about any command

   version   print the version number and exit (also --version)

Flags:

--ci	Skip the interactive TUI and validate against CI rules (same as env var CI=true)
--ci-config string	If CI=true in the environment, use the given yaml to drive validation rules. (default ".dive-ci")
--config string	config file (default is $HOME/.dive.yaml, ~/.config/dive/*.yaml, or $XDG_CONFIG_HOME/dive.yaml)
-h, --help	help for dive
--highestUserWastedPercent string	(only valid with --ci given) highest allowable percentage of bytes wasted (as a ratio between 0-1), otherwise CI validation will fail. (default "0.1")
--highestWastedBytes string	(only valid with --ci given) highest allowable bytes wasted, otherwise CI validation will fail. (default "disabled")
-j, --json string	Skip the interactive TUI and write the layer analysis statistics to a given file.

`--lowestEfficiency string`	(only valid with `--ci` given) lowest allowable image efficiency (as a ratio between 0-1), otherwise CI validation will fail. (default "0.9")
`--source string`	The container engine to fetch the image from. Allowed values: docker, podman, docker-archive (default "docker")
`-v, --version`	display version number

Use "`dive [command] --help`" for more information about a command.

The next step is to execute the mentioned container with a specific image identifier:

```
$ docker run --rm -it \
-v /var/run/docker.sock:/var/run/docker.sock \
quay.io/wagoodman/dive:latest <image_identifier>
```

We can obtain the metadata and layers from the image we are analyzing when executing Dive container with a specific image identifier:

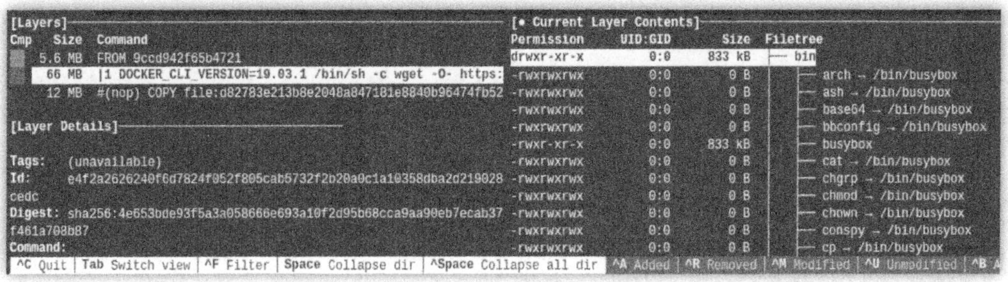

Figure 9.11: Layer details inside the image

We can see the layer details and the folder structure of a layer when selecting a specific layer inside an image. We can also see information related to the command that is generating that layer, image size, potentially wasted space, and the image efficiency score.

Container monitoring with Falco

From the monitoring perspective, we can find other tools, like Falco (**https://falco.org/**), that allow us to monitor all activities of containers, applications, and networks just like we would do with a combination of Unix tools like *Snort, tcpdump, htop, iftop, lsof,* and *strace.*

Falco focuses on the control at the level of behavior, which provides visibility within the containers through the instrumentation of system calls. The call instrumentation of the system is completely transparent to the containers in execution, so **we need not** modify the code or images.

A security event, such as an alert, is emitted when any abnormal activity is detected. The conditions that trigger the alert are defined by its falco policies, which are a collection of rules whose syntax is easy and works just like calls to tcpdump.

Falco policies are a collection of rules that act directly on the kernel system calls. These are the behaviors that Falco can detect:

- A shell that runs inside a container
- A process that generates another process with unexpected behavior
- Reading a confidential file in the operating system
- A process is using a file that is not a normal device type, indicating a possible rootkit activity

We can combine different conditions from various sources like events, metadata, and process information:

- **System call events**: `evt.type = listen`, `evt.type = mkdir`, `evt.type = setns`
- **Docker metadata**: `container.image`, `container.privileged`, `container.name`
- **Process tree information**: `proc.pname`, `proc.cmdline`

For example, we can create a Falco rule that detects any socket connection outside our listening context when:

- The image of the container is nginx
- The listening process inside that container is nginx

The syntax for creating this rule can be as follows:

```
condition: evt.type in (accept,listen) and (container.image!=myreg-
istry/nginx or proc.name!=nginx)
```

Launching Falco container

Falco can be started as a container in the Docker host. We can use the **falcosecurity/ falco** image, which we can find in the public repository in the Docker hub (**https:// hub.docker.com/r/falcosecurity/falco**) for this:

```
$ docker pull falcosecurity/falco:latest
```

```
latest: Pulling from falcosecurity/falco
f307d194cb74: Pull complete
ea175dc1421e: Pull complete
17ff026eb88f: Pull complete
6434e0fcbbd8: Pull complete
299368ac2043: Pull complete
b1f544f718fd: Pull complete
e6be5e7b42d5: Pull complete
09ee772e7af1: Pull complete
bde713efa6d9: Pull complete
91faf45782ea: Pull complete
a538cdc36e74: Pull complete
cfe3889a8f7a: Pull complete
Digest: sha256:49316a25c909b0a2a3b02f0c07548713a35bf4f08174774233119038f4f138fb
```

```
Status: Downloaded newer image for falcosecurity/falco:latest
docker.io/falcosecurity/falco:latest
```

Next, we can execute the following command to run the Falco container:

```
$ docker run --rm -i -t \
>       --privileged \
>       -v /var/run/docker.sock:/host/var/run/docker.sock \
>       -v /dev:/host/dev \
>       -v /proc:/host/proc:ro \
>       -v /boot:/host/boot:ro \
>       -v /lib/modules:/host/lib/modules:ro \
>       -v /usr:/host/usr:ro \
>       -v /etc:/host/etc:ro \
>       falcosecurity/falco:latest
* Setting up /usr/src links from host
```

```
* Running falco-driver-loader for: falco version=0.28.2, driver ver-
sion=13ec67ebd23417273275296813066e07cb85bc91

* Running falco-driver-loader with: driver=module, compile=yes,
download=yes

* Unloading falco module, if present

* Trying to load a system falco module, if present

* Looking for a falco module locally (kernel 4.4.0-193-generic)

* Trying to download a prebuilt falco module from https://down-
load.falco.org/driver/13ec67ebd23417273275296813066e07cb85bc91/fal-
co_ubuntu-generic_4.4.0-193-generic_224.ko

* Download succeeded

* Success: falco module found and inserted

2021-05-27T19:42:19+0000: Falco version 0.28.2 (driver version
13ec67ebd23417273275296813066e07cb85bc91)

2021-05-27T19:42:19+0000: Falco initialized with configuration file /
etc/falco/falco.yaml

2021-05-27T19:42:19+0000: Loading rules from file /etc/falco/falco_
rules.yaml:

2021-05-27T19:42:19+0000: Loading rules from file /etc/falco/falco_
rules.local.yaml:

2021-05-27T19:42:19+0000: Loading rules from file /etc/falco/k8s_au-
dit_rules.yaml:

2021-05-27T19:42:20+0000: Starting internal webserver, listening on
port 8765
```

Once we have Falco running, it will capture and display information related to system calls and events. This includes information like the name of the process, the thread identification, and the type of event.

Falco provides file configuration where we can find preconfigured rules that allow you to filter **system-specific** calls, similar to what we can do with the **tcpdump** command. The following files are available in the falco container:

```
$ docker exec -it 0b72c907a4f5 /bin/bash
root@0b72c907a4f5:/# ls
bin    build   docker-entrypoint.sh  home   lib    lib64   mnt   proc  run   srv   usr   var
boot   dev     etc                          host   lib32   media  opt   root  sbin  sys   usr
root@0b72c907a4f5:/# cd etc
root@0b72c907a4f5:/etc# ls
X11                      dkms          inputrc        machine-id     profile       selinux
adduser.conf             dpkg          iproute2       mke2fs.conf    profile.d     shadow
alternatives             environment   issue          modprobe.d     rc0.d         shadow-
apt                      falco         issue.net      modules        rc1.d         shells
bash.bashrc              fstab         ld.so.cache    motd           rc2.d         skel
bash_completion          gai.conf      ld.so.conf     mtab           rc3.d         ssl
bindresvport.blacklist   group         ld.so.conf.d   nsswitch.conf  rc4.d         subgid
ca-certificates          group-        ldap           opt            rc5.d         subuid
ca-certificates.conf     gshadow       libaudit.conf  os-release     rc6.d         systemd
cron.daily               gss           localtime      pam.conf       rcS.d         terminfo
debconf.conf             host.conf     logcheck       pam.d          resolv.conf   timezone
debian_version           hostname      login.defs     passwd         rmt           update-motd.d
default                  hosts         logrotate.d    passwd-        securetty     xattr.conf
deluser.conf             init.d                       perl           security
root@0b72c907a4f5:/etc# cd falco
root@0b72c907a4f5:/etc/falco# ls
falco.yaml               falco_rules.yaml       rules.available
falco_rules.local.yaml   k8s_audit_rules.yaml   rules.d
```

Figure 9.12: Checking files configuration inside the container

As you can see inside the container, **falco.yaml** configures the Falco service, and **falco_rules.yaml** contains the threat detection patterns.

The following code shows the content of the **falco.yaml** configuration file:

falco.yaml
rules_file:

- /etc/falco/falco_rules.yaml
- /etc/falco/falco_rules.local.yaml
- /etc/falco/k8s_audit_rules.yaml
- /etc/falco/rules.d

If true, the times displayed in log messages and output messages
will be in ISO 8601. By default, times are displayed in the local
time zone, as governed by /etc/localtime.
time_format_iso_8601: true

Whether to output events in json or text
json_output: false

...

The following code shows the content of the **falco_rules.yaml** configuration file:
falco_rules.yaml

```
# This rule helps detect CVE-2021-3156:
# A privilege escalation to root through heap-based buffer overflow
- rule: Sudo Potential Privilege Escalation
 desc: Privilege escalation vulnerability affecting sudo (<= 1.9.5p2).
Executing sudo using sudoedit -s or sudoedit -i command with command-
line argument that ends with a single backslash character from an
unprivileged user it's possible to elevate the user privileges to
root.
  condition: spawned_process and user.uid!= 0 and proc.name=sudoedit
and (proc.args contains -s or proc.args contains -i) and (proc.args
contains "\ " or proc.args endswith \)
   output: "Detect Sudo Privilege Escalation Exploit (CVE-2021-
3156) (user=%user.name parent=%proc.pname cmdline=%proc.cmdline
%container.info)"
  priority: CRITICAL
  tags: [filesystem, mitre_privilege_escalation]
- rule: Debugfs Launched in Privileged Container
 desc: Detect file system debugger debugfs launched inside a privileged
container which might lead to container escape.
  condition: >
    spawned_process and container
    and container.privileged=true
    and proc.name=debugfs
   output: Debugfs launched started in a privileged container
(user=%user.name user_loginuid=%user.loginuid command=%proc.cmdline
%container.info image=%container.image.repository:%container.image.
tag)
  priority: WARNING
  tags: [container, cis, mitre_lateral_movement]

- macro: mount_info
   condition: (proc.args="" or proc.args intersects ("-V", "-l", "-h"))


- rule: Mount Launched in Privileged Container
```

```
  desc: Detect file system mount happened inside a privilegd container
which might lead to container escape.
  condition: >
    spawned_process and container
    and container.privileged=true
    and proc.name=mount
    and not mount_info
 output: Mount was executed inside a privileged container (user=%user.
name user_loginuid=%user.loginuid command=%proc.cmdline %container.
info image=%container.image.repository:%container.image.tag)
  priority: WARNING
  tags: [container, cis, mitre_lateral_movement]
```

Here, we can see the rules that allow us to detect a potential Privilege Escalation in Docker containers.

Falco rules

Falco provides the `falco_rules.yaml` file with specific rules that detect system calls inside the containers. For example, the following rules allow checking whether a shell is running in a container:

```
- macro: container
  condition: container.id != host
- macro: spawned_process
  condition: evt.type = execve and evt.dir=<
- rule: run_shell_in_container
  desc: a shell was spawned by a non-shell program in a container.
  Container entrypoints are excluded.
  condition: container and proc.name = bash and spawned_process and
  proc.pname exists and not proc.pname in (bash, docker)
  output: "Shell spawned in a container other than entrypoint (us-
  er=%user.name container_id=%container.id container_name=%contain-
  er.name  shell=%proc.name  parent=%proc.pname  cmdline=%proc.cmd-
  line)"
  priority: WARNING
```

You can find more examples at **https://falco.org/docs/examples/**.

The full content of previous files are available in the following GitHub repository:

https://github.com/falcosecurity/falco/blob/master/falco.yaml

https://github.com/falcosecurity/falco/blob/master/rules/falco_rules.yaml

Nginx container monitoring

The following example shows how to monitor an **nginx** container. We will perform a basic exploration of containers and processes in containers, CPU monitoring, network, and I/O files.

The first step is create an **nginx** container with the following command:

```
$ docker run -d -P --name docker-nginx nginx

Unable to find image 'nginx:latest' locally

latest: Pulling from library/nginx

69692152171a: Pull complete
30afc0b18f67: Pull complete
596b1d696923: Pull complete
febe5bd23e98: Pull complete
8283eee92e2f: Pull complete
351ad75a6cfa: Pull complete
Digest:          sha256:6d75c99af15565a301e48297fa2d121e15d80ad526f-
8369c526324f0f7ccb750

Status: Downloaded newer image for nginx:latest
6b0eaf6ac580124298052de26f91f5b3b1c0146 c56c56fd62efd962ddbcf78b0
```

Next, we can use the **docker exec** command to execute the **nginx** container:

```
$ docker ps

CONTAINER ID        IMAGE            COMMAND                    CREATED
STATUS              PORTS               NAMES
6b0eaf6ac580        nginx                "/docker-entrypoint.…"    4
minutes ago     Up 4 minutes     0.0.0.0:32768->80/tcp   docker-
nginx
$ docker exec -it docker-nginx bash

root@6b0eaf6ac580:/#
```

Next, we will review how Falco is capturing system calls made within the Linux kernel. Falco can operate with both real-time data and previously captured data, so you can check how applications work within containers.

We should be able to read if we tail the log file with **`/var/log/falco_events.log`**:

```
2021-05-27T21:08:58.903066500+0000: Notice A shell was spawned in
a container with an attached terminal (user=root user_loginuid=-1
docker-nginx (id=788b39827bb5) shell=bash parent=runc cmdline=bash
terminal=34816 container_id=788b39827bb5 image=nginx)
```

At the end of the log file, we can see a summary of the events detected and the rules that have been triggered:

```
Events detected: 16

Rule counts by severity:

    WARNING: 1

    NOTICE: 15

Triggered rules by rule name:

    Set Setuid or Setgid bit: 14

    Delete or rename shell history: 1

    Terminal shell in container: 1

Syscall event drop monitoring:

    - event drop detected: 0 occurrences

    - num times actions taken: 0
```

In this section, we reviewed the Falco tool that lets us monitor and detect anomalies in containers, applications, hosts, and network activity.

Conclusion

In this chapter, we reviewed how the container gives a lot of information about CPU, processes, threads, memory, and network information for each container. In this chapter, you learned about some open source tools available for Docker container monitoring and others that allow filtering using information from different sources like system calls and events that occur in the container.

The main advantages of these tools is that they offer a container monitoring system that allows you to collect metrics to ensure that your application works correctly.

Most of the applications targeting container monitoring are tools related to **Application Performance Monitoring (APM)**. We can also find others that are aimed at monitoring activity to detect anomalous activity in containers, like Falco.

In the next chapter, we will review open source tools available for Docker container administration, such as rancher and portainer.io.

Points to remember

- We can use the `docker events` command to observe the events that arrive at the Docker engine in real-time. This command can be useful if we want to know what happened during the runtime of the container. Containers report a list of events, including the `attach, commit, copy, create, destroy, detach, die, exec_create, exec_detach, exec_start` commands.

- We can find tools in the Docker ecosystem that allow us to graphically visualize the use of CPU and memory by the containers in execution in the Docker host. We can highlight cAdvisor and Dive among these.

- There are other solutions for administration, such as the Dockstation **https:// dockstation.io** that provides a user interface for container management in Docker. You can access the public repository in GitHub **https://github.com/ DockStation/dockstation** for more information about installation and use.

- These tools allow us to check the resource consumption of each container as well as monitor the state of the containers in execution, checking the usage of resources, CPU, memory, and network.

Multiple choice questions

1. Which is the path where logs are located on the Docker host by default?

    a. /var/docker/containers/<container_id>

    b. /var/lib/containers/<container_id>/docker/

    c. /var/lib/docker/containers/<container_id>

    d. /var/lib/docker/<container_id>

2. Which command allows you to see what life cycle events are occurring in real-time inside the container?

    a. docker compose

    b. docker stats

    c. docker logs

d. docker events

Answers

1	c
2	d

Questions

- Which command allows you to obtain statistics for one or more containers in execution and get information like the use of CPU, memory, and I/O operations at the network level?

- Which is one of the most useful tools that enable container-oriented performance monitoring and runs as a daemon process that collects performance data in running containers?

- Which tool allows you to monitor all activities of containers, applications, and networks, as we would do with a combination of Unix tools like Snort, tcpdump, htop, iftop, lsof, and strace?

Key terms

- We can get real-time statistics of all the containers running in the Docker Host with the **docker stats** commands. The **docker stats** command accepts the following options:

  a. **--no-stream**: This option disables real-time statistics and will only show the first result

  b. **-a (--all)**: This option shows the statistics of all containers

- The Docker stats provides the **/stats** endpoint for getting detailed memory usage information as well as information about CPU usage.

- Docker events command will show processes that are running in real-time for tracking all actions and system calls captured.

- Falco is a behavioral activity monitor designed to detect anomalous activity in containers using a kernel module to intercept system calls. It supports Docker and Kubernetes and provides a rich ruleset and the ability to filter events for taking action auditing and monitoring tools, where tools like AppArmor and Seccomp are enforcement tools.

CHAPTER 10
Docker Container Administration

Containers constitute a complete execution environment, which includes an application, its dependencies, libraries, binary files, and configuration necessary for execution. This is called **containerization** and allows you to add a level of abstraction at the platform, operating system, and underlying infrastructure level.

However, appropriate management tools are required to move dockerized applications to production containers and ensure security, automation, orchestration, and administration. This chapter introduces some of the open source tools available for Docker container administration, such as *Portainer*, *Rancher*, and *Openshift*.

Structure

We will discuss the following topics in this chapter:

- Introducing container administration
- Container administration with Portainer
- Container administration with Rancher
- Container administration with Openshift

Objectives

This chapter will teach you about container administration with Portainer, Rancher, and Openshift.

Introducing container administration

Organizations and developers should consider the challenges associated with managing Docker environments and the need to implement business solutions that support effective management while deploying Docker containers, which must have technology that allows them to successfully manage the problems of dispersion, compliance, and governance of the same containers. The three stages of the container life cycle are as follows:

- **Development**: In the first stage, developers create and deploy Docker containers that include items like application codes and libraries. Then, they test the applications, correct errors, add functions or improvements, create new Docker images, and deploy them in new containers. This process continues until the required standards are met.

- **Application release**: In the second stage, managers coordinate the automation of application environments, which include Docker construction, testing, and deployment drivers.

- **IT operations**: In the last stage, the containers are deployed in production and remain operational and available until they are dismantled. This is the stage at which the final challenges are critical: orchestration and governance, security, and container monitoring.

To harness the potential of Docker's benefits, developers and organizations need solutions designed to address five major container management challenges:

- **Lack of control**: Developers need independence to quickly create, implement, and test application containers. In contrast, the operations team needs control and governance to avoid excessive consumption of resources.

- **Cycle from rise to production**: It is important to maintain quality and safety as changes in development increase.

- **Complexity of scale containers**: The virtualized or cloud infrastructure does not disappear and will continue to coexist with the Docker infrastructure. The implementation of complete applications covering Docker and other infrastructures requires more advanced capabilities to orchestrate applications and optimally manage running environments.

- **Vulnerability protection and compliance**: Docker containers can integrate vulnerabilities, such as Heartbleed and Ghost, because they include parts of the operating systems. The protection of the environment requires security in the host Docker layer, containers, and images. The container update creates a new management paradigm that can change the tasks of operations to development.

- **Monitoring Requirements**: Docker environments require special monitoring capabilities, such as API-level integration with Docker and instrumentation, built into the Docker image.

To take full advantage of Docker's benefits, organizations need the appropriate management and administration tools that allow them to manage the full life cycle of the Docker container and ensure the company's availability for both development and production environments.

In the next section, we will learn to use Portainer to manage our container stacks in Docker.

Container administration with Portainer

Portainer (**https://www.portainer.io**) is an open source web tool that can execute itself as a container and allow us to manage our Docker containers easily and intuitively through a graphical interface. You can find the source code in the GitHub repository at **https://github.com/portainer/portainer**.

We can find the official image for deploying this tool as Docker container in the Docker Hub repository at **https://hub.docker.com/r/portainer/portainer**.

In order to manage the local Docker server, you must include the `-v /var/run/docker.sock:/var/run/docker.sock` option in the `docker run` command. Then, we can proceed to download and start the container, as follows:

```
$ docker run -d -p 9000:9000 --name portainer --restart always -v
/var/run/docker.sock:/var/run/docker.sock  -v  portainer_data:/data
portainer/portainer
```

The `docker run` command options are the usual ones, such as:

- `-d` for running the container as a background process
- `--name portainer` to give a name to the container
- -p 9090:9000 to connect port 9090 on the Docker host with port 9000 exposed in the container

- **-v portainer-data:/data** will create a persistent Docker volume that will allow you to reinstall or update it without having to configure user and password again
- **-v /var/run/docker.sock:/var/run/docker.sock** mounts the Docker sock in the container
- **portainer/portainer** is the Docker Hub repository from where we download the image

The preceding command executes the container and listens on port 9000, so we can access **http://localhost:9000** in our browser to access it.

Another way to execute it is using the following command from the file that we can find at **https://downloads.portainer.io/docker-compose.yml**

```
$ docker-compose up -d

docker-compose.yml

version: '2'
services:
  portainer:
    image: portainer/portainer
    ports:
      - "9000:9000"
    command: -H unix:///var/run/docker.sock
    volumes:
      - /var/run/docker.sock:/var/run/docker.sock
      - portainer_data:/data
volumes:
  portainer_data:
```

You can use the following command to inspect the volume created by Portainer to see the directory where the files are located on the server:

```
$ docker volume ls
DRIVER        VOLUME NAME
local        portainer_data
$ docker volume inspect portainer_data
[
    {
        "CreatedAt": "2021-06-06T08:16:57+02:00",
        "Driver": "local",
        "Labels": {},
        "Mountpoint": "/var/lib/docker/volumes/portainer_data/_
                     data",
        "Name": "portainer_data",
        "Options": {},
        "Scope": "local"
    }
]
```

You will be asked to configure the administrator user and password when accessing the application via the web interface for the first time. Once the administrator user has been created, you will be asked to connect to the Docker environment you want to manage. The following figure shows that we have selected local installation to handle the containers:

Figure 10.1*: Local installation for managing Portainer*

The Portainer interface illustrated in *figure 10.2* gives us the information of its volumes, images, and containers.

Figure 10.2: Portainer interface

The **Dashboard** shown in *figure 10.3* is the main page of our Portainer instance that shows a summary of our Docker system: the total number of containers, images, networks, and volumes. This section is useful to show us the current status of Docker in our machine:

Figure 10.3: Portainer Dashboard

The containers menu will show us the list of all our containers, and we can execute several instructions that we usually execute through the command line, such as starting, stopping, or eliminating them. The following figure shows the container list in Portainer interface:

Figure 10.4: *Container list in Portainer interface*

We can get more details by clicking on the container name. The container details section allows us to perform some operations over the container, as follows:

- Executing common operations, such as stop, pause, kill, or delete the container
- See container information (**docker inspect**)
- Create a new image from the same container and add it to a record (**docker commit**)
- See container logs (**docker logs**)
- See container statistics (**docker stats**)
- Enter the container, choosing the shell or the user (**docker exec**)
- Connect/disconnect the container with a network (**docker network connect**)

The following figure depicts the container details in Portainer interface:

Figure 10.5: *Container details in Portainer interface*

You will see the following icons from left to right if you look at the quick actions:

- **Logs**: It allows us to see the container logs in real time and export previous logs
- **Inspect**: It gives us all the information of the container
- **Stats**: It shows the statistics of the container (memory usage, CPU, network, and processes)
- **Console**: It gives us access to the container console

The following figure shows the inspect section in Portainer interface:

Figure 10.6: Inspect details in Portainer interface

The **Images** section shown here would correspond to the **docker images** command:

Figure 10.7: Images section in Portainer interface

We can see the networks that we have already created in the **Network list** section. We can also remove them or add a new network through the interface. The following figure shows the network list in the Portainer interface:

Name ↕	Stack	Driver	Attachable	IPAM Driver	IPV4 IPAM Subnet	IPV4 IPAM Gateway	IPV6 IPAM Subnet	IPV6 IPAM Gateway	Ownership
bridge System	-	bridge	false	default	172.17.0.0/16	172.17.0.1	-	-	⊚ public
cda	-	bridge	false	default	172.18.0.0/16	172.18.0.1	-	-	administra
descargas_default	-	bridge	false	default	172.22.0.0/16	172.22.0.1	-	-	administra
dev_default	dev	bridge	true	default	172.19.0.0/16	172.19.0.1	-	-	administra
host System	-	host	false	default	-	-	-	-	⊚ public
iky_default	iky	bridge	true	default	172.21.0.0/16	172.21.0.1	-	-	administra
none System	-	null	false	default	-	-	-	-	⊚ public
yeti_default	yeti	bridge	true	default	172.20.0.0/16	172.20.0.1	-	-	administra

Figure 10.8: Network list section in Portainer interface

We can see the volumes that we have already created in the **Volumes list** section. We can also remove them or add a new volume through the web interface. The following figure shows the details from a specific volume in the Portainer interface:

Figure 10.9: Volume list section in Portainer interface

We can find a lot of templates available to download and install in the **Templates** section shown here:

Figure 10.10: App Templates section in Portainer interface

We must assign a network, volumes, and the ports that we will expose once the *nginx template* has been selected. In our case, port 80 is redirected to 9080 and 443 to 9443. The following figure shows the Port mapping assignment in the Portainer interface:

Figure 10.11: Port mapping in Portainer interface

We can see that an nginx server instance has been deployed in the container list shown here:

Figure 10.12: Container list with nginx deployed

The container related with nginx is running in the **Containers** list section once deployed:

Figure 10.13: Nginx container in execution

The following figure provides container details, where we can see information related to nginx image, port configuration, environment variables, and labels:

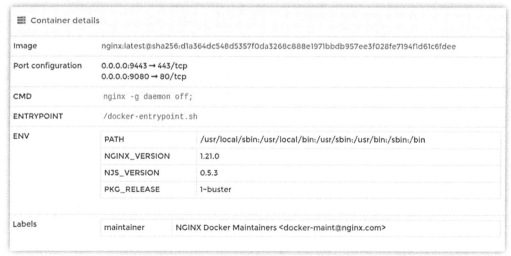

Figure 10.14: Deploying nginx application template

Tip: Portainer demo
You can try a Portainer demo with http://demo.portainer.io
(username :admin, password:tryportainer).

Deploying Portainer in Docker Swarm Cluster

Portainer is compatible with the Docker engine and Docker Swarm. Katacoda provides a scenario for deploying Portainer to Docker Swarm Cluster in **https://www.katacoda.com/portainer**.

The first step is to create a docker swarm cluster with the **docker swarm init** command. You can use the **docker node ls** command to view the status of the Swarm cluster.

The following figure shows the interface for deploying Portainer to Docker Swarm cluster:

Figure 10.15: Container list in Portainer interface

With the cluster configured, the next step is to deploy Portainer. By deploying Portainer as a Docker Service, Swarm will ensure that the service is always running on a manager, even if the host goes down.

The service exposes port 9000 and stores the internal Portainer data in the **/host/data** directory. When Portainer starts, it connects using the **docker.sock** file to the Docker Swarm Manager.

```
$ docker service create \
    --name portainer \
    --publish 9000:9000 \
    --constraint 'node.role == manager' \
    --mount type=bind,src=/host/data,dst=/data \
     --mounttype=bind,src=/var/run/docker.sock,dst=/var/run/dock-
    er.sock \
    portainer/portainer \
    -H unix:///var/run/docker.sock
```

When executing the preceding command, you can see that portainer container is executing on port 9000 with the `docker ps` command.

The following figure shows the `Container list` interface with the Portainer container in execution:

Figure 10.16: Portainer container in execution

With Portainer running, we can now access the dashboard and manage the cluster via the user interface.

Docker Swarm Administration with Portainer

Portainer provides us with a web GUI to manage a Docker Swarm cluster. For example, you can configure your environment with two nodes: one master and one worker. These two nodes are configured to serve requests from my containers, as shown here.

With the Portainer interface, we can see this configuration in the **Swarm** section:

Name ↕	Role	CPU	Memory	Engine	IP Address	Status	Availability
manager1	manager	4	8.3 GB	20.10.3	172.24.0.5	ready	active
worker1	worker	4	8.3 GB	20.10.3	172.24.0.4	ready	active

Figure 10.17: Portainer swarm nodes in execution

So, the Portainer installation can be done by deploying it as another service within our cluster with the following YML file:

```
$ curl -L https://downloads.portainer.io/portainer-agent-stack.
yml -o portainer-agent-stack.yml
```

If we look at the configuration file of the stack, we see that the agent is deployed in global mode for the entire cluster, and the container containing the administration services is deployed in replication mode. The content of the `portainer-agent-stack.yml` file is shown here:

```yaml
version: '3.2'
services:
  agent:
    image: portainer/agent
    volumes:
      - /var/run/docker.sock:/var/run/docker.sock
      - /var/lib/docker/volumes:/var/lib/docker/volumes
    networks:
      - agent_network
    deploy:
      mode: global
      placement:
        constraints: [node.platform.os == linux]
  portainer:
    image: portainer/portainer
    command: -H tcp://tasks.agent:9001 --tlsskipverify
    ports:
      - "9000:9000"
      - "8000:8000"
    volumes:
      - portainer_data:/data
    networks:
      - agent_network
    deploy:
      mode: replicated
      replicas: 1
      placement:
        constraints: [node.role == manager]
networks:
  agent_network:
```

```
      driver: overlay
      attachable: true

volumes:
  portainer_data:
```

We can use the following command to deploy portainer in the cluster using the preceding file configuration:

```
$ docker stack deploy --compose-file=portainer-agent-stack.yml por-
tainer
```

The previous file configuration allows us to see how two services and one network are deploying:

```
Creating network portainer_agent_network

Creating service portainer_agent

Creating service portainer_portainer
```

We can see how two services are deployed using the following command:

```
$ docker service ls

ID                 NAME              MODE           REPLICAS
IMAGE                    PORTS

ngvbdywoej8o       portainer_agent       global          2/2
portainer/agent:latest

uq7zsmd5badq       portainer_portainer   replicated      1/1
```

As we can see, the agent has two replicas running, one instance running in the swarm manager and the other in the worker. The data is balanced between the swarm Manager and more than one Worker if the agent had more than two replicas.

Once the deployment is done, we can see agent service as well as the Docker Swarm cluster status in *figure 10.18*:

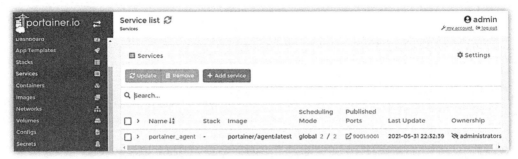

Figure 10.18: Agent service from docker swarm cluster

We can see the nodes that are part of the Swarm cluster and the services they are running in the cluster visualizer section shown here:

Figure 10.19: Cluster visualizer from docker swarm cluster

In the next section, we will learn to use Rancher to orchestrate our container stacks in Docker.

Container administration with Rancher

Rancher (**https://rancher.com**) is a platform that allows you to manage containers and stacks of containers on remote servers. With Rancher, you can initialize multiple clusters with one single central place to manage them. In production, Rancher would typically be run in its own highly-available kubernetes cluster.

You can find the installation requirements in your server at the following link:

- https://rancher.com/docs/rancher/v2.x/en/installation/requirements

You can install Rancher on your server in a Docker container with the following command:

```
$ docker run -d --restart=unless-stopped -p 8080:8080 rancher/
server:stable
```

The preceding command enables you to download the official image of Rancher and starts Rancher Server. You can also access the panel interface on port 8080. Use the following command to view the starting process:

```
$ docker logs rancher

…..

time="2021-06-01T19:19:29Z"    level=info    msg="Creating    schema
machine, roles [project member owner]" id=1ds31 service=gms

time="2021-06-01T19:19:29Z" level=info msg="Creating schema host,
roles [project member owner]" id=1ds32 service=gms

time="2021-06-01T19:19:29Z"    level=info    msg="Creating    schema
machine, roles [admin user readAdmin]" id=1ds33 service=gms

time="2021-06-01T19:19:29Z" level=info msg="Creating schema host,
roles [admin user readAdmin]" id=1ds34 service=gms

time="2021-06-01T19:19:30Z"    level=info    msg="Creating    schema
machine, roles [readonly]" id=1ds35 service=gms

time="2021-06-01T19:19:30Z" level=info msg="Creating schema host,
roles [readonly]" id=1ds36 service=gms

time="2021-06-01 19:25:26" level=info msg="Telemetry Client v0.4.0"

time="2021-06-01    19:25:26"    level=info    msg="Listening    on
0.0.0.0:8114"
```

Here are some of the main advantages that Rancher offers:

- It allows you to create as many environments as you need and manage users and roles for different environments
- It allows you to select the container orchestrator from several options, such as Cattle, Mesos, Kubernetes, and Docker Swarm
- There is a public catalog called **Rancher Community** where the community can contribute with its applications
- It makes single-cluster and multi-cluster deployments easy

- It facilitates cluster provisioning using the user interface
- Simplified cluster operations and security policy enforcement

The application provides a simple interface, wherein the hosts can create containers and start applications inside the containers on the one hand.

Rancher manages agents to establish communication between them and its hosts, so we must install that agent. It is a simple process—add the hosts from the Rancher console by following these steps:

1. We choose the Infrastructure> Hosts option in the menu.

2. We follow the steps marked by the wizard to install the agent on the host.

3. We execute the command on the host that we want Rancher to manage.

The following figure shows the steps for adding a host with the command we could execute for registering the host:

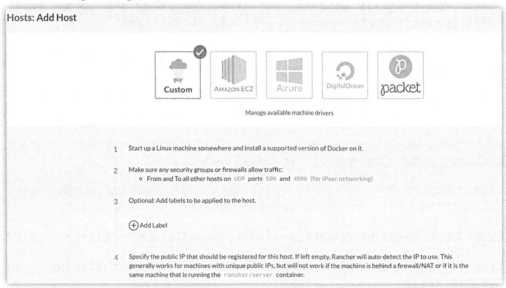

Figure 10.20: Adding host in Rancher interface

Execute the following command for adding a host:

```
$  sudo  docker  run  --rm  --privileged  -v  /var/run/docker.
sock:/var/run/docker.sock        -v        /var/lib/rancher:/var/
lib/rancher      rancher/agent:v1.2.11      https://2886795279-
8080-frugo01.environments.katacoda.com/v1/scripts/
D28EF1A78A369A4F6B46:1609372800000:pqDcPVPAzzVFHIE4YdRrvkg8Mo
```

INFO: Running Agent Registration Process, CATTLE_
URL=https://2886795279-8080-frugo01.environments.katacoda.com/v1

INFO: Attempting to connect to: https://2886795279-8080-frugo01.
environments.katacoda.com/v1

INFO: https://2886795279-8080-frugo01.environments.katacoda.com/
v1 is accessible

INFO: Configured Host Registration URL info: CATTLE_
URL=https://2886795279-8080-frugo01.environments.katacoda.com/
v1 ENV_URL=https://2886795279-8080-frugo01.environments.katacoda.
com/v1

INFO: Inspecting host capabilities

INFO: Boot2Docker: false

INFO: Host writable: true

INFO: Token: xxxxxxxx

INFO: Running registration

INFO: Printing Environment

INFO: ENV: CATTLE_ACCESS_KEY=85918AE54E3B58E24CBD

INFO: ENV: CATTLE_HOME=/var/lib/cattle

INFO: ENV: CATTLE_REGISTRATION_ACCESS_KEY=registrationToken

INFO: ENV: CATTLE_REGISTRATION_SECRET_KEY=xxxxxxx

INFO: ENV: CATTLE_SECRET_KEY=xxxxxxx

INFO: ENV: CATTLE_URL=https://2886795279-8080-frugo01.
environments.katacoda.com/v1

INFO: ENV: DETECTED_CATTLE_AGENT_IP=144.76.8.205

INFO: ENV: RANCHER_AGENT_IMAGE=rancher/agent:v1.2.11

INFO: Launched Rancher Agent:
98a601a4f5d0e3d79a99e2cca0131689e8c75718d03a08faa2b37ced4e61018e

We can see the host in the Rancher interface after executing the preceding command:

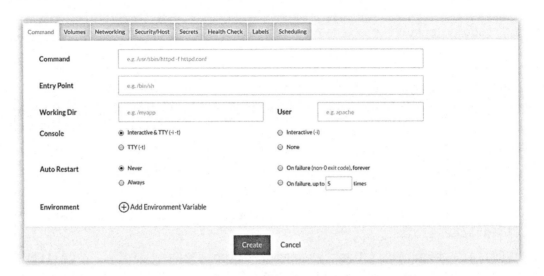

Figure 10.21: Information about host in Rancher interface

We can also configure and add different development environments using some environment templates, depending upon the orchestration platform we are using. The following figure shows the environments offered by Rancher by default:

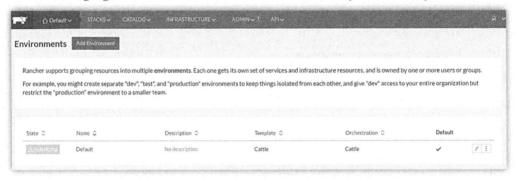

Figure 10.22: Environment templates in Rancher interface

The following figure shows the templates offered by Rancher by default:

| Command | Volumes | Networking | Security/Host | Secrets | Health Check | Labels | Scheduling |

Command   e.g. /usr/sbin/httpd -f httpd.conf

Entry Point   e.g. /bin/sh

Working Dir   e.g. /myapp   **User**   e.g. apache

Console   ◉ Interactive & TTY (-i -t)   ○ Interactive (-i)
                   ○ TTY (-t)   ○ None

Auto Restart   ◉ Never   ○ On failure (non-0 exit code), forever
                   ○ Always   ○ On failure, up to 5   times

Environment   ⊕ Add Environment Variable

Figure 10.23: Environment templates in Rancher interface

Another important aspect of Rancher is its catalog of applications. This catalog is public; the open source community can contribute its applications to all Rancher Community users. It also offers the possibility of having a private application catalog. The following figure shows the applications catalog available in Rancher interface.

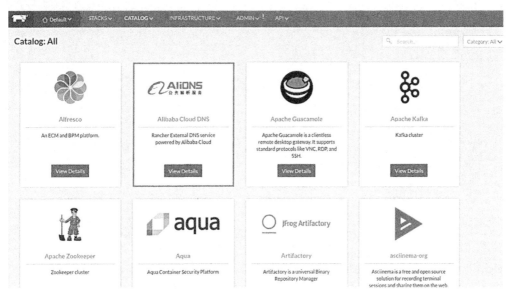

Figure 10.24: Applications catalog in Rancher interface

Rancher provides a web interface to control containers. The dashboard in the following figure shows starting, stopped, and running containers:

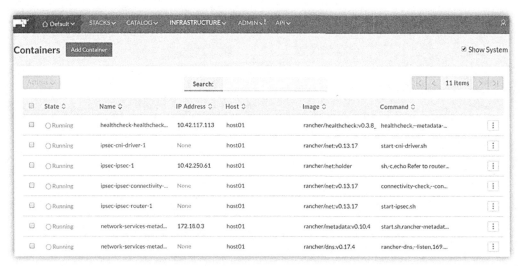

Figure 10.25: Container dashboard in Rancher interface

Clicking on **Add Container** will redirect you to a page where you can set the container run parameters, as shown here:

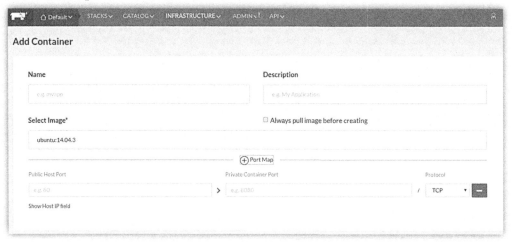

Figure 10.26: Adding Container in Rancher interface

Additionally, we can configure the command when adding a container, as shown here:

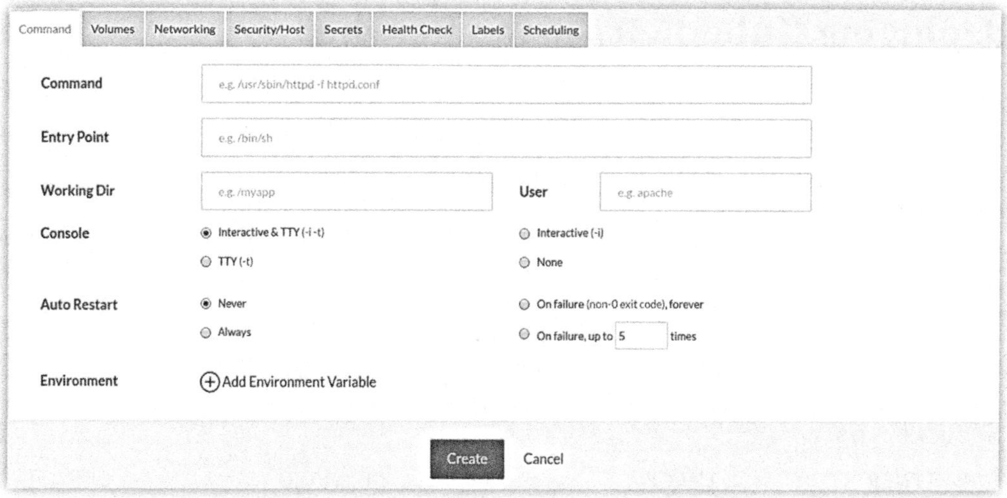

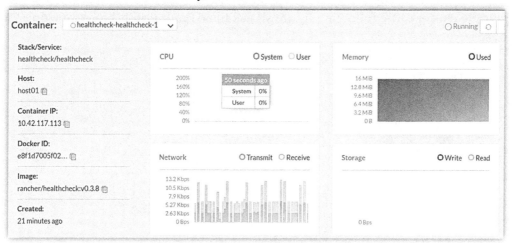

Figure 10.27: Container command options in Rancher interface

The containers section lists all your running containers. You can open a shell into a container, stop, restart, and delete the container and other options related to logs, and clone the container. The following figure depicts the container details with information about CPU, memory, and network:

Figure 10.28: Container details in Rancher interface

In this section, we reviewed how you can deploy a container from the container dashboard and see each container's status from the Rancher interface.

Deploying Kubernetes using Rancher

You can initialize multiple clusters with a central place to manage them with Rancher. The Rancher control plane is deployed as a Docker Container. You can execute the following commands to start Rancher and check boot process:

```
$ docker run -d -p 80:80 -p 443:443 --name=rancher rancher/
rancher:stable
$ docker logs rancher
```

We can see the Rancher container in execution with the following command:

```
$ docker ps
CONTAINER ID       IMAGE                       COMMAND           CREATED
STATUS       PORTS                                     NAMES
9f424719a637        rancher/rancher:stable    "entrypoint.sh"       6
seconds ago      Up 3 seconds     0.0.0.0:80->80/tcp, 0.0.0.0:443-
>443/tcp    rancher
```

Once the container is started, the first step is to configure a password for the admin user and select the option depending on whether we want to create or manage multiple clusters. The following figure shows the default options for managing the cluster:

Figure 10.29: Rancher welcome page

In the next step, you'll create a cluster to configure Kubernetes, as shown here:

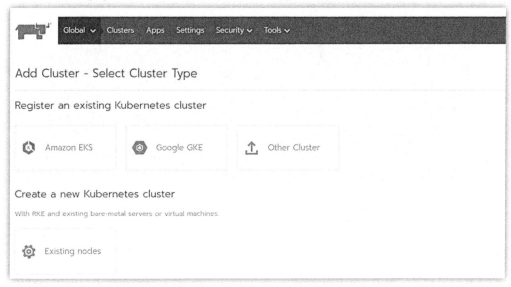

Figure 10.30: Add cluster-Select Cluster type

We'll deploy an on-premise solution in this scenario. Click on the **Add Cluster** button and select the cluster type of **Custom** to begin the installation, as shown here:

Figure 10.31: Add cluster-Custom

You can edit and customize the Kubernetes cluster options in the cluster configuration shown in *figure 10.32*:

```
Kubernetes Options
Customize the kubernetes cluster options

                                                    📋 Copy to Clipboard    ⬆  Read from a file

 1 #
 2 # Cluster Config
 3 #
 4 docker_root_dir: /var/lib/docker
 5 enable_cluster_alerting: false
 6 enable_cluster_monitoring: false
 7 enable_network_policy: false
 8 local_cluster_auth_endpoint:
 9   enabled: true
10 name: ' '
11 #
12 # Rancher Config
13 #
```

Figure 10.32: Cluster file configuration

The next step is to deploy Kubernetes. We'll start by configuring a single node instance of Kubernetes in this case.

A single node instance has etcd, the Kubernetes Control Plane, and a Kubernetes node to all run on the same machine. This would be deployed onto multiple nodes in production, but a single node is a great starting place for testing and experimenting.

The command to initialize the cluster at the top will change by selecting the etcd and control plane boxes. This command will deploy the correct configuration for our node cluster, as shown here:

```
▼ Customize Node Run Command
  Editing node options will update the command you will run on your existing machines

  ①  Node Options
      Choose what roles the node will have in the cluster.
      Node Role
             ☑ etcd              ☑ Control Plane         ☑ Worker
                                                         Show advanced options

  ②  Run this command on one or more existing machines already running a supported version of Docker.

        sudo docker run -d --privileged --restart=unless-stopped --
      net=host -v /etc/kubernetes:/etc/kubernetes -v /var/run:/var/run
      rancher/rancher-agent:v2.5.8 --server https://2886795291-443-
      elsy02.environments.katacoda.com --token
      mk5whn884mcrs4pzdsrxrcljnfs5fkkwtwrwdtsfn8bdxwmzh7skqx --ca-checksum
      0cce8e5186c16efdfb9332516288721133f244ba3371ee423b5f5f6b724fc4e7 --etcd --
      controlplane --worker
```

Figure 10.33: Cluster node configuration

You can run the command in the Terminal window when you're okay with the configuration. You can use the "**Copy to Clipboard**" button to make this process easier. The Rancher dashboard should report one new node being registered in the cluster after running the command, as follows:

Figure 10.34: *Registering Master Node in the cluster*

Rancher is now starting all the components of Kubernetes, which will take a couple of minutes. You will then have a fully functional Kubernetes cluster. You can select the newly deployed Cluster within the user interface to view the details and status. The following figure shows the cluster state in the Rancher interface:

Figure 10.35: *Cluster state in Rancher interface*

We can click on the name of the cluster to access a dashboard that offers us information, such as the configuration file, necessary to configure our kubectl client and start using our Kubernetes cluster. This is shown as follows:

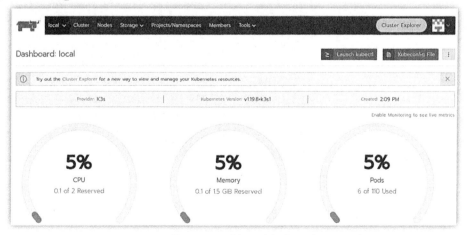

Figure 10.36: *Cluster Dashboard in Rancher interface*

We can see more details related to namespaces, nodes, deployments, and services in the cluster explorer option shown in *figure 10.37*:

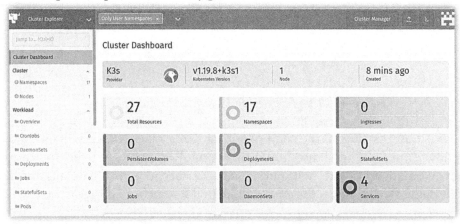

Figure 10.37: Cluster Explorer in Rancher interface

Tip: Deploying Kubernetes using Rancher

The following URL and figure 10.38 provide interactive learning scenarios that provide you with a pre-configured Rancher instance accessible from your browser without any downloads or configuration:

`https://www.katacoda.com/andymelichar/scenarios/rancher-rodeo`

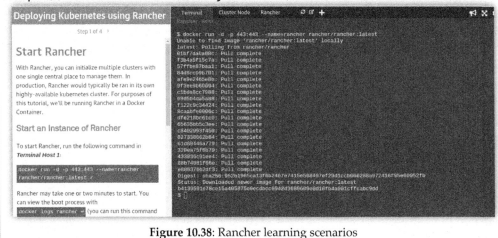

Figure 10.38: Rancher learning scenarios

In the next section, we will review Openshift as a container platform.

Container administration with OpenShift

Red Hat OpenShift container platform helps organizations develop, deploy, and manage the existing and new applications in physical, virtual, and public cloud infrastructures. OpenShift offers a common platform and a group of tools for the development and operations teams in your organization.

Using the container orchestration system of the Kubernetes project, OpenShift has a set of additional functionalities that makes it the ideal platform for the integration of DevOps environments such as:

- Provides a set of integrated middleware platforms for the development and deployment of applications
- Allows the construction of traditional applications and those oriented to the cloud
- Allows managing the life cycle of applications based on containers
- Includes tools for converting source code into running applications, thanks to the source-to-image process

DevOps tool offers organizations mechanisms to improve communication between development and operations and eliminate integration barriers between both departments with the help of the following features:

- **Self-provisioning**: The main problem that development finds is the waiting time since the application architect has developed the diagram architecture until the developer team can start the development process. At this point, OpenShift allows reducing this process to just a few minutes with a simple command from the developer, and you can provide the hardware, software, and network.
- **Multi-language**: OpenShift allows the use of different languages, platforms, and databases, allowing developers to use all the possibilities Docker is offering. So, OpenShift will not limit users to develop in a single platform, but it gives you the power to choose the programming language.
- **Automation**: OpenShift offers automated systems to manage the life cycle of applications in the most effective way.
- **Collaboration**: One of the functionalities is one that allows the management of roles that will enable a set of operations within the same project to a set of users. For example, you can allow a user of the QA/Testing team to monitor the status of a development project and promote it to the QA or production environments when the application is running in that environment.

- **Application portability**: Being built on Docker containers, this feature allows your application to be migrated in any system that uses Docker as a container platform.

- **Open source**: Offers all the possibilities and advantages that free software provides us.

- **Scalable**: Allows applications to scale easily and automatically.

As we have seen, the additional features offered by the Red Hat OpenShift Container platform, beyond the Docker containerization engine and the Kubernetes orchestration, make this technology ideal for the integration and promotion of DevOps environments.

Here are some of the many versions of OpenShift:

- **OpenShift Origin**: This version allows you to have an OpenShift cluster managed by Red Hat to deploy your applications.
  - https://github.com/openshift

- **OpenShift online**. It allows you to create and execute applications in the public cloud offered by Red Hat. You can test OpenShift online if you log in with RedHat account credentials.
  - https://manage.openshift.com

- **OpenShift dedicated**: It allows you to have an OpenShift cluster managed by Red Hat to deploy your applications.
  - https://www.openshift.com/products/dedicated

- **OpenShift container platform**: It allows you to have an OpenShift cluster in your own infrastructure managed by Red Hat.
  - https://www.openshift.com/products/container-platform

- OKD (https://www.okd.io) : This Kubernetes distribution is optimized for continuous application development and multi-tenant deployment. It also serves as the upstream codebase upon which Red Hat OpenShift Online and Red Hat OpenShift container platforms are built. Check the documentation at **https://docs.okd.io/index.html** for more information.

We have two options for deploying an OpenShift cluster instance in a local environment:

- Run OKD in a Container following documentation from docs.okd.io site `https://docs.okd.io/latest/welcome/index.html`.

- Try out a fully functioning OKD instance with an integrated container registry and run it locally on your machine with minishift. This tool allows you to build a cluster of single nodes on a virtual machine. Check documentation at **https://www.okd.io/minishift** for all the necessary details and the instructions to start it.

Tip: Learning scenarios

The following URL— https://learn.openshift.com and figure 10.39 have interactive learning scenarios that provide you with a pre-configured OpenShift instance accessible from your browser without any downloads or configuration. Use it to experiment, learn OpenShift, and see how we can help solve real-world problems. You can start learning the Openshift basics at https://developers.redhat.com/learn/openshift.

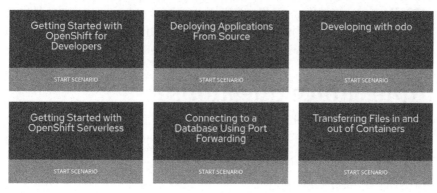

Figure 10.39: OpenShift learning scenarios

Conclusion

In this chapter, we have reviewed Portainer and Rancher open source tools for managing your Docker containers, images, volumes, and networks. These tools are compatible with other orchestration platforms like Docker Swarm and Kubernetes.

From the Container Administration point of view, Rancher provides an open source container management platform built for organizations that deploy containers in production. Additionally, Portainer allows you to manage containers, monitor logs, and containers in progress (CPU, memory, network use, and processes, etc.), run a console to access them, and work with volumes and other interesting features.

In the next chapter, we will introduce Kubernetes architecture and different tools for working with Kubernetes, such as kubectl, explaining minikube as the main tool for deploying a cluster.

Points to remember

- Within the Docker ecosystem, we can find some interesting tools for developers to safely manage the process of managing images and containers. Rancher and Portainer are some of the main tools for container administration.

- **Portainer (https://www.portainer.io)** is a user interface that allows you to manage different Docker environments (at the host level or at the cluster level with Swarm). This tool consists of a single container that can be run on any Docker engine, and it can be implemented as a Linux container or a native Windows container.

- **Rancher (http://rancher.com)** is an open source platform that runs on Docker and allows applications to be deployed on a container solution. The platform provides a section to manage the machines or instances of different cloud providers, such as AWS (Amazon), Azure (Microsoft), or Digitalocean.

Multiple choice questions

1. Which Rancher section allows you to deploy a container from the container dashboard and see the state of each one container from the Rancher interface?

   a. Catalog>containers

   b. Environment>containers

   c. Infrastructure>containers

   d. Stacks>containers

2. Which volumes do you need to mount in order for the Portainer to manage the local Docker server with the docker run command?

   a. /var/lib/docker.sock and portainer_data

   b. /var/run/docker.sock and portainer_data:/data

   c. /var/lib/docker.sock and /data

   d. /var/lib/docker.sock and portainer:/data

Answer

1	C
2	B

Questions

1. Which tool consists of a single container that can be run on any Docker engine and implemented as a Linux container or a native Windows container?

2. Which platform has a Hosts section to visually manage the machines or instances of different clouds, like AWS (Amazon), Azure (Microsoft), and Digitalocean?

3. Which check button do we need to activate to show templates related to container images like Docker registry or MySQL?

Key terms

- **Portainer**: It provides a web interface where an administrator can have an overview of containers that are running.

- **RedHat OpenShift**: It proposes a complete platform of containers integrating Docker and Kubernetes as native technologies of execution and container orchestration with a series of special functions to manage permissions, storage, application life cycle, and other functions of the enterprise base in Red Hat Enterprise Linux.

- **OKD**: It provides a complete open source container application platform. OKD is built around a core of OCI container packaging and Kubernetes container cluster management, and it is augmented by application lifecycle management functionality and DevOps tooling.

## CHAPTER 11

Kubernetes Architecture

In modern software development, K8s is a tool that becomes essential due to the many advantages it offers. It enables DevOps in large architectures, that is, it allows you to unify development and operations. It allows a team to be the owner of the project from development to deployment across different environments, including production.

This chapter introduces Kubernetes architecture, components, objects, and networking model. We will also review different tools for working with Kubernetes, explaining minikube as the main tool for deploying a cluster.

Structure

We will cover the following topics in this chapter:

- Kubernetes architecture
- Kubernetes objects
- Kubernetes networking model
- Tools for deploying Kubernetes

Objectives

After studying this chapter, you will understand Kubernetes architecture and Kubernetes objects. You will also learn about the Kubernetes networking model and tools for deploying Kubernetes.

Kubernetes architecture

Kubernetes is an orchestration tool that allows us to have our application infrastructure as code. This way, we can take our software solution to any platform as long as we have a Kubernetes cluster deployed.

The reality is that all major cloud computing providers are starting to offer Kubernetes as a service, freeing up the work that goes into maintaining and deploying the cluster. So, a software solution is achieved that avoids the *"Vendor lock-in"*, being able to migrate the solution to any Cloud.

In addition, Kubernetes performs a container monitoring task. This way, it always tries to ensure that the desired number of containers is up and running, bringing us closer to high availability.

A Kubernetes cluster is made up of different nodes, which, in turn, are made up of pods that offer services. A node corresponds to a real or virtual machine that contains all the services necessary to run the pods that it contains. A pod represents a process that is running within the cluster and can be made up of one or more running containers.

The use of Kubernetes is not only oriented to the needs of large companies but also for smaller-scale projects or for developers who want to create their own content outside the market.

Here are some of the main features that Kubernetes offers:

- **Secret and configuration management**: Secret objects in Kubernetes allow you to store and handle confidential information like passwords and authentication tokens securely. You can deploy and alter the application settings without having to rebuild the container images or exposing the stack configuration secrets.

- **Scaling**: It allows you to scale vertically and generate containers within minutes to meet the demand of our application.

- **Regeneration**: It allows us to recover from an error or crash in the server instantly by restarting or replicating the damaged containers.

- **Services and load balancing**: We don't need external tools to generate services and load balancing. K8s takes care of everything automatically and also assigns its own IP addresses and creates a DNS for the entire node.

- **Automatic deployments**: We can update our application or go back to a previous version progressively, giving our users continuous availability.

- **Secrets**: It allows us to handle sensitive information such as SSH keys or passwords, encoding the information and assigning it to a special resource called **secret**.

Components of a Kubernetes cluster

The elements that make up the architecture of a Kubernetes cluster fall into two categories: **Master components** and **Node components**.

The following diagram contains the different basic components of a Kubernetes cluster, which will be explained later:

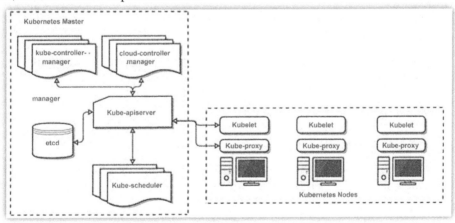

Figure 11.1: *Kubernetes architecture*

The Master nodes are in charge of deciding which node each container runs on, maintaining the state of the cluster, ensuring that the desired number of containers are running at all times, and updating applications in a coordinated manner when new versions are deployed. The following points refers to the processes running on the Master node:

- **kube-apiserver:** The Kubernetes API server verifies and configures data for API objects like pods, services, controllers, and other cluster-related items. This component exposes the Kubernetes API and serves as the Control Plane's front-end. At this point, controlplane nodes run the Kubernetes API server, scheduler, and controller manager. These nodes take care of routine tasks to ensure that the cluster maintains the configuration.

- **kube-controller-manager:** It's a process control loop that uses the API to monitor the cluster's shared state and makes modifications in order to move the cluster from its present state to the desired state.

- **cloud-controller-manager:** It's a daemon process that runs on the master node and is in charge of managing *"the cloud controllers"*. Those controllers have dependencies on cloud providers like Amazon, Google Cloud, or Azure.

- **kube-scheduler:** This module is in charge of workload distribution as well as maintaining the affinity between pods in order to boost cluster performance.

- **etcd:** Cluster data storage service is responsible for maintaining all the status information of the cluster and its configuration. In large clusters, it can be distributed among several nodes that do not necessarily have to be master nodes of the cluster itself. You can find more information at **https:// github.com/etcd-io/etcd**.

kube-controller-manager consists of a single process that includes the following controllers:

- **Node-Controller**: Responsible for notifying and responding when a node goes down

- **Replication-Controller**: Responsible for maintaining the correct number of Pods in the system

- **Endpoint-Controller**: Brings Pods and Kubernetes services together

- **Token and Service Account Controller**: Creates default accounts and API access tokens for each namespace

The following diagram contains the different basic controllers of the **kube-controller-manage** component and the connection with the API-Server:

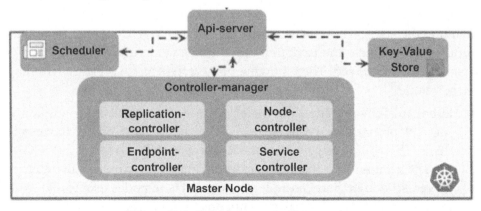

Figure 11.2: Kubernetes controller-manager

The previous figure highlights the presence of the **ETCD** or **Key-Value Store** component. Basically, this component is a **Distributed Key-Value Store** for the Cluster.

These master components are in charge of making global cluster choices as well as detecting and responding to various events. These components can operate on any server in the cluster, but they are often started on the same machine when deploying a Kubernetes cluster, and user containers are rarely executed on that machine.

The following refers to the processes running on the worker node:

- `kubelet:` It is the principal process that runs on each worker node, and it is responsible for managing the node's connectivity to the cluster as well as keeping the cluster informed about the various pods and workloads that are operating on its own node.

- `kube-proxy:` The proxy module is in charge of managing and balancing the various network flows by functioning as a network proxy. It keeps track of a set of network rules that allow Pods to communicate with one another from within or outside the cluster. In theory, it uses the operating system's packet filtering layer if it is available, but it redirects the traffic itself if it isn't.

- **Container runtime**: Software responsible for running the containers. Kubernetes supports different software for this purpose, such as Docker, containerd (**https://containerd.io**), and cri-o (**https://cri-o.io**).

These node components run on all nodes that user containers run on, allowing for Pod maintenance and providing a software container environment to Kubernetes.

You can find the official documentation about Kubernetes components at **https://kubernetes.io/docs/concepts/overview/components**.

Tip: Other Kubernetes elements

Apart from the previous elements, there is a set of add-ons that run on the cluster. These add-ons are like containers and are optional. They usually run in the kube-system namespace and offer traversal services. The best known ones are:

- **Kubernetes Dashboard: https://github.com/kubernetes/dashboard**
- **CoreDNS: https://coredns.io**

You can find different add-ons, organized by categories, at

`https://kubernetes.io/docs/concepts/cluster-administration/addons/.`

Kubernetes objects

Kubernetes objects are persistent entities on the cluster system that are used to display the cluster's state, including:

- What applications are running in containers and the node they are running on
- The resources available for those applications
- The policies and rules associated with those applications

Kubernetes verifies that an object exists and functions properly when it is formed in the cluster. The specification and the state of an object within the cluster define it.

The specification describes the desired state, that is, the features and configuration that you want to have in the object, while the state describes the point where the object is at the current moment. These two factors are supplied and updated by Kubernetes, which ensures that the current equal state and the specified or desired state match at all times.

Due to the large amount of information that is usually associated with each deployment, it is not convenient or practical to do it directly using commands, except in certain situations. So, the best solution is to configure a `.yaml` file. An example of a configuration file with an nginx deployment is shown below:

```
apiVersion: apps/v1
kind: Deployment
metadata:
  name: nginx-deployment
spec:
  selector:
    matchLabels:
      app: nginx
  replicas: 2 #controller instruction to execute 2 pods
  template:
    metadata:
      labels:
        app: nginx
    spec:
      containers:
      - name: nginx
        image: nginx:1.7.9
        ports:
        - containerPort: 80
```

Here, you can see an example of these YAML files with the description of a deployment type object, in which it is specified that two replicas of an Nginx web server are required, running inside two containers.

In the previous deployment file, we can highlight the apiVersion (with the version of the Kubernetes API that you intend to use), kind (with the type of object described), metadata, and spec fields as required.

Creating an object using a file similar to the previous one allows us to create a multitude of variants and perform almost any function we want, thanks to the versatility of the different objects. Not all of them need all the information shown, so the only mandatory fields common to all are:

- **apiVersion**: Specifies which version of the Kubernetes API to use to create the object
- **kind**: Specifies what type of object you want to create
- **metadata**: A single piece of data that allows the object to be differentiated by including a string of characters, such as name (name) or user ID (UID) and optionally, also a namespace.

The main Kubernetes objects needed to understand how they work are listed here:

- **Pods**: It's Kubernetes' fundamental unit, the smallest and most basic drop-down object in your model. A Pod contains a software container (or more), storage resources, and network resources (unique IP address and TCP/UDP ports).
- **Controllers**: These objects create and manage multiple Pods, handling replicas and providing automatic repair capability. For example, the controller can automatically replace a scheduled Pod on the node with an identical replacement on a different node if a node fails. There are different types of controllers, such as deployments, statefulSets (for stateful applications that save data related to their sessions), and daemonSets (they ensure that all nodes have a replica of the Pod, useful for monitoring or logging Pods, for example).
- **Service**: It's an abstract way of offering a network service for an application operating on a number of Pods. Kubernetes can assign a set of Pods on their own IP address and domain name and balance the load between them using services. The presence of Services is motivated by the fact that Pods in Kubernetes have a finite life cycle.

  Kubernetes provides name resolution of the services within the cluster in addition to the IP addresses assigned to them. We will be able to communicate among PODs using the names of the previously established Services in this way.

- **Ingress**: An Ingress provides externally accessible URLs, load balancing, TLS termination, and name-based virtual hosting to Kubernetes Services by exposing HTTP and HTTPS routes from outside the cluster to Kubernetes Services. It's the most common method for externally exposing HTTP or HTTPS ports.

- **Ingress Controller**: Ingress controller deploys a container into a Pod in the cluster. Several load balancing system providers, such as HAProxy and Nginx, have developed their own ingress controller.

All objects in Kubernetes consist of metadata, a specification, and a state. You must interact with the Kubernetes API by providing metadata and the spec in JSON format within the request field to create an object.

The most typical method is to use a command line client like kubectl, to which a file in the YAML format is supplied and then transformed into JSON to make the API request. There are, however, a variety of clients for various contexts and programming languages.

Pods

Pods (**https://kubernetes.io/docs/concepts/workloads/pods**) are the smallest deployment unit in Kubernetes. You can also specify Pods with many containers, which forces these containers to be deployed in the same node at all times. This is useful if containers communicate over the filesystem.

The following figure shows pod components:

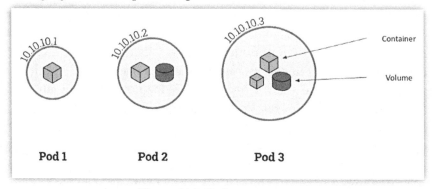

Figure 11.3: Pods components

Containers inside a Pod have access to network and storage resources. In terms of the network, each pod is assigned a unique IP address and each container uses the same network, both IP and port.

Within the definition of the Pods, we can define the containers through a multitude of options:

- **Name of the Pod**: Name of the Pod to identify it within the cluster

- **Image of the container to be displayed**: We define the name of the container that we want to deploy using the image key

- **Environment variables**: We can specify a list of variable names and values that will be injected into the container as environment variables using the '**env:**' key

- **Ports used by the container**: A list of ports used by the container can be included

- **PullPolicy**: Container unloading policy; for example, we can indicate that it always pulls the container image before deploying it

- **Reserve and resource limits**: We can define reserves in the resources (RAM and CPU) of the node in which the node will be deployed using the resources' key, and we can also define limits

- **Readiness and liveness**: Thanks to ReadinessProbes and LivenessProbes, the Kubernetes cluster can know when a container is ready to serve traffic after it is started and if it is still ready for this task. These tests can be REST calls to a certain endpoint or even commands executed within the container itself.

We can describe the structure of a pod in a YAML format file, like the **nginx.yaml** file, as follows:

```
apiVersion: v1
kind: Pod
metadata:
  name: nginx
  namespace: default
  labels:
    app: nginx
spec:
  containers:
    - image:   nginx
      name:   nginx
```

Each existing pod contains the needed application, storage resources, IP address, and other container-specific parameters. In Kubernetes, a pod represents a single instance of an application, which might be one or more containers sharing resources. Note that all the containers in a pod share the same IP address and are accessible with localhost addresses.

A pod cannot recover by itself when it dies for some reason; the Kubernetes controller decides whether to create a new one to meet the total number of pods desired by the user.

For storage, each pod can specify a shared storage (called a **volume**) that all existing containers can access and so, share the necessary data. The volumes created can be persistent to save the necessary information, even if the pod has to be restarted.

Pods are ephemeral, which means that all the information they contain is lost when they are destroyed. We have to use volumes if we want to develop persistent applications.

Volumes

The files on disk related to the containers that are running inside the various pods are ephemeral, which presents two main problems. First is that a container is restarted when it stops its execution, but it loses all the content it might have since it starts with the initial configuration. Second is that it is usually necessary for two containers running simultaneously in the same pod to exchange information.

In Kubernetes, a volume can be thought of as a directory that the various containers within a pod can access and save information in. Here are some of the main types of volume:

- **emptyDir:** A basic type of volume is created when a pod is first allocated to a node. It starts out as an empty directory, and then the containers fill it in with the necessary data. The volume will be active for as long as the pod that contains it is active, and the data will be finished once the pod is finished.

- **nfs:** This volume type lets you mount an existing **Network File System** (**NFS**) share on the pod. When a pod completes its execution, the volume is dismounted rather than removed, allowing the information it contains to be accessed by other pods at the same time.

- **persistentVolumeClaim:** This is used to mount a persistent volume, which is a way to use storage space in a durable way.

- **secret:** This is used to pass confidential information, such as passwords, access codes, or tokens, to the pods. They are stored in key-value pair format using tmpfs, which uses volatile memory.

Deployment

Deployment (**https://kubernetes.io/docs/concepts/workloads/controllers/deployment/**) defines the ReplicaSet, which is in charge of controlling the number of Pods and their allocation between the different nodes. We can mainly specify the following features in the definition of deployment:

- **Name of the deployment**: Name of the deployment to identify it within the cluster

- **Deployment tags**: We can define labels to be able to reference the Deployment in other components of the cluster using the `'labels'` key

- **Number of replicas desired**: The number of replicas of the POD that we want to deploy

- **Upgrade strategies**: We can choose between several strategies for updating the Deployment

- **Version history**: We can indicate how many previous versions are saved with the `'revisionHistoryLimit'` key in our Deployment definition file; we can go back to a previous version of Deployment quickly this way

ReplicaSet

ReplicaSet (**https://kubernetes.io/docs/concepts/workloads/controllers/replicaset/**) is a Kubernetes feature, which ensures that a number of replicas of a given pod is always executing in the cluster. This way, it ensures that our pods are always available.

Kubernetes uses the **kube-controller and kube scheduler** services for this. This way, if a deployment specifies that we need five replicas of a Pod, the ReplicaSet will ensure that there are always five active and executing replicas in the cluster.

In addition, the ReplicaSet is in charge of supporting the version history functionality mentioned in the Deployment, depending on how many versions we need to work, we can easily return to a previous version of the ReplicaSet.

A new ReplicaSet is created to manage the new replicas with the new image when a Deployment is updated with a new version of a container image. Later on, we'll go through how Kubernetes handles updates and version control.

The following figure shows Kubernetes ReplicaSet configuration for an application that provides front and backend services:

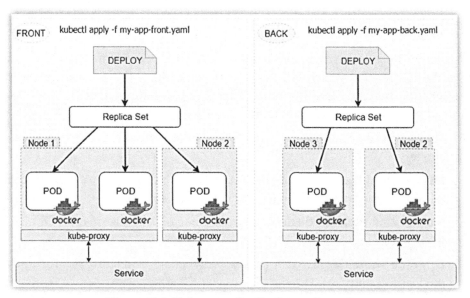

Figure 11.4: Kubernetes ReplicaSet configuration

Here, we can see a distribution that can withstand the collapse of any of the nodes in our application.

Services

A service in Kubernetes is an abstraction layer used to route traffic to the corresponding pods, so it is not necessary to find the IP address of each of them supporting TCP and UDP. Labels are commonly used to identify which pods should be routed, so the service simply needs that label to match, regardless of how the pods were formed.

The following figure shows the most important Kubernetes services:

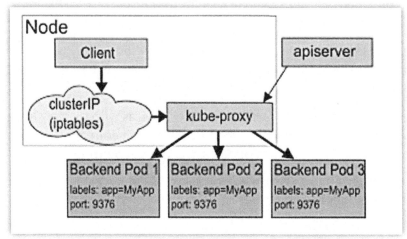

Figure 11.5: Kubernetes services

Here are some of the main types of services:

- **ClusterIP:** It is the default service type and exposes the service with an internal IP of the cluster, so it is accessible only by the objects inside it.

- **NodePort:** It exposes the service on each node using the node's own IP address and a static port, automatically creating a **ClusterIP** service to which the **NodePort** service is routed. The service can be accessed from outside the cluster using the **<NodeIP>: <NodePort>** path by exposing the node.

- **LoadBalancer:** It exposes the service externally using a load balancer provided by an external agent. The **NodePort** and **ClusterIP** services are automatically created to follow the path between the pod and the outside.

StatefulSets

ReplicaSets objects are intended for pods that have the same state and so can be exposed on K8s under the same IP with a balancer between them, while **StatefulSets** have a directly different approach.

What happens if one of the pods replicates the application deployed in it and has a different status than the rest ?. In this case, we cannot go to any of them under a single IP address with a balancer. Here, the idea is to manage the applications where this casuistry occurs.

StatefulSets (**https://kubernetes.io/docs/concepts/workloads/controllers/statefulset/**) are similar to deployment, with the exception that they are intended for Pods that require unique network identifiers, persistent storage, ordered deployments, or updates in a certain order.

In addition, the PODs maintain a unique identifier that persists even if they are reassigned to other nodes, unlike the PODs controlled by the deployment. The data volumes handled by these drivers must be of the PersistentVolume type.

Kubernetes networking model

Decoupled microservices-based applications rely heavily on networks to mimic the tight coupling that was once available in the monolithic era. Networks, in general, are not the easiest to understand and implement. Kubernetes is no exception as a Containerized Microservices Orchestrator must address four distinct network challenges:

- Container to container communication within Pods

- Pod to Pod communication in the same node and in all cluster nodes
- Pod-to-service communication within the same Namespace and between cluster Namespaces
- External communication to the service for clients to access applications in a cluster

All of these networking challenges need to be addressed before implementing a Kubernetes cluster. Next, we will review some of these models.

Container to container communication within Pods

A container environment creates an isolated network space for each container that it starts with the help of the kernel features of the underlying host operating system. On the Linux operating system, this isolated network space is called a **Network Namespace** and is shared between containers or with the host operating system.

A network namespace is created within the Pod when a Pod is started, and all containers running within the Pod will share that network namespace so that they can communicate with each other via localhost.

Pod to Pod communication through cluster nodes

Pods are assigned to nodes in a Kubernetes cluster in a random way, and they should be able to connect with all other Pods in the cluster regardless of their Host Node (host), all without the use of **Network Address Translation** (**NAT**). This is a prerequisite for any Kubernetes-based network implementation.

In this case, the Kubernetes network model aims to reduce complexity and treats Pods as it does **Virtual Machines** (**VMs**) on a network, where each VM receives an IP address; so, each Pod receives an IP address. This model ensures Pod-to-Pod communication in the same way that virtual machines can communicate with each other.

External communication from the Pod

Successfully deploying containerized applications running on Pods within a Kubernetes cluster requires accessibility to and from the external network.

In this case, services are processes that encapsulate network rule specification in the cluster nodes and are used by Kubernetes to provide connectivity in this situation. The apps become accessible from outside the cluster using a virtual IP after using the kube-proxy to expose the services to the external network.

Tools for deploying Kubernetes

The Kubernetes concept was born to serve as a platform for any deployment that is required, so any additional features needed in the implementation must be configured based on specific integrations, contextualizing the project in which they will work.

Cluster election

There are different technologies of Kubernetes depending on the tasks we want to perform. Each of these solutions has their own characteristics and advantages:

- **Minikube https://github.com/kubernetes/minikube** : You can execute this on Linux, Windows, and MacOS as it relies on virtualization to deploy a cluster on a Linux virtual machine. It can be run on a Linux operating system without the need for virtualization.

- **Kubeadm https://github.com/kubernetes/kubeadm** : This is the official CNCF tool for provisioning Kubernetes clusters in a variety of ways (single node, multi node, HA, self-hosted, etc.). Its main benefit is the ability to launch minimal viable Kubernetes pools anywhere.

- **Kops (Kubernetes Operations) https://github.com/kubernetes/kops** : It provides a set of tools for installing, operating, and removing Kubernetes clusters on cloud platforms. AWS, Google Cloud Platform, OpenStack, DigitalOCean are some of the platforms it supports.

- **Microk8s (https://microk8s.io)** : It is similar to Minikube in aspects like raising single node clusters and having its own set of add-ons that act as configuration plugins. It has the added difficulty of only being able to run on Linux.

- **K3s (https://k3s.io)** : It runs on any Linux distribution without any additional external dependencies. K3s replace Docker with containerd as container runtime and uses sqlite3 as default database. It is light, with a consumption of 512MB of RAM and 200MB of disk space.

- **Kind** (Kubernetes-in-Docker) **https://kind.sigs.k8s.io** : It runs Kubernetes clusters in Docker containers. It supports multi-node clusters as well as HA Clusters (High-Availability). Kind can run on Windows, Mac, and Linux operating systems because it runs on top of Docker.

- **K3d https://k3d.io** : It is a new project that aims to bring dockerized K3s.

The final choice of where to run Kubernetes varies according to the needs of each project, so there is no better or worse solution. That said, it is true that a cloud solution facilitates the creation and maintenance since it is in charge of the server where it is hosted, generally in the case of large companies.

Knowing the basic operation of Kubernetes, the next step is to create an environment that allows you to use the tool. This environment is called a cluster, and the options to create it exist both locally and on the cloud.

Working with Kubernetes using Minikube

The simplest way to start interacting with a Kubernetes cluster is through the Minikube. It is an official Kubernetes project that allows you to run a single node cluster in a local environment. It is a multiplatform tool and can be used on Windows, Linux, and macOS.

Minikube configures a single node cluster, so there are limitations that make the tool useless if you need to orchestrate applications that need heavy loading or in a production environment, but it is very useful for development and testing of software products.

Running the tool will launch a virtual machine with Kubernetes installed on which the cluster will work, unless otherwise specified with the **vm-driver = none** parameter. This will make Minikube directly use the Docker host installed on the computer.

This use is dangerous because the program is run as an administrator directly on the computer, which makes it vulnerable to possible attacks. However, it is necessary if you want to create the cluster in a virtual machine since another degree of virtualization is not allowed. In other words, the virtual machine on which you are working does not allow Minikube to create a machine where you can run Kubernetes.

These are the steps to follow for installing MiniKube:

```
#Download the package:
curl -Lo minikube
$    https://storage.googleapis.com/minikube/releases/latest/mini-
kube-linux-amd64
#Execution permissions
$ chmod +x minikube
#Copy the file in the /bin/ PATH
$ sudo cp minikube /usr/local/bin && rm minikube
#check command version
$ minikube version
```

Once installed, we can check if the system recognizes the minikube keyword. You only need the `minikube start` command to start the cluster. The necessary image is downloaded and the indicated settings are made in the startup process, and those that Minikube performs by default are considered if none are indicated.

The following output shows the command execution for starting minikube:

```
$ minikube start --wait=false

* minikube v1.8.1 on Ubuntu 18.04

* Using the none driver based on user configuration

* Running on localhost (CPUs=2, Memory=2460MB, Disk=145651MB) ...

* OS release is Ubuntu 18.04.4 LTS

* Preparing Kubernetes v1.17.3 on Docker 19.03.6 ...

  - kubelet.resolv-conf=/run/systemd/resolve/resolv.conf

* Launching Kubernetes ...

* Enabling addons: default-storageclass, storage-provisioner

* Configuring local host environment ...

* Done! kubectl is now configured to use "minikube"
```

This command starts minikube without any additional configuration, and both the chosen virtual machine and the required hardware resources or the cluster IP address are automatically configured according to the default values.

Kubectl should configure itself automatically when starting Minikube. We can use the following command that generates a dashboard to view the status of the cluster to move from the command line to a graphical user interface:

```
$ minikube dashboard

* Enabling dashboard ...

* Verifying dashboard health ...

* Launching proxy ...

* Verifying proxy health ...

http://127.0.0.1:42407/api/v1/namespaces/kubernetes-dashboard/
services/http:kubernetes-dashboard:/proxy
```

At this point, we will be able to interact with our cluster using kubectl.

Interacting with the cluster using kubectl

The way for a user to interact with the cluster is through the Kubernetes API. The **kubectl** command—a tool that translates commands entered by the client through a command line interface to the Kubernetes engine— facilitates this communication.

We can install kubectl with the following commands:

```
$ sudo apt-get update && sudo apt-get install -y apt-transport-https
```

```
$ curl -s https://packages.cloud.google.com/apt/doc/apt-key.gpg |
sudo apt-key add -
```

```
$ echo "deb https://apt.kubernetes.io/ kubernetes-xenial main" |
sudo tee -a /etc/apt/sources.list.d/kubernetes.list
```

```
$ sudo apt-get update
```

```
$ sudo apt-get install -y kubectl
```

Once installed, we can execute it for checking the options:

```
$ kubectl [command] [TYPE] [NAME] [flags]
```

Here:

- **command** specifies the operation to be performed over the cluster
- **TYPE** specifies the type of resource (pod, service, namespace …)
- **NAME** specifies the name of the resource; all resources of the indicated type will be displayed if this is omitted
- **flags** specify optional input parameters; you can see all the allowed parameters with the kubectl options command

We can verify the Kubernetes configuration before we start running the kubectl command. We have a file called **kubeconfig** for this task; it is used to configure access to Kubernetes. By default, kubectl checks the **~/.kube/config** path for a kubeconfig file, but you can use any directory you want using the **--kubeconfig** flag.

For example, you can use the following command to change the default path file configuration:

```
$ kubectl --kubeconfig /custom/path/kube.config get pods
```

The first thing we can do is obtain the nodes that are part of the cluster using the following command:

```
$ kubectl get nodes

NAME        STATUS    ROLES     AGE    VERSION

minikube    Ready     master    12m    v1.17.3
```

The output of the preceding command shows how we have a single node that acts as master and worker.

The following command displays cluster status information:

```
$ kubectl cluster-info

Kubernetes master is running at https://172.17.0.57:8443

KubeDNS is running at https://172.17.0.57:8443/api/v1/namespaces/
kube-system/services/kube-dns:dns/proxy
```

Another option is to create deployments through the terminal. To do this, the contents must already be integrated into a Docker image stored in a repository, as follows:

```
$ kubectl create deployment --image=<docker_image>
```

We can continue creating a deployment from a docker nginx image, as shown here:

```
$ kubectl create deployment myapp --image=nginx:latest
deployment.apps/myapp created
$ kubectl get deployments
NAME     READY   UP-TO-DATE   AVAILABLE   AGE
myapp    0/1     1            0           11s
$ kubectl describe deployment myapp
Name:                 myapp
Namespace:            default
CreationTimestamp:    Sat, 19 Jun 2021 19:46:06 +0000
Labels:               app=myapp
Annotations:          deployment.kubernetes.io/revision: 1
Selector:             app=myapp
Replicas:             1 desired | 1 updated | 1 total | 1 avail-
able | 0 unavailable
StrategyType:         RollingUpdate
MinReadySeconds:      0
```

```
RollingUpdateStrategy:   25% max unavailable, 25% max surge
Pod Template:
  Labels:  app=myapp
  Containers:
   nginx:
    Image:          nginx:latest
    Port:           <none>
    Host Port:      <none>
    Environment:    <none>
    Mounts:         <none>
   Volumes:         <none>
Conditions:
  Type            Status   Reason
  ----            ------   ------
  Available       True     MinimumReplicasAvailable
  Progressing     True     NewReplicaSetAvailable
OldReplicaSets:   <none>
NewReplicaSet:    myapp-7d88697bdc (1/1 replicas created)
Events:
  Type     Reason           Age    From                  Message
  ----     ------           ----   ----                  -------
Normal   ScalingReplicaSet  29s    deployment-controller  Scaled up
replica set myapp-7d88697bdc to 1
```

We can get information about the running pods with following command:

```
$ kubectl get pods --all-namespaces
NAMESPACE              NAME                           READY
STATUS      RESTARTS   AGE
default                myapp-7d88697bdc-zqsg8            1/1
Running     0          22m
kube-system            coredns-6955765f44-f2nxg          1/1
Running     0          44m
kube-system            coredns-6955765f44-tnlc7          1/1
Running     0          44m
```

```
kube-system              etcd-minikube                          1/1
Running     0            44m
kube-system              kube-apiserver-minikube                1/1
Running     0            44m
kube-system              kube-controller-manager-minikube       1/1
Running     0            44m
kube-system              kube-proxy-t7zdp                        1/1
Running     0            44m
kube-system              kube-scheduler-minikube                1/1
Running     0            44m
kube-system              storage-provisioner                    1/1
Running     1            44m
kubernetes-dashboard     dashboard-metrics-scraper-7b64584c5c-5h6lq
1/1        Running    0          32m
kubernetes-dashboard     kubernetes-dashboard-79d9cd965-jrvcf
1/1        Running    0          32m
```

We can also get information about the running services with the following command:

```
$ kubectl get services

NAME          TYPE         CLUSTER-IP    EXTERNAL-IP    PORT(S)    AGE

kubernetes    ClusterIP    10.96.0.1     <none>         443/TCP    55m
```

Once we have the pods running, we can increase the number of replicas for that specific deployment with the following command:

```
$ kubectl scale deployment myapp --replicas=2
```

We can also execute the same action by editing the deployment file:

```
$ kubectl edit deployment myapp
```

We will continue explaining how to create Pods and Replications Controllers. We can do it in two ways: with a file (YAML, JSON) or by command line. We can use the following kubectl command, which is the one in charge of interacting with the Kubernetes API, to do it through the command line:

```
$ kubectl run webserver-nginx --image=nginx --generator=run-pod/v1
```

We can use the following command to see if the pod is running correctly:

```
$ kubectl get pods -o wide

NAME                                 READY    STATUS             RESTARTS
AGE     IP              NODE      NOMINATED NODE   READINESS GATES

webserver-nginx                      1/1      Running                   0
8m11s   172.18.0.6      minikube  <none>           <none>
```

The previous output shows the pod status (Running), IP address (172.18.0.6) of the pod within our cluster, and in which node it is deployed (minikube).

This service is only visible from the internal network of the cluster, so we can use cURL to access the content that the pod is serving. It returns a message from nginx server in this case:

```
$ curl http://172.18.0.11:80
<!DOCTYPE html>
<html>
<head>
<title>Welcome to nginx!</title>
<style>
    body {
        width: 35em;
        margin: 0 auto;
        font-family: Tahoma, Verdana, Arial, sans-serif;
    }
</style>
```

We see that pods are all created with the same name and a unique identifier. We can execute the following command to see the information of a pod:

```
$ kubectl describe pod <pod_identifier>
$ kubectl describe pod webserver-nginx
Name:        webserver-nginx
Namespace:   default
Priority:    0
Node:        minikube/172.17.0.29
Start Time:  Sat, 19 Jun 2021 21:24:36 +0000
```

```
Labels:         run=webserver-nginx
Annotations:    <none>
Status:         Running
IP:             172.18.0.11
IPs:
  IP:   172.18.0.11
Containers:
  webserver-nginx:
    Container ID:       docker://72ff36a52aa5a0f09415f922e3e33a42c-
    f4523136879005ab47e8ef8c09b7edf
    Image:              nginx
    Image ID:           docker-pullable://nginx@sha256:6d75c99a-
    f15565a301e48297fa2d121e15d80ad526f8369c526324f0f7ccb750
    Port:               <none>
    Host Port:          <none>
    State:              Running
```

The next step can be to create a deployment using the kubectl apply command and associate a YAML file with it that contains all the necessary parameters for it. The following file contains a deployment configuration for the nginx server:

nginx-deployment.yaml

```
apiVersion: apps/v1
kind: Deployment
metadata:
  name: nginx-deployment
  labels:
    app: nginx
spec:
  replicas: 3
  selector:
    matchLabels:
      app: nginx
  template:
    metadata:
```

```
    labels:
      app: nginx
  spec:
    containers:
      - name: nginx
        image: nginx:latest
        ports:
          - containerPort: 80
```

You can see that the Deployment type contains this YAML. We are creating three replicas, and we are using an nginx container image using the port 80. We can launch this deployment with the following command:

```
$ kubectl apply -f nginx-deployment.yaml
```

If we obtain the pods now, there are three instances in running state corresponding to the number of replicas that we have added in the deployment file:

```
$ kubectl get pods -o wide

NAME                         READY    STATUS              RESTARTS    AGE    IP
NODE            NOMINATED NODE   READINESS GATES

nginx-deployment-59c9f8dff-77f55    1/1       Running                    0
16m   172.18.0.9    minikube   <none>              <none>

nginx-deployment-59c9f8dff-dfcw8    1/1       Running                    0
16m   172.18.0.8    minikube   <none>              <none>

nginx-deployment-59c9f8dff-pbrtj    1/1       Running                    0
16m   172.18.0.10   minikube   <none>              <none>
```

At this point, the ideal thing to do would be to have a balancer that allows us access to the deployment. To do this, a service will have to be created through the kubectl expose command, which will be of ClusterIP type by default, and the port through which we want to access must be specified as follows:

```
$ kubectl expose deployment nginx-deployment --port=8000

service/nginx-deployment exposed
```

In this case, we are exposing the deployment through port 8000 of the service. By doing this, we will see the following output if we visualize the services:

```
$ kubectl get services

NAME                TYPE       CLUSTER-IP     EXTERNAL-IP  PORT(S)   AGE

kubernetes          ClusterIP  10.96.0.1      <none>       443/TCP   43m

nginx-deployment  ClusterIP  10.107.75.11  <none>       8000/TCP  26s
```

> **Tip**
>
> **Play with Kubernetes clusters**
>
> The http://play-with-k8s.com site allows you to mount Kubernetes clusters and launch replicated services quickly and easily. It is an environment where we can test and play for four hours with several Docker instances on which we can use kubeadm to install and configure Kubernetes, creating a cluster in less than a minute.
>
> Visit the Play with Kubernetes Classroom at https://training.play-with-kubernetes.com if you want to learn more about Kubernetes. It provides more direct learning using an integrated Play with Kubernetes command line.
>
> **Kubectl commands**
>
> The https://kubernetes.io/docs/reference/generated/kubectl/kubectl-commands site provides a complete reference of the commands to execute on a Kubernetes cluster using the kubectl command. These commands help users in writing K8s resources (YAML files).
>
> For example, we can use kubectl api-resources to obtain a list of the resources that we have available on the server and with the kubectl api-versions command to get supported API versions on the server.

Conclusion

The use of Kubernetes is not only oriented to the needs of large companies but also for smaller-scale projects or developers who want to create their own content outside the market. Kubernetes provides the necessary software to build, implement, and configure reliable and scalable distributed systems as it contains the most important needs to run containerized applications, like the following:

- Deployment of containers
- Persistent storage

- Container status monitoring
- Resource management
- Automatic scaling
- Cluster robustness

In this chapter, we reviewed Kubernetes as an open source system originally developed by Google and used to automate the deployment, scaling, and management of containerized applications across multiple hosts. Like containers, Kubernetes is designed to run anywhere from scratch, whether on a local computer, the public cloud, or a hybrid.

In the next chapter, we will review Kubernetes security patterns and best practices for securing components and pods, applying the principle of least privilege in Kubernetes.

Points to remember

- A Kubernetes Pod is a logical grouping of components. Pods contain at least one container, and its components are deployed on the same host sharing resources. These containers share network and storage.

- Volumes allow you to assign persistent storage to pods. The data contained in this storage is not lost when the pod is restarted, and it can also be used as shared storage for containers within the pod itself.

- A service is a collection of pods that work together to provide a specific service. The service can be exposed internally to the Kubernetes cluster with DNS or externally to be visible from clients outside the cluster.

- kubelet is responsible for managing pods and their containers, their images, their volumes, etc. Each node runs a kubelet, which is responsible for registering each node and managing the pods running on that node. Kubelets asks the API server for pods to be created and deployed by the Scheduler and for pods to be deleted based on cluster events. It also manages and communicates the use of resources, the status of the nodes, and the pods running on it.

- etcd is a highly available database (distributed in multiple nodes) that stores key-values in which Kubernetes stores information (configuration and metadata) about itself, pods, services, networks, etc. so that it can be used by any node in the cluster. This functionality coordinates the components in the event of changes in these values. Kubernetes uses etcd to store cluster state as well.

- Kube-scheduler is responsible for distributing the pods among the nodes, and it assigns the pods to the nodes, reads the pod requirements, analyzes the cluster, and selects the acceptable nodes. It communicates with the API server in search of un-deployed pods to be deployed on the node that best satisfies the requirements. It is also responsible for monitoring the resource utilization of each host to ensure that pods do not exceed the available resources.

- The most widely used local solutions for working with kubernetes include kubeadm, which allows several nodes to be included in the cluster, meaning that it has a master and different workers. Minikube is another local solution for working with kubernetes, and it is made up of only one node and is the ideal solution for development and test environments outside the business environment.

- Whichever option is chosen, a point in common is the obligation of having to communicate with the Kubernetes API to satisfy the requests. This communication is done through kubectl.

Multiple choice questions

1. A Deployment is a Kubernetes object that provides updates to which of the following?

   a. Secrets and Pods

   b. ConfigMaps and Secrets

   c. ReplicaSets and ConfigMaps

   d. Pods and ReplicaSets

2. Which of the following are Kubernetes objects?

   a. Namespaces and ConfigMaps

   b. Kubelets and Clusters

   c. Namespaces and Clusters

   d. ConfigMaps and Kubelets

Answers

1	d
2	A

Questions

1. Which kubectl command creates an object using the details in the pod.json file?

2. Which Kubernetes object represents a single instance of processes running in a container?

3. What does create do in this sample kubectl command: kubectl create -f nginx. yaml?

Key terms

*   The official Kubernetes documentation describes Kubernetes as "a portable, extensible, open source platform for managing containerized workloads and services that facilitates both declarative configuration and automation.

*   "etcd" is a highly available key value store that contains all the cluster data. When you tell Kubernetes to deploy your application, that deployment configuration is stored in etcd. So, etcd is the source of truth for the state in a Kubernetes cluster, and the system works to bring the cluster state

*   Kubernetes objects are persistent entities in Kubernetes. "Persistent" means that when you create an object, Kubernetes continually works to ensure that that object exists in the system, unless you modify or remove that object. This way, Kubernetes objects define the state of your cluster. Pods, namespaces, Deployments, ConfigMaps, and volumes are a few examples of Kubernetes objects.

*   The Pod represents a single instance of an application within Kubernetes that can consist of a single container or a small number of containers that share resources.

*   kubectl provides a wide range of functionality for working with Kubernetes clusters and managing the workloads that run in a cluster. For example, you can simply run the **"kubectl run nginx --image nginx"** command to create a Pod that runs a specific container, in this case, **"nginx"**.

*   Another way to deploy an application is using a specific YAML file that contains the object configuration, and it specifies that this object should be created. This is an improvement over basic imperative commands because the configuration template makes replicating the changes much simpler. All the configuration is available in the file, so it's easy to perform this operation multiple times or in multiple environments.

*   The most supported solutions by the Kubernetes community for creating a local cluster are as follows:

a. **Minikube**: Tool to create a single node cluster (being the same master and slave node) ideal for development and testing. Installation is automated and does not require a cloud provider.

b. **Kubeadm**: A multi-node (master and slave) cluster that only requires the use of the Docker engine, that is, it only requires Docker to be installed. For cloud services, the popularity belongs to large companies like Google, Microsoft, IBM, or Amazon.

CHAPTER 12
Kubernetes Security

Kubernetes has become a standard way of implementing applications in containers at scale and helps us handle complex container deployments. As Kubernetes grows and evolves, some of its excesses are likely to be controlled from within. That said, some people are not expecting Kubernetes to become easier to use and have released their own solutions to many common problems with Kubernetes in production.

In this chapter, we will learn about Kubernetes security and best practices for securing components and pods by applying the principle of least privilege in Kubernetes.

Structure

We will cover the following topics in this chapter:

- Introducing Kubernetes security
- Kubernetes security best practices
- Kubernetes security risks
- Analyzing Kubernetes components security

Objectives

After studying this chapter, you will understand the principles and best practices of Kubernetes security and learn about security risks in Kubernetes and Kubernetes components security.

Introducing Kubernetes security

Kubernetes and Docker are revolutionizing the world of computing, application development, and specifically, DevSecOps. Both technologies combined offer us benefits like scaling and managing the implementation of an application or a service by using containers, to the point of becoming a true standard for orchestration. Like any other infrastructure, we must take precautions while implementing them to try to make it as secure as possible while offering the best final performance.

From the perspective of DevOps, Kubernetes has the following characteristics:

- **Operating in the DevOps model**: In the DevOps model, software developers assume greater responsibility for building and deploying applications.

- **Creation of common service sets**: Applications request a service from another application pointing to an IP address and port number. With Kubernetes, we can build applications in containers that provide services that are available for other containers to use.

- **Data-center pre-configuration**: Kubernetes aims to create consistent **Application Programming Interfaces (APIs)** that result in stable environments for running applications in containers. Developers should be able to create applications that work in any cloud provider that supports those APIs. This reliable framework means developers can identify the version of Kubernetes, along with the services they need, and not have to worry about the specific configuration of the data center.

Configuring Kubernetes

While Docker manages entities referred to as images and containers, Kubernetes wraps those entities in what is referred to as pods. A pod can contain one or more running containers and is the unit that manages Kubernetes. Kubernetes brings several advantages to container management as pods:

- **Multiple nodes**: Instead of simply deploying a container on a single host, Kubernetes can implement a set of pods on multiple nodes. Essentially, a node provides the environment where a container is executed.

- **Replication**: Kubernetes can act as a replication controller for a pod. This means you can set how many replicas of a specific pod should be running at all times.

- **Services**: The word *"service"* in the context of Kubernetes implies that you can assign a service name (ID) to a specific IP address and port and then assign a pod to provide that service. Kubernetes internally tracks the location of that service and can redirect requests from another pod of that service to the correct address and port.

You must understand the following concepts if you choose to configure Kubernetes:

- **Kubernetes controller**: A Kubernetes controller acts as a node from which the pods, replication controllers, services, and other components of a Kubernetes environment are implemented and managed. You must configure and run the `systemd, kube-api-server, kube-controller-manager`, and `kube-scheduler` services to create a Kubernetes controller.

- **Kubernetes nodes**: A Kubernetes node provides the environment in which the containers run. To run a machine as a Kubernetes node, it must be configured to run the Docker, `kube-proxy`, and `kubelet` services. These services must be run on the Kubernetes cluster's each node.

- **kubectl command**: Most Kubernetes administration is performed on the master node using the `kubectl` command. With kubectl, we can create, obtain, describe, or eliminate any of the resources that Kubernetes manages (pods, replication controllers, services, and so on).

- **Resource files (YAML or JSON)**: The `kubectl` command expects the information needed to create that resource to be in one of these two types of formats when you create a pod, a replication controller, service, or another resource in Kubernetes.

The classical way to see how Kubernetes works is to configure a Kubernetes cluster that has a master controller node and has at least two nodes, each operating on separate systems. The latest methods of setting up a highly available Kubernetes cluster allow splitting up the master component onto multiple nodes of Orchestrator / Control Plane and ETCD.

The Kubernetes API, managed by a kubelet, must be protected to ensure that it is not accessed in an unauthorized way to perform malicious actions. If unauthorized access was made to one of the containers running in a pod of a Kubernetes environment, the API can be attacked by means of some simple commands to be able to visualize the information about the entire environment.

Security in Kubernetes should be focused on preventing image manipulation and unauthorized access to the entire environment. Regarding runtime protection, it is essential not to deploy pods with root permissions, checking that pods have defined security policies and that Kubernetes is using secrets for credential and password management.

For example, attackers can execute remote code execution attacks that can give them access to the cluster anonymously if we have a misconfigured kubelet. The kubelet maintains a set of pods within a Kubernetes cluster and functions as a local agent that monitors the pod specifications through the Kubernetes API server.

Tip: Kubernetes in practice

You can play with Kubernetes with an online service that allows you to have 4-hour environments, totally free, where you can quickly create a cluster with several nodes.

The following links provide some resources related to executing Kubernetes online, and you can play with some scenarios that are configured in the online environment:

- `https://labs.play-with-k8s.com`
- `https://training.play-with-kubernetes.com`

Kubernetes security best practices

It is advisable to follow some best practices at the security level due to the impact that some implementations that can be carried out in an organization can cause. In the following sections, we will comment on the main security practices with Kubernetes.

Using secrets

If we want to start securing our Kubernetes projects, we can start with good practices like not storing objects with sensitive data like passwords, SSH keys, or OAuth tokens in the clear. The use of secrets allows you to control how sensitive data is used, and it significantly reduces the risk of exposure of that sensitive data to unauthorized users.

Firewall ports

This security practice is frequently used since it is not advisable to expose a port that does not need to be exposed. It is best to define the port's exposure to prevent this from happening.

The first thing you should do is check the existence of some interface or define an IP to link the service; for example, the localhost interface **127.0.0.1**. Some processes are opening so many ports on all interfaces that they should rather have a public access firewall. Although they only allow purely confidential information, they also allow you direct access to your set of computers.

Restrict the Docker pull <image> command

Docker is a resource that can sometimes be uncontrolled by the ease of access it has. That is, anyone with access to the Kubernetes API or Docker connector can obtain the image they want, generating traffic from infected images or serious security problems for Kubernetes. Many clusters have also become a network of Bitcoin miners.

Although it is a problem that seems not to be solved, the Image Policy plugin can significantly improve that situation, connecting directly with the Docker API. This plugin imposes a series of strict security rules that reflect a black and white list of images that can be extracted.

Another solution is to use the Image Policy Webhook through Admission Controller, which intercepts all image extractions and takes care of security just like the plugin mentioned earlier.

API authorization and anonymous authentication

You should know what authorization mode your system is using. This can be done by verifying the parameters, where you can also check if authentication is configured anonymously.

It is important to know that this configuration will not affect the kubelet authorization mode since it exposes an API on its own that executes commands that kubelet can completely ignore.

More specifically, a kubelet provides a command API used by **kubi-apiserver**, in which arbitrary commands are executed on a specific node. This configuration can be designed as **--authorization-mode = Webhook** and **--anonymous-auth = false**.

When we talk about giving permissions in a Kubernetes cluster, we will have to talk about **Role Based Access Control** or **RBAC**, which manages security policies for users, groups or Pods. It is implemented in a stable way in the latest versions of Kubernetes. You can use Roles and ClusterRoles to define access profiles.

We are defining specific rules for accessing our pods in the following example:

```
apiVersion: rbac.authorization.k8s.io/v1
kind: ClusterRole
metadata:
  name: cluster-role
rules:
- apiGroups: [""]
  resources: ["pods"]
  verbs: ["get", "list"]
```

You can use open source tools like **rbac-manager** **https://github.com/FairwindsOps/rbac-manager** to help you simplify the authorization process in Kubernetes using RBAC to facilitate RBAC configuration.

This is an operator that supports declarative configuration for RBAC with new custom resources. Instead of managing role bindings or service accounts directly, you can specify a desired state and the RBAC manager will make the necessary changes to achieve that state.

Management of resources and limits

It is important to manage the resources and limits that we are going to assign to our applications when creating a container in a Kubernetes infrastructure, especially in production. At the security level, it is important because a single container can generate a denial of service when sharing a host with other containers. In the generation of the Pod, we can easily control it through the requests and limits sections in the deployment execution file.

Security features built into k8s

Kubernetes offers native security features to protect against some of the threats described earlier or at least mitigate the potential impact of a breach. The main safety features include:

- **Role-Based Access Control (RBAC)**: Kubernetes allows administrators to define what are called **Roles** and **ClusterRoles** that specify which users can access which resources within a namespace or an entire cluster. This way, RBAC provides a way to regulate access to resources.

- **Pod security policies and network policies**: Administrators can configure pod security policies and network policies, which place restrictions on how containers and pods can behave. For example, pod security policies can be used to prevent containers from running as root users, and network policies can restrict communication between pods.

- **Network encryption**: Kubernetes uses TLS encryption by default, which provides additional protection for encryption of network traffic.

These built-in Kubernetes security features provide layers of defense against certain types of attacks, but they do not cover all threats. Kubernetes does not offer native protections against the following types of attacks:

- **Malicious code or incorrect settings inside containers or container images**: A third-party container scanning tool must be used to scan them.

- **Security vulnerabilities in host operating systems**: Again, these need to be searched with other tools. Some Kubernetes distributions like OpenShift integrate security solutions like SELinux at the kernel level to provide more security at the host level, but this is not a feature of Kubernetes itself.

- **Container runtime vulnerabilities**: In this case, Kubernetes has no way of alerting if a vulnerability exists within its runtime or if an attacker is trying to exploit a vulnerability at the time of execution.

- **Kubernetes API abuse**: Kubernetes does nothing to detect or respond to API abuse beyond following any RBAC and security policy settings that you define.

- **Management tools vulnerabilities or configuration errors**: Kubernetes cannot guarantee that management tools like Kubectl are free from security issues.

Managing secrets

A secret is everything that nobody else in the cluster should know, neither the rest of the applications nor users that access the cluster. For example, a password from a certificate store, an API key so that an application can consume third-party resources, and so on.

Let's say that someone discharges those resources along with certain permissions. From there, it is the application that requests those secrets from K8s by presenting the information that authorizes them to consume those resources.

Authorization management is done through what is known as **Role-Based Access Control (RBAC)**, that is, the application can access certain types of resources only if it has a certain role. Additionally, it's important to configure these roles and release the secret before the application is deployed.

Kubernetes secrets

Using secrets allows you to control how sensitive data is used and significantly reduces the risk of exposure of sensitive data to unauthorized users. This information is often placed in pod specifications or container images. A secret can be generated both by a user and by the system itself.

When the system does this, secrets are automatically generated by service accounts with API credentials. Kubernetes automatically creates secrets that contain credentials to access the API and modifies your Pods to use this type of secret.

The following image illustrates a basic diagram for storing secrets in the cluster:

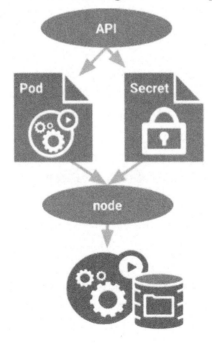

Figure 12.1: Storing secrets in the cluster

Other interesting facts about secrets:

- Secrets are objects with namespaces, that is, they exist in the context of a namespace
- You can access them through a volume or environment variable from a container running in a pod.

In the following example, we will create a secret with the username and password for our postgres database. The first thing we will do is create two files: one that contains the username, and another with the password to access this database:

```
$ echo -n 'user' > ./user.txt

$ echo -n 'password' > ./password.txt
```

We can create the secret in the kubernetes cluster from these two files, as follows:

```
$ kubectl create secret generic db-user-password --from-file=./
user.txt --from-file=./password.txt

secret/db-user-password created
```

We can obtain the secrets that we have stored with the following command:

```
$ kubectl get secrets

NAME                 TYPE                                     DATA  AGE

db-user-password     Opaque                                     2   15s

default-token-c4jc5  kubernetes.io/service-account-token  3   15m
```

Once our secret is created, there are two ways to consume the secrets: on the one hand we can mount them as a volume, and on the other hand, we can access them from the pod as if it were another file or through environment variables.

In this case, we will use them during the creation of the pod as environment variables to define the username and password that we want to use to access the database :

deployment-pod.yaml

```
apiVersion: apps/v1
kind: Deployment
metadata:
  name: postgres-deployment
  labels:
    app: postgres
```

```
spec:
  replicas: 1
  selector:
    matchLabels:
      app: postgres
  template:
    metadata:
      labels:
        app: postgres
    spec:
      containers:
      - name: mypostgres
        image: postgres
        env:
        - name: POSTGRES_USER
          valueFrom:
            secretKeyRef:
              name: db-user-password
              key: user.txt
        - name: POSTGRES_PASSWORD
          valueFrom:
            secretKeyRef:
              name: db-user-password
              key: password.txt
        volumeMounts:
          - name: postgres-data
            mountPath: /var/lib/postgresql/data
            subPath: postgres
      volumes:
      - name: postgres-data
        persistentVolumeClaim:
          claimName: azure-managed-disk
```

In the preceding deployment file, we see how we are using the **db-user-password** secret in the env section of the pod definition to specify both the username and the password. We can see the keys that we have stored inside a secret through the following command:

```
$ kubectl describe secret db-user-password
Name:          db-user-password
Namespace:     default
Labels:        <none>
Annotations:   <none>


Type:   Opaque


Data
====
password.txt:   8 bytes
user.txt:       4 bytes
```

The following command executes the deployment file in the cluster:

```
$ kubectl apply -f deployment-pod.yaml
deployment.apps/postgres-deployment created
```

Finally, we can expose the deployment through the following command and see the services that are deployed:

```
$ kubectl expose deployment/postgres-deployment --type LoadBalanc-
er --rt 5432 --protocol TCP
service/postgres-deployment exposed


$ kubectl get services
NAME                    TYPE            CLUSTER-IP      EXTERNAL-IP
PORT(S)            AGE
kubernetes              ClusterIP       10.96.0.1       <none>          443/
TCP            34m
postgres-deployment     LoadBalancer    10.110.247.6    172.17.0.29
5432:31197/TCP     26s
```

The use of environment variables for storing secrets in memory can result in their accidentally leaking. The recommended approach is to mount them as a Volume. This is the content of the **secret-pod.yaml** configuration file:

```
apiVersion: v1
kind: Pod
metadata:
  name: secret-vol-pod
spec:
  volumes:
  - name: secret-volume
    secret:
      secretName: test-secret
  containers:
    - name: test-container
      image: alpine:latest
      command: ["sleep", "9999"]
      volumeMounts:
        - name: secret-volume
          mountPath: /etc/secret-volume
```

From the previous file, we can create our new Pod using the following command:

```
$ kubectl create -f secret-pod.yaml
pod/secret-vol-pod created
```

Once started you can interact with the mounted secrets. For example, you can list all the secrets available as if they're regular data. For example:

```
$ kubectl exec -it secret-vol-pod ls /etc/secret-volume
password  username
```

Reading the files allows us to access the decoded secret value. To access username and password we could use the following commands:

```
$ kubectl exec -it secret-vol-pod cat /etc/secret-volume/username
admin

$ kubectl exec -it secret-vol-pod cat /etc/secret-volume/password
a62fjbd37942dcs
```

> **Tip: Kubernetes secrets in practice**
>
> In this scenario, you'll learn how to manage secrets using Kubernetes (refer to figure 12.2). Kubernetes allows you to create secrets that are mounted to a pod via environment variables or as a volume.
>
> This allows secrets, such as SSL certificates or passwords, to only be managed securely via an infrastructure team instead of having the passwords stored within the application's deployment artefacts.
>
> https://www.katacoda.com/courses/kubernetes/managing-secrets
>
>

Figure 12.2: Kubernetes secrets in practice

Other projects for managing Kubernetes secrets

Within the Kubernetes ecosystem, we can find different projects that allow the management of secrets securely. For example, the KubeSealed **https://github.com/bitnami-labs/sealed-secrets** project is a tool that allows you to encrypt secrets using a resource called **SealedSecret**.

The solution is based on a Public Key Infrastructure (PKI) and shares a public key to encrypt and install a private key on the cluster. What this tool does is encrypt using a public key for the cluster, using the certificate of the Kubernetes cluster where it is applied. Additionally, we must save the secrets in a JSON file to work with the tool.

Another interesting project is Kubernetes external secrets **https://github.com/external-secrets/kubernetes-external-secrets**, which allows you to use an external secrets management system to add new secrets to the cluster securely. The tool supports different providers in the cloud, including:

- AWS Secrets Manager
- AWS System Manager
- GCP Secret Manager
- Azure Key Vault
- Hashicorp Vault

With external secrets, you can store the secrets in different providers in the cloud and use them within your Kubernetes cluster in such a way that you can centrally manage the secrets that your applications, CICD, etc. need.

With this approach, you will avoid storing secrets in different places and confidential data in your code repositories.

Handle security risks in Kubernetes

Here are the main strategies that we can follow to manage the risks of putting your application with Kubernetes in production:

- **Integrate security from the early stages of development**: With Kubernetes, it is necessary to integrate security at each stage of the software development process. It is a mistake to leave security settings for the last step as it may be too late.

- **Consider a commercial platform of Kubernetes**: When you participate in a Kubernetes trading platform, the most important benefit you get is the rapid structural responses from development to any threat or problem. Kubernetes will be updated quickly to any vulnerability, and you will always have the latest security updates for your company.

- **Do not trust your old tools and practices**: The attackers update faster than the software, so the same moves at any time may be obsolete. You should not assume that your conventional security tools will protect you. Many open source tools evaluate Kubernetes clusters or perform penetration tests on clusters and nodes. Experts point out that it is necessary to keep your software updated and patched, for example, and new approaches and tools are also necessary.

Here is a summary of the key parts of a Kubernetes environment and the most common security risks that affect them:

- **Containers**: Containers can contain malicious code that was included in your container images. They can also be subject to misconfigurations that allow attackers to gain unauthorized access under certain conditions.

- **Host operating systems**: Vulnerabilities or malicious code within operating systems installed on Kubernetes nodes can provide attackers with a path to Kubernetes clusters.

- **Container runtimes**: Kubernetes supports a variety of container runtimes. All of them can contain vulnerabilities that allow attackers to take control of individual containers, escalate attacks from container to container, and even gain control of the Kubernetes environment.

- **Network layer**: Kubernetes relies on internal networks to facilitate communication between nodes, pods, and containers. It also often exposes applications to public networks so that they can be accessed over the Internet. Both network layers can allow attackers to gain access to the cluster or escalate attacks from one part of the cluster to others.

- **Kubectl Dashboard and other management tools**: They may be subject to vulnerabilities that allow abuse in a Kubernetes cluster.

Analyzing Kubernetes components security

Pods are the main component of Kubernetes and represent one or more containers that share network and storage configurations. So, their security is very important and needs to be implemented from the first steps of its design, using security policies.

The official documentation provides some examples of how to apply these security policies in our implementation with Kubernetes. It is available at **https://kubernetes. io/docs/concepts/policy/pod-security-policy.**

According to official documentation, a pod security policy is a cluster-level resource that controls aspects of a pod's security. These security policies are defined through the **PodSecurityPolicy** object, through which we can define the conditions which a pod must meet to be accepted in the system. It also allows us to define the default values of fields that are not explicitly assigned.

A security policy is defined as practically everything in Kubernetes, through a manifest file, usually in YAML format. Let's consider an example:

```yaml
apiVersion: policy/v1beta1
    kind: PodSecurityPolicy
    metadata:
      name: permissive
    spec:
      privileged: true
```

```
hostNetwork: true

hostIPC: true

hostPID: true

seLinux:

  rule: RunAsAny

supplementalGroups:

  rule: RunAsAny

runAsUser:

  rule: RunAsAny

fsGroup:

  rule: RunAsAny

hostPorts:

- min: 0

  max: 65535

volumes:

- '*'
```

In this example, you can see how the defined policy is very permissive. It practically allows us to run a pod with all kinds of privileges. For example, we can execute it in privileged mode (privileged: true) so that we can have access to parts of the host; share the space of network names, processes, and **Inter-Process Communication** (**IPC**) of the host; run the container or containers as root; etc. Such configurations should be avoided unless there is a good reason.

Pod security policies

Pod security policies allow administrators to control the following aspects:

- **Containers in privileged mode**: This feature allows or does not allow the execution of containers in privileged mode. The field that sets this aspect is called **privileged**. The containers run in non-privileged mode by default. Here are some of the main values that this feature can take:

  - **Host namespace**: There are four fields that allow us to define the behavior of a container with respect to access to certain parts of the host:

    - **HostPID**: This controls whether the pod containers share the same process space (IDs) of the host.

- **HostIPC**: This controls whether the containers in a pod share the host's IPC space.

- **HostNetwork**: This controls whether a pod can use the same host network space. It implies that the pod would have access to the loopback device and the processes running on that host.

- **HostPorts**: This defines the range of ports allowed in the host network space. This range is given by the `HostPortRange` field, and the min and max attributes that define the range of ports are included in the range.

- **Volumes and filesystems**: Here are some of the main values that this feature can take:

  - **Volumes**: This provides a list of permitted volumes, and they correspond to the source used to create the volume.

  - **FSGroup**: Allows you to indicate the groups where to apply certain volumes.

  - **AllowedHostPaths**: Specifies a list of paths allowed to be used by volumes. An empty list would imply that there are no restrictions. This list is defined by two attributes: `pathPrefix` and `readOnly`.

  - **ReadOnlyRootFilesystem**: This requires that the containers run with the root filesystem in read-only mode.

- **Users and groups**: Some of the main values of this feature are:

  - **RunAsUser**: Specifies which user the containers run inside the pod

  - **RunAsGroup**: Specifies with which group ID the containers run within the pod

- **Privilege escalation**: Basically, it controls the `no_new_privs` option of the container process. This option prevents binaries with the setuid option from changing the user's effective ID and prevents enabling new extra capabilities. Here are some of the main values that this feature can take:

  - `allowPrivilegeEscalation:` Specifies whether or not to set the security context of the container. By default, `allowPrivilegeEscalation = true` to avoid problems with binaries with setuid active.

  - `DefaultAllowPrivilegeEscalation:` This allows you to set the default option of `allowPrivilegeEscalation`.

- **Capabilities**: GNU/Linux capabilities are a series of superuser privileges that can be enabled or disabled independently. The following fields accept the capabilities as a list, without the CAP_ prefix (all capabilities in GNU/Linux begin with that prefix):

- **AllowedCapabilities:** List of capacities that can be added to a container. All capacities are allowed by default. If this field is specified empty, it implies that you cannot add capacities to a container beyond those defined by default. The asterisk (*) can be used to refer to all capabilities.

- **RequiredDropCapabilities:** List of capacities that must be removed from the container. These are removed from the default capacity group. The capabilities included in this field should not be included in **AllowedCapabilities** or **DefaultAddCapabilities**.

- **DefaultAddCapabilities:** Capabilities added to a default container by default.

Static analysis with kube-score

kube-score is a tool that performs static code analysis of your Kubernetes object definitions. The output is a list of recommendations of what you can improve to make your application more secure and resilient.

Check **https://github.com/zegl/kube-score** on GitHub for more information about how to use **kube-score**. Use this website to easily test **kube-score**; you can just paste your object definition YAML or JSON document. For example, we can analyze the following nginx deployment file:

```
apiVersion: apps/v1
kind: Deployment
metadata:
  name: nginx-deployment
spec:
  selector:
    matchLabels:
      app: nginx
  replicas:
  template:
    metadata:
      labels:
        app: nginx
    spec:
```

```
    containers:
    - name: nginx
      image: nginx:1.7.9
      ports:
      - containerPort: 80
```

This tool detects the following security issues in the preceding deployment file:

```
apps/v1/Deployment nginx-deployment
    [CRITICAL] Container Resources
        · nginx -> CPU limit is not set
            Resource limits are recommended to avoid resource DDOS.
            Set resources.limits.cpu
        · nginx -> Memory limit is not set
            Resource limits are recommended to avoid resource DDOS.
            Set resources.limits.memory
        · nginx -> CPU request is not set
            Resource requests are recommended to make sure that the
            application can start and run without
            crashing. Set resources.requests.cpu
        · nginx -> Memory request is not set
            Resource requests are recommended to make sure that the
            application can start and run without
            crashing. Set resources.requests.memory
    [CRITICAL] Container Image Pull Policy
        · nginx -> ImagePullPolicy is not set to Always
            It's recommended to always set the ImagePullPolicy to
            Always, to make sure that the
            imagePullSecrets are always correct, and to always get
            the image you want.
    [CRITICAL] Pod NetworkPolicy
        · The pod does not have a matching NetworkPolicy
            Create a NetworkPolicy that targets this pod to control
            who/what can communicate with this pod.
            Note, this feature needs to be supported by the CNI
            implementation used in the Kubernetes cluster
            to have an effect.
```

```
[CRITICAL] Container Security Context
    · nginx -> Container has no configured security context
        Set securityContext to run the container in a more se-
        cure context.
[WARNING] Deployment has host PodAntiAffinity
    · Deployment does not have a host podAntiAffinity set
        It's recommended to set a podAntiAffinity that stops mul-
        tiple pods from a deployment from being
        scheduled on the same node. This increases availability
        in case the node becomes unavailable.
[CRITICAL] Deployment has PodDisruptionBudget
    · No matching PodDisruptionBudget was found
        It's recommended to define a PodDisruptionBudget to avoid
        unexpected downtime during Kubernetes
        maintenance operations, such as when draining a node.
```

Auditing the state of the cluster

You may have to perform a small internal audit of the state of the cluster when you work with Kubernetes clusters. We can use the Polaris tool available in the GitHub repository at **https://github.com/FairwindsOps/polaris** to do this.

This tool can be used in three ways:

- In audit mode, where it shows us the state of the cluster and whether there is any aspect that we can improve.

- In validation mode, that allows us to validate what we are going to execute complies with the standard.

- In YAML file testing mode via command console, where it allows us to check our developments locally.

We can deploy the tool in our Kubernetes cluster by executing the following commands:

```
$ kubectl apply -f https://github.com/FairwindsOps/polaris/releas-
es/latest/download/dashboard.yaml

$ kubectl port-forward --namespace polaris svc/polaris-dashboard
8080:80
```

Tools like Kube Bench, **https://github.com/aquasecurity/kube-bench** that allow us to quickly check our infrastructure at the security level.

There are several best practices to follow when running a Kubernetes cluster. Here are some of the best security practices for your Kubernetes cluster:

- Use the minimum privilege principle for your service accounts
- Disable Kubernetes dashboard
- Create a cluster network policy

The *principle of minimum privilege* helps reduce the impact of a potential vulnerability or data that has been compromised. So, it will be more difficult for a potential attacker to escalate privileges if a certain component is compromised.

If you are using the Google Cloud Platform, each Kubernetes Engine node has an associated service account. The first thing that should be done is analyze the accesses that the account has by default and see the permissions that are really necessary to run your Kubernetes cluster.

At this point, it is recommended to use a service account with the minimum privileges to run the Kubernetes Engine Cluster instead of the default service account. The following urls contain the documentation for logging and monitoring in Google Cloud.

- https://cloud.google.com/monitoring/access-control#overview
- https://cloud.google.com/logging/docs/access-control#overview

The following commands will create a GCP service account for you with the minimum permissions necessary to operate Kubernetes engine:

```
$ gcloud iam service-accounts create "${SA_NAME}" \
--display-name="${SA_NAME}"

$ gcloud projects add-iam-policy-binding "${PROJECT_ID}" \
   --member "serviceAccount:${SA_NAME}@${PROJECT_ID}.iam.gservice-
   account.com" \
   --role roles/logging.logWriter

$ gcloud projects add-iam-policy-binding "${PROJECT_ID}" \
   --member "serviceAccount:${SA_NAME}@${PROJECT_ID}.iam.gservice-
   account.com" \
   --role roles/monitoring.metricWriter

$ gcloud projects add-iam-policy-binding "${PROJECT_ID}" \
   --member "serviceAccount:${SA_NAME}@${PROJECT_ID}.iam.gservice-
   account.com" \
   --role roles/monitoring.viewer
```

If you need your Kubernetes engine cluster to have access to other Google Cloud services, we recommend that you create an additional role and supply it to workloads through the Kubernetes secrets. You can do it by following the official documentation:

https://cloud.google.com/kubernetes-engine/docs/tutorials/authenticating-to-cloud-platform.

Regarding the Kubernetes dashboard, it's important to know how to disable the Kubernetes web user interface when it runs on Kubernetes Engine. The cloud console provides many of the same features, so you don't need these permissions if you are running the Kubernetes engine.

More information about this tool is available in the Kubernetes documentation at **https://kubernetes.io/docs/tasks/access-application-cluster/web-ui-dashboard/**.

The following command disables the Kubernetes web user interface:

```
$ gcloud container clusters update "${CLUSTER_NAME}"  --update-ad-
dons=KubernetesDashboard=DISABLED
```

Additionally, it is important to create *network policies* to control the communication between the pods and services in your cluster. The application of network policies makes it much more difficult for a potential attacker to obtain high privileges within the cluster.

We can also use the Kubernetes network policy API (**https://cloud.google.com/kubernetes-engine/docs/how-to/network-policy**) to create firewall rules at the pod level in the Kubernetes engine. These firewall rules will determine which pods and services can communicate with each other within the cluster.

You can specify the **---enable-network-policy** flag using **gcloud** command to enable the application of network policies when creating a new cluster:

```
$ gcloud container clusters create "${CLUSTER_NAME}" \
   --project="${PROJECT_ID}" \
   --zone="${ZONE}" \
   --enable-network-policy
```

Using livenessProbe and readinessProbe

Health checks are very important in Kubernetes. Two types of controls are provided at this point: `livenessProbe` and `readinessProbe`:

- **livenessProbe** is used to check if the application is still running or has stopped. Kubernetes does nothing if the application runs successfully, but it will launch a new pod and run the application in it if your application is stopped.

- **readinessProbe** is used to verify that the application is ready to start sending traffic. Kubernetes will stop sending traffic to the pod until this health check fails.

Tip: Checking container health in practice

In this scenario, you'll learn how Kubernetes checks container health using Readiness and Liveness Probes:

Readiness Probes checks if an application is ready to start processing traffic. This probe solves the problem of the container having started, but the process is still warming up and configuring itself, meaning it's not ready to receive traffic.

Liveness Probes ensure that the application is healthy and capable of processing requests. Kubernetes will destroy and recreate the failed container if the Probe fails.

`https://www.katacoda.com/courses/kubernetes/liveness-readiness-healthchecks`

Figure 12.3: Checking container health in practice

If these checks are not successful, pods can terminate or begin receiving user requests even before they are ready. In the following configuration example, when Kubernetes pings a route to the HTTP server and gets an HTTP response, it will say that the application is ok:

```
apiVersion: v1
kind: Pod
metadata:
 name: container10
spec:
 containers:
   - image: ubuntu
     name: container10
    livenessProbe:
      httpGet:
        path: /prodhealth
        port: 8080
```

For example, you can check the status of the Pod with the following command if Pod is an HTTP service that returns a 500 error, indicating that it hasn't started correctly:

```
$ kubectl get pods --selector="name=bad-frontend"
NAME                 READY    STATUS     RESTARTS    AGE
bad-frontend-klggv   0/1      Pending    0           7s
```

Kubectl will return the Pods deployed with our particular name selector. The health check is failing, so it will say that zero containers are ready. It will also indicate the number of restart attempts of the container. We can use the following command to find more details of why it's failing:

```
$ pod=$(kubectl get pods --selector="name=bad-frontend" --output=-
jsonpath={.items..metadata.name})
controlplane $ kubectl describe pod $pod
Name:               bad-frontend-pvrbp
Namespace:          default
Priority:           0
PriorityClassName:  <none>
Node:               controlplane/172.17.0.32
Start Time:         Tue, 13 Jul 2021 20:34:48 +0000
Labels:             name=bad-frontend
Annotations:        <none>
```

```
Status:              Running
IP:                  10.32.0.6
Controlled By:       ReplicationController/bad-frontend
Containers:
  bad-frontend:
    Container ID:    docker://59a241eac6dfeb43119eb10322c3b325aed
                     72c4a0df9f85ec92e67c8ce042e4d
    Image:           katacoda/docker-http-server:unhealthy
    Image ID:        docker-pullable://katacoda/docker-http-serv-
                     er@sha256      :bea95c69c299c690103c39ebb3159c-
                     39c5061fee1dad13aa1b0625e0c6b52f22
    Port:            <none>
    Host Port:       <none>
    State:           Waiting
      Reason:        CrashLoopBackOff
    Last State:      Terminated
      Reason:        Error
      Exit Code:     2
      Started:       Tue, 13 Jul 2021 20:38:45 +0000
      Finished:      Tue, 13 Jul 2021 20:39:15 +0000
    Ready:           False
    Restart Count:   6
    Liveness:        http-get http://:80/ delay=1s timeout=1s peri-
                     od=10s #success=1 #failure=3
    Readiness:       http-get http://:80/ delay=1s timeout=1s peri-
                     od=10s #success=1 #failure=3
    Environment:     <none>
    Mounts:
      /var/run/secrets/kubernetes.io/serviceaccount from default-to-
      ken-5gbbc (ro)
Conditions:
  Type              Status
  Initialized       True
  Ready             False
  ContainersReady   False
  PodScheduled      True
```

```
Volumes:
  default-token-5gbbc:
    Type:          Secret (a volume populated by a Secret)
    SecretName:    default-token-5gbbc
    Optional:      false
QoS Class:         BestEffort
Node-Selectors:    <none>
Tolerations:       node.kubernetes.io/not-ready:NoExecute for 300s
                   node.kubernetes.io/unreachable:NoExecute for 300s
Events:
  Type      Reason      Age               From               Message
  ----      ------      ----              ----               -------
  Normal    Scheduled   5m18s                          default-scheduler
Successfully assigned default/bad-frontend-pvrbp to controlplane
  Normal    Pulling     5m16s                         kubelet, controlplane
Pulling image "katacoda/docker-http-server:unhealthy"
  Normal    Pulled      5m11s                         kubelet, controlplane
Successfully pulled image "katacoda/docker-http-server:unhealthy"
  Normal    Created     4m11s (x3 over 5m11s) kubelet, controlplane
Created container bad-frontend
  Normal    Started     4m11s (x3 over 5m11s) kubelet, controlplane
Started container bad-frontend
  Warning   Unhealthy   4m11s (x6 over 5m1s)   kubelet, controlplane
Liveness probe failed: HTTP probe failed with statuscode: 500
  Normal    Killing     4m11s (x2 over 4m41s) kubelet, controlplane
Container bad-frontend failed liveness probe, will be restarted
  Normal    Pulled      4m11s (x2 over 4m41s) kubelet, controlplane
Container  image  "katacoda/docker-http-server:unhealthy"  already
present on machine
  Warning   Unhealthy   4m4s (x7 over 5m4s)    kubelet, controlplane
Readiness probe failed: HTTP probe failed with statuscode: 500
  Warning   BackOff     11s (x10 over 2m41s)   kubelet, controlplane
Back-off restarting failed container
```

Here, we are checking whether the pod has some error and could not be started.

Setting limits and resource requests

The application will stop working when you are deploying a large application on a resource-constrained production cluster where nodes run out of memory or CPU. This application downtime can have a huge impact on your business, but you can solve this by having requests and resource limits.

Requests and resource limits are the Kubernetes mechanisms for controlling the use of resources like memory and CPU. If one pod consumes all CPU and memory, the other pods will run out of resources and be unable to run the application.

We can set requests and limits for each container in a pod to improve this aspect. CPU is defined using millicores and memory using bytes (megabyte / mebibyte). In the following example, we are setting a CPU limit of 500 millicores and 128 mebibytes, and we are setting a quota for CPU requests of 300 millicores and 64 mebibytes:

```
containers:
- name: prodcontainer1
    image: ubuntu
    resources:
        requests:
            memory: "64Mi"
            cpu: "300m"
        limits:
            memory: "128Mi"
            cpu: "500m"
```

Applying affinity rules between nodes and pods

One of the main mechanisms in Kubernetes for associating a pod with a node within the cluster is to define the affinity for better performance. We can use node affinity to define the criteria that a pod will follow to associate with a certain node in a Kubernetes cluster:

```
apiVersion: v1
kind: Pod
metadata:
  name: ubuntu
spec:
```

```
  affinity:
    nodeAffinity:
preferredDuringSchedulingIgnoredDuringExecution:
      - weight: 2
        preference:
matchExpressions:
          - key: disktype
            operator: In
             values:
            - ssd
  containers:
  - name: ubuntu
    image: ubuntu
    imagePullPolicy: IfNotPresent
```

We can use **pod affinity** to schedule multiple pods on the same node (to improve latency) or decide to keep pods on separate nodes (for high availability) to increase performance.

```
apiVersion: v1
kind: Pod
metadata:
  name: ubuntu-pod
spec:
  affinity:
    podAffinity:


requiredDuringSchedulingIgnoredDuringExecution:
      - labelSelector:


matchExpressions:
          - key: security
            operator: In
            values:
            - S1
```

```
        topologyKey: failure-domain.beta.kubernetes.io/zone
containers:
- name: ubuntu-pod
  image: ubuntu
```

After analyzing the cluster workload, we will have to decide on the best affinity strategy to use.

Conclusion

With the objective that developers and DevOps get the best possible performance and security in the Kubernetes infrastructure, we have analyzed the state of Kubernetes security in this chapter, including best practices and the main projects we can find in Kubernetes ecosystem for checking the security of a Kubernetes cluster.

In the next chapter, we will review the state of Kubernetes security and some tools to check whether Kubernetes is implemented in a secure way by following some best practices documented in the CIS Kubernetes Benchmark guide.

Points to remember

- Security in Kubernetes must extend beyond images and workloads and protect the entire environment, including the cluster infrastructure. Here are some of the main actions that we can take to add different security layers:
  - **Update Kubernetes**: It is important to update to the latest version whenever possible, including security patches for recent vulnerabilities. This way, our version will receive the patch as soon as the fix is released if a critical vulnerability is discovered in the Kubernetes core.
  - **Securely configure the Kubernetes API server**: It is important to disable unauthenticated or anonymous access to the cluster and use TLS encryption for connections between the kubelets and the API server.
  - **Kubelet security**: As a head node agent running on every node, an incorrect kubelet configuration can expose the cluster to an application backdoor.

Multiple choice questions

1. Which command can you use for creating a secret from a file?
   a. $ kubectl create generic mysecret --from-file=./file.txt

    b. $ kubectl create secret --from-file=./file.txt mysecret

    c. $ kubectl create secret generic mysecret --from-file=./file.txt

    d. $ kubectl create secret --from-file=./file.txt

2. Which is the command Google cloud provides for disabling the Kubernetes web user interface?

    a. $ gcloud container clusters update "${CLUSTER_NAME}" --Kubernetes Dashboard=FALSE

    b. $ gcloud container clusters update "${CLUSTER_NAME}" --Kubernetes Dashboard=DISABLED

    c. $ gcloud container clusters update "${CLUSTER_NAME}" --update-addons=KubernetesDashboard=FALSE

    d. $ gcloud container clusters update "${CLUSTER_NAME}" --update-addons=KubernetesDashboard=DISABLED

Answer

1	C
2	D

Questions

1. Which is the best configuration for API authorization mode and anonymous authentication?

2. Which tools allow the checking and auditing of the state of the cluster?

3. What is the new mechanism that Kubernetes provides to assign permissions and privileges to roles instead of specific users?

Key terms

- kube-score is a Kubernetes tool object analysis with recommendations for improved reliability and security.

- Network policies represent a series of firewall rules for Kubernetes, so it is good that you consult the network policies of Kubernetes to configure them correctly from the beginning. Consider switching to a network provider who supports network policies if your current one does not.

- A new feature called RBAC has been released from Kubernetes version 1.8. RBAC is a new mechanism that Kubernetes provides to assign permissions and privileges to roles instead of specific users.

## CHAPTER 13

Auditing and Analyzing Vulnerabilities in Kubernetes

Vulnerability detection is one of the most important parts of any container-based application. At this point, it is important to identify the main vulnerabilities in Kubernetes and the tools that we can use to identify them.

In this chapter, we will introduce Kubernetes security and Kubernetes bench for security project to execute controls documented in CIS Kubernetes Benchmark guide. We will also review main security projects for analyzing security in Kubernetes components and more critical vulnerabilities discovered in Kubernetes in the last few years.

Structure

We will cover the following topics in this chapter:

- KubeBench Security
- Kubernetes Security projects
- Analyzing Kubernetes vulnerabilities and CVEs

Objectives

After studying this chapter, you will understand KubeBench security and the main vulnerabilities discovered in Kubernetes. You will also learn about Kubernetes security projects and plugins for testing the security of your Kubernetes cluster.

KubeBench security

KubeBench (**https://github.com/aquasecurity/kube-bench**) is a Kubernetes security scanner that allows us to eliminate about 95% of configuration defects, generating specific guidelines to ensure the configuration of your computer network through the application of Kubernetes benchmark.

CIS benchmarks for Kubernetes with KubeBench

CIS benchmarks are security standards for different systems carried out by the Center for Internet Security, which aim to harden our operating systems. Compliance with these standards is common in environments that have to meet PCI-DSS, GDPR, or are for government use. So, if we are concerned about security, we will always be right if we meet CIS Benchmarks.

We can use KubeBench to verify the rules of CIS Benchmark.. It is a tool that will automate the entire process of validating CIS Benchmark rules for Kubernetes. We can install KubeBench through this dedicated container by executing the following container:

https://hub.docker.com/r/aquasec/kube-bench

This tool supports tests for multiple versions of Kubernetes defined in the CIS guides, and the easiest way to run this tool is to run it from a container and launch the tests on the Kubernetes cluster with the following command:

```
$ docker run --rm -v `pwd`:/host aquasec/kube-bench:latest install
Unable to find image 'aquasec/kube-bench:latest' locally
latest: Pulling from aquasec/kube-bench
540db60ca938: Pull complete
1a54aff31526: Pull complete
eaeda0957c43: Pull complete
f0f0bea18150: Pull complete
74607f20dee7: Pull complete
7705a0d556dc: Pull complete
d42def918d40: Pull complete
1c3af4762903: Pull complete
bd03f4ea544b: Pull complete
162fd9b40ec9: Pull complete
6021a5e04eb0: Pull complete
```

```
Digest: sha256:e02aa2eb58c9a6bee9e2b060684051be14b266f0e9952cadd8f71
f32f578b5d7
Status: Downloaded newer image for aquasec/kube-bench:latest
===============================================
kube-bench is now installed on your host
Run ./kube-bench to perform a security check
===============================================
```

This way, we can execute the command for analyzing the master node or a :worker node. First, we will analyze the Master node as follows:

```
$ ./kube-bench master
```

We will get the following output:

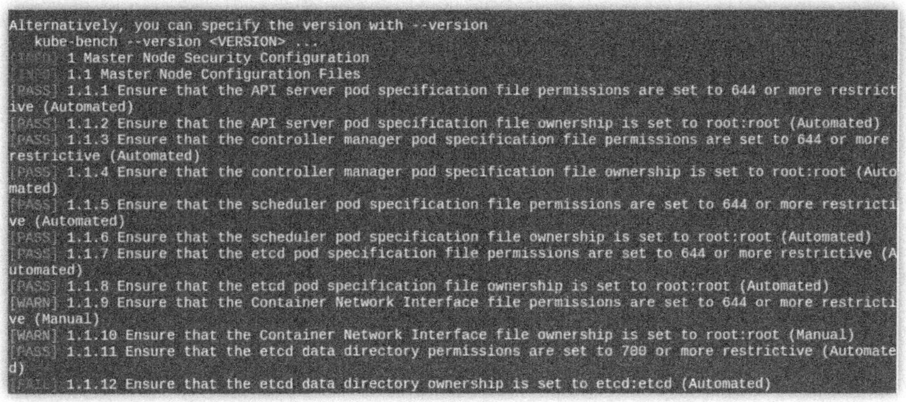

```
Alternatively, you can specify the version with --version
   kube-bench --version <VERSION> ...
[INFO] 1 Master Node Security Configuration
[INFO] 1.1 Master Node Configuration Files
[PASS] 1.1.1 Ensure that the API server pod specification file permissions are set to 644 or more restrict
ive (Automated)
[PASS] 1.1.2 Ensure that the API server pod specification file ownership is set to root:root (Automated)
[PASS] 1.1.3 Ensure that the controller manager pod specification file permissions are set to 644 or more
restrictive (Automated)
[PASS] 1.1.4 Ensure that the controller manager pod specification file ownership is set to root:root (Auto
mated)
[PASS] 1.1.5 Ensure that the scheduler pod specification file permissions are set to 644 or more restricti
ve (Automated)
[PASS] 1.1.6 Ensure that the scheduler pod specification file ownership is set to root:root (Automated)
[PASS] 1.1.7 Ensure that the etcd pod specification file permissions are set to 644 or more restrictive (A
utomated)
[PASS] 1.1.8 Ensure that the etcd pod specification file ownership is set to root:root (Automated)
[WARN] 1.1.9 Ensure that the Container Network Interface file permissions are set to 644 or more restricti
ve (Manual)
[WARN] 1.1.10 Ensure that the Container Network Interface file ownership is set to root:root (Manual)
[PASS] 1.1.11 Ensure that the etcd data directory permissions are set to 700 or more restrictive (Automate
d)
[FAIL] 1.1.12 Ensure that the etcd data directory ownership is set to etcd:etcd (Automated)
```

Figure 13.1: *Kube-bench master node execution*

We can also analyze the worker node with the same command:

```
$ ./kube-bench node
```

We will get the following output:

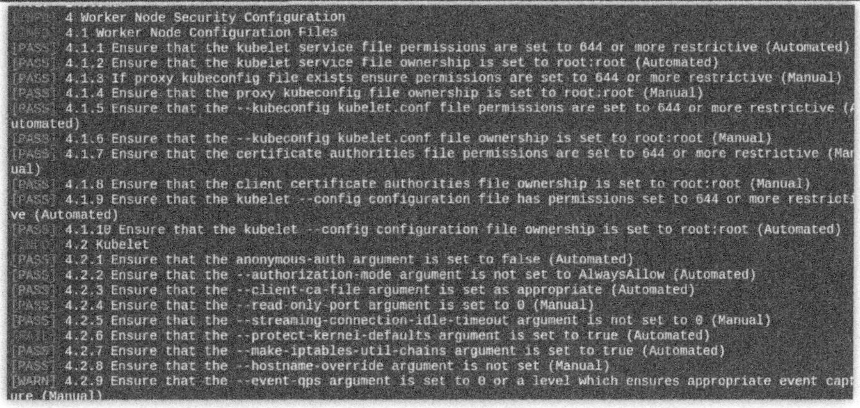

```
[INFO] 4 Worker Node Security Configuration
[INFO] 4.1 Worker Node Configuration Files
[PASS] 4.1.1 Ensure that the kubelet service file permissions are set to 644 or more restrictive (Automated)
[PASS] 4.1.2 Ensure that the kubelet service file ownership is set to root:root (Automated)
[PASS] 4.1.3 If proxy kubeconfig file exists ensure permissions are set to 644 or more restrictive (Manual)
[PASS] 4.1.4 Ensure that the proxy kubeconfig file ownership is set to root:root (Manual)
[PASS] 4.1.5 Ensure that the --kubeconfig kubelet.conf file permissions are set to 644 or more restrictive (A
utomated)
[PASS] 4.1.6 Ensure that the --kubeconfig kubelet.conf file ownership is set to root:root (Manual)
[PASS] 4.1.7 Ensure that the certificate authorities file permissions are set to 644 or more restrictive (Mar
ual)
[PASS] 4.1.8 Ensure that the client certificate authorities file ownership is set to root:root (Manual)
[PASS] 4.1.9 Ensure that the kubelet --config configuration file has permissions set to 644 or more restricti
ve (Automated)
[PASS] 4.1.10 Ensure that the kubelet --config configuration file ownership is set to root:root (Automated)
[INFO] 4.2 Kubelet
[PASS] 4.2.1 Ensure that the anonymous-auth argument is set to false (Automated)
[PASS] 4.2.2 Ensure that the --authorization-mode argument is not set to AlwaysAllow (Automated)
[PASS] 4.2.3 Ensure that the --client-ca-file argument is set as appropriate (Automated)
[PASS] 4.2.4 Ensure that the --read-only-port argument is set to 0 (Manual)
[PASS] 4.2.5 Ensure that the --streaming-connection-idle-timeout argument is not set to 0 (Manual)
[FAIL] 4.2.6 Ensure that the --protect-kernel-defaults argument is set to true (Automated)
[PASS] 4.2.7 Ensure that the --make-iptables-util-chains argument is set to true (Automated)
[PASS] 4.2.8 Ensure that the --hostname-override argument is not set (Manual)
[WARN] 4.2.9 Ensure that the --event-qps argument is set to 0 or a level which ensures appropriate event capt
ure (Manual)
```

Figure 13.2: *Kube-bench worker node execution*

The tests are configured with YAML and JSON files, making it easy to update this tool as the test specifications evolve. When the script is executed, it shows information about the security compliance of the cluster and mentions the best practices and remediations for solving the security issues:

```
== Remediations master ==
```

1.1.9 Run the following command (based on the file location on your system) on the master node.

For example,

```
chmod 644 <path/to/cni/files>
```


1.1.10 Run the following command (based on the file location on your system) on the master node.

For example,

```
chown root:root <path/to/cni/files>
```


1.1.12 On the etcd server node, get the etcd data directory, passed as an argument --data-dir,

from the following command:

```
ps -ef | grep etcd
```

Run the following command (based on the etcd data directory found earlier).

```
For example, chown etcd:etcd /var/lib/etcd
```

1.2.1 Edit the API server pod specification file /etc/kubernetes/manifests/kube-apiserver.yaml

on the master node and set the following parameter.

```
--anonymous-auth=false
```


1.2.6 Follow the Kubernetes documentation and set up the TLS connection between

the apiserver and kubelets. Then, edit the API server pod specification file

```
/etc/kubernetes/manifests/kube-apiserver.yaml on the master node
and set the
```

```
--kubelet-certificate-authority parameter to the path to the cert
file for the certificate authority.
```

```
--kubelet-certificate-authority=<ca-string>
```

1.2.10 Follow the Kubernetes documentation and set the desired limits in a configuration file.

Then, edit the API server pod specification file /etc/kubernetes/manifests/kube-apiserver.yaml

and set the following parameters:
```
--enable-admission-plugins=...,EventRateLimit,...
--admission-control-config-file=<path/to/configuration/file>
```

1.2.12 Edit the API server pod specification file /etc/kubernetes/manifests/kube-apiserver.yaml

on the master node and set the --enable-admission-plugins parameter to include

AlwaysPullImages.
```
--enable-admission-plugins=...,AlwaysPullImages,...
```

1.2.13 Edit the API server pod specification file /etc/kubernetes/manifests/kube-apiserver.yaml

on the master node and set the --enable-admission-plugins parameter to include
```
SecurityContextDeny, unless PodSecurityPolwwicy is already in place.
--enable-admission-plugins=...,SecurityContextDeny,...
```

1.2.16 Follow the documentation and create Pod Security Policy objects as per your environment.
Then, edit the API server pod specification file /etc/kubernetes/manifests/kube-apiserver.yaml
on the master node and set the --enable-admission-plugins parameter to a
value that includes PodSecurityPolicy:
```
--enable-admission-plugins=...,PodSecurityPolicy,...
Then, restart the API Server.
```

1.2.21 Edit the API server pod specification file /etc/kubernetes/manifests/kube-apiserver.yaml
on the master node and set the following parameter:
```
--profiling=false
```

1.2.22 Edit the API server pod specification file /etc/kubernetes/manifests/kube-apiserver.yaml

on the master node and set the --audit-log-path parameter to a suitable path and

file where you would like audit logs to be written, for example:

```
--audit-log-path=/var/log/apiserver/audit.log
```

1.2.23 Edit the API server pod specification file /etc/kubernetes/manifests/kube-apiserver.yaml

on the master node and set the --audit-log-maxage parameter to 30 or as an appropriate number of days:

```
--audit-log-maxage=30
```

1.2.24 Edit the API server pod specification file /etc/kubernetes/manifests/kube-apiserver.yaml

on the master node and set the --audit-log-maxbackup parameter to 10 or to an appropriate value.

```
--audit-log-maxbackup=10
```

1.2.25 Edit the API server pod specification file /etc/kubernetes/manifests/kube-apiserver.yaml
on the master node and set the --audit-log-maxsize parameter to an appropriate size in MB.
For example, to set it to 100 MB:

```
--audit-log-maxsize=100
```

1.2.26 Edit the API server pod specification file /etc/kubernetes/manifests/kube-apiserver.yaml
and set the following parameter as appropriate and if needed.
For example,

```
--request-timeout=300s
```

1.2.33 Follow the Kubernetes documentation and configure an EncryptionConfig file.
Then, edit the API server pod specification file /etc/kubernetes/manifests/kube-apiserver.yaml

on the master node and set the --encryption-provider-config parameter to the path of that file: --encryption-provider-config=</path/to/EncryptionConfig/File>

1.2.34 Follow the Kubernetes documentation and configure an EncryptionConfig file. In this file, choose aes, cbc, kms, or secretbox as the encryption provider.

1.2.35 Edit the API server pod specification file /etc/kubernetes/manifests/kube-apiserver.yaml
on the master node and set the following parameter:
--tls-cipher-suites=TLS_ECDHE_ECDSA_WITH_AES_128_GCM_SHA256,TLS_ECDHE_RSA_WITH_AES_128_GCM
_SHA256,TLS_ECDHE_ECDSA_WITH_CHACHA20_POLY1305,TLS_ECDHE_RSA_WITH_AES_256_GCM
_SHA384,TLS_ECDHE_RSA_WITH_CHACHA20_POLY1305,TLS_ECDHE_ECDSA_WITH_AES_256_GCM
_SHA384

1.3.1 Edit the Controller Manager pod specification file /etc/kubernetes/manifests/kube-controller-manager.yaml
on the master node and set --terminated-pod-gc-threshold to an appropriate threshold,
for example:
--terminated-pod-gc-threshold=10

1.3.2 Edit the Controller Manager pod specification file /etc/kubernetes/manifests/kube-controller-manager.yaml
on the master node and set the following parameter:

```
--profiling=false
```

1.4.1 Edit the Scheduler pod specification file /etc/kubernetes/manifests/kube-scheduler.yaml file
on the master node and set the following parameter:

```
--profiling=false
```

At the end of the report, it shows information about the script numbers that have passed checking and other that have failed:

```
== Summary master ==
44 checks PASS
10 checks FAIL
11 checks WARN
0 checks INFO
== Summary total ==
44 checks PASS
10 checks FAIL
11 checks WARN
0 checks INFO
```

Another way to execute Kube-bench is through a YAML configuration file that you can find in the GitHub repository:

https://github.com/aquasecurity/kube-bench/blob/main/job.yaml

```
$ kubectl apply -f job.yaml
job.batch/kube-bench created
$ kubectl get pods
NAME                      READY    STATUS            RESTARTS    AGE
kube-bench-j76s9    0/1      ContainerCreating    0            3s
# Wait for a few seconds for the job to complete
$ kubectl get pods
```

```
NAME                      READY    STATUS      RESTARTS    AGE
kube-bench-j76s9    0/1      Completed    0            11s

# The results are held in the pod's logs
kubectl logs kube-bench-j76s9
[INFO] 1 Master Node Security Configuration
[INFO] 1.1 API Server
```

Kubernetes security projects

In this section, we will review different security projects that can help us, both to secure our Kubernetes cluster and to offer the best possible performance to our infrastructure.

Kube-hunter

Kubernetes clusters are mounted on a set of nodes or servers in which at least one has to take the role of master. The rest are defined as workers and have visibility with each other in order to communicate.

Kube-hunter (**https://github.com/aquasecurity/kube-hunter**) is a Python script developed by Aqua Security that allows you to analyze the potential vulnerabilities in a Kubernetes Cluster.

This tool relies on known attack vectors and information about the attack surface of its environment and allows you to perform a security vulnerability analysis in a Kubernetes installation.

It allows remote, internal, or CIDR scanning over a Kubernetes cluster and incorporates an active option through which it tries to exploit the findings. It can be run locally or through the deployment of a container that is already prepared.

We can run this tool in several ways: locally from the source code, using a container, or using a pod. In the case of the basic installation from source code, we have to install a series of dependencies, clone the GitHub repository, and run the kube-hunter script. The commands to execute in this case are:

```
$ git clone https://github.com/aquasecurity/kube-hunter.git
$ cd ./kube-hunter && pip install -r requirements.txt
$ ./kube-hunter.py
```

We can use the following command in the case of using a Docker container:

```
$ docker run –rm aquasec/kube-hunter
```

We can use the **–cidr** parameter to specify a network to scan, as shown here:

```
$ docker run –rm aquasec/kube-hunter –cidr 192.168.0.0/24
```

Regarding the scan options, **kube-hunter** will open an interactive session, where you can select one of the following scan options. For example, you can specify remote machines using the **-remote** option, as follows:

```
$ kube-hunter.py -remote domain.com
```

To control the log, we can specify a log level using the **-log** option. Consider this example:

```
$ kube-hunter.py -active -log WARNING
```

The following image shows an example of a report where we can see some vulnerabilities related to information disclosure in our cluster:

```
Vulnerabilities
+-----------+----------------+----------------+------------------+---------------+
| LOCATION  | CATEGORY       | VULNERABILITY  | DESCRIPTION      | EVIDENCE      |
+-----------+----------------+----------------+------------------+---------------+
|    :10255 | Information    | K8s Version    | The kubernetes   | v1.15.8-gke.2 |
|           | Disclosure     | Disclosure     | version could be |               |
|           |                |                | obtained from    |               |
|           |                |                | logs in the      |               |
|           |                |                | /metrics         |               |
|           |                |                | endpoint         |               |
+-----------+----------------+----------------+------------------+---------------+
|    :10255 | Information    | Exposed Pods   | An attacker      | count: 13     |
|           | Disclosure     |                | could view       |               |
|           |                |                | sensitive        |               |
|           |                |                | information      |               |
|           |                |                | about pods that  |               |
|           |                |                | are bound to a   |               |
|           |                |                | Node using the   |               |
|           |                |                | /pods endpoint   |               |
+-----------+----------------+----------------+------------------+---------------+
```

Figure 13.3: Kube-hunter vulnerabilities report

Tip: Kube-Bench and KubeHunter in MiniKube

This interactive scenario aims to deploy a local development Kubernetes cluster using minikube and run Kube-Bench and KubeHunter:

`https://www.katacoda.com/kubesec/scenarios/kubebench`

Kubesec

This tool (**https://kubesec.io**) allows you to analyze the security risk for Kubernetes resources. Here are some of the main features:

- Helps you quantify the risk for Kubernetes resources
- Runs against your Kubernetes applications (deployments and pods)
- Can be used as a standalone application or as kubectl plugin
  https://github.com/controlplaneio/kubectl-kubesec

In the following URL, we can execute kubesec over a Kubernetes security scenario:
https://www.katacoda.com/controlplane/scenarios/kube-sec-deploy

Figure 13.4: Kubernetes security scenario for executing kubesec

In the next section, we will review different plugins that can help us secure our Kubernetes cluster and offer the best possible performance to our infrastructure.

Kubectl plugins for managing Kubernetes

There are many plugins for **kubectl** to interact with and perform all kinds of operations against our cluster. We have seen that **kubectl** is the command-line tool to interact directly with Kubernetes, and it also allows you to create custom plugins, increasing your possibilities by adding ad-hoc commands to the existing ones.

We can review some plugins that offer us different security and control features to make our implementation with Kubernetes much safer. Some plugins are focused, for example, on the security of the pods, and others in RABC, and we will even see one that will allow us to sniff all the network traffic generated to or from a pod.

kubectl-trace

kubectl-trace (**https://github.com/iovisor/kubectl-trace**) is a plugin that allows using **bpftrace** in a Kubernetes cluster with the aim of creating control points in the execution to manage its flow, or even stop it, detect problems, and make an in-depth analysis of the infrastructure. You can find the complete **bpftrace** manual at **https://github.com/iovisor/bpftrace/blob/master/docs/reference_guide.md**.

Kubectl-debug

kubectl-debug (**https://github.com/aylei/kubectl-debug**) is a plugin that complements perfectly with **kubectl-trace** for debugging tasks. This allows you to execute a container within a pod that is running. It shares the namespace of the processes (PID), network, user, and IPC of the container to be analyzed, allowing us to debug them without having to install anything beforehand.

You can see a demonstration of its use at **https://github.com/aylei/kubectl-debug/blob/master/docs/kube-debug.gif**.

Ksniff

There is another plugin called **ksniff https://github.com/eldadru/ksniff** that lets us analyze all the network traffic of a Kubernetes pod using **tcpdump** and Wireshark.

Ksniff uses the data collected by **tcpdump** associated with a pod and then sends it to Wireshark to perform the analysis. This plugin is essential if you are working with microservices since it is tremendously useful for identifying errors and problems between them as well as their dependencies.

kubectl-dig

Sometimes, getting the information from a Kubernetes cluster requires the use of several commands, which, in turn, return all kinds of information.

Thanks to this plugin **https://github.com/sysdiglabs/kubectl-dig**; you can install a user-friendly user interface to easily see all the information related to the Kubernetes cluster.

The following screenshot shows the execution of this plugin for getting informamtion from a Kubernetes cluster:

Figure 13.5: kubectl-dig plugin execution

We only need to pass the node name as a parameter for the plugin execution, and it will obtain all detailed and formatted information about it.

Rakkess

Access control to all the elements of a Kubernetes cluster is one of the main tasks in securing it. From kubectl, we can obtain this information from a resource, but we cannot get an overview. Rakkess plugin (**https://github.com/corneliusweig/rakkess**) allows us to obtain a complete list in a matrix form of the current situation of access permissions between users and all server resources.

The following screenshot depicts the execution of this plugin:

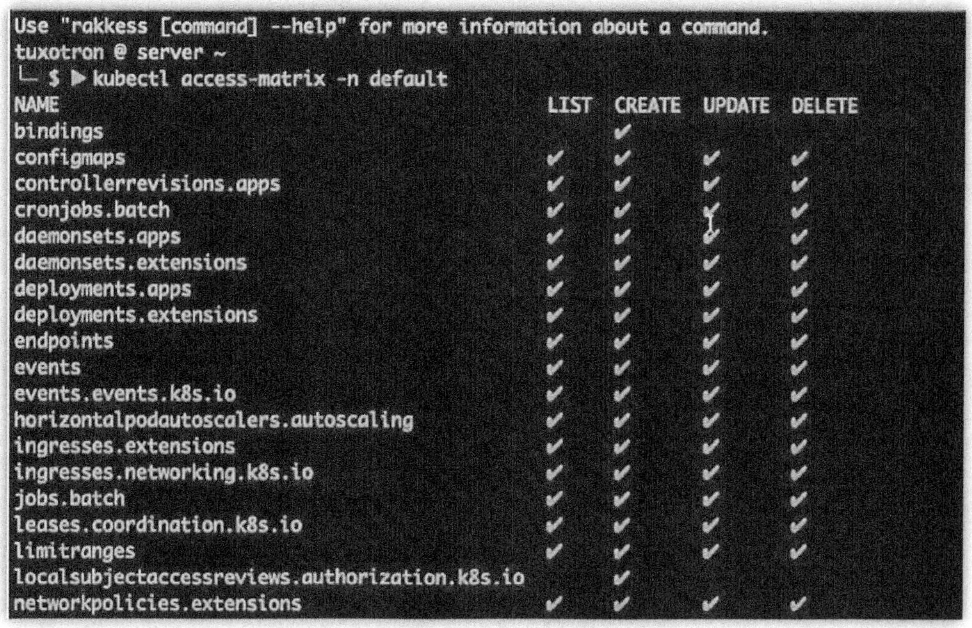

Figure 13.6: Rakkess plugin execution

Here, we can see permissions for listing, creating, updating and deleting for each resource.

Kubestriker

Kubestriker (**https://github.com/vchinnipilli/kubestriker**) is a platform-agnostic tool designed to tackle Kubernetes cluster security issues due to misconfigurations and helps strengthen the overall IT infrastructure of any organization.

It performs numerous in-depth checks on a range of services and open ports well across more than one platform, such as self-hosted Kubernetes, Amazon EKS, Azure AKS, Google GKE, and so on, to identify any misconfigurations that make organizations an easy target for attackers.

In addition, it helps safeguard against potential attacks on Kubernetes clusters by continuously scanning for anomalies. Furthermore, it comprises the ability to see some components of Kubernetes infrastructure and provides visualized attack paths of how hackers can advance their attacks.

There are several ways to install and run this tool. For example, we can run a Docker container with the following commands:

```
$ docker run -it --rm -v /Users/<yourusername>/.kube/config:/root/.
kube/config -v "$(pwd)":/kubestriker --name kubestriker cloudsecguy/
kubestriker:v1.0.0


$ python -m kubestriker
```

The following image shows this tool in execution:

Figure 13.7: Kubestriker execution

Another way to install it is using a Python environment and install dependencies from source code:

```
# Create python virtual environment
$ python3 -m venv env


# Activate python virtual environment
$ source env/bin/activate


# Clone this repository
$ git clone https://github.com/vchinnipilli/kubestriker.git
```

```
# Go into the repository
$ cd kubestriker


# Install dependencies
$ pip install -r requirements.txt
$ pip install prompt-toolkit==1.0.15
$ pip install -r requirements.txt


# Gearing up Kubestriker
$ python -m kubestriker
```

The tool will perform different tests to verify the security of the cluster. To do this, you get the Kubernetes running services in the first instance, as shown in the following figure:

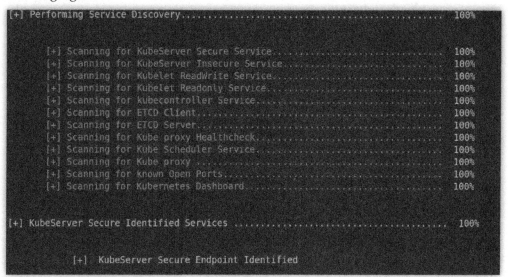

Figure 13.8: Kubestriker execution for Performing Service Discovery section

Here are some of the main configurations that it analyzes:

- Scans for IAM Misconfigurations in the cluster, as shown in the following figure:

```
[+] Gearing up for Api Server Secure Scan...........................................  100%


[+] Scanning for IAM Misconfigurations ...........................................

        [+] Scanning for Admin Roles...........................................  100%
        [+] Scanning for Read only Admin Roles.................................  100%
        [+] Scanning for Destructive Roles.....................................  100%
        [+] Scanning for Secrets Roles.........................................  100%
        [+] Scanning for Impersonate Roles.....................................  100%
        [+] Scanning for PSP atached Roles.....................................  100%
        [+] Scanning for Privileged Roles......................................  100%


[+] Identified IAM Misconfigurations ...........................................  100%


            [+]  Admin Roles Identified in the cluster
            [+]  Read Only Admin roles Identified in the cluster
            [+]  Destructive roles Identified in the cluster
```

Figure 13.9: Kubestriker execution for Scanning for IAM Misconfigurations section

It returns the identified IAM misconfigurations detected after process scanning, as shown in the following figure:

```
[+] Identified IAM Misconfigurations ...........................................  100%


            [+]  Admin Roles Identified in the cluster
            [+]  Read Only Admin roles Identified in the cluster
            [+]  Destructive roles Identified in the cluster
            [+]  Secrets roles Identified in the cluster
            [+]  Impersonate roles Identified in the cluster
            [+]  PSP attached roles Identified in the cluster
            [+]  Privileged roles Identified in the cluster

[+] Scanning for Misonfigured containers ...........................................
```

Figure 13.10: Kubestriker execution for Identified IAM Misconfigurations section

- Scans for misconfigured containers, as shown in the following figure:

```
        [+] Scanning for readiness Probe ....................................  100%
        [+] Scanning for CPU Limit .........................................  100%
        [+] Scanning for Memory Limit ......................................  100%
        [+] Scanning for Priorityclassname .................................  100%
        [+] Scanning for ServiceAccount Mount ..............................  100%
        [+] Scanning for Secrets Mounted ...................................  100%
        [+] Scanning for docker Socket Mount ...............................  100%

[+] Identified Misonfigured containers ...........................................

            [+]  Containers with High Privileges Identified in the cluster
            [+]  Containers with missing liveness Probe Identified in the cluster
            [+]  Containers with missing readiness Probe Identified in the cluster
            [+]  Containers with missing CPU Limit Identified in the cluster
            [+]  Containers with missing Memory Limit Identified in the cluster
            [+]  Containers with missing Priorityclassname Identified in the cluster
            [+]  Containers with ServiceAccount Mounted Identified in the cluster
            [+]  Containers with Secrets Mounted Identified in the cluster
```

Figure 13.11: Kubestriker execution for Identified Misconfigured containers section

- Scans for **Pod Security Policies, Misconfigured Pod Security Policies,** and **Network Policies**, as shown in the following figure:

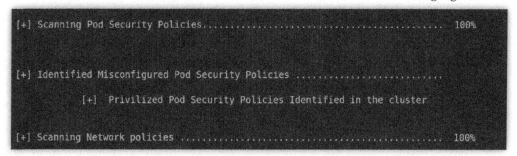

Figure 13.12: Kubestriker execution scanning Policies sections

Other tools

Within the Kubernetes ecosystem, we have different tools that can help us, depending on the security of our infrastructure. Here are some of them:

- **Checkov (https://www.checkov.io)** is a tool that allows us to analyze security at the infrastructure level as code.We can use it to avoid incorrect configurations in the cloud if we are using solutions like Terraform or Cloudformation. It is developed in Python and aims to increase the adoption of security and compliance with best practices.

- **Managed Kubernetes Inspection Tool (https://github.com/darkbitio/mkit)** enables you to quickly identify key security risks to Kubernetes clusters and their resources; for example, evaluating misconfigurations in the cluster and workloads.

- **Kubei (https://github.com/Portshift/kubei)** allows you to scan all images used by the Kubernetes cluster, application pods, and system pods. It comes with multiple options to customize the scan in terms of the criticality level of the vulnerabilities.

- **Project Calico (https://docs.projectcalico.org/getting-started/kubernetes)** is a network policy engine for Kubernetes that can be used as a code network and network security solution for containers, virtual machines, and native host-based workloads.

- **Kubeaudit (https://github.com/Shopify/kubeaudit)** is a command line tool and a Go package to audit Kubernetes clusters for various security concerns. It allows us to find security misconfigurations in Kubernetes resources and gives tips on how to resolve these issues.

- **Audit2rbac (https://github.com/liggitt/audit2rbac)** takes a Kubernetes audit log and username as input and generates RBAC roles and binding objects that cover all the API requests made by that user.

Here are some of the main advantages of using this type of tool:

- Identifies misconfigurations and vulnerabilities in clusters, containers, and pods
- Provides solutions to correct misconfigurations and eliminate vulnerabilities
- Provides a real-time view of the status of the cluster
- Gives more confidence to the DevOps team to develop and deploy the applications in a Kubernetes cluster

Analyzing Kubernetes vulnerabilities and CVEs

In this section, we will review vulnerabilities we can find in Kubernetes and the solutions provided for solving these security issues. You can see the vulnerabilities and CVEs related to Kubernetes, organized by categories, at the following links:

- `https://www.cvedetails.com/vendor/15867/Kubernetes.html`

The following image shows the number of vulnerabilities organized by category in the last years:

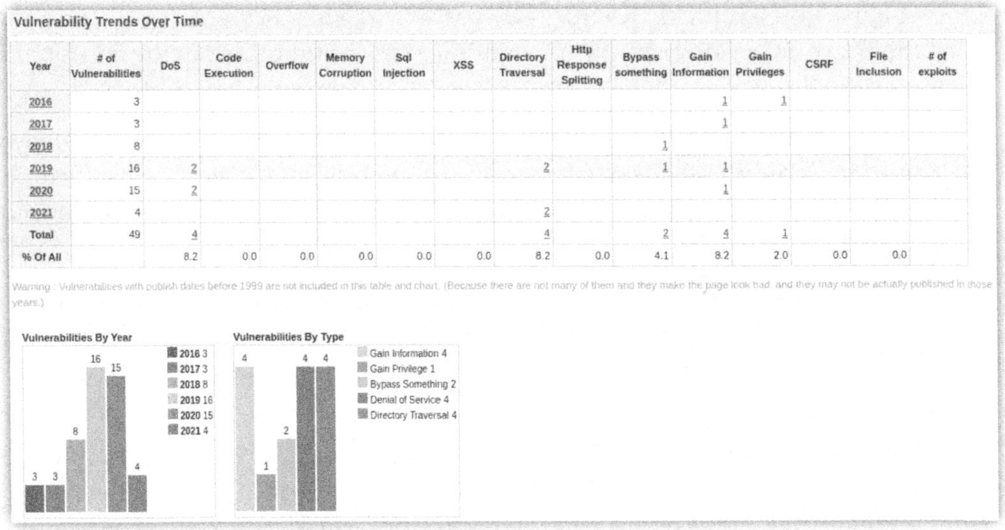

Vulnerability Trends Over Time

Year	# of Vulnerabilities	DoS	Code Execution	Overflow	Memory Corruption	Sql Injection	XSS	Directory Traversal	Http Response Splitting	Bypass something	Gain Information	Gain Privileges	CSRF	File Inclusion	# of exploits
2016	3										1	1			
2017	3										1				
2018	8									1					
2019	16	2						2		1	1				
2020	15	2									1				
2021	4							2							
Total	49	4						4		2	4	1			
% Of All		8.2	0.0	0.0	0.0	0.0	0.0	8.2	0.0	4.1	8.2	2.0	0.0	0.0	

Warning : Vulnerabilities with publish dates before 1999 are not included in this table and chart. (Because there are not many of them and they make the page look bad; and they may not be actually published in those years.)

Figure 13.13: Kubernetes vulnerabilities organized by categories

Kubernetes vulnerabilities

One of the most critical vulnerabilities detected in Kubernetes has been the one we can find in the CVE database with the code `CVE-2018-1002105` (`http://cve.mitre.org/cgi-bin/cvename.cgi?name=CVE-2018-1002105`).

The vulnerability has been identified in the Kubernetes API server and has been categorized as critical with punctuation CVSS 9.8. The vulnerability allows any authenticated Kubernetes user to obtain administrative access to the cluster using standard security settings and allows the escalation of Kubernetes privileges through a specially designed proxy request.

Note that all Kubernetes-based services and products, including Red Hat products such as OpenShift container platform, are affected, so we can also find the reference in the RedHat database.

We can see affected products by this vulnerability at `https://access.redhat.com/security/cve/cve-2018-1002105`.

The following image shows the information related with these Red Hat products:

Platform	Package	State	Errata	Release Date
Red Hat OpenShift Enterprise 3.0	openshift CVSS v3: 8.8 See score details	Will not fix		
Red Hat OpenShift Container Platform 3.11	atomic-openshift CVSS v3: 8.8 See score details	Fixed	RHSA-2018:3537	20 de noviembre de 2018
Red Hat OpenShift Container Platform 3.2	atomic-openshift CVSS v3: 8.8 See score details	Fixed	RHSA-2018:3742	3 de diciembre de 2018
Red Hat OpenShift Container Platform 3.3	atomic-openshift CVSS v3: 8.8 See score details	Fixed	RHSA-2018:3754	3 de diciembre de 2018
Red Hat OpenShift Container Platform 3.4	atomic-openshift CVSS v3: 8.8 See score details	Fixed	RHSA-2018:3752	3 de diciembre de 2018
Red Hat OpenShift Container Platform 3.5	atomic-openshift CVSS v3: 8.8 See score details	Fixed	RHSA-2018:3624	3 de diciembre de 2018
Red Hat OpenShift Container Platform 3.10	atomic-openshift	Fixed	RHSA-2018:3549	20 de noviembre de 2018

Figure 13.14: Red Hat products affected

The vulnerability is due to a vulnerable TCP connection, through which a remote attacker could send specially manipulated requests to one of the added APIs of the Kubernetes API server and escalate privileges using that service's TLS credentials. The problem is that an unauthenticated user can access the API to create new services that could be used to inject malicious code.

Any user can establish a connection through the Kubernetes API to a server in the backend. Once the connection is established, an attacker can send arbitrary requests directly to that service, and these requests are authenticated with the **Transport Layer Security (TLS)** credentials of the Kubernetes server.

The bug can be used in two ways: one related to users with execution permissions over a group of containers that share storage and network resources. You can realize privilege escalation at the cluster-admin level and execute any process in a container.

Ultimately, an attacker who manages privilege escalation through any of the APIs could access a pod in execution, list the pods in a specific node, and execute arbitrary commands or reveal sensitive information.

The vulnerability has already been solved by the Kubernetes development team, and it is recommended to update it with patched versions. You can find more information in the Kubernetes GitHub repository at **https://github.com/kubernetes/kubernetes/issues/71411**.

Another critical vulnerability discovered in Kubernetes is the CVE-2020-10749 (**https://nvd.nist.gov/vuln/detail/CVE-2020-10749**). This vulnerability enables **Man-In-The-Middle (MITM)** attacks, where an attacker can intercept network traffic to a pod in a Kubernetes cluster and impersonate clients.

This vulnerability was found in all versions of the `networking/plugins` container before version 0.8.6, which allows malicious containers in Kubernetes clusters to perform MITM attacks. A malicious container can exploit this flaw by sending rogue IPv6 router advertisements to the host or other containers to redirect traffic to the malicious container.

Consider an IPv4-only cluster, where IPv6 addresses have never been routed. If an attacker gains access to one of your pods with the CAP_NET_RAW capability, it can send *"malicious"* IPv6 packets, indicating that the attacker's pod is an IPv6 router that knows how to resolve all IPv6 addresses.

This way, vulnerable container network deployments could send all traffic for which DNS returns an IPv6 record to the attacker's pod, allowing them to see this traffic and spoofing client-server communication.

An attacker would have to control one of the pods in their cluster to exploit this vulnerability. This can happen if they unintentionally install a malicious pod or if an attacker uses other means to gain control of one of their pods.

The result is that any user could mount a directory of the host machine from the container and access the filesystem, managing to escape from the container.

This vulnerability could disable the CAP_NET_RAW capability on your pods by default, enabling it only for pods that need it. From a certificate point of view, it is important to use TLS with certificate validation in requests made to the Kubernetes API.

Another vulnerability that is considered critical is that of the CVE-2020-8559 code that allows the escalation of privileges of a compromised node within the cluster.

This vulnerability is based on the fact that if an attacker can intercept certain requests to the Kubelet process, they can also send a redirect response using the original request's credentials.

If multiple clusters share the same certificate authority and authentication credentials trusted by the client, this vulnerability can allow an attacker to redirect the client to another cluster over which requests would be spoofed using the original credentials.

With this configuration, this vulnerability should be considered high severity and requires an attacker to first compromise a node in the cluster. We can find different proofs of concept that aim to exploit this vulnerability in the following repositories:

- `https://github.com/tabbysable/POC-2020-8559`
- `https://github.com/tdwyer/CVE-2020-8559`

Vulnerability with PodSecurityPolicy

Another vulnerability is related to the HostPath type of PersistentVolumes that allows you to bypass the PodSecurityPolicy directive.

In Kubernetes, PodSecurityPolicy is one of the resources that allows the admission controller to decide whether a pod can be created by a service account depending on its configuration. For example, if privileged mode pods are not allowed in a PodSecurityPolicy, any pod that tries to create privileged mode from that service account will fail.

This usually works, but some security audits have found cases in which the mounting of hostPath volumes is done instead of using a persistent volume even though the definition of the pod is restricted. This restriction is not taken into account if you are working with a **Persistent Volume Claim (PVC)**.

The result is that any user could mount a directory of the host machine from the container and have access to the filesystem, managing to escape from the container.

The solution to this vulnerability has been to document the PodSecurityPolicy does not limit the types of persistent volumes, and these should only give allowed users access to cluster resources.

Vulnerability in the use of certificates

The different Kubernetes services use X.509 certificates to ensure the authentication, authorization, and security of the data transported between them. The API server acts as the certifying entity and signs and sends the certificates to the rest of the services.

The problem occurs when one of the nodes is compromised (by an intrusion, a suspicious use of resources, a strange behavior of a container, etc.). If it is suspected that the certificate may have been compromised, one of the certificates cannot be revoked individually. Instead, the entire chain of system certificates must be revoked, regenerated, and sent again to the different nodes and services.

The solution will go through having a list of revoked certificates. This would imply having a certificate server in which you could individually revoke whatever you wanted, and that would stamp the date and time of the certificate before use to ensure that it is still valid.

Conclusion

With the objective of ensuring that developers and DevOps get the best possible performance and security in the Kubernetes infrastructure, we have analyzed the state of Kubernetes security in this chapter. This includes best practices, the latest vulnerabilities discovered, and the main projects we can find in the Kubernetes ecosystem for checking the security of a Kubernetes cluster.

From the user's point of view, it is important to keep track of the vulnerabilities that arise, in addition to being well documented in order to understand the internal structure of Kubernetes with the strengths and weaknesses of its components, its attack surface, and the possible threats that exist in a system where we have deployed applications that use Kubernetes and container-based systems as a base.

In this chapter, we reviewed Kubernetes security principles and some tools, like Kubernetes bench for security project as an application that checks whether Kubernetes is implemented securely and other plugins for managing the Kubernetes cluster securely.

In the next chapter, we will review tools related to observability and monitoring in Kubernetes for getting metrics about applications deployed in the cluster.

Points to remember

- **KubeBench** is a tool that performs an in-depth analysis of your Kubernetes environment. The tool integrates more than 100 security tests and parameters, so you get a clear picture of how safe your environment is at the end of the process.

- **Kube-hunter** offers a list of tests that are run both actively and passively and allow us to identify most of the vulnerabilities that we can find in a Kubernetes cluster.

Multiple choice questions

1. Which tool is a platform-agnostic tool designed to tackle Kubernetes cluster security issues due to misconfigurations and helps strengthen the overall IT infrastructure of any organization?

    a. Kubesec

    b. Kubestriker

    c. Kube-bench

    d. Kube-hunter

2. Which is the command you can use for deploying jube-hunter as a Docker container?

    a. $ docker run –rm docker/kube-hunter

    b. $ docker run –rm kube-hunter

    c. $ docker run –rm kube-hunter/aquasec

    d. $ docker run –rm aquasec/kube-hunter

Answers

1	b
2	d

Questions

1. Which tool checks if Kubernetes is implemented securely by executing controls documented in CIS Kubernetes Benchmark?

2. Which tool is a Python script developed by Aqua Security that allows you to analyze the potential vulnerabilities in a Kubernetes Cluster?

3. Which tool allows us to analyze security at the infrastructure level as code and can be used to avoid incorrect configurations?

Key terms

- **KubeBench** is an application developed in Golang that checks if Kubernetes is implemented securely by executing controls documented in CIS Kubernetes Benchmark.

- **Kubesec** is an open source security risk analysis tool for Kubernetes resources. Validate the configuration and manifest files used for Kubernetes cluster operations and deployment, and you can install it on your system using its container image, its binary package, or a kubectl plugin.

CHAPTER 14
Observability and Monitoring in Kubernetes

Observability and monitoring are important parts of the maintenance of applications for getting metrics about application behavior.

This chapter reviews capabilities that are recommended to be implemented when running Kubernetes in production. We will first analyze observability and monitoring in the context of Kubernetes, and then we will review Kubernetes dashboard for getting metrics in your cluster. Finally, we will look at the Kubernetes stack for observability and monitoring with Prometheus and Grafana.

Structure

We will cover the following topics in this chapter:

- Introducing observability and monitoring
- Observability in a Kubernetes cluster
- Monitoring resources in a Kubernetes cluster
- Kubernetes dashboard
- Enhancing observability and monitoring with Prometheus and Grafana

Objectives

After studying this chapter, you will understand observability and monitoring and learn about observability in a Kubernetes Cluster, Kubernetes dashboard, and enhancing observability and monitoring with Prometheus and Grafana.

Introducing observability and monitoring

Monitoring is an essential part of the infrastructure. Thanks to it, we can obtain information to take scaling measures, and it will help us understand what is happening and how our cluster behaves.

By definition, monitoring is a real-time process that encompasses the collection, processing, and analysis of quantifiable data from a system. It involves many aspects, and it can contemplate everything from knowing the status of infrastructure and services to having a complex, resilient system capable of anticipating events, depending on the needs and ambitions of who needs it.

Monitoring has ceased to be something purely technical and has become a way of obtaining valuable information that supports decision making and contributes to improving the conditions of our customers, reducing costs, evolving our products, and even creating new ones. In this sense, a monitoring system aims to be able to know our system and its behavior in the face of interactions with our clients.

When facing the construction of a monitoring system, it is important to take into account the objective we are pursuing and the users of the information. Once these are identified, we can define the metrics and tools that help us collect data in each part of our application architecture.

Currently, development or architecture based on microservices is one of the strongest and most used paradigms. Similarly, different design patterns have emerged to be able to implement these types of architectures based on microservices and the cloud.

Microservices architectures can grow rapidly, so we need to know that everything is working correctly. It is also important to determine if our system is degrading or if, for example, we are not capable of complying with **Service Level Agreement (SLAs)**.

The monitoring of our system will be constantly providing metrics and values to analyze the correct operation. In recent years, other patterns have emerged to be able to know if all our development is working as it should. At this point, observability can be considered as a new form of monitoring.

Observability details when and why an error occurs. Four fundamental components are needed to achieve observability:

- **Open instrumentation**: Open instrumentation collects vendor-specific or open source telemetry data from a service, host, application, container, or any other entity that produces data. This enables full-face visibility of critical infrastructure and applications. It also prepares teams for the future as you introduce new platforms and data types to the system.

- **Correlation and context**: The collected telemetry data must be analyzed so that all data sources can be connected. You also need to incorporate metadata to allow correlation between various parts of the system and your data. Together, these actions create context and shape meaning.

- **Programmability**: Organizations need the flexibility to create their own context with custom applications based on their goals. For example, an application can help teams calculate and visualize the impact of errors on the end user.

- **Artificial intelligence for IT operations (AIOps)**. Unlike traditional incident management tools, AIOps solutions use machine learning models to automate IT operations processes. We can automatically correlate, add, and prioritize incident data with AIOps.

Observability in a Kubernetes cluster

The Kubernetes cluster itself exposes cluster metrics and Kubernetes has Metrics-Server, an aggregator of data on the use of resources, since version 1.8. Thanks to Metrics-Server, Kubernetes can provide information on the use of resources through the CLI kubectl.

For example, kube-state-metrics exposes the data obtained by the Kubernetes API so that other tools like Prometheus or another data collector can consume this data.

We can use the open source software Prometheus to collect metrics. It is a monitoring system that communicates with the Kubernetes API to record the metrics that the user requests, and it uses time series databases to store them.

It uses its own query language, PromQL, and exposes an HTTP API for integration with other services that allow creating new requests, consulting already registered metrics, configuring alerts, and so on. Grafana is one of the services it is regularly integrated with.

Cluster monitoring

Monitoring of the containers allows us to know the status of each one individually, but the problem of having multiple containers arises when creating a cluster, so reviewing all of them can be a repetitive and tedious task prone to errors.

Within a Kubernetes cluster, multiple objects can be running concurrently; a single namespace with a service includes, at least, that there is a pod executing a deployment with a container, therefore, with the presence of so many objects, which can also vary over time (e.g. rescaled), find where an error occurs when the cluster fails it becomes an impossible task.

In addition, due to the ephemeral nature of containers, the container may disappear from the moment the failure occurs until the moment of debugging. This makes log files a fundamental and indispensable tool.

Despite all this, Kubernetes has a great capacity to automatically recover from failures, such as restarting a pod or balancing the load on the nodes. However, sometimes it is not enough, and the process must be performed manually; For these cases, it is necessary to monitor the execution of the cluster using different tools, from Kubernetes own, such as the control panel, to specialized external software.

Two main factors must be taken into account to monitor a process: what can be monitored and how to do it. As for what to monitor, Kubernetes itself offers the ability to know:

- **CPU usage**: Monitoring reveals system and user CPU usage as well as read and write waits. It is useful for finding bottlenecks in deployment.

- **Memory usage**: Shows the amount of memory available and in use for both free memory and cache.

- **Disk usage**: Indicates disk space. The lack of disk space can cause a failure in the execution of a program, so we must keep an eye on it.

- **Network bandwidth**: Offers the bandwidth in use and the bandwidth available. Although it seems impossible to consume the bandwidth now, it is important to monitor it if suspicious behavior, such as a DDoS attack, occurs.

- **Pods resources**: You can access the different resources that a specific Pod is using, this information being used by the scheduler and placing the pods in nodes where there are available resources (auto-scaling).

Regarding how to do it, the easiest way for the above-mentioned metrics is to use the Kubernetes control panel.

However, the monitoring metrics that we have by default are sometimes insufficient and we need to expand the capabilities, which is why Kubernetes allows the use of custom metrics. This is where the questions come up again:

- What custom metrics can the cluster read?
- How do you read them?

The available metrics are the ones written in such a way that Kubernetes API can access them, and external programs must be used to access them. As mentioned earlier, the one most used by the community is Prometheus **https://prometheus.io**.

Kubernetes dashboard

In addition to the command line, Kubernetes provides a web user interface where you can view and interact with the cluster. It can be used both to deploy applications to a Kubernetes cluster and to troubleshoot or manage the existing resources.

`https://github.com/kubernetes/dashboard`

The interface shows the current state of the cluster in real-time as well as all the objects that compose it, being able to interact with them so a service can be scaled or a pod can be restarted. Start it using the following command to use it:

```
$ kubectl apply -f

https://raw.githubusercontent.com/kubernetes/dashboard/master/aio/
deploy/recommended.yaml
```

In the preceding command, we can see we are using the YAML file from the official Kubernetes website. Next, we can verify that it has been deployed correctly. The containers that are part of this solution are:

```
$ docker ps

docker.io/kubernetesui/dashboard                              v2.0.0-beta3
6feddba9df747        32MB

docker.io/kubernetesui/metrics-scraper                            v1.0.1
709901356c115          16.1MB
```

This tool provides an interface with token authentication and a dashboard where we have all the main elements of Kubernetes. Additionally, when we select a node, it returns us a large amount of information about it:

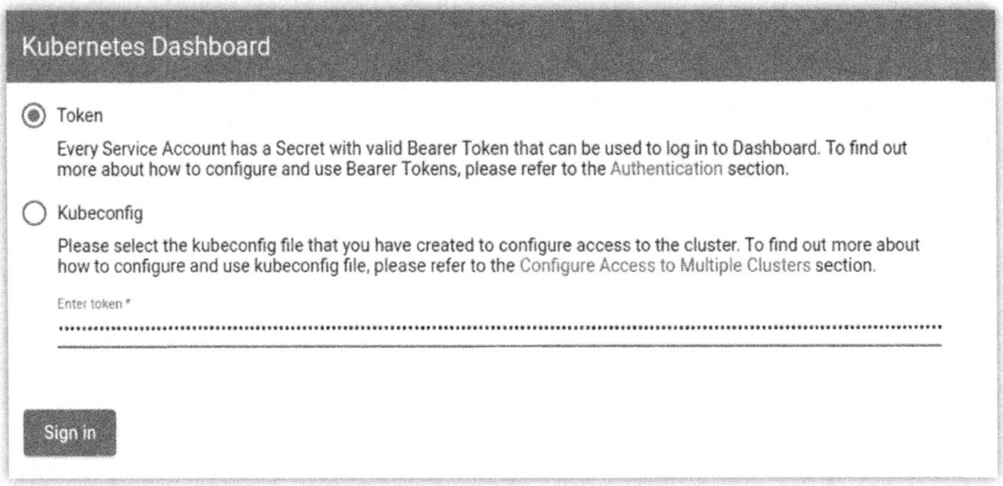

Figure 14.1: Accessing Kubernetes Dashboard with authentication token

The preceding command will create a pod from the official Kubernetes repository specs on GitHub. You can check the system pods through the following command to verify that Kubernetes Dashboard has been deployed correctly:

```
$ kubectl get pods --all-namespaces

NAMESPACE    NAME                                         READY  STATUS   RESTARTS  AGE

kube-system  coredns-66bff467f8-47mbp                     1/1    Running  0         55m

kube-system  coredns-66bff467f8-wws72                     1/1    Running  0         55m

kube-system  dash-kubernetes-dashboard-6cc989d574-vp5t8  1/1    Running  0         55m

kube-system  etcd-controlplane                            1/1    Running  0         55m

kube-system  kube-apiserver-controlplane                  1/1    Running  0         55m

kube-system  kube-controller-manager-controlplane         1/1    Running  0         55m

kube-system  kube-flannel-ds-amd64-6msg8                  1/1    Running  0         55m

kube-system  kube-flannel-ds-amd64-hj2gx                  1/1    Running  0         55m

kube-system  kube-proxy-8zpvj                             1/1    Running  0         55m

kube-system  kube-proxy-ct5fk                             1/1    Running  0         55m

kube-system  kube-scheduler-controlplane                  1/1    Running  0         55m
```

We can also use the system namespace, which is **kube-system**, with the following command to check these pods:

```
$ kubectl get pods --namespace kube-system

NAME                                        READY   STATUS    RESTARTS   AGE

coredns-66bff467f8-h8n2h                    1/1     Running   0          2m37s

coredns-66bff467f8-tzlcf                    1/1     Running   0          2m37s

dash-kubernetes-dashboard-6cc989d574-nxsxt  1/1     Running   0          2m37s

etcd-controlplane                           1/1     Running   0          2m47s

kube-apiserver-controlplane                 1/1     Running   0          2m47s

kube-controller-manager-controlplane        1/1     Running   0          2m47s

kube-flannel-ds-amd64-96r74                 1/1     Running   0          2m26s

kube-flannel-ds-amd64-tphcr                 1/1     Running   0          2m37s

kube-proxy-476mg                            1/1     Running   0          2m37s

kube-proxy-4dm82                            1/1     Running   0          2m26s

kube-scheduler-controlplane                 1/1     Running   0          2m47s
```

In both cases, you should see a pod named `dash-kubernetes-dashboard-*` in the running state:

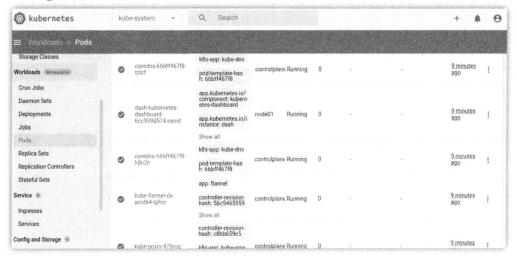

Figure 14.2: Pods in Kubernetes Dashboard

The interface allows multiple options to choose from, both pods and nodes, volumes or namespaces. However, the part that interests us for the monitoring is the visualization of the memory and CPU usage of the deployments within the cluster.

We can check the nodes and their status with the following command:

```
$ kubectl get nodes
NAME            STATUS    ROLES     AGE    VERSION
controlplane    Ready     master    13m    v1.18.0
node01          Ready     <none>    12m    v1.18.0
```

Similarly, we can use the interface to verify this aspect:

Figure 14.3: Nodes in Kubernetes Dashboard

We can see details about **dash-kubernetes-dashboard** deployment in the **Deployments** section:

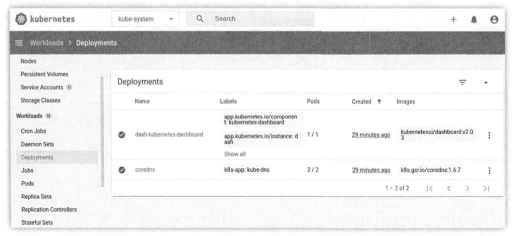

Figure 14.4: Deployments in Kubernetes Dashboard

Figure 14.5: Deployments in Kubernetes Dashboard

To test this tool, we can launch a couple of pods to be able to see the operation of the dashboard and then deploy the dashboard to be able to observe what happens in our infrastructure.

We can create the YAML file where we will define some pods with nginx and deploy it through a **ReplicationController**:

```
$ cat nginx_rc.yaml
apiVersion: v1
kind: ReplicationController
metadata:
  name: nginx
spec:
  replicas: 2
  selector:
    app: nginx
  template:
    metadata:
      name: nginx
      labels:
        app: nginx
    spec:
      containers:
      - name: nginx
        image: nginx
        ports:
        - containerPort: 80
```

We can also use the Kubernetes Dashboard interface to create the replica controller:

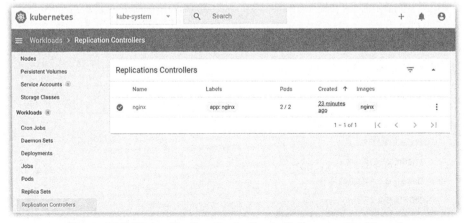

Figure 14.6: Creating Replica Controller in Kubernetes Dashboard

The following commands are used to create the pods and verify that they have been deployed successfully:

```
$ kubectl create -f nginx_rc.yaml
$ kubectl get rc
NAME      DESIRED   CURRENT   READY    AGE
nginx     2         2         2        4m25s
$ kubectl get pods
NAME           READY    STATUS     RESTARTS   AGE
nginx-bbhsw    1/1      Running    0          4m44s
nginx-cksz6    1/1      Running    0          4m44s
```

In the **Replication Controllers** section, we can see details about nginx deployment with two pods:

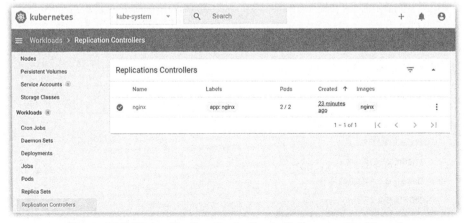

Figure 14.7: Nginx Replica Controller in Kubernetes Dashboard

We can see the two pods in execution if we go into the details:

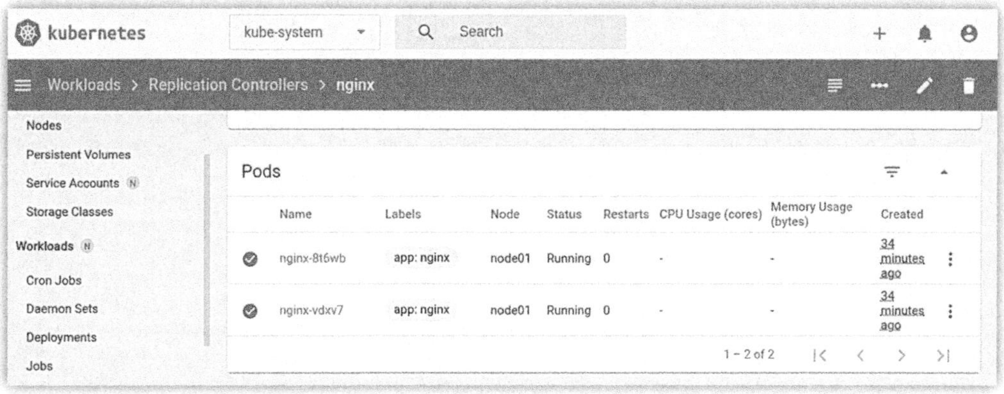

Figure 14.8: Nginx Pods in Kubernetes Dashboard

An interesting operation that we can perform from the same interface is one that allows us to scale to more nodes in order to increase availability within the cluster.

We can execute one instance of the nginx container with the following command:

```
$ kubectl create deployment nginx --image=nginx
deployment.apps/nginx created
```

Figure 14.9: Scale a resource in Kubernetes Dashboard

The preceding action is equivalent to the following command:

```
$ kubectl scale -n default deployment nginx --replicas=3
deployment.apps/nginx scaled
```

Within the detail of the cluster nodes we can obtain the resources that are used at the memory and CPU level:

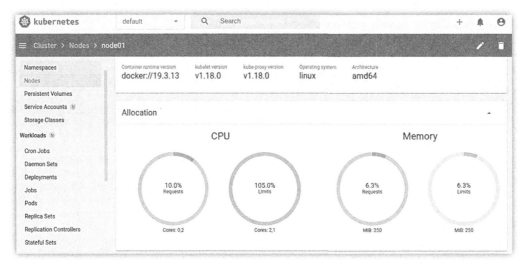

Figure 14.10: Nodes Allocation in Kubernetes Dashboard

This information would be the equivalent to what we can see when executing the following command:

```
$ kubectl describe node node01
Name:              node01
Roles:             <none>
Labels:            beta.kubernetes.io/arch=amd64
                   beta.kubernetes.io/os=linux
                   kubernetes.io/arch=amd64
                   kubernetes.io/hostname=node01
                   kubernetes.io/os=linux
Annotations:       flannel.alpha.coreos.com/backend-data: null
                   flannel.alpha.coreos.com/backend-type: host-gw
                   flannel.alpha.coreos.com/kube-subnet-manager:true
                   flannel.alpha.coreos.com/public-ip: 172.17.0.29
                   kubeadm.alpha.kubernetes.io/cri-socket:  /var/
                   run/dockershim.sock
                   node.alpha.kubernetes.io/ttl: 0
                   volumes.kubernetes.io/controller-managed-at-
                   tach-detach: true
```

```
Addresses:
  InternalIP:  172.17.0.29
  Hostname:    node01
Capacity:
  cpu:                 2
  ephemeral-storage:   199545168Ki
  hugepages-1Gi:       0
  hugepages-2Mi:       0
  memory:              4039104Ki
  pods:                110
Allocatable:
  cpu:                 2
  ephemeral-storage:   183900826525
  hugepages-1Gi:       0
  hugepages-2Mi:       0
  memory:              3936704Ki
 pods:                110
System Info:
  Machine ID:                 df10c9c4bf9f5645d7ec1ae361195adf
  System UUID:                df10c9c4bf9f5645d7ec1ae361195adf
  Boot ID:                    b5c41011-96ac-49ba-bcfd-dbfb7594a8b8
  Kernel Version:             4.15.0-122-generic
  OS Image:                   Ubuntu 18.04.5 LTS
  Operating System:           linux
  Architecture:               amd64
  Container Runtime Version:  docker://19.3.13
  Kubelet Version:            v1.18.0
  Kube-Proxy Version:         v1.18.0
PodCIDR:                      10.244.1.0/24
PodCIDRs:                     10.244.1.0/24
Non-terminated Pods:          (11 in total)
  Namespace                                                     Name
CPU Requests  CPU Limits  Memory Requests  Memory Limits  AGE
```

```
   ---------              ----                        -------
-----  ----------   ---------------  -------------   ---
   default                                              nginx-57jlq
0 (0%)         0 (0%)        0 (0%)          0 (0%)      26m
   default                 nginx-6znxm                           0
(0%)         0 (0%)        0 (0%)          0 (0%)      26m
   default                                     nginx-f89759699-987rb
0 (0%)         0 (0%)        0 (0%)          0 (0%)      16m
   default                                     nginx-f89759699-mkrq2
0 (0%)         0 (0%)        0 (0%)          0 (0%)      13m
   default                                     nginx-f89759699-tbjlh
0 (0%)         0 (0%)        0 (0%)          0 (0%)      16m
   default                          random-logger-7687d48b59-dlmc8
0 (0%)         0 (0%)        0 (0%)          0 (0%)      17m
   default                          random-logger-7687d48b59-frgds
0 (0%)         0 (0%)        0 (0%)          0 (0%)      20m
   default                          random-logger-7687d48b59-s2lwd
0 (0%)         0 (0%)        0 (0%)          0 (0%)      17m
   kube-system              dash-kubernetes-dashboard-6cc989d574-gdm64
100m (5%)      2 (100%)    200Mi (5%)      200Mi (5%)   37m
   kube-system                          kube-flannel-ds-amd64-zm7c2
100m (5%)      100m (5%)   50Mi (1%)       50Mi (1%)    37m
   kube-system                              kube-proxy-hc2jh
0 (0%)         0 (0%)        0 (0%)          0 (0%)      37m
Allocated resources:
  (Total limits may be over 100 percent, i.e., overcommitted.)
  Resource             Requests     Limits
  --------             --------     ------
  cpu                  200m (10%)   2100m (105%)
  memory               250Mi (6%)   250Mi (6%)
  ephemeral-storage    0 (0%)       0 (0%)
  hugepages-1Gi        0 (0%)       0 (0%)
  hugepages-2Mi        0 (0%)       0 (0%)
Events:
  Type    Reason                 Age           From           Message
  ----    ------                 ----          ----           -------
```

```
   Normal   Starting                    37m                      kubelet, node01
Starting kubelet.

   Normal   NodeHasSufficientMemory   37m (x2 over 37m)    kubelet, node01
Node node01 status is now: NodeHasSufficientMemory

   Normal   NodeHasNoDiskPressure     37m (x2 over 37m)    kubelet, node01
Node node01 status is now: NodeHasNoDiskPressure

   Normal   NodeHasSufficientPID      37m (x2 over 37m)    kubelet, node01
Node node01 status is now: NodeHasSufficientPID

   Normal   NodeAllocatableEnforced   37m                      kubelet, node01
Updated Node Allocatable limit across pods

   Normal   Starting                    37m                   kube-proxy, node01
Starting kube-proxy.

   Normal   NodeReady                   37m                      kubelet, node01
Node node01 status is now: NodeReady
```

Tip: Basic Kubernetes Observability

This interactive scenario aims to explore the basic techniques for observing the state of Kubernetes using metrics.

https://www.katacoda.com/javajon/courses/kubernetes-observability/basics

---

Other Kubernetes Dashboards

Here are some of the other dashboards we can find in the Kubernetes ecosystem:

- **Kube-ops-view https://codeberg.org/hjacobs/kube-ops-view** : This project presents us with a dashboard designed for large servers, where we have a significant volume of pods that we need to review at a glance.

- **Kubeview https://github.com/benc-uk/kubeview** : This project focuses on representing relationships between objects in Kubernetes.

- **Weave Scope https://github.com/weaveworks/scope** : It is intended to be a tool that covers all possible elements in a deployment with docker as runtime and weave as network manager.

- **Skooner https://github.com/skooner-k8s/skooner** : It is a dashboard similar to the official one and offers the possibility of viewing all the objects, along with the related events.

- **Ktop https://github.com/ynqa/ktop** : Application that allows showing the status of a Kubernetes cluster that works directly in the terminal.

- **Kubenav https://github.com/kubenav/kubenav** : Application that provides an overview of all the resources in a Kubernetes cluster, including current status information for workloads. The details view for resources provides additional information. We can view logs and events or get a shell into a container. We can also edit and delete resources or scale our workloads within the app.

- **K9s https://k9scli.io** : K9s is a terminal-based UI to interact with our Kubernetes clusters. This project aims to make it easier to navigate, observe, and manage your deployed applications in the wild. K9s continually watches Kubernetes for changes and offers subsequent commands to interact with your observed resources.

Enhancing observability and monitoring with Prometheus and Grafana

We need external tools to have panels with cluster information, as well as alarms that give us precise information on the status of the cluster. The Prometheus-Grafana combination is the most widely used today. These two tools are open source and have a large community that is improving and adapting them to the new needs of users.

Prometheus

Prometheus is an open source monitoring and alert toolkit. It was developed in 2012 by the *SoundCloud* company, but later it would become an open source project, joining the Cloud Native Computing Foundation in 2016 as the second project hosted after Kubernetes.

Prometheus has the metrics constantly and actively, that is, it is in charge of reading the required data at all times instead of waiting for a response that may not match the waiting times estimated by the user. Furthermore, the software can send alerts according to preconfigured rules to the manager called **alertmanager**.

This manager is in charge of managing the alarms, grouping the received ones, and sending them to another application in charge of transmitting the message. It is also possible to use other software that allows you to view all the data read, such as the Kubernetes user interface itself.

- `https://prometheus.io/docs/introduction/overview`
- `https://github.com/prometheus/prometheus`

Prometheus allows two types of possible rules to be configured and evaluated at predefined time intervals:

- **Recording rules**, which allows you to execute actions that are required repeatedly or are computationally expensive and save the result as a new one.

- **Alert rules**, which allow defining conditions under which the program sends a notification. These alerts have to be written in the Prometheus language for Prometheus to understand and execute them.

The software contains a local database on disk to store the corresponding data, but it can also be used on remote systems. There are several functionalities that make up Prometheus, the most notable ones being:

- **Alertmanager** manages the alerts sent by the applications or the Prometheus server itself.

- **The Prometheus operator** provides monitoring definitions to the Kubernetes services and the Prometheus deployment, making the configuration within the cluster native by managing the necessary instances.

One of the outstanding advantages of Prometheus is its query language, which is quite flexible. It also has a pull model for metric collectors and a discovery service for the objectives that greatly facilitates integration with tools such as Kubernetes, which has elements that are created and destroyed, such as Pods.

Its architecture is designed to be highly scalable, which is ideal for environments where the probability of scaling is high and for already scaled environments that require efficient configurations.

Prometheus architecture

Prometheus works well to record numerical time series, for example, those based on time series data, both machine-centric monitoring and microservice-based architectures monitoring. Here are some of the main features:

- It provides a multidimensional data model and a **powerful query language (PromQL)**.

- Collects information from more than 5000 metrics automatically, with zero configuration, zero dependencies, and zero maintenance.

- Prometheus libraries offer four types of metrics: counter, gauge, histogram, and summary.

Prometheus is made up of multiple components, including:

- **Prometheus server**: It is the main component in charge of collecting and storing application metrics in a time series database.

- **Service discovery**: Prometheus has connectors with the main service discovery on the market and can auto-discover applications automatically in real time. This is essential when working with containers that are constantly changing their IP address.

- **Client libraries**: These are the libraries in charge of exposing the internal metrics of the application to be monitored in Prometheus format (CPU, Memory, Threads, GC) so that they can be collected by the Prometheus server.

- **Alert manager**: It is the component in charge of managing the alerts sent by the Prometheus server.

Prometheus installation

One of the ways to start a Prometheus server on Kubernetes is through the Prometheus operator, which provides native Kubernetes deployment and management, along with related monitoring components.

`https://github.com/prometheus-operator/prometheus-operator`

This project aims to simplify and automate the configuration of a prometheus-based monitoring stack for Kubernetes clusters. The installation of the operator can also be done through the following Helm chart developed for it using the following YAML file.

`https://github.com/helm/charts/blob/master/stable/prometheus-operator/values.yaml`

By default, this chart will display both the operator and the Prometheus itself, with the corresponding alertManager and grafana, all configurable in the **values.yaml** file discussed earlier.

You can find more information about the helm prometheus chart at **https://artifacthub.io/packages/helm/edu/prometheus**.

These are the helm commands that we can use to install this operator. The first step is to create the namespace where Prometheus will be deployed:

```
# Create namespace
kubectl create namespace prometheus-system
```

We can use the following command using the **values.yaml** file to deploy it in Kubernetes:

```
# Install Prometheus operator using helm

helm install stable/prometheus-operator --name=prometheus-operator
--namespace=monitoring -f prometheus/values.yml
```

A specific namespace called **monitoring** has been created for this deployment with the preceding command. Once it is finished, you will be able to access the server using these two commands:

```
$ export POD_NAME=$(kubectl get pods --namespace monitoring -l
"app=prometheus,component=server" -o jsonpath="{.items[0].metada-
ta.name}")

$ kubectl --namespace monitoring port-forward $POD_NAME 9090
```

Another way to start Prometheus is through a Docker Container with a user interface available on port 9090. Prometheus uses the following configuration file to scrape the targets and collect and store the metrics before making them available via API that allows dashboards, graphing, and alerting.

prometheus.yml

```
global:
  scrape_interval:     15s
  evaluation_interval: 15s

scrape_configs:
  - job_name: 'prometheus'

    static_configs:
      - targets: ['127.0.0.1:9090', '127.0.0.1:9100']
        labels:
          group: 'prometheus'
```

The following command launches the container with the prometheus configuration. Any data created by prometheus will be stored on the host, in the **/prometheus/data** directory. The data will be persisted when we update the container.

```
$ docker run -d --net=host \
>       -v /root/prometheus.yml:/etc/prometheus/prometheus.yml \
>       --name prometheus-server \
>       prom/prometheus
```

After executing the previous command, we have the Prometheus server running:

```
# docker ps

CONTAINER ID          IMAGE               COMMAND                      CREATED
STATUS                PORTS               NAMES

94c3270d8855          prom/prometheus     "/bin/prometheus --c…"  9 minutes
ago         Up 9 minutes                              prometheus-server
```

You should see the Prometheus interface if you access **http://localhost:9090**:

Figure 14.11: Prometheus interface

We need to run a Prometheus node exporter to collect metrics related to a node. Prometheus has many exporters that are designed to output metrics for a particular system, such as Postgres or MySQL.

We are starting the Node Exporter container with the following command. By mounting the host **/proc** and **/sys** directory, the container has access to the necessary information to report on.

```
$ docker run -d \
>     -v "/proc:/host/proc" \
>     -v "/sys:/host/sys" \
>     -v "/:/rootfs" \
>     --net="host" \
>     --name=prometheus \
>     quay.io/prometheus/node-exporter:v0.13.0 \
>       -collector.procfs /host/proc \
>       -collector.sysfs /host/sys \
>       -collector.filesystem.ignored-mount-points "^/(sys|proc|dev|
      host|etc)($|/)"
```

You can view the raw metrics with the following command:

```
$ curl localhost:9100/metrics
```

The following interface shows a text box where you can enter queries about the metrics it is collecting:

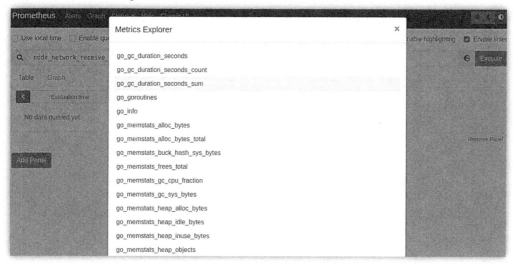

Figure 14.12: Prometheus metrics

The interface offers the possibility of obtaining the different metrics through auto completion:

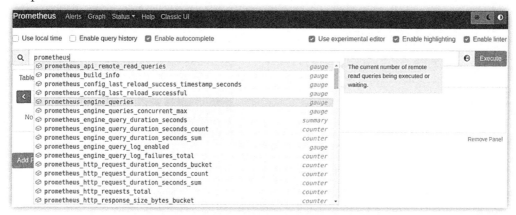

Figure 14.13: Prometheus metrics searching

By selecting a metric, we can see the values it returns through the different endpoints:

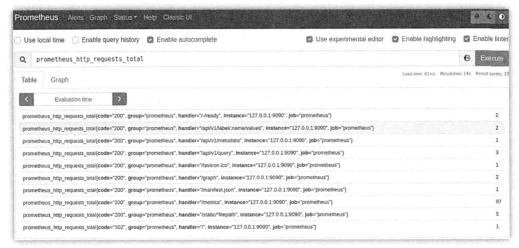

Figure 14.14: Prometheus details metrics

You can see examples of queries to the Prometheus API in the official documentation at **https://prometheus.io/docs/prometheus/latest/querying/basics**.

In the **Graph** tab, we can see the graphs that are generated for the different metrics:

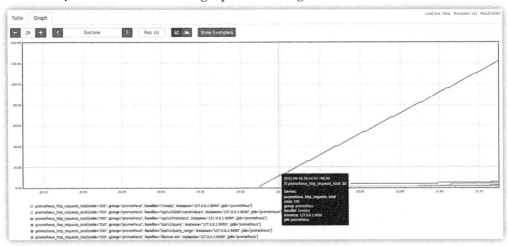

Figure 14.15: Prometheus details metrics

Tip: Getting started with Prometheus

The goal of this interactive scenario is to learn how to start collecting system metrics with Prometheus.

- `https://www.katacoda.com/courses/prometheus/getting-started`

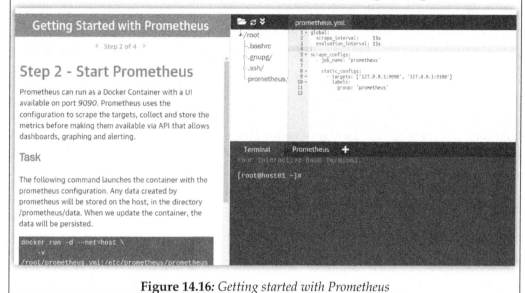

Figure 14.16: *Getting started with Prometheus*

Collecting metrics

In this process, one of the main tasks is the identification of metrics. When we talk about metrics, we refer to data that is obtained from the source and has not been processed (number of requests, available disk space, number of connections, etc.). In turn, metrics can be absolute or relative.

The absolute ones are those for which there is no previous reference value, for example, the number of transactions carried out, number of connected users, etc. On the other hand, the relative ones refer to those that are based on a previous value and have a value at a given moment, for example, the availability of 45% of memory.

The indicators, on the other hand, are the result of manipulating the metrics (attention capacity = number of requests/connections) to obtain information on behavior based on different variables. Both the metrics and the indicators can give us information to make business decisions related to the functionalities of the product or platform where it is located.

The performance metrics give us information about the operation of the components of our system (infrastructure, devices, networks), for example, the use of the CPU, the amount of memory consumed, the available disk capacity, the number of active processes and devices, the number of failures in the system, the number of available networks, the status of communication between devices, and so on.

These values allow us to have a vision on the use of resources and support the tasks of the operations team. It's simple reading guides us in the management of the capacity of the platform to obtain better results in cost or performance at a certain moment.

With technological evolution, the amount of information begins to grow and more data is obtained, therefore, it is necessary to measure other aspects related to the application and interaction with the user: the services that are available, the number of users who use it an application, the number of requests we can support simultaneously, the response time, the number of errors and their type, and the time it takes to recover and many others.

Information is acquired at different levels of the system architecture, at the lowest layer through communication protocols and at the application level through the registry and the application server information itself.

Although these metrics continue to provide low-level information, they help understand the behavior of the system and its interaction. If we analyze this data, we will have information that continues to support operational management and involves development teams who begin to know when and how the user is using their application.

> **Tip: Graphing Docker metrics with Prometheus**
>
> The goal of this interactive scenario is to collect and graph Docker Metrics with Prometheus
>
> `https://www.katacoda.com/courses/prometheus/docker-metrics`

Exploring metrics with Grafana

Grafana `https://grafana.com` is an open source tool that lets us display graphs of data collected from Prometheus, ElasticSearch, and InfluxDB, among others.

Metrics can help you set reasonable performance targets, while log analysis can uncover issues affecting your workloads. Our deployment proposes two types of metrics through our Grafana dashboards:

- The system metrics include the utilization of CPU/memory/disk of both the master of K8s and the workers.
- The cluster metrics include data at the container level and K8s cAdvisor endpoints.

These metrics, for example, can be exploited in a dashboard, which will help us understand the performance and behavior of our infrastructure at a low level. These metrics will help us determine if the system or performance is degrading and can cause the system to fail. It is important to use low-level data to help us prevent any failure before it occurs.

Grafana also makes it easy to obtain data from different data sources, which can be mixed on the same dashboard. You can also define alert rules visually for the most important metrics. Grafana evaluates these rules permanently and continuously and sends notifications in different ways.

With your hostname, you can access the tool using admin as username and the password that you just recovered. Click on **Add data source** to configure Prometheus as a data source, and the first option that will appear is Prometheus.

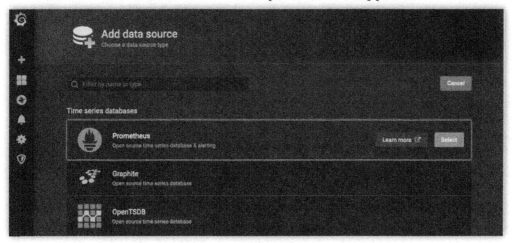

Figure 14.17: Add data source in Grafana interface

We can configure Prometheus as Grafana data sources. In this way, we can configure Grafana to query the Prometheus database for metrics.

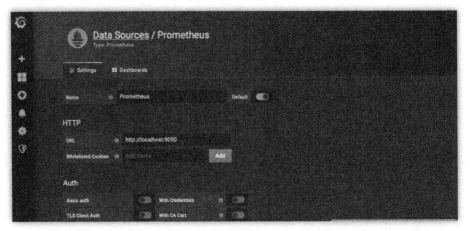

Figure 14.18: Grafana settings

Once we have connected Grafana with Prometheus, we can add a dashboard with the metrics that hosts Prometheus and Grafana.

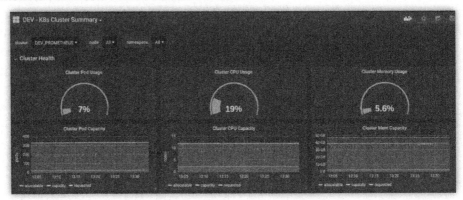

Figure 14.19: Grafana metrics

For example, we can show the CPU usage of a container or pod within Kubernetes in real-time or the evolution of the values over time. We can install Grafana from a Docker image **https://github.com/monitoringartist/grafana-xxl** using the following command:

```
$ docker run -d --name=grafana-xxl -p 3000:3000 monitoringartist/
grafana-xxl:latest
Unable to find image 'monitoringartist/grafana-xxl:latest' locally
latest: Pulling from monitoringartist/grafana-xxl
c5e155d5a1d1: Pull complete
636812ca4cd8: Pull complete
89336075b74f: Pull complete
```

```
Digest: sha256:0ca7441bf76ae97473350078dca504974de65d7748927361fe00ae
1dcdec92c9
```

```
Status: Downloaded newer image for monitoringartist/grafana-xxl:latest
WARNING: IPv4 forwarding is disabled. Networking will not work.
```
```
cc76fe06387535f8c0984238d5979b86ba9591ea2db0f39fc0fc05897291a6cf
```

Later, we can verify that we have the container running on port 3000:

```
$ docker ps -a
CONTAINER ID IMAGE COMMAND CREATED STATUS PORTS NAMES
cc76fe063875 monitoringartist/grafana-xxl:latest "/run.sh"
3 minutes ago Up 3 minutes 0.0.0.0:3000->3000/tcp grafana-xxl
```

We can also install Grafana using a helm chart we can find at
https://github.com/helm/charts/blob/master/stable/grafana/values.yaml.

To deploy the chart, we can use the same namespace where we locate the Prometheus
server:

```
helm install --namespace monitoring --name grafana stable/grafana
-f grafana/values.yml
```

Once you deploy it, you will need to recover the administrator password through
this command:

```
$ kubectl get secret grafana -n monitoring -o jsonpath="{.data.
admin-password}" | base64 --decode ; echo
```

We can define different panels with different metrics. Within each panel, we can add
and edit different types of graphs, such as tables, heat maps, or typical graphs. The
following figure depicts a section of a typical panel:

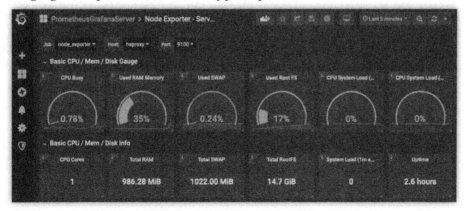

Figure 14.20: Grafana metrics

In the preceding figure, see, for example, the total consumption of CPU, RAM, and storage capacity. We can also see the CPU consumption of each Pod individually. Similarly, the panel contains the memory usage of the Pods as well as the network usage.

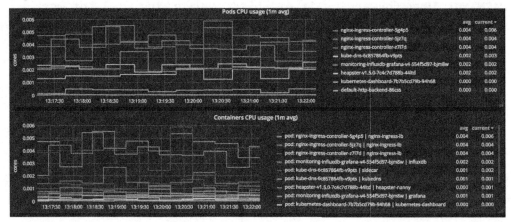

Figure 14.21: Grafana pods metrics

Behind Grafana, there is a very active community that shares different panels and configurations, which allows you to take better advantage of the tool. Each panel can be defined, exported, and imported in JSON format. This tool is very well adapted to platforms like Docker and can be easily configured and deployed.

It contains an initialization file to configure the different options. However, all the options that exist in that initialization file can also be configured through environment variables.

All the configuration can be transferred to code, but if we want it to persist in case of server failures, we can take advantage of the functionalities that Kubernetes offers and link it to an external volume.This way, we will never lose the state of our Grafana dashboard.

With Grafana, we can define alarms about our metrics. Alarms are a very useful resource when monitoring a system. We can send notifications to our email, mobile, or internal chats to our organization with alarms. The alarms that we can define are:

- **CPU usage per node**: The use of the CPU is always important, a notification that tells us that the cluster is close to the maximum possible consumption of CPU can be interesting.

- **RAM memory usage per node**: Although there are options that make the nodes of a Kubernetes cluster not reach 100% RAM memory usage, it is interesting to control when any node is close to its limit.

- **Use of the file system per node**: File system usage is an important metric. Saturation can cause workloads running on the node to fail. With a simple alarm, we are aware of this metric.

- **PODs not available**: It is always interesting to know when we have a POD not available within our cluster and if it has been able to regenerate.

- **Less desired PODs available per deployment**: This metric is more interesting than the previous one since we can have PODs not available in cases of updates, but this does not mean that the desired number of PODs are not in operation.

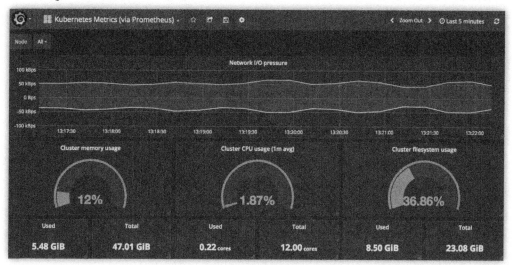

Figure 14.22: Grafana Kubernetes metrics

As we've seen, updates to Kubernetes generate additional PODs that boot while the old ones serve traffic. With this metric, we ensure that the expected number of replicas are up and running.

> **Tip: Monitoring with Prometheus and Grafana**
>
> The goal of this interactive scenario is to monitor an application based on a local development Kubernetes cluster running Prometheus and Grafana:
>
> - `https://www.katacoda.com/datastax/courses/cassandra-ops-k8s/cassandra-ops-prometheus-grafana`

Other tools

Within the observability and monitoring ecosystem, we have different tools that can help us, depending on the needs of our project and the infrastructure configuration. We can highlight the following among them:

- **Datadog (https://www.datadoghq.com)** is a monitoring and analytics tool that can be used to obtain performance metrics in applications and event monitoring for infrastructure and cloud services.

- **New Relic (https://newrelic.com)** is a tool that allows you to measure the performance of applications deployed in the cloud and allows you to analyze and visualize different metrics in the software development environment.

- **InfluxDB (https://www.influxdata.com)** can be considered a database that stores time series (TSDB). These databases allow you to store and evaluate data from sensors or protocols with timestamps for a certain period of time. The main advantage of these databases is that they are much faster than relational databases when storing and processing data with timestamps.

- **Splunk (https://www.splunk.com)** is a big data software that can capture, index, and correlate log data. It is also capable of manipulating data in log files and generating charts, reports, alerts, and dashboards.

Conclusion

In this chapter, we reviewed tools like Kubernetes Dashboard, Prometheus, and Grafana as open source tools for the analysis and visualization of metrics.

The monitoring and observability tools analyzed are beginning to be fundamental pieces in the implementation of the infrastructure of the systems and applications, offering a set of advantages:

- Control over what is happening in real time

- Agility in error prevention and detection processes

- Systems efficiency improvement and cost reduction

As we have seen, these tools offer the ability to create generic dashboards that can be quickly changed to display different statistics for a specific cluster, server, or applications.

Points to remember

- Prometheus exposes information related to its internal metrics and performance and allows it to monitor itself.

- Grafana is a tool that allows us to visualize time series data.We will obtain a graphical overview of the situation of the data. We can see the running application and the possibilities it offers at **https://play.grafana.org**.

Multiple choice questions

1. What is the command we need to run to check if Kubernetes Dashboard has been deployed correctly?

   a. `kubectl get pods --namespace kube-system`

   b. `kubectl get --all-namespaces`

   c. `kubectl get pods --namespace kubernetes-dashboard`

   d. `kubectl get pods --namespace kube-dashboard`

2. What command do we have to execute to create a namespace for prometheus in the case of installing through the operator?

   a. `kubectl create namespace prometheus`

   b. `kubectl create namespace prometheus-operator`

   c. `kubectl create namespace prometheus-kubernetes-operator`

   d. `kubectl create namespace prometheus-system`

Answer

1	a
2	d

Questions

1. Describe the main elements of the Prometheus and Grafana architectures.

2. Describe the main metrics that we can obtain for a pod within Kubernetes.

3. Explain the types of possible rules to be configured and evaluated in Prometheus.

Key terms

- Monitoring our infrastructure plays a crucial role in determining thr quality of the service we are providing. In addition, thanks to alarms and automation, we can know what is happening at all times and to take corrective measures.

- The Kubernetes Dashboard is a Kubernetes web user interface panel. The dashboard enables you, among other things, to distribute containerized applications across a Kubernetes cluster, search for errors in containerized applications, and manage the cluster.

- Prometheus is an OpenSource tool with which we can collect and store metrics. It has multiple integrations and is one of the most used tools by the community for this purpose. It has an integrated database and its own query system to extract the information. It uses a data exporter called node exporter to collect information. This tool must be deployed within the Kubernetes cluster.

- Grafana is a multiplatform and extensible software through plugins in which users can build their data visualization panel in a personalized way and share it easily. Grafana is widely used in network service monitoring systems such as Prometheus or Zabbix. Here are some of the main features:

  a. We will have different graphics for data visualization.

  b. It makes dynamic and reusable panels available to us.

  c. It is extensible, and we can use different panels and plugins available in the official library.

  d. We can authenticate through LDAP, Google Auth, Grafana.com, and Github.

  e. Visualization of multiple types of graphs (histograms, geographical maps, heat maps ...) with a multitude of options with which they can be enriched and extended.

  f. Creation of dynamic and reusable dashboards with the possibility of sharing them.

  g. Use of diverse and multiple data sources from which you can obtain personalized metrics as well as filter data and make annotations in real time.

  h. Definition of alerts and notifications.

Index

Printed in Great Britain
by Amazon